The Fiction of Tokuda Shūsei

and the Emergence of Japan's New Middle Class

The Fiction of Tokuda Shūsei

and the Emergence of Japan's New Middle Class

RICHARD TORRANCE

University of Washington Press

Seattle and London

This book is published with the assistance of a grant from the College of Humanities and the Office of Research and Graduate Studies of the Ohio State University.

Copyright © 1994 by the University of Washington Press
Printed in the United States of America

Library of Congress Cataloging-in-Publication Data

Torrance, Richard.
  The fiction of Tokuda Shūsei, and the emergence of Japan's new middle class / Richard Torrance.
    p. cm.
  Includes bibliographical references and index.
  ISBN 0–295–97296–3
  1. Tokuda, Shūsei, 1872–1943—Criticism and interpretation.
2. Middle classes in literature. I. Title.
PL817.036Z88 1994   93–20845
895.6′342—dc20   CIP

The paper used in this publication meets the minimum requirements of American National Standard for Information Sciences—Permanence of Paper for Printed Library Materials, ANSI Z39.48–1984.

Title page illustration: Shūsei in 1938 in the study of his house in Morikawa-chō *for Emiko, Mashiho, and Noah*

Contents

Acknowledgments

There are many people and several institutions that deserve thanks for this book. Support for two years of research in Japan from 1985 to 1987 was provided by a Fulbright-Hays Training Fellowship and a Japan Foundation Fellowship. The writing of the dissertation from which this study has evolved was supported at Yale University by an East Asian Prize Fellowship. I would like to thank Professors Paul Anderer and Robert Danly for their suggestions and helpful criticism of drafts of several chapters of the dissertation on the occasions of my examinations for this fellowship. Professor Anderer has continued to follow the progress of this study and has provided many valuable insights at various stages of completion. Ms. Naomi Pascal and Ms. Pamela Bruton at the University of Washington Press offered steady hands and excellent editorial assistance.

Over a decade ago, I first learned of Tokuda Shūsei from Professor Jay Rubin at the University of Washington. Professor Rubin's later advice and encouragement after reading a draft manuscript of the present book are much appreciated.

In Japan, Nishikōri Shūichi, Kageyama Susumu, Jean Marie Mahieu, and Wada Hideo have been sources of instruction and help over the years. Noguchi Fujio took considerable time from his busy schedule to respond in writing to my questions about Tokuda Shūsei. Tokuda Masahiko has been immensely generous with his time and in allowing me to quote at length from his father's works. He was also kind enough to provide the photographs of his family in this volume.

This book would have been something very different without the guidance of Professor Etō Jun. For two years, during weekly discussions of Shūsei's texts at the Tokyo Institute of Technology, I was privileged to receive instruction from the most discerning, intelligent, and knowledgeable critic and reader I have ever encountered. I am also grateful to Professor Etō for reading this study in draft form and as a dissertation and for permission to quote at length from his essays on Tokuda Shūsei.

Hamako Ito Chaplin taught me a great deal during the several years I studied under her at Yale. Professor Edward Kamens, a reader of the dissertation, was of invaluable assistance, helping me to clarify my thinking page by page. Professor John Treat, then my teacher at Yale, has been a constant supporter of this project and provided the enthusiasm necessary to shepherd it from dissertation to book. At the Ohio State University, Professor James Morita read the dissertation and offered a number of perceptive suggestions.

If this book has been able to impart some measure of Tokuda Shūsei's importance as a novelist, it is largely due to Edwin McClellan, Sumitomo Professor of Japanese at Yale University. He suggested Shūsei as a dissertation topic, compelled me to read Shūsei's literature carefully, recommended the general framework upon which this study is based, and extended advice, support, and friendship over the years.

Infelicities and errors, however, are my own.

Note on Japanese Names

Japanese words are romanized according to the modified Hepburn system used in the standard Kenkyūsha *New Japanese-English Dictionary*. Macrons are not used for well-known Japanese place-names. Names of Japanese persons are given in the Japanese order, surname first. Titles of Japanese periodicals are not translated unless the meaning of the title is relevant to the discussion.

The Fiction of Tokuda Shūsei

and the Emergence of Japan's New Middle Class

Introduction

This study examines class-cultural milieux in modern, pre–World War II Japan as portrayed by the novelist Tokuda Shūsei (1872–1943). Throughout much of his adult life, Shūsei remained committed to depicting the world of the lower classes. "It is said that art is eternal," he wrote in 1906, "but that is a concept of the past, and we can no longer be satisfied with such vague formulations. Today we must investigate the problem of bread and consider whether we are being governed justly or not."[1] In 1934, in response to the head of the Police Bureau, Matsumoto Gaku, who had plans to organize Japanese writers in support of the state, Shūsei replied: "Japanese literature was born among the common people and has grown up without the least 'protection' from the government. . . . What we would really like is for you to leave us alone."[2] In 1936, in a preface to a collection of his short stories, he wrote that "this volume reflects my deep interest in the lower classes and my growing conviction that I have lived my life together with the masses."[3] As will be documented, Shūsei's belief that literature should speak for the powerless and represent common experience was forged by a number of oppositional political and literary movements, such as the People's Rights movement of the 1870s, the *shajitsu* (realism) movement of the 1880s, naturalism during the first decade of the twentieth century, and social realism in the 1920s and 1930s.

Shūsei's novels have much to teach about class structure in modern Japanese society. Yet the notion of "class" is fraught with scientist implications, and if one brings extraneous models of social stratification to bear on Shūsei's work, one will soon become disoriented and confused, concerning both its form and its content. Reading his novels according to a proletariat/petite bourgeoisie/bourgeoisie/aristocracy paradigm or even a lower class/middle class/upper class paradigm will lead one to mistake his highly original work for melodrama, classical European naturalism, or social realism: his mature novels will inevitably disappoint such generic expectations.

Of necessity, then, the nature of this project is descriptive of patterns of life. The first chapter examines Shūsei's own class background: his birth and upbringing in Kanazawa. Chapter 2 analyzes Shūsei's relation to the masses as he struggled to become established as a professional novelist. The last four chapters concern the mature works of Tokuda Shūsei. These novels are invariably described as representing "common (*shomin*) life," a term, it will be argued, referring to that class of people in Japan who became the urban "new middle class" after the end of World War II. The secrets of the people who live in major urban centers are the substance of Tokuda Shūsei's mature fiction. The domestic history of the modern Japanese masses is one of urbanization, the fears engendered by this process, and the unsuccessful ideological and structural measures attempted by the state to counter it. To my knowledge, Tokuda Shūsei is the only novelist who managed to portray the sheer chaos, indeterminacy, and beautiful, breathless excitement precipitated by increasing urbanization. In doing so, he created a new genre of realism that has never been and probably never will be duplicated.

Tokuda Shūsei was a professional novelist who supported himself and his rather large family almost solely by his writing from about the turn of the century to his death in 1943. As we shall see in the course of this study, his literary career constitutes a history in microcosm of modern Japanese literary culture from the Meiji period through the middle of the Great Pacific War. It is fashionable to argue that the pre–World War II Japanese literary world (*bundan*) was a particularly oppressive institution.[4] On the contrary, it is maintained here that the Japanese literary world gave Tokuda Shūsei the freedom to create and that his works cannot be understood without considering the *bundan,* of which he was a part for almost fifty years.

A crucial part of the process of description is the presentation of the responses of Japanese critics to Shūsei and his work. Fortunately, a great deal has been written about Shūsei over the years, and this material is liberally used. This body of writing provides a critical vocabulary that serves as a bridge between the texts of Shūsei's works and the class realities of his contemporary society. It also allows for a general assessment of the relative importance of Shūsei's literary career.

This brings us to the question of Shūsei's place in the discourse on the Japanese novel in Japan and the United States. Kawabata Yasunari, the Nobel laureate for literature, has written that there are three pinnacles in the history of the Japanese novel: Murasaki Shikibu, Ihara Saikaku, and Tokuda Shūsei.[5] This opinion was shared by a great many of Japan's most influential professional writers and critics. Such agreement is not often the case among academics. The Japanese novel makes claim to a kind of knowledge so universal and encyclopedic as to tempt the critic to use it to create generalizations about "the Japanese." It is the distinctive nature of the novel as a genre to invite such criticism, and this study, as well, has used Shūsei's work to arrive at conclusions concerning Japanese society. However, as we shall see, the discourse on the Japanese novel, especially among some academics, has been influenced extensively by nonliterary political debates defining the structure of Japanese society. These have tended to concentrate on what the Japanese personality or Japanese society "lacks" that might have prevented Japanese history and literature from advancing along the same evolutionary course as the West.

The mode of analysis that finds absence at the heart of the Japanese novel has invariably been mirrored in American writings. In the late sixties, it was argued that the Japanese novel reflected the inability of Japanese writers to find a true bourgeois sense of self, and this in turn testified to the low level of political consciousness among Japanese intellectuals.[6] The debate over whether or how "the Japanese self" appears in the Japanese novel has since undergone a permutation in its level of determinism; the notion of "self" has come to transcend sociological, phenomenological, and psychological categories and has become a genetic/linguistic trait that somehow the Japanese novel is not marked with.[7]

Given the centrality of Shūsei's career and works to the Japanese literary scene from the turn of the century to 1943, his reputation, especially as it relates to his role as one of the most important figures of Japanese naturalism, has inevitably been subjected to a great deal of criticism for personifying the most "Japanese tendencies" in leading the Japanese novel in the wrong evolutionary direction: away from society to the nonexistent self. Since this study directly concerns the social significance of Shūsei's work, it is incumbent upon it to address the degenerate and mesmerizing explanatory power of negation that colors much academic Shūsei criticism.

Although Shūsei had a remarkable memory for language use, temporal associations, people's mannerisms, and conversations, he does not seem to have had a good memory for dates, and some of the information he provided about his life was mistaken. These errors influenced many secondary sources at least until the early sixties. This study is not a biography, and if, at times, it seems to have become too absorbed in "irrelevant facts," this stems from the impulse to "set the record straight," out of the conviction that Tokuda Shūsei, the literary figure, deserves as accurate a treatment as that accorded to any major twentieth-century writer.

In the end, however, Tokuda Shūsei's novels are best apprehended not as a manifestation of himself but in their sheer diversity and sensitivity to social change and in Shūsei's willingness to experiment to reveal those deep realms of everyday experience that are so often hidden from us.

1
Born into Kanazawa's Decline

> On noticing an almost imperceptible change in the season from a
> scent borne on a slight breeze, he could sense again the cold, rough
> winds of the northern province where he was born, and with a
> faint longing came fragmentary memories of certain houses, gar-
> dens, and people of the place where he had spent his bleak youth,
> but with remembrance of this distant past, representing continuity
> with his present self, also came the certainty that, for him, during
> his boyhood, his birthplace was a degenerating, isolated graveyard.
> —Tokuda Shūsei, "Shotō no kibun"
> (Feelings at the Start of Winter)

In examining Shūsei's own class origins, it is necessary to recognize that
in his writings—including his memoirs and autobiographical fiction,
from which this portrait of his childhood and youth is drawn—class
standing is almost always a coalescence of a variety of factors. It has
been frequently asserted that Shūsei was of lower-class *bushi* (gentry, or
samurai) birth, but a closer examination reveals a more complicated
situation.[1] James L. McClain has explained one of the important rules of
thumb for ranking gentry in the city of Kanazawa, where Shūsei was
born: "the distance of a samurai's residence from the castle ought to be
proportional to his status within the warrior hierarchy."[2] At the time of
Shūsei's birth, his father still retained the family's hereditary house in a
bushi neighborhood that was relatively close to the castle. Kanazawa
was the castle town of the Maeda *daimyō*, hereditary lords of the Kaga
domain, which, with an annual assessed rice income of more than
1,000,000 *koku,* was second only to the Tokugawa shogunate in wealth.
The city was designed to protect and supply the Maeda castle, which
even today, in ruins, is an impressive structure, with its watchtowers and
massive walls towering over the city that spreads out below it. The
isolation of the city was the result of the intentional use of natural
defenses to protect it. To the north and northwest is the Japan Sea, an
important supply route for the city that was patrolled by the domain's
own navy. To the east, west, and south are mountains, and the Sai and
Asano rivers form another line of defense, running parallel to each other
and enclosing the city from the mountains to the sea.

Kanazawa's population, estimated at about 120,000 at the end of the Edo period, was arranged in the city to protect the castle and to maintain civil order. The Maeda had twelve retainers with incomes of 10,000 *koku* or more, incomes as large as those of many independent *daimyō*. The substantial residences and estates of these major retainers were located in strategic areas of the city so that they might bear the preliminary brunt of an attack. The compound of the Yokoyama family (30,000 *koku*), where Shūsei was born, was adjacent to the castle to the southwest, the vast residences and gardens of the Honda family were located to the south of the castle, and the Chō and Imaeda families protected the eastern approach to the castle. Residences of lesser direct retainers were organized to form warrior/gentry neighborhoods, and these also were located at strategic points in the city. Those of minor *bushi* status lived in neighborhoods some distance from the castle, often on the banks of the Asano River and Sai River furthest from the castle. These persons constituted the lower class of the *bushi* hierarchy in Kanazawa.

Before the Meiji Restoration of 1868, Kanazawa was a well-ordered and beautiful city, and the Maeda lords took pride in governing it along strict Neo-Confucian lines. The Maeda were widely recognized for their generous provisions for the poor and sick, for the large libraries and schools they established to promote Neo-Confucian learning, and for their sponsorship of artists and craftsmen who, in turn, founded distinctive schools of the *nō* and tea ceremony and who created textiles, pottery, and metalwork of high quality. It was the relative success of this traditional centralized government, which bled the countryside to support a high standard of living in the city and which cut the warrior/gentry class off from most ties with the land, that left the city so ill-prepared to make the transition to life under the new Meiji government.

There was a pro-imperial faction in the domain, but most of the domain's retainers remained satisfied with the long-standing military and marriage ties the Maeda house had maintained with the Tokugawa shogunate, and the conservatives put the "radicals" to death on the occasion of the abortive uprising against the shogunate by the Chōshū domain in the eighth month of 1863. The last lord of the domain, Maeda Yasuyoshi, wisely attempted to steer a neutral course through the armed turmoil that resulted in the birth of the Meiji state, and he thus spared his domain invasion by pro-imperial armies. But the domain as a whole was left with few connections to figures in the new central government who would help Kanazawa men obtain government positions and capital in the new order. Under the prefectural system of administration, Maeda Yasuyoshi stayed on as governor until 1871, but he was then replaced by Uchida Masakaze, a Satsuma man, who moved the capital of the newly named Kanazawa prefecture to Migawa, because, it was declared, the *bushi* of the city of Kanazawa were arrogant, obstructionist, and lacking in ambition, talent, and patriotism. The Maeda took the 1,194,000 yen they received from the central government in 1876 in compensation for the income of their domain (a figure that represents slightly over 1 percent of the public bonds issued for the commutation of all *daimyō* holdings and *bushi* stipends) and moved more or less permanently to Tokyo as members of a new, artificially created aristocracy. Their major retainers later followed them to Tokyo.

With the end of the feudal order and the removal of the Maeda family to palatial residences in Tokyo, what was without doubt the most elegant and populous city on Japan's northern coast of the Japan Sea became an empty shell. Its reason for existence had evaporated. Of the estimated 60,000 *bushi* and their dependents in Kanazawa at the time of the Restoration, many with the means to emigrate probably did so, for the city's population had declined by approximately 40,000 by the middle of the Meiji period. Those who were left behind inhabited a beautiful, isolated *bushi* slum.[3]

Tokuda Shūsei was born into this disintegrating social situation as Tokuda Sueo, his given name meaning "the last son." The official date of his birth was the twelfth month, twenty-third day, fourth year of Meiji, or, according to the Gregorian calendar, February 1, 1872.[4] He was the third son and sixth child of Tokuda Unpei Fujiwara Katsunao (1818–91), a retainer of the Yokoyama family, which was one of the major retainers of the Maeda. In terms of both his stipend of 70 *koku* and his status as an indirect retainer to the Maeda, Unpei was in the lower-middle level of the domain's *bushi* hierarchy. The Tokuda family could trace its history as local warriors in the Kaga/Noto region back to 1580, when Tokuda Shima died in battle against the forces of Oda Nobunaga's general Shibata Katsuie. Tokuda Jūeimon brought the family under the protection of the Yokoyama in 1713, and Unpei inherited the family's stipend as the tenth-generation head of the Tokuda house. Shūsei's mother, Take (b. ca. 1838–41, d. 1916), was of better birth than her husband. She was the third daughter of Tsuda Uneme, a direct retainer to Maeda with a stipend of 700 *koku* (later reduced to 400).[5]

Shūsei, then, was of respectable *bushi,* or samurai, birth, and, to a certain extent, one must agree with Tōda Yasutaka's assessment of him: "In the depths of Shūsei's mind, there was a consciousness of being one of the elite, a sense of being a leader, which cannot be conceived of without taking into consideration the age and place in which he was raised and his status as *shizoku* [the legal status granted *bushi* in 1869]."[6] The validity of Tōda's statement lies in the fact that Shūsei's status disposed him, as it did numerous other young *shizoku,* to participate in the People's Rights movement. Tetsuo Najita has described the results of this disposition as follows: "Through the theory of natural right . . . the bruising psychological reality of declassment was explained as part of progress, the poverty of military rebellion was exposed, and the value of loyal action was directed toward participation in a radical popular movement."[7] The naive mixture of nativistic egalitarianism and hero worship Shūsei embraced during his adolescence was a natural outgrowth of his birth-given right to public leadership. It also led him to an early commitment to literary realism, varying concepts of which he remained faithful to throughout his life.

But Shūsei was a complex person given to much self-analysis, and if, in his maturity, he was tempted to feel superior to the commoners around him because of the status accorded him by birth, such impulses were severely repressed. Shūsei stated that he did not enjoy writing about his youth, because it contained only unpleasant memories (15:448).[8] But by the 1930s, Shūsei overcame this reluctance, perhaps because he perceived that he was one of the few remaining voices capable of providing testimony about the sacrifices that resulted from Japan's political revolution of 1868. Through a number of memoirs, short stories, and autobiographical novels, a fairly clear picture of his formative experiences in Kanazawa emerges. One of the most detailed of these works is Shūsei's *Hikari o ōte* (In Pursuit of Light, 1938–40). In the afterword to this long novel, Shūsei invited readers to look upon the work's hero, Hitoshi (meaning "equal," "no better than others"), as his own alter ego, and this literary creation attaches little or no importance to questions of family origin:[9]

Hitoshi knew nothing of his ancestors. When his mother died in an epidemic and her possessions were put out in the garden to be disinfected in the sunlight, he found among them his family's genealogy stored in a fine paulownia wood box. He watched with a mixed sense of regret and relief as the junkman took the box away, but that it was of no great significance was testified to by his father's life. (18:5)

Tokuda Unpei was in his late fifties when the carrying of swords was prohibited and all *bushi* stipends were converted to currency and government bonds. He was too old to make the transition to a new way of life under the evolving capitalistic national economy. He attempted to start several enterprises—among them, raising chickens and growing mulberry trees—but these failed, and he spent much of his time in the mountains hunting (2:515). Possessing no business acumen or experience, the elderly father had little choice but to rely on advice from local government officials on financial matters, and, more often than not, the advice was probably wrong:

> Hitoshi's father's expression was always grave, but for all his worry, the family's circumstances did not change for the better, and his father's strength finally gave out. He could never have had many resources. After one of his periodic visits to his former lord's house, he returned despairing of his lord's declining fortunes, and when they vacated their house and moved to a small residence in an undistinguished neighborhood, his father wept in spite of himself. Years later, on his way to play at the home of a relative, Hitoshi passed what was probably the site of the house where he was born. Part of the property had been turned into rice fields, and much of the rest was covered by deep grass. Clear water from an abandoned well flowed up through the grass, and large Japanese hemlocks towered over what must have been the garden.
>
> The person to whom his father had entrusted his small sum of government bonds was a prefectural official named Kawakoshi, who had lived near that house. Perhaps Kawakoshi had invested the bonds in some venture started by *shizoku,* but in any case the result was that his father lost most of them and in recompense received the house by the Asano River to which Hitoshi and his family moved. At the end of the year, Hitoshi observed that his parents, with bleak-looking faces, had collected the money from somewhere to pay family debts, and he nagged his mother to take him to the theater. "The theater!" she exclaimed. "That's beyond our means," and she ignored his importunity. His parents must have been fairly pressed by that time. (18:24–25)

When Tokuda Unpei's lord, Yokoyama Takahira, was forced to give up his large estate close to the castle, the Tokuda family had to vacate its inherited home, which was on that estate, and move far away from the castle to a low-class neighborhood formerly reserved for *ashigaru* (foot soldiers) and others of marginal *bushi* status. It is doubtful that Shūsei, who was only two or three at the time of this move, remembered the house in which he was born, but even six decades after the event, he could well imagine his father's tears, for this move to the east bank of the Asano River represented a major fall for the family, which was no longer able to maintain the proper appearances of its class.[10] And by the time Shūsei was about seven, his indulgent parents had lost the financial wherewithal to allow for such small pleasures as trips to the nearby theater.

In 1883, when Shūsei was eleven, the family moved again, this time to a house in the Okachi district that it had received in compensation for Unpei's bonds. Shūsei felt he had emerged into a bright new world (18:28), probably because the house was in a proper gentry neighborhood and had a gate (*mon*), the mark of respectability. Unpei, however, was able to hold on to this residence for only about seven or eight months, and the family moved again to a respectable house in the Misokura district across the river. Shūsei believed that this move may have been occasioned by his eldest half brother's failure to pass an examination to become a lawyer (18:33–34), and thus we can probably conclude that this half brother, Naomatsu, had become the main provider of financial support for the family. After Naomatsu's departure for Osaka, where he became a policeman, Unpei was no longer able to maintain his family as an independent household, and toward the beginning of 1886, when Shūsei was about fourteen, Unpei, Take, Shūsei, and Shūsei's youngest sister, Fude, moved in with Shūsei's elder half sister Ōta Kin and her husband, Ōta Tameyuki. At about this time, Unpei suffered a stroke, which left him partially paralyzed. Fortunately, he had found Shūsei's half brother Juntarō and Ōta Tameyuki positions in a mining venture started by his former lord, Yokoyama, and one can probably assume that the family subsisted on the earnings of these two men. Shūsei spent much of his adolescence, then, dependent on half brothers, a half sister, and an in-law. His circumstances could only have been very impoverished, but Shūsei does not touch at any length on his domestic living arrangements during this period, perhaps because he was afraid of falling into self-pitying sentimentality (15:448).

By the time Unpei died in 1891 of yet another stroke, the main Tokuda house in Kanazawa was on the verge of penury with little prospect of being capable of keeping Shūsei in school, even if Shūsei had wanted to stay (18:61). Toward the end of March 1892, at the age of twenty, Shūsei, ignoring his mother's urgings to stay in school, set off with his friend Kiryū Yūyū and another companion for Tokyo (18:71–72). His youthful experiences in Kanazawa had been largely those of social and familial disruption, declassment, and poverty. But he also described feeling a sense of liberation in Kanazawa, a freedom to play, pretend, and imagine revolution, which was probably a factor in his decision to become a novelist.

By the mid-1880s, the economic situation for many of the gentry class throughout Japan, but particularly in Kanazawa, was desperate. Histories of the city tell of whole families drowning themselves in the great moat around the castle, former warriors reduced to begging on the street, and long lines of gentry forming at street kitchens where free rice gruel was dispensed.[11] In Shūsei's memoirs, deprivation and declassment are often accompanied by descriptions of degeneracy and the collapse of the Neo-Confucian moral order, as in the following passage describing the effects of the compulsory amortization of *bushi* stipends enforced in 1876:

The castle town was inundated with gold. Currency and bonds flowed into the purses of all the gentry in exchange for their rice stipends. Men higher up in the domain's hierarchy, those with some financial sense, and even those who were of low station but who had grown used to living prudently managed adequately, but there were a great many of the gentry living beneath the castle who had grown utterly dependent on their stipends, gave no thought to the future, and, with no experience with currency and in a world at peace, had become accustomed to luxurious clothing and personal possessions and had developed a taste for fine foods and wine.

The small theater which later planted the seeds of decadence in young Hitoshi's mind made its appearance during this time of prosperity. At first, it was located at the top of a hill close to the city. At the foot of the hill was a restaurant that specialized in fine Edo cuisine (this establishment was to survive for many years), and its exquisite ceramics were unequaled for their extravagance. Not far from the restaurant was the pleasure quarter, the latticed fronts of its dimly lit buildings painted in Indian red in the Kyoto fashion, and its entrances concealed by light yellow beaded curtains. (18:13)

Elsewhere in his memoirs, Shūsei recounts the story of his maternal grandfather, Tsuda Uneme. Tsuda lost his only son and adopted Iori, the husband of his daughter Masa, as heir to the Tsuda house. Iori was ordered into house confinement for "dissolute behavior" by domain authorities, and Uneme committed *seppuku* (ritual suicide by disembowelment) to atone for his adopted son's crime (15:453–54). Shūsei gives no hint what this "dissolute behavior" was, but the contrast between moral standards before and after the Restoration is striking. The perhaps cruel sanctions maintained by the domain against the establishment of new theaters, popular entertainments, gambling, and whoring disappeared with hereditary rice stipends, and many *shizoku* took advantage of this new freedom.[12] And in the end, did it make much difference whether the gentry drank their meager capital or saw it depreciate or disappear in the inflations and deflations surrounding the Seinan War of 1877?

In his forties, Shūsei confessed that he was addicted to traditional Japanese music and to the theater (he was to write numerous reviews of traditional Japanese plays and entertainments), and when he traced the origin of this addiction, he encountered the disintegration of the Neo-Confucian moral order that had prevailed in Kanazawa before the Restoration.[13] Many of Shūsei's memories of his youth in Kanazawa seem colored by the sexual abandon that was such an integral part of the world of the traditional popular arts and the demimonde. He remembered the excitement of being taken to the nearby theater by his mother or sister (18:14–15), the pleasure of performing roles from popular plays for young girls, his main playmates in the Asano neighborhood, and the images of young dancing girls performing in the local pleasure quarter, to which his father took him (15:449–50). And yet even these memories of childhood longings which seem so intimately tied to performance and pretending bring forth associations of the human devastation brought about by Kanazawa's decline:

Two sisters with white round faces were Hitoshi's playmates. He would occasionally read storybooks with their older brother, but more often he played house or hide-and-seek with the younger of the two sisters. He and the girl would spread a straw mat in the narrow open space outside the fence of the girl's house and play with dolls or pretend to cook dinner. Hitoshi was the father, and she was the mother. They would lie down together, their eyes closed tight facing the blue sky. . . .

Years later, both girls were sold into the dark world of prostitution in a neighboring province. (18:16)

Or again, some years later in a different neighborhood:

One day a startlingly beautiful young woman, her freshly washed hair falling loosely down her back, came to the front entrance and briefly conversed with his mother, who had come out to greet her there. She was in a hurry and left promptly, and Hitoshi only caught a glimpse of her from behind his mother's skirt, but her beauty would remain in his memory for the rest of his life. It was his cousin Onobu, who had been divorced by the younger of his two half brothers. . . . She had come that day to say farewell, for she was leaving to take up residence in a pleasure quarter in Tokyo.

Onobu was not the only daughter of gentry family on the verge of ruin to sink into the demimonde. So many women of gentry birth were separated from their families and scattered about in pleasure districts throughout the nation. They were like the sons of gentry, who emigrated to cities to become policemen in such numbers that cops were said to be the special regional product of Kanazawa, or like the swords, tea utensils, mirrors, antique chests, and hair ornaments furtively smuggled out of homes through the rear entrance and sold to the junkman or buyers of secondhand furniture, possessions which subsequently found their way into the storehouses of the rural bourgeoisie, or like the priceless treasures kept in families for generations that found their way to the central cities and made lovers of objets d'art and antique dealers salivate with desire. (18:40–41)

Everywhere he looked, the adolescent Shūsei saw respectable families breaking up and their daughters being sold into prostitution or semi-prostitution: his boyhood playmates mentioned above, Onobu (the daughter of his paternal uncle), his cousin Suga (Tsuda Masa's daughter), Gin (the daughter of another paternal uncle), and his distant relatives Kawasaki Tora and Kiyokawa Ito.[14] Shūsei's reputation as a novelist was largely predicated on his portrayal of women and his love affairs with them. In the course of this study, the class-cultural milieux explored will generally be seen through the eyes of a number of memorable women. From an early age, Shūsei apparently enjoyed the company of girls and women more than that of boys his own age, and as we shall see below, he was raised mainly by maternal authority figures, and yet, during his adolescence, he witnessed the decimation of Kanazawa's young female population. If Shūsei's memoirs are to be believed, perhaps his sympathy for women and his willingness to see things from a feminine point of view came, in part, from the early perception that men may suffer psychological pain from declassment, but, in the end, it was déclassé women's sacrifices and strength that offered sustenance in times of social and moral disintegration.

Impoverishment, a sense of moral abandon, and the consequent spread of the morally intolerable practice of selling daughters and wives into prostitution seem to have been accompanied in Shūsei's memory with physical violence:

The mood of bloodletting engendered by the upheaval of the Restoration did not allow for the establishment of public order. When the weather turned warm, young men would set up armed camps in every district of the city, and there would be pitched battles between neighborhoods waged with rocks, bamboo swords, and the occasional knife. (18:31)

Kanazawa was a conservative place before the Restoration, and afterward it appears to have turned nastily reactionary. Elements of the gentry class attempted to organize in resistance to the policies of the central government, but this seems to have translated quickly into assassination: Shimada Ichirō, a low-level Kanazawa samurai who headed a reactionary movement within the city, led the band, including five other Kanazawa men, that cut down the prominent pro-imperial politician Ōkubo Toshimichi on May 14, 1878, ostensibly to avenge the death of Saigō Takamori.[15] Shūsei recorded blades flashing at political rallies and men with drawn swords chasing after the rickshas of visiting national political figures (18:62–63). Izumi Kyōka (1873–1939), another famous novelist, simply despaired of the city:

I was born in Kanazawa and was raised there until I was seventeen, but, to put it bluntly, I hate the natives of the place. I may sound as though I am a traitor to my hometown, but the people there are arrogant, conceited, inhumane, stubborn, and blockheaded. The gentry, in particular, were haughty and overweening and treated us merchants and craftsmen as if we were not even human beings.[16]

It is not difficult to imagine why sensitive, frail young men such as Shūsei, Kiryū Yūyū, and Kyōka desired to leave Kanazawa as soon as they could.

At least for the casual visitor, it is difficult to discover the dark and desperate Kanazawa of Shūsei's memory in what seems the clean, healthy, and cordial Kanazawa of today. But the somber beauty of its natural setting remains unchanged. The present Higashiyama district roughly corresponds to the older Asano, Okachi, and Baba districts, where Shūsei lived for approximately fifteen of his twenty years in Kanazawa. If one were to visit the city in the late autumn or early winter and cross the Asano River to find lodgings in a fairly traditional house or inn in this district, one might discover a quality of light, the light of storytellers, that appears in Shūsei's autobiographical short story "Shotō no kibun" (Feelings at the Start of Winter, 1923) and in other places in his fiction. In the following passage, Ono is a thinly disguised alter ego of Shūsei:

There is, of course, none of nature's brilliant clarity that washes the towns and cities on the southern coast, nor are there the magnificent mountain ranges that tower over the high plateau of the central region, but with the winter comes a sense of isolated warmth unique to this northerly coast of the Japan Sea, the sensation of a dimly lit room where one is satisfied to remain through the long winter, reading, telling stories, eating and drinking, a sensation born of the natural surroundings of the district in which Ono had lived. After the leaves had been blown from the trees of the gardens in gentry neighborhoods and uncannily dark clouds had closed in the mountains that wind to the east, west, and south, the rains of late autumn fell so quietly on eaves and bushes in the garden, as if trying to conceal their presence or as if softly weeping. And as the days grew colder, on quiet nights, from his bed, he could hear the lonely sound of huge waves pounding the shore some two and a half miles away. Sleet or hail would lash the persimmon tree in the back garden and the shuttered front entrance. Now, as he was growing older, Ono remembered all the more vividly eating from a common cooking pot, with the rest of his family, the wild ducks his father had shot. (6:380–81)

The provincial city of Kanazawa in the last decades of the nineteenth century, darkly beautiful, elegant, and permeated by fantasy and acting but morally degenerate and violent, all covered over by a thin veneer of Neo-Confucianism, must be regarded as the entrance to the maze that is Tokuda Shūsei.

Family

He was born a sickly child, with few prospects of surviving to maturity, the second of three children his father's third wife would bear into a family already consisting of an elder half sister by his father's first wife, who had died, and two elder half brothers and an elder half sister by his father's second wife, who had also died. There were, of course, numerous other infants born into the nation on the date of his birth. And disregarding for the moment differences of class and wealth, some of these children must have been welcomed into the world with joy and celebration by their parents and other family members. In imagining the circumstances of his own birth, however, he could only conclude that it cast a shadow across the hearts of most members of his immediate family. If there was someone who was secretly pleased, it was his mother, and perhaps his father, who felt that his wife's position as stepmother would be made less difficult by the birth of her own son. (18:3–4)[17]

It would seem from this passage from *Hikari o ōte* that Shūsei was obsessed with the same theme that dominates many of Japan's greatest autobiographical novels: sons alienated from their fathers at birth. After reading on, however, one discovers that one is in a different world from that occupied by the stern, uncaring patriarchs and resentful younger sons in Natsume Sōseki's *Michikusa,* Shiga Naoya's *Anya kōro,* and Dazai Osamu's *Ningen shikkaku.*[18]

Shūsei recalls that his father had nothing to give his children but a simple set of moral standards and an instinctive, biological love for his offspring (2:519). Apparently because of his straitened economic circumstances, Unpei seems to have promised to give up his sixth child, Shūsei, for adoption to a farmer while the child was still in the womb, but on seeing his infant son's face, he was unable to part with his child, and he went back on his promise (18:34). It would appear that the natural love of a father for his children set a tone in the Tokuda household which kept the disparate family members together on fairly cordial, even loving, terms. Although Unpei did marry Shūsei's half sisters and sister off at younger and younger ages—Shizu in 1861 at the age of eighteen, Kin in 1878 at the age of fifteen, Kaori in 1880 at the age of thirteen—he did not sell them to reverse the decline of the Tokuda house. Finding respectable *shizoku* husbands for his daughters must have entailed some expense. To the end of his life, he insisted that Shūsei remain in school, though the family could barely afford the cost (2:517).[19]

Unpei does not appear to have been a distant authority figure. Shūsei began sleeping with his father at the age of seven, when he left his mother's bedding to make room for his newborn sister, Fude (18:6). Since the family could not afford servants, the task of caring for the young boy was shared by all members of the family, including the father, who took his frail, youngest son on regular visits to the doctor, to school, and to the sites of local amusements or curiosities:

He remembered being led, his tiny hand enveloped by his father's long, delicate fingers, to attend the theater or to see the acrobats in front of the Matsuji Temple or to view the elephant which had just arrived at the local museum [it contained a zoo] and which everyone was talking about. He remembered the tall figure of his father walking through the town, the skirts of his kimono tucked up, his bare knees protruding, and his leather sandals slapping the dusty road. It was also his father who took him on a cold winter evening to buy an English dictionary. When they returned home, he opened the new dictionary under the dim light of the lamp and began to translate his English reader. In his joy at understanding enough to find the contents interesting, he studied late into the night, straining to keep his eyes open. His father, wrinkles forming at the corners of his eyes and exhaling thick tobacco smoke through his nostrils, came over to peer at what his son was doing. (2:518)

The railroad would not reach Kanazawa until several years after Shūsei had left for Tokyo, and it is difficult to say whether the elephant walked to the isolated city or was carried in by horse-drawn wagon, but, in any case, the animal must have been a great curiosity indeed. The so-called civilization and enlightenment (*bunmei kaika*) movement was just beginning to be felt in the Kaga region, and it consisted of rough red blankets mass-produced for the army, the eating of meat, kerosene lamps, and English dictionaries. Buying such a book, probably imported from abroad, must have represented a great economic sacrifice for Unpei, and it was an act of generosity in another sense as well, for apparently the elderly man was not in the least intimidated by the notion that his youngest son might become infinitely better educated than himself. Unpei may not have been a heroic father figure—his final years after his stroke were pathetic (2:517)—but he was a man Shūsei remembered with affection.

If there is a hero in Shūsei's memoirs concerning his childhood and youth, it is his eldest half brother Tokuda Naomatsu (1855–1921). Shūsei attempted a number of times to memorialize Naomatsu in short stories, notably in a 1902 adaption of Alphonse Daudet's "Le Petit Chose," but this was a melodramatic failure.[20] The clearest portrait of his half brother emerges from Shūsei's memoirs and autobiographical novels:

Ken'ichi [Naomatsu] was studying the law. Among his acquaintances were civil servants, prefectural assemblymen, and lawyers, and he had even begun to take on legal cases and appear in court. Even now, Hitoshi was moved to tears when he remembered how assiduously Ken'ichi had studied for his examination to become a lawyer. A red blanket over his shoulders, Ken'ichi would sit up all night at his desk while the rest of the family slept. The family had begun to use gas lamps in place of candles about then, and it was Hitoshi's daily chore to clean and fill with kerosene the three lamps his brother used. Ken'ichi would sometimes come over and send Hitoshi off to the butcher shop across the river to buy beef. The butcher invariably gave him free spring onions with his order, and on his return he and Ken'ichi would cook and eat the meat and onions over the fire of the open hearth. (18:28–29)

Naomatsu was struggling to keep the Tokuda family together in their respectable residence in the Okachi district by finding some foothold in the local prefectural administration. He failed to pass his examination in 1885, however, and he was forced to emigrate to Osaka to take a position as a police officer: "Kanazawa's regional specialty." Naomatsu had protected Shūsei and Shūsei's mother from his younger brother Juntarō, Shūsei's elder half brother, who was the only family member to display open hostility to his stepmother and Shūsei, and Naomatsu continued to act as the main support of the family after he moved to Osaka, sending part of his salary to keep Shūsei in school. In 1892 and 1893, he supported Shūsei in Osaka after Shūsei failed in his first attempt to become established as a writer in Tokyo, and there are descriptions in Shūsei's memoirs and autobiographical fiction of Naomatsu finding Shūsei a job as a clerk, providing him with his first suit, and praising his fledgling literary efforts. It seems that Naomatsu's career taught Shūsei a lesson that would become a seminal theme in his early literature: "civilization and enlightenment" was a political power struggle in which kind, decent, self-sacrificing people, such as his half brother, lost out.[21]

"Kanshō-teki no koto" (A Sentimental Story, 1921), one of Shūsei's finest autobiographical short stories, reveals the ambivalence in his feelings about his mother:

She gave me no concept of the realities of life. I didn't even learn how to count money until I was almost grown up. From my middle-school years, my family endured considerable poverty, and this had an influence on me as a young man. But my mother never failed to try to shield her children from the harsh reality of impoverished circumstances. Of course, she herself regarded poverty neither as something to be ashamed of nor as a source of tribulation. Born of relatively good gentry family, she herself had only a vague sense of economic realities. She was "poor and improvident," if put uncharitably, but "generously easygoing," if put charitably, and believing that poverty was a condition to be proud of— proof of honesty and gentility—she made no attempt to escape from a life that year by year was growing more desperate. I acknowledge that putting the blame for our family's situation entirely on her shoulders is cruel. But I slowly became

aware that in her natural generosity and indulgence there was growing an
infinite love which sought to bind all of her children—and me as her only son in
particular—securely to her forever. I came to reproach her not for the way she
raised us but for the absurdity of her own life.

"The poor woman," I concluded whenever I thought of my mother, and I
was compelled to confront my own selfishness and indolence, but I felt that
even if I approached her, we would have little to say to each other. (6:407–8)

It is little wonder that Shūsei was reluctant to recall his youth in
Kanazawa, for in remembering his indulgent father, the caresses of his
sisters and half sisters, the protection he received from his eldest half
brother, and the "infinite love" of his mother, he had to confront his
own betrayal of their generosity and affection. In contrast to many
bourgeois and large landowning families, which became exclusionary
and cold to younger sons in the wake of the vast changes brought about
by the Restoration, most members of Shūsei's immediate family closed
ranks to protect and educate its youngest male. Undoubtedly, this was
done in part in the hope that Shūsei would complete an elite educational course, take up a responsible position in society, help restore the
fortunes of the Tokuda house, and provide generously for his aging
mother. He disappointed all of these expectations. He simply "let go"
and went into a free fall into the bohemian circles of the literary world
in Tokyo. Shūsei himself has offered several reasons for his decision to
drop out of school: he hated the discipline maintained in the state-run
school system; he could not master mathematics; money from his half
brother ceased coming and his family could not hope to send him to
university; and he was by nature given to vain daydreaming.[22]

The realization of Shūsei's aspiration to become a professional novelist meant that ultimately he had to cast himself as a rebellious youth, or
at least an unfilial son, in his memoirs and autobiographical fiction
about his boyhood and adolescence, and yet in several respects he remained remarkably faithful in his personal life and his literature to the
experiences of his youth. As did his mother and half brother, he took a
gentrylike pride in poverty, though he was by no means always poor,
and in keeping with his background as a déclassé ex-samurai, he generally disdained the ostentation and high living associated with new
wealth. He married a woman who was, if anything, more generous and
easygoing than his mother. He maintained a large family—four sons
and three daughters—and, like his father, was personally concerned
with the welfare of his children and could not bring himself to give

them up for adoption. Finally, in his literature, he consistently portrayed families that, like his own, had been marginalized by social and economic changes beyond their control.

Education

One morning, Hitoshi was caught by his mother. As usual, he had been trying to stay out of her sight and was fiddling around by the desk in the front room. She was suddenly behind him, and scooping him up under one arm, she carried him over to the edge of the well off the kitchen, where she forced him to stare down into its cool depths.

"You're your mother's shame! If you won't go to school, we'll die together now!"

The determination in her eyes and voice was more than enough to frighten the timid Hitoshi. But that was the first and last time she chastised him so severely. She disliked disciplining her children.

"I'll go, I'll go!"

Hitoshi was at last forgiven. (18:17)

That Shūsei's gentle mother should resort to such an extreme measure to force her son to attend school is compelling evidence that self-improvement through education was broadly seen as the primary means for young men of *shizoku* class to succeed in life, even in such backward regions as Kanazawa. The scarce resources of the Tokuda family were invested in the education of the youngest son. Unpei's second son, Juntarō, twelve years Shūsei's senior, was probably judged not able enough to undergo the educational process, a decision which indicates that Unpei, Naomatsu, and Take thought that Shūsei was bright enough to warrant their confidence. In making the yearly decision to forgo whatever income the young Shūsei would have been able to earn and to pay fees for tutors and tuition, they probably hoped that Shūsei would graduate from the elite educational course and eventually find a position in the prefectural or central government bureaucracy.

The steps in this course in Ishikawa prefecture changed frequently during Shūsei's years in school in accord with changing national educational policy, but they can be roughly outlined as follows: four years of compulsory primary education (in Shūsei's case, at the Yōsei Shōgakkō), entrance by examination to a four-year middle school (Kanazawa Shōgakkō), and entrance by examination to a four-year university preparatory school (Ishikawa Senmon Gakkō, ultimately to become the

Fourth Higher School in 1894, one of five state-run university preparatory schools). Graduation from the equivalent of the Fourth Higher
School would have practically ensured Shūsei's entrance to Tokyo Imperial University, the only state-sponsored university in Japan at the time,
but Shūsei dropped out of the system in 1891 in his second year of the
three-year university preparatory course. He was nineteen at the time,
and his progress through the educational system had been delayed by
poor grades, ill health, and the necessity of taking remedial classes.
Shūsei, then, never received a university education, and this meant that
he was never to be intensely exposed to various "Western worldviews,"
such as Spencer's Social Darwinism. His "lack of education," however,
should be kept in perspective, for far fewer than 1 percent of the students
who matriculated into primary schools throughout the country in the
same year as Shūsei made it as far up the state-sponsored educational
ladder as he did.[23]

Kanazawa, as noted above, was a conservative place, and Shūsei's
early education probably differed little from the pre-Restoration *tera-
koya* tradition of rote learning of classical Chinese texts. But even this
basic curriculum had to be supplemented by study in a private academy:

His teacher was a fiftyish, short, plump man with disheveled thinning hair, an
elementary-school teacher who taught private students in the mornings and
evenings before and after his official duties. No matter how cold the morning,
Hitoshi would set off before breakfast, often while it was still dark, to take his
place in a room with twenty other sleepy students who were all reading their
texts at desks, each of which had its own small kerosene lamp. These students
were much older than Hitoshi, and most did not appear to be attending school.
Hitoshi was taught such works as the *Wen hsuan* [Literary Selections] and the
Yuan Ming shih lueh [The Abbreviated History of the Yuan and Ming Dynas-
ties]. When his teacher, who reeked of wine from early morning, reached Wen
T'ien Hsiang's "Song of the Just," he became quite enthusiastic in his recitation,
and Hitoshi was annoyed by flying saliva. (18:43)

Shūsei seems to have been thrown back on his own resources and
those of his family when it came to mastering enough English and
mathematics to pass the competitive entrance examinations for the
higher, noncompulsory schools of learning. He began to study English
under his brother-in-law Ōta Tameyuki, a former student of the scholar
of Dutch learning Takamine Seiichi (18:22), and he was fortunate to
have had such an erudite relative, for there were few teachers in

Kanazawa with a knowledge of the fundamentals of English. Tsuda Jū, a doctor of Chinese medicine, taught him mathematics and English at another private academy (18:45). There were no official school textbooks, and Shūsei was dependent on the school library, a lending library, and the private libraries of friends and relatives (18:57–58).

Having passed the entrance examination (Izumi Kyōka was to fail the same examination a year later), Shūsei entered Kanazawa Technical College in January of 1886. This was about the same time that the Tokuda family was forced to move into the house of Shūsei's half sister, where Shūsei would live until he left Kanazawa. At college, Shūsei encountered an ideological atmosphere that was semifeudal, young men bent on imitating the extreme nationalism and worship of martial values advocated by the unregenerate samurai of the Satsuma domain (15:427). The dominant faction in the school Shūsei termed the Seiken Igen group after the Neo-Confucianist Asami Keisai's (1652–1711) anthology of the biographies and final testaments of heroic Chinese historical figures who gave their lives in the service of lord and country. This group would strut around the school acting as if they were the young heroes of the Restoration, even threatening to drive off the single foreign English teacher in the name of ridding the nation of barbarians (jōi) (18:48). The complete rejection of femininity in favor of masculine values led to widespread homosexuality: "During our schooldays—that is, our middle-school years—we had almost no contact with the opposite sex, but there was homosexuality in the Kyūshū manner [in the manner of samurai of the Satsuma domain]" (15:425).

Shūsei dropped out of school before a new generation of teachers (he mentions Nishida Kitarō and Fujioka Sakutarō) arrived to lecture on positivism, Spencer, Kant, and Japanese literature. In his accounts of his years at higher school, Shūsei expressed great respect for the abilities of only one of his Japanese teachers, Miyake Shōtarō, a brilliant scholar of classical Chinese who taught his students both the *Shih-chi* (Historical Records) and how to read modern Chinese newspapers (18:53). Shūsei quarreled with this teacher, however, because the man refused to recognize as literarily grammatical the new style of writing being developed by Yamada Bimyō (18:60). Shūsei had fond memories of a young Canadian who taught him English grammar, a person who was later employed by a Christian church in Tokyo (18:49), but the Christianity that was inspiring such future novelists as Tōson, Hakuchō, Doppo, and Hōmei in other parts of the country is mentioned just once in *Hikari o ōte:* "[O]n a snowy evening in January, he was taken by his mother through the gathering drifts to see a Western magic show; everyone in the audience called it Christianity" (18:29).

Much of Shūsei's literary education during adolescence was gained through relatives and friends who introduced him to books in personal and lending libraries. He was stimulated to read a great deal by "poverty and literature" (18:50). The stimulation of poverty can probably be interpreted as an enthusiasm for a mixture of nativistic egalitarianism and naive hero worship. Shūsei's middle-school years correspond to the height of the People's Rights movement, and Shūsei has recorded an outburst of political enthusiasm and opposition to the Satsuma-Chōshū oligarchy among young men in Kanazawa (15:443). Influenced by the journal *Eisai Shinshi* (New Writings of Gifted Young People), one of the first of dozens of Tokyo magazines specializing in the publication of contributions from the youthful literate public as a whole, Shūsei began to think about basic political and philosophical questions and made speeches in front of his class advocating "wildly radical, impractical doctrines" (18:33).

Especially after the issuance of the Education Ordinances of 1886, political activity by students was strictly prohibited. Shūsei broke the rules by attending political rallies while he was in school (18:62), and approximately a year after leaving school, he was working for Jiyū-tō (Liberal party) newspapers, first in Kanazawa and later in Nagaoka in Niigata prefecture, employment which continued intermittently for about fifteen months.[24] Thus, Shūsei was schooled in an opposition, nativistic, egalitarian political movement, a fact that, we will see, is a key to understanding his later commitment to literary realism. His political enthusiasm, however, was in no way exceptional; rather, his response to declassment was probably typical of a great many marginalized *shizoku*.[25]

Classical Chinese political philosophy was also an important early influence on Shūsei. At about the age of sixteen, through the library of a friend, Shūsei discovered in the unorthodox classical Chinese tradition the means to subvert the "modern oppositions"—individual versus state, self versus collectivity, subjectivity versus objectivity, rural virtue versus urban vice—that a reconstituted Neo-Confucianism in the form of state ideology imposed and that recourse to Western metaphysics often opposed.[26] In his early fifties, Shūsei stated that *Lao Tzu* and *Chuang Tzu* had had more influence on him than any other system of thought, and perhaps his tendency in his mature works to ignore or gently satirize the dominant discourses of his day owed something to those aspects of the Taoist tradition which were an implicit critique of Neo-Confucian metaphysics.[27]

If poverty stimulated Shūsei to read widely in Sino-Japanese political philosophy and to consider the proper social ordering of the world, a love of the theater and fantasy led him to devour novels and works of other genres of the literary arts. This reading was done largely at random and was again determined by the access he had to other people's libraries. Shūsei tells us that the study of Chinese learning was widespread in Kanazawa but that classical Japanese literature was not much read (18:51). For this reason, there were few of his fellow students who shared his enthusiasm for the native literary arts, and perhaps because of the scarcity of such young men, his reading almost always involved "literary comrades," or close friendships formed around reading and discussing books. First, there was Naomatsu, who taught Shūsei the rules for writing classical Chinese poetry and left his young half brother a small library when he departed for Osaka:

There were the classical Chinese poems of the heroes of the Restoration, which his brother had copied by hand, and loosely bound pornographic works. He found the Mito retainer Hasuda Ichigorō's letter to his mother from prison and Yamagata Aritomo's letter admonishing Saigō Takamori. Then new books came into his hands, adventure tales about the exploration of the North Pole, journeys to the depths of the sea, or flights into the sky. (18:46)[28]

Shortly after entering college, where he was determined to devote himself to his studies, Shūsei made friends with Gotō Tomomatsu, a fellow student who lent Shūsei books and encouraged him to read such influential works as Suehiro Tetchō's *Setchūbai,* Tōkai Sanshi's *Kajin no kigū,* and Nishimura Tenshū's *Kuzuya no kago* (18:47).[29] He also urged Shūsei to borrow and read Futabatei Shimei's *Ukigumo* and Tsubouchi Shōyō's *Shosei katagi.* Shūsei, who by this time was literate in several pseudoclassical languages, frankly admitted that he could not understand these two pioneering novels (15:421–22).[30] When the business his family started in Kanazawa failed, Gotō moved to Nanao.

Shūsei later formed new literary friendships in Kanazawa. Though he composed Chinese poetry and haiku with friends, he appears to have been primarily attracted to the narrative arts. A young man named Sagaki Kiichi informed Shūsei about the exciting new figures and events on the central Tokyo literary scene. He explained Tsubouchi Shōyō's concept of realism (*shajitsu*), guided Shūsei to the new publication *Kokumin no Tomo,* and, on a summer evening on a bridge over the Asano River, suggested that the young Shūsei become a professional novelist. Shūsei recalled turning red with embarrassment as if whispered to by his first love, but he did not believe at that point that he had the ability to become a professional writer (15:432, 18:56).

It was during his last three or four years in Kanazawa that Shūsei began to feel, in local book-lending shops, the vitality and productivity of the Tokyo literary scene:

At about that time, new publications were overflowing from the shelves of Teradaya Lending Library and the bookstore Tanada close to his school. The progressive *Kokumin no Tomo* [1887], the conservative *Nipponjin* [1888], and the literary magazines *Waseda Bungaku* [1891], *Mezamashigusa* [1896], *Shinshōsetsu* [1889], and *Miyako no Hana* [1888] were appearing, and printed editions of Chikamatsu and Saikaku and other classics had been transported into the town. Hitoshi was more idly addicted to literature than he was a scholarly reader, and so all kinds of books came and went across his desk. *Tosa nikki, Ise monogatari, Makura no sōshi,* Chikamatsu's *Tenchi Tennō* and *Sekihachi tsunagiuma,* Saikaku's *Honchō wakafuzoku,* and *Gonin onna* were some of the classics he read. In place of the Chinese novels such as *Sangokushi* and *Suikoden* he once read under his bedding late into the night, Mokuami's plays or Kōson's *Muratake* now occupied his summer nights. . . . On the other hand, there were the collected essays of Addison and novels by Dickens and Lytton, which at some point had gotten mixed in with textbooks and which he could never have hoped to understand even if he had looked up every word in the dictionary. (18:57)[31]

The years the periodicals mentioned above first appeared are noted in brackets, and Shūsei probably confused *Mezamashigusa* with *Shigarami Sōshi* (1889), an earlier literary periodical also closely associated with Mori Ōgai. (That Shūsei was reading Ōgai somewhere seems certain because he remembered memorizing portions of *Maihime*.)[32] Shūsei's memory substantiates the impression that in the last decade of the nineteenth century the Japanese publishing industry was on the verge of a boom unprecedented certainly in the history of East Asia and perhaps in the history of the world.[33] Given the expansion of literacy around the turn of the century, the result of the most successful compulsory education system in East Asia, and given the large number of publications—newspapers, magazines, and literary journals—carrying fiction during this period, Shūsei's ambition to become a professional novelist was perhaps not as unrealistic as he portrayed it to be in his memoirs.[34]

Of all of Shūsei's literary friendships in Kanazawa, the one he formed with Kiryū Yūyū (1873–1941) was the most intimate and long lasting.

Kiryū, who later became a well-known journalist, editor, and a consistent critic of Japanese militarism, had contempt for Shūsei's acquaintances among the Seiken Igen group. He maintained that their patriotic fervor was a mere mask for repressed sexual desire (18:68). Shūsei and Kiryū discussed the works of Saikaku, Chikamatsu, and Ozaki Kōyō on long walks to the sea (where Shūsei would swim as a form of therapy), and together they attempted a translation of Shakespeare's *A Midsummer Night's Dream,* which they were unable to complete because the original proved too difficult. Kiryū introduced Shūsei to Mori Ōgai's translations of Karl Robert Eduard von Hartmann's writings on aesthetics and encouraged Shūsei's interest in haiku (18:68–69). The two young men made the long journey to Tokyo together in hopes of gaining Ozaki Kōyō's support, but they were turned away at Kōyō's door by Izumi Kyōka, who had already become Kōyō's disciple. They hung on in Tokyo, sharing lodgings for about a month in 1892 before Kiryū returned to Kanazawa and Shūsei, who was suffering from a mild infection of smallpox, received money from Naomatsu to travel to Osaka. They remained close friends even after Kiryū's antimilitarism led him into trouble with the army in 1933, when he was forced to resign from his position as editor of a major daily paper because of his outspoken political views.[35]

Shūsei's autobiographical works go on to chronicle his dark years of purposeless wandering through Osaka, Kanazawa, and Nagaoka, how the success of Izumi Kyōka's *Teriha-kyōgen* (1896) inspired him to return to Tokyo and make a second attempt at a literary career, how he got a position as a copywriter and proofreader at the publishing firm Hakubunkan through his connections with the Niigata politician Koganei Kenzaburō, his early contacts with Taoka Reiun, and his apprenticeship to Ozaki Kōyō.[36] However, enough biographical information has been presented here to provide a good idea of Shūsei's own social position.

Shūsei received a largely literary education that was very eclectic. He was not an intellectual. The fact that he dropped out from the elite educational course left him uneducated by the standards of the intelligentsia who encountered the "West" through the university or Christianity. His formal education, however, was more than adequate to enable him to join a number of bright, radicalized young people who were finding positions on the margins of the publishing boom in Tokyo. Shūsei found a foothold on the edge of the Tokyo literary world because he had received a better education in foreign languages—English and classical Chinese—than that received by most popular writers of his day.[37]

He was born as well as or better than most of the people he portrayed and the writers he associated with, but he suffered no illusion that this fact had any real significance. He was used to poverty, and for most of his life he judged himself to be poor, but he saw this condition more as a source of pride and was "prejudiced" against the rich and obvious ostentation. In reality, he commanded relatively high fees for his writing, and he always managed to keep his large family in fairly respectable circumstances.[38]

Shūsei generally did not participate in debates about literary theory, and his tendency to avoid intellectual discourses led a writer and critic associated with Japanese naturalism to conclude that Shūsei lacked intelligence: " 'Shūsei doesn't have it up here,' Iwano Hōmei once stated, tapping his finger against his head."[39] Adding to this impression, Shūsei displayed a certain shyness and was overmodest in public situations. He frequently referred to his laziness and lack of diligence as a writer, his timidity, and the fact that he could not bear to read his own work after he had written it.[40] Such self-deprecatory remarks can perhaps be seen as an aspect of what Shūsei's biographer Noguchi Fujio has termed "a sense of inferiority brought about by Shūsei's dark upbringing in an impoverished family, his physical frailty, and being in the position of the son of his father's [fourth] wife, a sense of inferiority which became the foundation of a view of life that contained a passive, negative phototropism, the undercurrent of that quality of his work later evaluated as the color of somber silver, or his subdued literary style."[41]

Shūsei recalled that in his childhood he experienced a physical aversion to bright light.[42] His mature fiction contains few moments of hard intellectual clarity. Rather, his novels and short stories concern the confusing muddle of the commonplace, the "taken for granted," those moments that almost always seem to escape articulation. During a visit to Akita prefecture in 1926 or so, Shūsei wrote an essay in which he expressed his abiding interest in "the myriad grasses," a traditional metaphor for the masses:[43]

I became a conscious human being [*hito*] in the provinces, and I feel a strange sense of familiarity with the nameless wild grasses and weeds growing in such profusion on vacant fields, hills, in rice paddies, beside the road, along paths, or at the foot of a hedge or a fence. Trees, wild shrubs, or weeds are more or less the same wherever one goes in this country, and on encountering the summer grasses that had sprung up along the water close to where I am staying here in the provinces, I was struck by their similarity to the wild grasses of my provincial hometown. The sight gave me a feeling of security associated with the earth.... I was raised in a provincial city with its own distinctive cultural tradition, but my family lost its stipend soon after my birth, and my childhood was spent in a household which always seemed on the verge of financial ruin. Probably for economic reasons, my family moved to a desolate neighborhood some distance from the center of the city. I have fond memories of the fruit trees in our garden, but what stands out most clearly in my memory of that dilapidated, old neighborhood are the ruins of deserted samurai residences that had been taken over by the vines and brambles of wild vegetation, and, quite naturally, I spent my youth playing with other children in fields overgrown by tall grass.... No matter how beautiful the natural setting from afar, if one draws close, one will discover at its base an undergrowth of a trailing profusion of unattractive small trees, wild bushes, and weeds. I was raised among just such a profusion, and, needless to say, my tastes and interests as a youth were rustic and uncultivated. After thirty years of urban life, perhaps I have distanced myself from that mood of wild undergrowth and have become somewhat more sophisticated. Still, I don't suppose I will ever rid my nature of the roughness of my childhood spent playing in dirt covered by tall grasses. Of course, I am impressed by the majestic beauty of the mountain Chōkaisan here in Akita, but I have to feel a deeper familiarity with the tall grasses growing here and there by the side of the water or by the road on the outskirts of town. (10:563–64)

If Shūsei was at times shy and reserved, he was also an extraordinary combination of will, tenacity, and flexibility, qualities which enabled him to write primarily about "merely ordinary" people and to survive as an important presence, sometimes as the preeminent presence, on the Japanese literary scene for forty-odd years. His novels and short stories have been praised as the culmination of modern Japanese realism both in aesthetic terms by Kawabata Yasunari and in terms of content by critics associated with the nondogmatic Left.[44] Serious realism has class implications, and in the next chapter the development of Shūsei's realistic popular fiction will be examined in the light of these implications.

2

Popular Entertainment:
1895–1908

> Description of locality, deliberate analysis of character or motive,
> demanded far too great an effort for his present condition. He kept
> as much as possible to dialogue; the space is filled so much more
> quickly, and at a pinch one can make people talk about the paltriest
> incidents in life.
>
> —George Gissing, *New Grub Street*

On turning from Shūsei's memory of his early career to the literary
works he actually wrote during this period, one is immediately struck by
the sense of dislocation that comes from the gap between remembrance
articulated in a mature style and the dusty fictions of the past, which are
marked by hackneyed plots and melodramatic excess. There is intrinsi-
cally little of interest in the hundreds of political melodramas, mysteries,
long serial romances, ghost stories, war stories, children's adventure
stories, fairy tales, and translations which Shūsei churned out during
this period, and yet it is paradoxical that the works produced during
these thirteen years from 1895 to 1908 established Shūsei's reputation
as a professional novelist. Shūsei at his worst has always been, in some
respects, more popular than Shūsei at his best. But it is the nature of
popular entertainment to be quickly forgotten, and most of these works
have been.[1]

From time to time, Shūsei would take positions with publishing
houses, but he soon quit to get back to his real work: writing fiction. Earning a living as a professional novelist required that he
write very swiftly, and he produced an enormous quantity of narrative during his career. Scholars have estimated that over two thousand different titles were published under his name, though some of
these were almost certainly written by others.[2] We will probably
never know how much he actually wrote, but a cursory count of the
titles in the most accurate bibliographical source reveals the following numbers for the period from 1895 to 1908: 160 short stories
and novellas, 16 children's stories, 22 translations, 110 haiku, and 24
long novels.[3]

Tokuda Shūsei and the Early Japanese Literary World

Shūsei's career illustrates the difficulty of maintaining that there was an absolute distinction between writers of "pure," or serious, fiction and writers of popular fiction and their respective rights to be members of the "literary world" (*bundan*). The *bundan* developed out of a series of literary guilds organized by writers for mutual self-help in reaction to rapacious publishing houses such as Hakubunkan and Shun'yōdō that were scrambling to meet the seemingly insatiable desire of the literate Japanese public.

Let us take a brief look at some of the more prominent popular periodicals Shūsei was writing for in 1898: *Shōnen Bunshū* (Collected Young People's Writings, a journal carrying contributions from the general public), *Yomiuri Shinbun* (Shūsei serialized two novels in this daily newspaper in 1898), *Shinshōsetsu* (The New Novel, published by Shun'yōdō), *Jogaku Kōgi* (Lectures for Young Ladies), *Joshi no Tomo* (The Girl's Friend, published by Jitsugyō Nipponsha), and *Kokumin Shinbun* (Tokutomi Sohō's daily newspaper, with a circulation of 25,000). In previous and subsequent years he frequently published in *Bungei Kurabu* (Literary Club, Hakubunkan's star literary journal). If Tokuda Shūsei had not been associated with Ozaki Kōyō's literary guild, his work probably would not have been accepted by any of these publications.[4]

Shūsei and his friend Kiryū Yūyū had been rudely rejected in their first attempt to gain entry to Kōyō's guild in 1892. However, Shūsei had hung on. Living with his brother in Osaka, Shūsei published serialized novels in two of Osaka's daily papers. Back in Tokyo after stints with progressive provincial newspapers, he published in 1895 criticism praising Kōda Rohan and urging greater realism in the Japanese novel. Then he aligned himself with Ozaki Kōyō's bitter enemy, Taoka Reiun, and began serializing a "protest novel" in the journal Reiun was editing, *Seinenbun* (Youth's Literature), a monthly magazine that solicited contributions from the general public. He managed to use a political connection, Shibuya Mokuan, to gain an introduction to Koganei Kenzaburō, a powerful Diet member from Niigata. Koganei, in turn, introduced Shūsei to Ōhashi Sahei, father of the founder, Ōhashi Shintarō, of the publishing house Hakubunkan. Employed as a copywriter and proofreader at Hakubunkan, Shūsei regularly associated with Iwaya Sazanami, cofounder with Ozaki Kōyō of *Garakuta Bunko* (Library of Odds and Ends) and the powerful literary guild Ken'yūsha (Friends of the Inkstone). While Shūsei was at Hakubunkan, he was knocking on Ozaki

Kōyō's door without going near Ozaki's house. It was only a matter of time before Izumi Kyōka, on a visit to his publisher Hakubunkan, encountered Shūsei and urged him to pay another call on Kōyō. In June of 1895, Shūsei was accepted into Ozaki's latest guild of younger writers, later known as the Sōsha. By the end of the next year, 1896, he had left Hakubunkan and was supporting himself by his writing. He continued this lifestyle until his death in 1943.[5]

The reasons Shūsei wanted to become a member of Kōyō's guild seem clear enough. Ozaki Kōyō was the most popular writer of the day, and his popularity enabled him to negotiate with publishers so that people associated with him found places to publish and received higher fees for their writing.[6] In December of 1896, Shūsei moved into a residence-workplace in the back of Kōyō's house. He thus became a live-in apprentice in the craft of the novel with three other young writers: Oguri Fūyō, Yanagawa Shun'yō, and Tanaka Ryōyō.[7] Toward the end of 1897, through 1898, and decreasingly in 1899, Shūsei published numerous works under his own name with the added attribution "assisted by Ozaki Kōyō" (Ozaki Kōyō ho). After Shūsei established himself as an independent novelist, he was known as one of the Four Devas (shi-tennō) of Kōyō's guild, the other three being Izumi Kyōka, Oguri Fūyō, and Yanagawa Shun'yō.[8] Shūsei remained firmly identified in the public mind as a writer from Kōyō's stable well after Kōyō's death in 1903.

Citing the fact that Taoka Reiun, Shūsei's former supporter, was an implacable enemy of Kōyō, several Japanese scholars have argued that Shūsei's apprenticeship to Kōyō was a betrayal of Shūsei's political convictions or of his so-called innate tendency to naturalism. This view is substantiated by a statement Shūsei made in 1908: "Ozaki Kōyō told me on several occasions, 'This won't sell,' and when I look back on it now, I realize that the works I wrote then were my efforts to produce salable fiction. Of course I started out at an infantile level, so saying this may seem rather silly, but I feel now that I deceived myself a great deal to produce things that would sell."[9]

This statement seems rather naive. Aside from a youthful political passion and a faith in the realism of polemic and problem fiction, Shūsei had little to betray in 1896.[10] Artistic integrity was something he had to build up incrementally by mastering an inventory of literary techniques obtained painfully by writing an enormous amount of "stuff" he had no particular investment or interest in. If his association with Ozaki Kōyō and the publishing boom Kōyō's immense popularity helped create had not provided Shūsei with the ability to earn enough money to keep on writing and honing his craft, he would not have been able to produce his mature fiction. As Matsumoto Tōru has argued, Shūsei could not allow himself to stop and reflect on what he was doing—selling out—for it would have deprived him of the only way he knew to grow: the act of writing.[11] By 1908, this "vicious circle" had created in Shūsei a novelist of enormous originality, power, and narrative skill, but his twelve years of training in the craft of narrative prose fiction must have been torturous.[12]

Ozaki Kōyō is reported to have once declared, "Shūsei is always at a disadvantage. Even when he has money, he appears to have none. How can a person be so somber all the time?"[13] Why did Kōyō take the angry, politically radical Shūsei under his wing? Kōyō probably saw Shūsei as a valuable addition to his guild because Shūsei had a better formal education than other writers associated with it.[14] Kōyō's pretensions to a mastery of Western literature irritated Shūsei, for Shūsei was convinced that Kōyō had only a weak command of foreign languages.[15] Shūsei's function was probably to work on the borders of languages. After receiving instruction in pseudoclassical rhetoric, Shūsei was sent by Kōyō to help Kōyō's friend Osada Shūtō, a European-educated professor of French at Waseda, embellish the Japanese literary style of Osada's translations from French.[16] Shūsei also translated portions of Victor Hugo's *Notre Dame de Paris* from an English translation, and these were ultimately published under the title of *Shōrōmori* (The Belfry Keeper), with credit for the translation taken by Kōyō and Osada.[17]

In 1900, in the weekly magazine *Taiyō* (The Sun), there appeared a satirical cartoon entitled "A Cabinet Formed by Literary Figures." In the cartoon, Osada Shūtō was given the post of minister of foreign affairs, Uchida Roan the post of vice-minister of foreign affairs, Tokutomi Roka the post of imperial councillor to the Ministry of Foreign Affairs, and Tokuda Shūsei the post of private secretary to the minister of foreign affairs.[18] At the turn of the century, Shūsei was closely associated with the importation and translation of European and American literature. This meant that Shūsei was often involved in plagiarism or an activity close to plagiarism. Shūsei can aptly be described as a fiction-making factory licensed by Kōyō to manufacture Japanese stories drawn from foreign sources.

Shūsei would at times translate or adapt European or American works and provide no other attribution than his name. This was standard practice for this period. In most cases, it was probably fairly evident to readers that Shūsei was at least imitating foreign works. For example, in 1899 Shūsei adapted a foreign work probably entitled *The Secret of Smugglers* (author and date unknown). He titled the serialized Japanese version of this work *Kyūakuzuka* (An Old Grave for the Wicked) and gave no indication that it was based on another novel. However, the fact that it was set in Great Britain and the main characters had kabuki-like names such as Yumichi Hidaroku probably informed most readers of the work's foreign origins. Audiences at this time seem to have delighted in exotic illustrations of English men and women with Japanese names. Shūsei got a great deal of mileage out of this work. Two years later, he rewrote the novel in modern inflections, changed the names of the characters, and moved the setting to Japan. With a new title, *Nochi no zange* (Repentance after the Fact), it was serialized in a newspaper in Kyūshū. In 1904, he published the same work in book form as *Chichū no bijin* (The Subterranean Beauty). There are other examples of Shūsei adapting or translating a foreign novel and then selling it, with minor revisions, as his own work to several publications.[19]

In a telling moment in his memoir, Shūsei recounts how Kōyō first tested his abilities. Kōyō told Shūsei that Iwaya Sazanami, a member of the older literary guild Ken'yūsha, wanted to commission a story for serialization in a newspaper Iwaya was editing. Kōyō gave Shūsei a "cheap American storybook" and told him to turn a ten-page story into a "Japanese-like adaptation." Shūsei used the English-language story to create a narrative suitable for fourteen or fifteen days' serialization. Iwaya bought it, Shūsei passed his test, and Kōyō gave Shūsei five yen, the first cash payment Shūsei received for his writing (18:142–43). It is not recorded under whose name the story appeared. Authorship may well have been claimed by Iwaya or another of Kōyō's apprentices. The concept of the immorality of plagiarism had not yet taken root in the popular Japanese literary world.[20] One can probably conclude that as a member of the literary guild Sōsha, Shūsei was expected to do translation work for which he was poorly paid and which often appeared under someone else's name.

At about the turn of the century, European thought and literature held great attraction for such young intellectuals as Natsume Sōseki, Mori Ōgai, and Shimazaki Tōson. Shūsei's encounter with the West was of an entirely different kind. If anything, Shūsei resented his main conduit to Western culture: the arrogant Osada Shūtō, a Francophile who was about Shūsei's own age. For Shūsei, English was not the path or opening to a bright, advanced civilization; rather it was merely one more language among the many he had to learn to enable him to grind out yet another "dumb story," its plot often stolen from Washington Irving, Hawthorne, Dickens, Pushkin, Gorky, Daudet, Maupassant, or some now obscure European or American author.[21] The English language was "just another tool of the trade."

In 1900, then, Shūsei occupied a low-level position in the literary "Ministry of Foreign Affairs," and he was being pressured by his superiors to read a great deal of literature in English. He may have read as much foreign literature as any novelist at that time. It was probably with a great sense of relief that he gradually gave up reading and stealing from foreign literature in the years following the Russo-Japanese War. After 1907, he concentrated almost exclusively on his own original work. He became, in his phrase, a person who disliked Western literature without reading it (*yomazu-girai*).[22]

Kōyō did not understand Shūsei's personality, and he thought that Shūsei's literature "smelled a little Western" (*sukoshi seiyō kusakute ikenai*).[23] Yet Kōyō did what he could to teach Shūsei the craft of writing and to see to it that Shūsei was able to sell his fledgling literary efforts. Though Shūsei's public statements and literary portrayal of his famous teacher reveal a marked ambivalence toward this much lionized "literary genius," Shūsei did assess Kōyō's stylistic influence in positive terms: "In terms of style, Kōyō was of great help to me in planning my work. . . . He generally wanted the light touch, but he would talk about his ideas and was willing to listen to ours. He was not much concerned with content, but I learned a great many techniques from him that enabled me to express myself more effectively."[24]

Shūsei recalled that after Kōyō had found him a position as a literary columnist for *Yomiuri Shinbun* in 1899, he had difficulty at his new job in finding works to write about. Kōyō heard a story concerning an aging actress, quickly wrote it down, and gave it to his apprentice. This ten-page piece was a literary gem just as Kōyō had written it, and Shūsei published it in his column, stretching out its serialization for as long as he could.[25] This anecdote provides an impression of the manner in which Kōyō perhaps "assisted" Shūsei in the group of works cosigned by Kōyō and published between the years 1897 and 1899.

Shūsei denied that Kōyō extensively revised his writing, or at least that is the way he wanted to remember it. As a young man, he was very protective of his independence and refused to run errands or perform domestic chores for his teacher.[26] In the seriously realistic works Shūsei was writing during this period, Kōyō probably exerted little direct influence other than heightening Shūsei's awareness of the importance of rhetoric in the novel. In the works Shūsei wrote for a popular audience, however, Kōyō's influence is palpable.[27]

Shūsei lived in Kōyō's school, the so-called Tochimandō-juku, also known as the Shiseidō, in back of Kōyō's house for approximately two years, and Kōyō was not a hands-off teacher. He would visit his students on a daily basis and often led all-night discussions on literature which were concluded in the morning when he and the younger men went together to a public bath.[28]

Tokuda Shūsei and Japanese Melodrama

Social problems such as industrialism, materialism, conformism, racism, and women's liberation—all a direct function of life under capitalism—form the core of the plots in Shūsei's works during this period. Elsewhere, as a question of the incorporation of extraliterary language diversity in narrative, I have traced Shūsei's stylistic development from radical political polemic to problem fiction centered on the tragic end of a young woman of stigmatized (*eta* or *burakumin*) birth to the pseudoclassical novel being developed by Ozaki Kōyō to "slum realism" and the influence of the *shaseibun* (sketch-from-life) movement.[29] Here, I will focus on the content of several of Shūsei's Western-influenced novels and will show that despite their popular success, Shūsei and his critics felt such works did not reflect their perceptions of reality.

Shūsei was a participant in the golden age of Japanese melodrama (1895–1905), when most of the major melodramatic character types that are so prominent even today were born. These include the *aisu*, or evil moneylender, the forerunner of today's *sarakin*, the venal politician; the innocent young countrywoman who is deceived by promises of marriage from a citified cad; the earnest young man who has come to Tokyo to work his way through college (*kugaku*); the mother and daughter who support the young man from the country on the understanding that he will marry the daughter after he graduates and who are invariably deceived; the wicked aristocrat who seduces the innocent maiden with promises of marriage; the liberated woman intellectual (often a schoolteacher) who finally realizes that her ultimate happiness is to be found in motherhood; the detective; the oh-so-respectable young lady (*ojōsama*) or young wife who is blackmailed for an indiscretion; the wicked banker; and the wicked lawyer. On any given night of the week, one or several of these "modern" character types can be found on Japanese television.

The melodramatic novel that developed at about the turn of the century should be distinguished from the *sewamono* plays of the kabuki and *jōruri* theaters and from other traditional forms of Japanese melodrama for at least three reasons. First, an important function of many genres of the theatrical and narrative arts is the creation or maintenance of a popular mythology satisfying a widespread desire to see a decadent elite chastised while allowing the public to participate vicariously in the decadence. In the melodramas created during this period, however, the elites being chastised were not feudal or even primarily political; rather they were the products of modern capitalism or technological innovation. The villains were most often those who possessed wealth earned or inherited immorally under capitalism or those who had gained specialized knowledge—medicine, dentistry, engineering, or the law—largely from the West.[30]

Second, as Peter Brooks has observed, melodrama is particularly suited to modern society, for it offers "the nearest approach to sacred and cosmic values in a world where they no longer have any certain ontology or epistemology."[31] In contrast to traditional forms of melodrama, the standards of personal and political morality expressed through modern melodrama were remarkably democratic. The heroes and heroines believe in ability and not class privilege, and it is the meek, poor, and oppressed who are portrayed as virtuous.[32] Shūsei's melodramas are conspicuously progressive.

Third, Shūsei is reported to have said that works of literature which amplified or enlarged on the ideas of the day or philosophical concepts, be these Neo-Confucian or Western, tended to degenerate into melodrama (*tsūzoku shōsetsu*).[33] He spoke from experience. The impersonal, external forces so essential to his melodramas were ideas borrowed from Western sources. That is to say, the key concepts against which the protagonists of his melodramas struggled were products of contemporary Western scientific, philosophical, and political discourses: Society, Heredity, Class, Bestial Sexual Urges, Love, and so on.

From his "Namakemono" (The Irresolute Man, 1899) on through many of the popular serial novels he wrote during the Meiji period, Shūsei reworked again and again a familiar melodramatic situation. A young person, usually impoverished and fatherless, comes from the provinces to Tokyo and has an opportunity, or believes he or she has an opportunity, to marry a wealthy or aristocratic person. Since the ensuing conflict almost always involves a high-status person deceiving a low-status person in order to marry a person of high status, a low-status person deceiving a person of similar status to marry a person of high status, or a person of low status deciding that he or she "truly loves" a person of similar status after a dalliance with a person of high status, Matsumoto Tōru's characterization of this genre of Shūsei's fiction as the novel of the love triangle is an appropriate way to think about the class relations in these works.[34] Though these love affairs are always heterosexual, there are variations in the sex of those in positions of power: some works have a woman in the higher-status position; some have a man.

When Shūsei began working with this formula, he created fictions that were close to structured social novels. Perhaps the skill displayed in these early works was due to the fact that the form seemed innovative to him, or perhaps it was because he was convinced he was going to die young and wanted to leave a work behind that would memorialize his name.[35] Especially in *Kumo no yukue* (Where the Clouds Go, 1900), the first work he wrote that was popular enough to establish him as a prominent young novelist (his *shussesaku*), there is an energy and sophistication of plot and characterization that show that Shūsei was becoming a writer of some imagination and skill.[36]

Once Shūsei had the formula down for this politically progressive melodrama, he began churning out scores of such works for serialized publication in Tokyo and regional newspapers. Since he was generally paid by the manuscript page, which filled faster with dialogue than with narration, he gave in to the temptation to pad with dialogue, often letting narrative function merely as stage directions. Shūsei had a fine ear for the rhythms of natural Japanese speech. Ideas translated into melodrama robbed him of even this natural talent, however, as is clear in the following passage from Shūsei's 1902 *Shunkō* (Spring Light):

They both fell silent, and Tochiyama turned his eyes to the garden. "Summer has come!"

"Yes, summer has come," Fuyuko replied, lowering her gaze and not caring to say more.

"You're a terrible egotist, you know. Here in this garden with the leaves of the trees bursting forth in splendor and the red flowers in bloom, how can you not believe in an omnipotent Creator who made all of this for a purpose!"

"Exactly what relationship does nonbelief have with egotism?" Fuyuko asked smiling.

"Relationship? It is not so much a relationship as the fact that you cannot believe."

"I won't believe!"

"Then how can you denounce society as cruel and callous?"

"But it's true!"

"Even if it is true," blurted out Tochiyama, becoming impatient, "it is all the more reason why you should lay your anguish on the shoulders of the omnipotent God. Then you will find peace!" Tochiyama pulled out his handkerchief and blew his nose noisily with it. (This was a bad habit this fellow had.)

"It's impossible," she said, her eyes laughing scornfully, but then they clouded and the crease in her forehead expressed her loathing. (1:371–72)

Fuyuko has been deceived by a rich young man and has had to bear his child after he deserted her. She has awakened to the oppression of women in Japanese society and is determined to remain independent of men, family, and marriage. She supports herself and her child by working as a journalist advocating progressive causes. *Shunkō* is largely made up of Fuyuko's angry arguments with a Christian minister, who urges her to find God, with her elder brother, who denounces her as a trollop, and with the rich young man who abandoned her and now lectures her on her responsibilities to his daughter. This novella was well received and perhaps helped form the prototype of the independent, existential woman that would emerge a month later in Nagai Kafū's *Jigoku no hana* (The Flower from Hell). Given the fact that the percentage of Japanese women at the turn of the century who received postsecondary, Western educations was infinitesimal, one wonders what appeal this kind of heroine had for the reading public. Perhaps it was precisely the scarcity of women who could aspire to play the role of Nora in Japan that made the role seem fascinatingly exotic or erotic. In any case, this is the progressive type Shūsei would reject in his later serious fiction as being untrue to Japanese society.

Shūsei's translation of foreign concepts into melodrama culminated with his serialized novel *Shōkazoku* (The Minor Aristocrat, 1904–5). "Nietzsche fever" overcame the literary world in Japan in 1901 and 1902, and Shūsei was infected by it too. The big names of the intelligentsia— Takayama Chogyū, Hasegawa Tenkei, Shimamura Hōgetsu, Ueda Bin, Tsubouchi Shōyō, and Mori Ōgai—turned out a profusion of articles and books on Nietzsche's life and thought. This activity influenced several works Shūsei wrote at about the turn of the century.[37]

Shōkazoku is interesting because it shows that Shūsei interpreted Nietzschean thought as the ideology of the villain. Shūsei conceived of the hero of this work as a Nietzschean figure, but when it came to putting the plan for the novel into execution, Shūsei simply took his standard "young-countryperson-up-to-Tokyo-to-marry-the-aristocrat" formula, switched the sexes in the various love triangles, substituted a woman aristocrat for a male one, and focused the action on the villain, the fatherless Odagaki Ken, who is also the protagonist.[38]

Odagaki Ken leaves the country for Tokyo, where he plans to work his way through university. In the provinces, he has become engaged to Misawa Yoshiko, whose mother has given him a large portion of her family's scarce resources to pay for his education. True to the formula, Odagaki abandons Yoshiko for a rich heiress. Akioka Matsue, daughter of Viscount Akioka by his Kyoto mistress, Ochō, and heiress to the Akioka house, shows up in the country and is introduced to Odagaki by an artist friend. Matsue and Odagaki travel to Tokyo together. Matsue, impressed by Odagaki's ambition and intelligence, introduces him to Kosone, the editor of a women's magazine. Kosone, who loves Matsue, gives Odagaki a job to impress her. Odagaki soon establishes himself as one of the brightest young critics of the day, but he has his sights on higher things than journalism or a literary career. He determines to marry Matsue and use his status as her husband to become a diplomat and advance Japan's fortunes abroad. Viscount Akioka takes a liking to Odagaki and concludes that this poor but ambitious young man will make a worthy successor to the Akioka house. Soon after Odagaki and Matsue are married, Akioka dies and Odagaki inherits everything.

Odagaki's sudden rise in the world arouses envy and ill-feeling from many quarters, especially from Umebara, a young lawyer from Odagaki's hometown. In contrast to Odagaki, Umebara did work his way through university but now finds that his degree is worthless. He determines to make a career out of attacking Odagaki, who had coldly refused to help him find employment. He decides to cause problems for the Akioka house through Ochō, Matsue's true mother. Ochō's brother has been arrested for embezzlement, and Umebara convinces her to allow him to represent her in attempting to force the Akioka house to pay off the brother's debts. Odagaki refuses to have anything to do with the "extortionist" Umebara and advises Matsue's stepmother to give Ochō nothing.

The stepmother savagely berates Ochō for bringing a stranger into a family dispute. Ochō drowns herself in a well. Her brother, the embezzler, incited by Umebara, shoots and kills Matsue's stepmother. The scandal these incidents creates in the press almost brings about the ruin of the Akioka house. The family elders meet and decide that Odagaki must divorce Matsue and resign as head of the family. Matsue protests and begs Odagaki to stay, but he takes the "separation money" the family offers and leaves. When his former lover, Yoshiko, hears that Odagaki will divorce Matsue, she goes to him and confesses that she still loves him. Odagaki bluntly tells her he has no affection left for her.

Yoshiko, heartbroken, drowns herself in the sea. Odagaki leaves for America to avoid the scandal (16:5–280).

Shōkazoku was the most popular work of fiction Shūsei had written up to that time. It probably earned him at least a hundred yen a month, a large sum rarely commanded by writers at that time, and later, in September 1905, it was adapted to the stage of the *shinpa-geki* (new-school theater) by the successful playwright Iwasaki Shunka (1894–1923). The lead role was played by Takata Minoru (1871–1916), one of the most popular actors of the day.[39] *Shōkazoku* clearly demonstrates that Shūsei had mastered the melodramatic mode. One should not underestimate the linguistic and literary facility necessary to keep moral imperatives in constant collision for the course of a rather long novel. Should Odagaki marry his country sweetheart or further his career? Should Odagaki betray his benefactor Kosone by marrying the woman Kosone loves? Should Odagaki ignore the claims of hometown and blood motherhood in the name of economic rationality? If Odagaki truly loves Matsue, should he divorce her and leave for America? Can one automatically conclude that this novel is less sophisticated than the popular paperback novels one sees in the supermarkets of the United States or than other popular fictions on Japanese television that obsess the popular imagination? Probably not. And Shūsei's serialized melodramas may tell us something about the obsessions that haunted the Meiji imagination: fears of the consequences of the dissolution of the received class order, unchecked migration from the provinces, and a lack of morality among the young.

Nonetheless, if Shūsei had remained satisfied with the realism and "ideas" of progressive melodrama, he would have undoubtedly fallen into the obscurity that awaited Oguri Fūyō, Kosugi Tengai, and so many other writers associated with Ozaki Kōyō. Fortunately, he was profoundly dissatisfied with what he was writing at this time. In the preface of *Shōkazoku*, which appeared as an independent volume in September 1905, Shūsei more or less disowned the work that had brought him more money and fame than he had ever had before. Serialized novels, he wrote in his preface, were appropriate for presenting interesting plots, which were growing ever more complex, and for introducing "fresh," original material on a "broad stage," but they were entirely inadequate for the serious representation and analysis of human affairs (*shinshi naru jinsei no byōsha setsumei*), and, he concluded, *Shōkazoku* as well was a failure in this regard. He declared that he saw no hope for the genre and that he planned to concentrate on writing short stories in the future.[40]

Writing was not a theoretical proposition for Shūsei, and his statements about the "future of the novel" or the intrinsic nature of certain genres have to be compared to the fiction he was actually writing. In fact, between 1906 and 1915, he produced a series of melodramas for publication in newspapers. He continued to portray romances among the upper classes, kill off evil aristocrats, and show poor laborers groaning under the oppression of venal capitalists and politicians. He wrote dozens of these long works, but he did so only for money and tried to keep them as far from the central Tokyo literary scene as possible, serializing some of them in newspapers in Hokkaido and even as far afield as Korea and Manchuria.[41]

The many works Shūsei wrote for a popular audience will no longer be of concern to this study. Ideas, the anguished confessions of intellectuals, romantic heroism, and political convictions were for him the province of genres other than the serious novel.

Tokuda Shūsei and Japanese Realism

From the perspective of the Japanese literary world in 1905, 1906, and 1907, Shūsei was a well-established professional novelist with a reputation as a realist.[42] He had made a living as a writer from 1900 on, had major successes in 1900 and 1905, had published numerous novels as books, and was invited to become a member of Prime Minister Saionji's "Gathering in the Murmuring Rain" (Useikai, begun in 1907), an honor placing him among the leading novelists of the day.[43]

A photograph of a meeting of the Useikai held on June 18, 1907, is an interesting artifact that provides information concerning Shūsei's standing in the literary world at the time.[44] The narrative arts, the novel in particular, were being carried in almost every newspaper and magazine throughout the country, and literature was reaching an unprecedentedly large readership. Writers of fiction were giving government officials headaches, and the prime minister, Saionji Kinmochi, a liberal known for his relative open-mindedness, had initiated a meeting with eminent men of letters to discuss problems of censorship and how writers might better serve the nation. The prime minister was granting novelists a new dignity by seeking out their views. What did he want in return? Some thought his motives were sinister.[45]

In the photograph, those in attendance are seated in an L-shaped configuration with their backs to the walls. The pseudoclassical novelist Tsukahara Jūshien is seated in the corner of the room at the center of the L and the photograph. The prime minister is seated to Tsukahara's immediate left. (How shabby all the writers seem when compared to the dignified and elegant aristocrat Saionji.) To Tsukahara's right are several writers who had come up through Kōyō's guilds: Kawakami Bizan, a founding member of the Ken'yūsha; Hirotsu Ryūrō, who early on had received Kōyō's support; and Yanagawa Shun'yō and Izumi Kyōka, both members with Shūsei of the Sōsha. The literary establishment was still dominated by writers once associated with Kōyō, but two newcomers had forced their way in. At the end of this row is Tayama Katai, the leading figure of Japanese naturalism, the literary movement which seemed so troublesome to government authorities. To his immediate left is Kunikida Doppo, the "father" of Japanese naturalism, who would die about a year after the photograph was taken. To Saionji's left are seated such respected literary figures as Kōda Rohan, Uchida Roan, Iwaya Sazanami, and finally Tokuda Shūsei. Shūsei barely made it into the photograph, and his uneasiness and shyness in this situation are apparent in his expression and downcast eyes.

Shūsei and Katai, then, are at opposite sides of the room, and this seating arrangement was probably appropriate at this time. Shūsei was acquainted with Katai, who sometimes visited the "school" in back of Kōyō's house, but Katai was far closer to Doppo, who had nothing but contempt for the professional novelists once associated with Kōyō.[46] The enormous success of literary naturalism in the years following the Russo-Japanese War was a threat most immediately to the writers formerly in Kōyō's guilds, who had been pushing the novel in a more serious, realistic direction in the late 1890s and early twentieth century, writers such as Shūsei. When the realism of these writers was judged to be superseded by naturalism, almost all of them fell out of fashion and into silence. Kawakami Bizan committed suicide less than a year after the photograph was taken. Hirotsu Ryūrō cut off all contact with the literary world and had ceased writing fiction by 1909. Who could have foreseen that the shy little man in the last seat, way down at the end, almost out of the photograph, would survive as a professional novelist longer than any other writer in attendance at the Useikai that day?

Shūsei was in his midthirties, had a wife and two children to support, and had done little else but write fiction for the previous ten years. It was imperative for him to respond to naturalism in order to maintain his public identity as a serious, realistic novelist. He must have felt threatened by naturalism. However, it is important to keep in mind that Shūsei responded to naturalism on his own terms as a *well-established* realistic novelist.

By the time naturalism had caught on as a popular literary movement in the years following the Russo-Japanese War, Shūsei had already successfully written his way through a number of calls for greater realism in Japanese literature. There had been the *shajitsu* movement advocated by Tsubouchi Shōyō and Futabatei Shimei, which Shūsei had interpreted as a call for radical polemic.[47] There had been the "awakening of the individual," promoted by Kitamura Tōkoku and other young Christian romantics.[48] Its influence is perhaps perceptible in such works as Shūsei's *Shunkō*. There had been the sketch-from-life movement, an appeal to a nativistic literary realism that coincided with the stylistic transformation in Shūsei's writing at the turn of the century.[49] In the first years of the twentieth century, there had been "Zolaism" (*zoraizumu*), which, together with other Western ideas, inspired Shūsei's melodramas.[50] Shūsei's response to the new challenge of naturalism caused him to move in a radical direction that can be described as antinaturalistic as easily as it can be described as naturalistic.

Without exception, Japanese literary histories classify Tokuda Shūsei as a writer of the school of Japanese naturalism. Upon scrutiny, however, one discovers the following contradictions and ambiguities in the association of Shūsei with naturalism as a national literary movement:

First, almost all of the major writers associated with naturalism—Kunikida Doppo, Shimazaki Tōson, Tayama Katai, Masamune Hakuchō, Iwano Hōmei—were, at one point or another, heavily influenced by Christianity or the brand of romanticism advocated by Kitamura Tōkoku in his literary journal *Bungakukai*. Shūsei's background—his early adoption of a native variety of utopian socialism and his training as a purely professional writer under Ozaki Kōyō—was different. As a consequence, according to Masamune Hakuchō's memoirs, Shūsei was not considered to be a part of the new literary movement by writers enthusiastically advocating it until "naturalism" had lost much of its force as a rallying cry for young writers.[51]

Second, Japanese naturalism was greatly indebted to a massive increase in the importation and translation of late nineteenth-century European literature and literary theory between 1902 and 1908, and European influence is clearly discernible in Katai's theoretical writings, in Tōson's literary style, and in Doppo's debt to Wordsworth.[52] In contrast, although Shūsei did a great deal of translation from English and later freely admitted the influence of Zola, Maupassant, Nietzsche, and Daudet on his early works, he denied the influence of foreign models on his mature novels, and there is no such influence apparent on examining these works.[53]

Third, distortions of European literary theory, a tendency to stylistic simplicity, and a certain smuttiness on the part of some self-proclaimed naturalistic writers gave rise to an "antinaturalism." Though Shūsei was not above publishing smutty stories under his own name from time to time (one of these was brought to an obscenity trial, where Shūsei was successfully prosecuted), it was the antinaturalists Takahama Kyoshi and Natsume Sōseki who commissioned and published the first two works, *Arajotai* (The New Household, 1908) and *Kabi* (Mold, 1911), that firmly established Shūsei's reputation as a novelist of great originality. Shūsei had to sell his *Ashiato* (Footprints, 1910), which was written between *Arajotai* and *Kabi,* by making the rounds of newspaper publishers as if he were a peddler trying to arouse interest in his product. *Yomiuri Shinbun* finally bought the novel as a stand-in for a novel it had commissioned from Kōda Rohan and which Rohan was tardy in delivering, but during *Ashiato*'s serialization there was almost no critical response to or support for this novel, which today is recognized as one of the masterpieces of Japanese naturalism. In short, Kyoshi and Sōseki recognized Shūsei's potential as a modern novelist before the writers and critics associated with naturalism, and it was Kyoshi's and Sōseki's support which enabled Shūsei to make the transition to a new, experimental conception of the novel.[54]

Fourth, as will be demonstrated below, Shūsei was ambivalent toward the literary techniques advocated by the theoreticians of naturalism.

From 1907 until the completion of *Arajotai,* during a crucial period of change in the literary world when young writers proclaiming the tenets of naturalism were taking over the pages of the periodicals Kōyō once opened to the members of his guild, Shūsei sustained his literary reputation with short stories. In April 1907, two critics in the literary journal *Shinsei* observed that the Ken'yūsha was finished as a meaningful presence on the literary scene and concluded that Shūsei and Oguri Fūyō were the only writers associated with the guild who had managed to make the transition to the new literary movement. Both critics praised Shūsei in particular for his intelligence and his grasp of foreign languages.[55] In a perceptive piece of criticism appearing in March 1908, Sōma Gyofū declared that in serialized novels, Shūsei was still putting concepts first, and he advised Shūsei to approach the novel with the same attitude that lay behind Shūsei's approach to the material in his short stories.[56] Concerning Shūsei's short stories, Sōma had no reservations: in September 1908, he called Shūsei and Hakuchō the two most distinctive short story writers on the literary scene at that time.[57] In October, a critic with *Chūō Kōron,* in a review of a collection of Shūsei's short stories, the *Shūsei shū,* would exclaim: "These stories do not read

like literary works; they read like real life. There is no other writer
working today who can do this."[58] By January 1909, Takita Choin
would conclude that there was no finer short story writer than Shūsei in
Japan.[59] Many of the basic features of the literary criticism favorable to
Shūsei were established before he had completed *Arajotai*. Matsubara
Shibun in his "Tokuda Shūsei ron" argued as follows in November
1908:

Natives of Kaga are somber [*jimi*] and restrained, but there is an extravagance in
these qualities. They are subdued, but they are not seedy. Tokuda Sueo [Shūsei]
is this kind of person. His works have the taste of somberness and restraint, but
they are certainly not lean. . . . They are not dry and desiccated, and when the
surface gloss [*tsuya*] is removed, a vivid luster is revealed. . . .

Shūsei is not one to abandon himself and weep in a loud voice. . . . In the
face of the pitiful condition of humankind, Shūsei intently absorbs the pain and
turns away with tears in his eyes. The strength of his writing lies in this. And in
this, he represents the best of the school of naturalism. . . .

Shūsei takes in an aspect of life at a sharp glance, and when he represents this
aspect, the other aspects of this human situation emerge as shadows. This is
Shūsei's tendency to impressionism.[60]

These are the prototypes for the tropes used to express the admirable qualities of Shūsei's work that have come to dominate secondary
literature and criticism on Shūsei down to the present. The term *jimi* is
employed by many critics to describe Shūsei's works and character.
The subtle beauty of Shūsei's writing is often referred to in terms of
"light cast by burnished silver," which is similar to Matsubara's "vivid
luster" beneath the "surface gloss." Shūsei's love and sympathy for the
common person are frequently commented on and correspond to Matsubara's description of Shūsei weeping out of pity for the human
condition. Finally, references to the sharp, penetrating nature of
Shūsei's vision abound in the secondary literature.

From 1906 to 1908, in his short stories dealing with low-class characters, Shūsei was loosening the strictures of plot and European-influenced
melodrama and looking on the problem of class difference in a fresh, new
way. However, other than convincing Shūsei of the desirability of experimentation, it is difficult to define exactly how the imported doctrines of
naturalism affected his writing. In an interview published in March 1908,
Shūsei stated: "We often speak of human truth or the realities of life, but
there is something unknowable about human beings. . . . When I deter-

mine to write about a 'mysterious something' in the human condition, I certainly do not intend to expose that something to the light. It is sufficient to portray life in all its indeterminacy. I am satisfied if I can show that 'mysterious something' as it is in life."[61]

At the height of naturalism as a literary movement, then, Shūsei saw the object of literary representation as being "something" not cognitively graspable and lying still deeper than portrayals of character or psychology. He was quite distant from the program being called for by the popularizers of naturalism, Hasegawa Tenkei and Tayama Katai, who seemed in their public statements to believe that a scientifically observable "reality" was possible.

Indeed, one doubts whether Shūsei ever really believed in a strictly delimited objectivity as opposed to a strictly delimited subjectivity, polar concepts so essential to the theory and criticism of naturalism. The following, from an interview published in August 1909, is Shūsei's odd response to Tayama Katai's call for *heimen byōsha* (surface description to the exclusion of the author's subjective judgments):

The term *heimen byōsha* is often used these days, though I really do not know what it means. Does it mean that one should describe only the surfaces of what one sees or comes in contact with? . . . It is impossible, after all, to remove the author's view of life or subjectivity from the work and proceed to portray human reality. The literary work must contain the writer's *color*. (Shūsei's emphasis)[62]

In 1909 Shūsei wrote:

Thus, when it comes to the problem of whether local regional color is portrayed, it must be the particular local color the author can adapt himself or herself to. In other words, the author must be the local color. . . . I savor the wise proposition: *it is a matter of the author's own local color.* (Shūsei's emphasis)[63]

The "inner self" is a spectrum of colors, permeable, presumably able to merge with outer colors, to color, and be colored. The "outer world" is equally elusive and inseparable from the individual human subject who is the object of the author's literary representation. As Shūsei wrote in December 1908:

All things have shadows [*in'ei*]. The pine tree in the garden, for instance, that pine has shadows. People too are inevitably surrounded by shadows. And the shadows cannot be separated from their subject. . . . When one is using a model in writing a novel, one must not neglect to portray the shadows that surround it.[64]

On occasion, Shūsei would describe one of his novels or short stories as purely objective, but from the context of these and other statements, one suspects that colors and shadows (almost innumerable literary techniques by which authorial voice is refracted) were the stuff of his "objectivity." Shūsei's position was antithetical to the mainstream of Japanese naturalism, which would reach a logical conclusion in the writings of Iwano Hōmei, who provided the theoretical basis for legitimizing the Japanese autobiographical novel (*shishōsetsu*). In response to what he saw as the moral and philosophical chaos of constantly changing points of view, Hōmei called for narrative perspective to be fixed and limited to one character.[65] Perhaps because Shūsei recognized that "a correct literary point of view" would make his own type of "objectivity" impossible, he early on argued that novelists should be allowed freedom in the matter. In 1910, he wrote: "I don't believe there is a need to decide on any one form for literary representation [*byōsha*], whether it be surface representation or any other. One should be able to use any form one wants depending on the situation."[66]

From the *shajitsu* movement of the 1880s to Japanese naturalism in the years immediately following the Russo-Japanese War of 1904–5, the mainstream of the Japanese literary world was vitally concerned with the definition and redefinition of realism, and Shūsei's career illustrates how diverse this process was.

Naturalism as a Form of Japanese Nationalism

In October 1908, Takahama Kyoshi took up the position as literary editor of Tokutomi Sohō's *Kokumin Shinbun*. The first work other than his own that he commissioned for the newspaper was Shūsei's *Arajotai,* which was serialized from October 16, 1908, to December 6, 1908. Kyoshi visited Shūsei at Shūsei's home and asked him to write a novel, not so long that the readers would tire of it and one that would be of true literary merit and that would avoid cliff-hanging sensationalism and other kinds of pandering to popular tastes.[67] (Kyoshi was obviously aware of Shūsei's weaknesses as well as his strengths.) Shūsei enthusiastically agreed to take on the assignment, and he filled Kyoshi's order to perfection, writing a novella that today is regarded as one of the finest products of Japanese naturalism.[68]

Oguri Fūyō, who was paying a visit to Shūsei when Kyoshi came to call, was associated in the public mind with naturalism, and he was a more salable novelist at that time, but Kyoshi did not like Fūyō's novels, which were similar to the melodramas Shūsei was writing in 1905 and 1906. In general, Kyoshi was hostile to naturalism, declaring in 1908 of such writers as Tayama Katai and Masamune Hakuchō: "Their descriptive technique [*byōsha*] is clumsy, especially in regard to their lack of composure. Those of us involved in the sketch-from-life movement, which places particular emphasis on literary representation, find their works unsatisfactory in this regard, and we soon tire of them." Again in 1908, Kyoshi dismissed Shimazaki Tōson with the comment, "His works are too subjective."[69] Kyoshi entrusted Shūsei with the important task of writing the first substantial novel to appear under his editorship because he believed in the "power of Shūsei's literary technique," which, he wrote in 1913, "allows the reader to become intimately involved in Shūsei's works."[70]

Shūsei, always the professional, gave Kyoshi exactly the novella he wanted, one that would establish *Kokumin Shinbun* as a forum for serious literature. In writing *Arajotai,* Shūsei's career took a new direction. *Arajotai* begins as follows:

Shinkichi took Osaku as his wife during the winter four years ago, when he was twenty-five and she twenty.

At the age of fourteen, the impressionable adolescent had been inspired by a success story in some biography of a rich entrepreneur, and he had dashed off from the provinces to Tokyo, where he labored with extraordinary diligence as an apprentice to a wine wholesaler in Shinkawa. After eleven years of working like hell, he managed to start his own business, renting a small shop in Omote-chō, there selling sake and soy sauce, firewood and charcoal, salt and other necessities. He worked all the harder, even begrudging himself the time spent for eating his meals; he would hastily gulp down his food at the front of his shop, not pausing to untie the cords holding up his sleeves or to put on his sandals. (7:453)

The transformation in Shūsei's writing in 1907 and 1908 was probably a manifestation of Japanese nationalism in the years after Japan's victory over Russia. Everyday Japanese experience was important in a new way. More specifically, the Japanese experience of most of the individuals living in cities was important in a new way. The day-by-day experience of the wine merchant across the street, the daily experience of the next-door maid, the pedestrian experience of a former prostitute, the quotidian adventures of a seamstress—these seemingly little stories suddenly became the subjects of Shūsei's major novels.

The first sentence of *Arajotai* indicates how confident Shūsei had become in his ability. He gave his plot away. He no longer needed the "cheap," melodramatic tension provided by the question of whether Shinkichi will marry Osaku or not. Shūsei was certain he could hold his readers with wonderful descriptions of how the marriage is arranged or with the fascinating and funny account of how Shinkichi acts as his own private detective and goes to investigate his prospective wife's family. He did set up a love triangle, but nothing really happens: Shinkichi stays married to his dull, unattractive wife. *Arajotai* marks the end of stories told from the perspective of the outside observer. In *Arajotai,* the reader is dragged into Shinkichi's world and is allowed to judge him only by the hard standards and language of his world. One soon learns that he is as complex, intelligent, and morally sensitive as any intellectual.

After 1908, Shūsei's best work was modeled on identifiable, real people. As Noguchi Fujio has argued, when Shūsei had a model—his wife, the wife of his brother-in-law, a lover, himself—this material forced him to experiment to present these original voices in an authentic manner. When Shūsei did not have a model in real life, he tended to "get caught" by the literary models of the past.[71] As he instructed young people in 1913, "You must work, as a human being and an author, to avoid being caught by form. It is so easy to get caught."[72] When Shūsei abandoned the political idea of the "lower classes" and opened his eyes and ears to the people around him, his fiction became aesthetically interesting and a source of historical knowledge.

In 1911, Ikuta Chōkō wrote that Tokuda Shūsei was a "born naturalist."[73] We have seen that his recommitment to realism occurred at the height of Japanese naturalism, Japan's first truly national literary movement under capitalism. If one feels compelled to classify Shūsei as a "naturalist," however, it should be done with the qualification that his naturalism was a form of nationalism.[74] It was turning inward to Japanese class realities rather than looking abroad for new ideas. His "strange innate talent for objectifying himself," as Itō Sei put it, was a literary sophistication and taste built up over a decade or more of hard literary labor to refract his own voice and enter the consciousness of a given character.[75] The next part of this study will immerse itself in the sea of language that constitutes Shūsei's novels of common life and will formally explore the class structures implicit in these works.

3

Four Novels about Common Life

> Any stylistics capable of dealing with the distinctiveness of the
> novel as a genre must be a *sociological stylistics*.
> —M. M. Bakhtin, "Discourse in the Novel"

The tone of much Shūsei criticism in the Japanese literary world is often
on the rhetorical level of homage. Professional writers and critics mar-
veled at the seemingly infinite "tricks" Shūsei developed to give to his
characters, who, like most people, are not very articulate, a narrative
language of great complexity and beauty. Shūsei came to be recognized as
one of Japan's most original and talented novelists. The novelist, critic,
and scholar Kojima Masajirō praised Shūsei as the great master (*kamisama*)
of the Japanese novel.[1] Kawabata Yasunari as well wrote that Shūsei was a
master of the novel, a master who maintained no school and who was the
most Japanese of all modern novelists in the sense of being the most
closely in touch with his own society.[2] Best-selling novelist Funabashi
Seiichi described Shūsei as a towering beam of light shining down on
Japan's literary world.[3] Nakamura Murao, professional critic, editor, and
essayist, wrote that after Saikaku only Shūsei portrayed the true characteristics of the Japanese people.[4] Murō Saisei, Uno Kōji, Chikamatsu
Shūkō, Hirotsu Kazuo, Aono Suekichi, Takeda Rintarō, Takami Jun,
Shinoda Hajime—one could go on and on listing prominent Japanese
writers and critics who have expressed enormous respect, admiration,
and even love for Shūsei's mature literature.[5]

A feature of this kind of criticism, once so common in the Japanese
literary world, is that when the writer or critic tries to go beyond the
rhetoric of rapture and wonderment and give some kind of rational
reason why the writing is so remarkable, there is a pause, a groping, and
then one sees some brilliant minds collapse. Here is an example from an
"interpretation" (*kaisetsu*) Kawabata wrote in 1966. Kawabata begins
an impressionistic argument which will conclude that Shūsei's *Shukuzu*
(A Microcosm, 1941) was Japan's finest modern novel and that Shūsei
was in touch with Japan's highest aesthetic, but suddenly his narrative
breaks down, and he declares: "I do not intend to write an interpretation of Shūsei's works here. I have only one wish of my readers. Please
read Shūsei's works slowly, ever so slowly. In Shūsei's case, this is far

more valuable and sincere advice than any number of interpretations I could write."[6]

This abandonment of rationality for higher, more imaginative tropes is frequently apparent in Hirotsu Kazuo's writings on Shūsei. In 1937, after years of reviewing Shūsei's individual works favorably, Hirotsu determined to write a full-scale assessment of Shūsei as a novelist (*Shūsei ron*), but he discovered that "the first emotion that comes over one is how extraordinarily difficult it is to assess Shūsei. I must confess that I'm in the same position now as I was four or five months ago when I began to reread Shūsei's past work in preparation to write this essay: no unified critical vision of Shūsei as an author emerges."[7]

Even the academic Shinoda Hajime, an extraordinarily well-read critic with a formalist perspective, is left speechless. He describes Shūsei's mature novelistic language as "beautiful," "miraculous," "exquisite," but when he asks rhetorically where the genres Shūsei was creating came from, he is at a loss; he does not know.[8] The experience of reading Shūsei, searching for a rational critical language to describe the experience, and coming up empty-handed is perhaps best described by Takami Jun, who wrote to the effect that reading Shūsei is like entering a vast sea; there is nothing to grasp hold of, and all the reader can do is float.[9]

The strategy adopted here is to read and interpret Shūsei's mature novels as forming a "myth of common life in Japan" and to see in this myth the archetype of the modern "myth of the middle class." Otherwise, one has to conclude that his novels have little ideological significance. Either one views Shūsei as an enormously ambitious writer who constantly struggled and experimented to find new ways of articulating and incorporating into the novel the experiences, values, and thinking of the vast majority of urban residents in Japan at the turn of and first decades of the twentieth century, or his works collapse into random incidents and beautiful scenes with no greater unity. If Shūsei's works constitute a myth, it is a colossal one, and if they do not, they are only of marginal interest.[10]

Japanese writers and critics are almost unanimous in describing the masses depicted in Shūsei's mature novels as *shomin* (commoners). Much of the rest of this study will be an exploration of what this term means in the context of Shūsei's fiction. *Shomin* is derived from the Chinese *shumin,* which appears in the *Shi ching* with the meaning of "myriad" or "masses of people." In Japan, the term came to be used for a class position that contrasted with various elites. Before the Meiji Restoration of 1868, the opposition was between *bushi* and *shomin* (an opposition reflected in the term *shisho,* the *shi* from *bushi* meaning "martial gentry" and the *sho* from *shomin* meaning "the myriad," "everyone else"), and even today a man in the street in a television interview will use the term *shomin* to describe his ordinary circumstances in contrast to the wealthy, highborn, or government elites. Especially during the Meiji period, the word *shomin* took on cultural connotations that other terms for the masses do not have. It suggests popular art forms such as Ozaki Kōyō's novels, magic lantern shows, the *yose* and other forms of popular theater, popular eating places, *shitamachi* (artisan and merchant) neighborhoods, and hundreds of similar associations that stand in contrast to Japanese high culture and especially Western high culture, which, in the Meiji period, was appreciated only by the wealthy and the intelligentsia.

If there is little disagreement that Shūsei's novels represent the unique Japanese cultural milieu of *shomin* life, there is some controversy over whether this cultural milieu is relevant or desirable for the present. After World War II, it became extremely unfashionable to be a mere commoner, and, in the new democratic Japan, young intellectuals urged urban residents to shed the shackles of feudalism and aspire to become true *citoyens* (*shimin,* "citizen," as opposed to *shomin,* "commoner"). For a time, the use of the word *shomin* was so stigmatized among some Western-educated intellectuals that Ara Masahito could seriously declare in 1949 that he became nauseated with self-revulsion when he discovered in himself the same *shomin* qualities he perceived in Shūsei's fiction.[11] Such expressions of class self-hatred need not concern us further.

Shūsei's mature fiction is most directly the product of *shomin* life in the sense that Shūsei lived the life of a commoner and modeled his best novels and short stories on the common people around him. In the early summer of 1906, Shūsei rented a house in the Morikawa district of the Hongō ward, a residence about five minutes' walk from the main entrance of Tokyo Imperial University. This was the seventh move Shūsei had made since his return from his second visit to Osaka in 1902, and now, with a wife and two children, he was not disposed to move again. He bought the house in 1920, and he died in the same residence in 1943. After 1907, Shūsei discovered the material for his great novels of common life within this house or within a fifteen- or twenty-minute walk of it.

Some critics might cite this sudden conscious delimitation of subject material on Shūsei's part as an indication of the failure of his, and the collective Japanese, imagination, but, in truth, such an argument probably reflects a failure on the part of the critic to imagine the sheer richness, heterogeneity, and complexity of class antagonisms in Shūsei's portrayals of this area of the city. A short distance above Shūsei's house, at the top of the hill, was the focal point of the Japanese elites: Tokyo Imperial University and the First Higher School. Across the street from these institutions were the shops that served the brilliant, ambitious young students: bookstores carrying the latest ideas from the West, tailor shops producing Western-style uniforms, and coffee shops that served as meeting places for the excitable, intellectual young men. Coming back into the complex web of meandering streets that constituted Shūsei's neighborhood, one found the sudden quiet of moderately respectable, discreet households with gates, a symbol of gentility that Shūsei insisted upon having. There was the domesticity of small shops selling foodstuffs and other items required by respectable housewives and their maids and the discipline of orderly boardinghouses for students, inns catering to people who had come up from the provinces to visit the academic institutions, and small private hospitals. A short walk from Shūsei's house down the hill, after crossing over the border into Koishikawa, one of the poorest wards in the city, one discovered a completely different world: noisy, dirty industrial districts drawing rough migrant laborers from the north, hawkers shouting from street stalls at the lively crowd of shoppers, each of whom had to use a little bit of money as economically as possible, and prostitution of every kind, legal and illegal. Close to his house in the Morikawa district, Shūsei had more stories than he could ever hope to tell in several lifetimes. In apprehending the diversity around him in these neighborhoods, he discovered an authentic imagination, not a melodramatic one.

Shūsei's marriage to Ozawa [Tokuda] Hama (1881–1926), the daughter of Shūsei's former maid, Ozawa Sachi (1852–1924), was his single most important passage across sexual, topographical, and class boundaries to new and variegated social environments. She was the model for Shūsei's first successful experiment, in *Ashiato* (Footprints, 1910), in the fixing of narrative perspective firmly in a single woman protagonist, Oshō, for the length of a long novel. Through Hama's memory, Shūsei made the acquaintance of the eccentric old merchants, alcoholics, homicidal maniacs, and dozens of other odd characters that populate that novel. Hama served as the model for Ogin in Shūsei's *Kabi* (Mold, 1911), and this secondary woman character stole the stage from the author/protagonist in this autobiographical novel. Hama introduced Shūsei to the model for *Tadare* (Festering, 1913), an ex-Yoshiwara prostitute whom Hama had met at her aunt's house in the nearby Yushima district and with whom she became good friends. The heroine of *Arakure* (Rough Living, 1915) was modeled on Hama's "sister-in-law," Suzuki Chiyo, the common-law wife of Hama's brother, Ozawa Takeo. Noguchi Fujio speculates that perhaps no Japanese novelist's wife provided her husband with as much rich literary material as Hama provided Shūsei.[12] Perhaps it would be more appropriate to say that she introduced him to extraliterary material, for she herself was almost illiterate (5:176–77).

Shūsei's children served as a bridge across generational barriers. The names and dates of Shūsei's children are as follows: Tokuda Kazuho (1904–1981), Tokuda Mizuko (1905–1916), Tokuda Jōji (1908–1974), Tokuda Kiyoko (1911–), Tokuda Sansaku (1913–1931), Tokuda Masahiko (1915–), and Tokuda Momoko (1918–). They begin to appear more and more in Shūsei's work, especially after the death in 1916 of his beloved daughter Mizuko. Kazuho, who himself became a professional writer, was especially influential in keeping Shūsei apprised of intellectual currents among younger literary circles. Shūsei and Hama, sometimes Hama's mother, a live-in maid, and all of these children occupied a living space of approximately 425 square feet until extra rooms in a shed in back of the house were made available to Shūsei in 1923. Visitors to Shūsei's house during the period under discussion describe a fairly chaotic situation: Shūsei receiving callers in his small study often already crowded with people waiting to meet the by-now famous literary figure, frequent interruptions by his children, and the noise of busy activity from the kitchen adjoining his study. Almost every account also describes the cordiality and courtesy with which Shūsei or Hama greeted even the least important of visitors.[13]

Takebayashi Musōan, a translator and critic, recalls that when he returned to Japan from abroad, he would go to call on Shūsei just to be reminded of what an ordinary urban Japanese household was like.[14] From 1906 or so until 1926, the year of Hama's death, Shūsei took pride in maintaining a common, ordinary, *shomin* (henceforth, these terms will be used interchangeably) life, and he stayed in close touch with common voices. His sense of identification with the class-cultural milieu of *shomin* life remained remarkably strong for most of his life. He argued that true Japanese refinement was a product of poverty and austerity, and he refused to accept a proposal of marriage offered for his daughter Kiyoko from the son of a wealthy family because, he reasoned, the two young people came from different worlds and would have no common language in which to communicate (10:587–89). There can be no doubt that Shūsei found his daughter's language to be the more authentic.

Undeniably, all of this is fairly pedestrian in the biographical sense. With the exception of a brief, sordid love affair with a prostitute, nothing much happened in Shūsei's life during this period.[15] In his fiction, however, Shūsei managed to assert the primacy of that realm of experience which usually escapes articulation in the disguise of "nothing much happened." The class-cultural milieu of *shomin* life is irrevocably linked in Shūsei's mature fiction with the "ordinary" perception of time. The patterns and cycles of time of *shomin* life hold absolute hegemony in Shūsei's vision of Japanese society. Shūsei did not intend his common characters to be representative in a sociological or statistical sense; rather they were elevated to the level at which they could be representative in the archetypic or mythic sense. For Shūsei, from 1908 to 1926, common Japanese characters were the only ones that mattered.

Social Mobility, Insecurity, and "Individualism"

Shūsei's determination to bring narrative perspective down to the level of common life is evident from the first lines of *Arajotai* (The New Household, 1908). Shinkichi, the protagonist of the novella, inspired as a young man by the early Meiji ideology of success, migrates from a northern province to Tokyo to make his fortune. After eleven years as an apprentice to a wine wholesaler, he saves enough money to open his own shop in Omote-chō, a newly developing district in the Koishikawa ward.[16]

At this point in the description one might conclude that this is among the thousands of such stories of ambitious young men who flocked to the cities in hopes of restoring the fortunes of once prosperous families gone into decline in the aftermath of the Meiji Restoration. Shinkichi's central problem seems clear enough, and its solution is largely beyond his control. If the newly developing Omote district grows, attracting more of the working-class families that will frequent his shop to buy small daily quantities of charcoal or soy sauce—all they can afford—and if businesses operating in the surrounding area, notably the nearby armory and manufacturer of government armaments, hire more of the rough laborers who come to his shop in the mornings and evenings to drink carefully measured cups of rice wine with pinches of salt, then Shinkichi's business will grow; if local industries do not prosper and more cheap rental housing is not constructed, Shinkichi's small business will fail.

But there is a disturbing and exciting anger in this portrayal that will not allow one to shrug off Shinkichi's story with a sigh. In the following, Shinkichi and his best friend, Ono, are preparing for Shinkichi's wedding to Osaku:

Shinkichi began grumbling again. Snatching up the paper on which Ono had written out his estimates, he went over the figures once more in his mind. Since he had started his business, he had managed, little by little, by observing every economy, to save about forty yen. To have to pay out almost all of it for the ceremony was painful. It had not been his intention that the wedding be such a large-scale affair. He would have preferred welcoming the bride into his house quietly and then conducting a simple, informal ceremony. And it was not just that he regretted the expense. By nature modest and reserved, Shinkichi was not inclined to enjoy gay occasions or gaudy displays. He wanted to work out of people's sight, saving his money as privately as possible. Revealing to others the sums he earned or the figure in his savings account made him uncomfortable. An odd, distorted kind of thinking, something like the spirit of independence or individualism, had been deeply implanted in his mind from the time of his apprenticeship. He resented Ono's interference in his affairs. But without the fellow's help, he was at a loss in this social situation. Though Shinkichi grumbled, he did not dare to flatly defy Ono. (7:460–61)

Appropriating the terms "spirit of independence" (*dokuritsu-shin*) and "individualism" (*kojin-shugi*) from the Meirokusha discourse of the intellectual proselytizers of "enlightenment and civilization" and applying them to Shinkichi was a brilliant move. "Individualism" had become naturalized, had drifted down to become a part of even Shinkichi's vocabulary, where it mocks the original loan translation.[17] Shinkichi's individualism has nothing to do with social progress or spiritual enlightenment or a weakening of the collective will to serve the state; rather it concerns a loneliness that is so deeply rooted in the political economic order that Shinkichi can never hope to overcome it. And Shinkichi's individualism, formed over a decade and more of hard work and bitter disappointment, is infinitely more important than the "individualism" of Christian romanticism or the "anti-individualism" of the state, first, because it is far more real than abstractions and, second, because it represents the experience of the vast majority of young people who have migrated to the city and stayed. As the prominent writer Furui Yoshikichi observed in 1974, "I have come to think that the new household described in *Arajotai* is the most archetypical formulation that I know of for the households of merchants and salaried employees—modern urban residents—living in the city today."[18]

Shinkichi is all alone. He has not returned to the north to see his family for eight years. His best friend is involved in various shady business deals, one of which lands him in prison. Shinkichi believes the head of the local wine retailers' union is intent on cheating him. Soon after his marriage, he becomes convinced that his new wife wants to leave him. Years of frugality and hard labor have taught him that he can trust nothing but his own bank account. What sustains Shinkichi is his belief in the possibility of success, a rather amorphous concept for him in the present, but something he hopes to attain in the future after years of work. It consists simply of establishing a house—business and family—on a foundation firm enough to withstand the hurricanes of change that have been blowing him and everyone he knows around for as long as he can remember. Throughout this novella, a severe distinction is drawn between those who can aspire to common respectability, the ethic of *shomin* life, and the truly destitute.

The work is probably set in the period immediately following the Russo-Japanese War (7:505), a time when a sizable industrial working class did not yet exist. Workers, along with ricksha pullers, day laborers, street peddlers, and the like, were perceived as a stigmatized minority.[19] In Koishikawa, official statistics for 1911 state that out of a population of 111,582 for the entire ward, 18,762, or approximately 17 percent, were truly impoverished, the standard of poverty being an income of less than twenty yen per month and a monthly rent of three yen or more.[20] This was a rather high rate when compared to the Hongō ward's 1.5 percent of the population living in poverty.

Much of Shinkichi's business comes from this impoverished minority, but he himself is not a part of it. Shinkichi is not a lower-class character or even a working-class character. He is a *shomin* character, which means he is under constant pressure to maintain himself and his wife in the realm of the commonly respectable. This is not an easy task, and his problem is that he is intelligent enough to imagine falling into the laboring classes, a world which is portrayed from Shinkichi's perspective as dark, shadowy, and threatening. His wife, Osaku, does not have the capacity to understand how precarious Shinkichi's social position is. She cannot comprehend his sense of urgency and his irrational rages over errors she makes in running the shop and household. Osaku cannot imagine descending into the lower classes. Working-class people simply repel her. Since she is so completely the product of an older, rurally based class order, she continues to function according to a traditional standard that is radically out of synchrony with her husband and the city:

While under the care of her parents and during her three years in service at the university professor's residence in the Komagome Nishikata district in Hongō, Osaku had simply done her best at whatever task was given her, and if she worked seriously and earnestly, her efforts were sufficient. Her parents had praised her for being a proper, ladylike daughter, and the professor had been quite fond of her, remarking on her kindness and good nature. When she had left service to marry, he had given her an unusually large sum as a parting gift and had predicted that her husband would find her to be a capable and caring wife. She had received ornamental combs and other gifts from her mistress, who had even seen her off at the front gate, a courtesy almost never accorded to domestics. When Shinkichi exploded and criticized her so severely, she was thrown into confusion, just didn't know what to think. Maybe he was trying to show her who was boss. Or perhaps he scolded her with the intent of frightening her into submission. The tasks he gave her were simple enough—she had made mistakes today, but she was certain she could master the work after two or three tries. In any case, she knew now what the old woman had meant when she had taken her aside on the day after the wedding and warned her that Shinkichi was irritable and quick to anger, and so Osaku did not take his criticisms deeply to heart. Shinkichi's fits of rage left her trembling, but the weight of fear soon lifted, and although she felt unsure for a time, this was not enough to undermine her sense of self-respect.

Still, she rested her needle in her lap from time to time and sighed. And on occasion, on quiet afternoons as she sat alone by the hibachi with no work to do, she felt tears rising to her eyes. At times she felt life would be easier if she returned to her parents or went back into service at the house of the professor. She often sat in front of her mirror. Looking around to make certain that no one was present, she would then quietly lift the cloth cover and stare at her reflection. Enraptured, she rearranged her hair and applied white makeup to her face. She went over in her mind again the day of the wedding and the happy dreams she had embraced during the first six months of the marriage. Her own image and scenes from that promising night appeared again before her eyes—that she now saw little of that promise in the mirror made her want to cry in disappointment. There was a loud sigh from the shop, where Shinkichi was keeping the books, and he peered with a disgruntled expression into the room. Osaku reddened and quickly covered the mirror.

"Get me some tea, will you," he demanded in a difficult tone and went back to his calculations.

When he joined Osaku by the hibachi, there was a strained silence. The coals of the fire had gone out, and the iron kettle was cold. (7:475–76)

Osaku is from a small landowning family, recently somewhat reduced, which in addition to farming also runs a kitchenware shop near
Hachiōji, at this time still a rural region but within easy traveling distance of Tokyo. What Shinkichi discovers in his investigation of Osaku
before he marries her seems promising enough: she will have learned
the basics of housekeeping and accounting, and while Shinkichi has
nothing but contempt for the rural manners of her family, he assumes
that Osaku herself should have become suitably urbanized through her
three years of service in the very respectable professor's house. First and
foremost, he expects Osaku to become an asset to his business, to work
hard and to exhibit a certain sociability that will gain him customers and
respect in the developing neighborhood. Osaku disappoints his expectation. Careless errors in measuring basic commodities, letting the fire go
out in the hibachi, and taking naps in the afternoon—such human
lapses have little significance in a backwater rural economy or in the
professor's comfortable home. When Osaku comes down from the
Hongō ward on the hill into Shinkichi's business, based largely on
profits taken from people earning subsistence wages, such errors become major infractions of the prevailing ethic of success and austerity.

Shinkichi's speech, clothing, and manners are roughly businesslike
and masculine, but he is not a cruel or sadistic person, as is stressed
again and again by the descriptions of his gentle eyes. His outbursts of
anger—when Osaku lets the coals go out in the hibachi, for instance, he
declares that he would be better off keeping a cat—stem from his own
insecurity as a lonely individual and his sense that letting the coals grow
cold is a violation of the rules of order of the household, the only
security Shinkichi knows. Later, he regrets his harsh words. Osaku, the
only major character in the work with firm family roots in the nearby
country, is too secure in her position. She is learning too slowly for this
rapidly evolving, fiercely capitalistic neighborhood made up of immigrants. She simply dismisses her husband's complaints as quirks of an
unreasonable temper.

There are really two "new households" in *Arajotai*. An alternative
"course to success" is represented by Shinkichi's friend Ono, a fellow
emigrant from Shinkichi's hometown.[21] Ono and his wife, Okuni, set
up a house in the Kyōbashi ward. Ono is a minor financial speculator
who keeps up a superficial appearance of prosperity. The rigors of life
do not allow Ono to pretend to succeed for long. He is soon arrested
for participating in an illegal business transaction. While the pregnant
Osaku is away at her home in the country, where she plans to give birth,
Ono's wife, Okuni, comes to Shinkichi with Ono's request that Shinkichi

house and support her until Ono is released. To Shinkichi's inexperienced eyes, Okuni is one of the Meiji "new women," whose status as a respectable woman or as a woman of the demimonde cannot be determined from her hairstyle, clothing, and manner, but she is from Ise (a region associated with prostitution) and her background is mysterious, and these facts along with her subsequent actions strongly suggest that she has made at least a part of her way through life in the demimonde. Okuni is everything Osaku is not: quick, hardworking, a good cook, efficient, attractive, and sociable with customers. But if Osaku's countrylike torpidity fills Shinkichi with something like self-hatred for his own provincial upbringing, Okuni's easy urbanity fills him with fear:

> Okuni drank several cups of wine, which she poured with her own hand. Shinkichi pretended not to notice. The rims of her eyes took on a reddish tinge, and her lips, moistened by the wine, gleamed with a charming allure. When she bowed her head to sip from her cup, her eyes, with their long lashes, and the way her hair framed her forehead were almost indescribably lovely. While he was noticing these details, however, there was something cold running through Shinkichi's mind. He couldn't shake the suspicion that during the last three or four days the household had been manipulated by this woman and was beyond his control, and when he saw how she drank, his displeasure became all the more deeply rooted. He felt antagonism and contempt for her. "This woman . . . where in the hell has she come from?" (7:499)

In many respectable urban families, a woman pouring herself enough to drink to grow a little tipsy or calling a blind masseur for a massage (another of Okuni's habits that shocks Shinkichi) would be nothing out of the ordinary; but for the provincial Shinkichi, Okuni's "degeneracy" marks her as a semimystical temptress. He is attracted to Okuni, but he remains on his guard. His fears are not unjustified, for when Okuni learns that Ono will probably have to serve several years in prison, she does attempt to seduce Shinkichi and take Osaku's place as mistress of the house. Shinkichi finally succumbs to Okuni's manipulation and "knows, for the first time, the feeling of being encompassed by a certain warmth that is woman" (7:517).

When Osaku returns after suffering a miscarriage, she finds, much to her chagrin, that Okuni is occupying the proper wife's place by the hibachi and is performing the wife's task of serving Shinkichi at meals. The two women occupy the same house for over a week, and the expected war of nerves results, which, by the logic of Social Darwinism,

Okuni, the abler and more articulate of the two, should win. Common life does not follow schemes of evolution, however, and Shinkichi's attitude remains unchanged: if Osaku stays with him, he will honor his commitments to her and her family. The dictates of common respectability favor the weak over the strong. As Shinkichi declares to the woman who has given him more pleasure than any other person during his adult life, "I personally don't care how long you stay here. But, unlike Ono's, my house is also my business, and it doesn't look good having a woman nobody knows anything about hanging around" (7:527). When Okuni understands that Shinkichi will always subordinate pleasure to business, the wicked temptress becomes a mere frightened young woman who is growing "a little strange" under the strain of not knowing what the future holds.

Perhaps the primary reason Shinkichi does not divorce Osaku is that she provides him with a link, however tenuous, to some sort of community, a link which the rootless Okuni cannot provide. The following portrays Shinkichi's departure after a visit to Osaku in the rural village to which she has withdrawn to give birth to their child:

Shinkichi arrived in a ricksha at the train station at about the time lamps were being lit, and points of light were visible here and there from houses in the shade of the surrounding forest. Good smells of simple foods boiling in soy sauce drifted out from the rough tavern in front of him, and he saw the shadows of laborers who were standing at the bar, drinking and joking in thick voices. Four or five maids were caring for children in the cold public square, and on hearing the plaintive melody of a lullaby, he remembered his own impoverished, provincial upbringing. He was suddenly struck by the impression that his shadow seemed isolated and alone. "Osaku and her family are about the only family I've got," he muttered to himself. (7:510)

Arajotai concerns inarticulate people, and yet, from their perspectives, in passage after passage, there emerges what might be termed an aesthetic of loneliness. Not even Osaku, with her firm ties to family, is immune to the loneliness of "individualism." Osaku defeats her rival, but in her victory she suffers her first major loss of self-confidence, for she understands that the pensive, depressed Shinkichi misses Okuni. To console her wounded pride, she goes to visit her former mistress at the professor's house. She is ignored and rudely dismissed. Osaku walks back down the hill to resume life as one more isolated, atomized individual struggling to maintain some sense of self-worth in her own common neighborhood on far lower ground. After Okuni departs permanently for a demimonde establishment in Chiba prefecture, Shinkichi lies down with a feeling that his body, with no other place to go, has been left exposed on a vast deserted plain. When Osaku approaches to spread a blanket over him, he kisses her cheek but finds it as cold as ice. An epilogue records that Osaku is pregnant again on the third anniversary of the opening of Shinkichi's shop.

Arajotai is one of the most important works of Shūsei's career. He remembered the novella as a literary experiment, which it was in at least two respects.[22] First, in this relatively short work, Shūsei was able to incorporate an enormous range of extraliterary language diversity. Shinkichi's dialogue, for example, is a highly varied mix of modern colloquial represented by *boku* (I, me), an older *shitamachi* dialect represented by *asshi* (I, me), and a northern dialect, elements of which (*uchi wa shōbaiya da mon da de,* "My house is my business, and so"; 7:527) emerge when Shinkichi is excited or under pressure. Second, the work was experimental in the sense that Shūsei was breaking away from plot devices he had depended on in the past. It seems that the real-life model upon which Osaku was based actually died in childbirth. Before he started to write the novella, Shūsei probably intended to set up a love triangle between Shinkichi, Osaku, and Okuni and then kill Osaku off.[23] In the process of writing the work, however, he apparently became interested in the subtle social relationships and complex personal loyalties that might work to keep two such ill-suited people as Shinkichi and Osaku together—a far more realistic and revealing proposition.

Shūsei also remembered *Arajotai* as his first "humanistic" (*jinseiha-teki*) literary effort, and one can probably infer from this vague statement that in this work, Shūsei, for the first time, employed his considerable literary technique to create common characters who were as complex, sensitive, and intelligent as more dramatic figures.[24] In the context of Shūsei's literature, here, in *Arajotai,* the experience of the keeper of a little shop across the street was made important in a new way. Perhaps no literary work provides a more complete understanding of the difficult struggles and frustrated expectations involved in trying to establish, on one's own, an independent household in a major Japanese city, or, to paraphrase Furui Yoshikichi, no other novel so vividly represents the cold, harsh winds that threaten to blow away the lives of ordinary "salary men" doing business in Japanese cities even today.[25]

Arajotai contains the basic formal class structures that underlie all of Shūsei's great novels of common life. *Shomin* life has internalized and does not question the values and assumptions of capitalism. It is generally constituted by immigrants to the city from the provinces and is distinguished by social mobility within fairly strict boundaries and horizons. The upper border of common life is the intelligentsia, aristocracy, high bourgeoisie, and government bureaucratic elites. These—which yield character types that appear quite often in Shūsei's popular melodramas (usually to be killed off)—almost never play a role in his serious, mature fiction, and when they do (e.g., when Osaku visits her former mistress on the hill), they are invariably exclusionary toward those of class status lower than themselves. The boundary on the lower extreme of common life is the hand-to-mouth existence of day laborers and ricksha pullers, what Yokoyama Gennosuke called the "lowest stratum of society" (kasō shakai) and what Matsubara Iwagorō called "Tokyo at its darkest" (saiankoku no Tokyo), a world Shūsei treated in his short stories but which in the novels under discussion here appears as one of dark, shadowy figures, such as the working-class men in the tavern scene quoted above, a kind of insubstantial, transient, and yet threatening presence.[26] On one horizon are the rural provinces, a time and space which commoners in the city hold in contempt and which they will go to great lengths to avoid living in permanently. On the other horizon is the demimonde, for women a black hole into which one falls. When characters in the novels under discussion here cross these borders or merge with these horizons, they cease to exist in common life. The world of the shomin, then, is one of common, urban respectability, a respectability ordinary people cling to and fight to retain.

The critical success of Arajotai provided Shūsei with the impetus to break decisively with received literary tradition and push the Japanese novel in a new direction. Shūsei's Ashiato (Footprints, 1910) was based on the life of his wife, Tokuda Hama, during the years before Shūsei knew her. A close reading of this novel and Noguchi Fujio's research based on it provides an accurate and detailed portrait of Hama's early life. (Names in parentheses refer to the corresponding fictional names in Ashiato.) Tokuda Hama (Oshō) was born Ozawa Hama to Ozawa Kōzaburō (Tame-sā) and Ozawa Sachi (Oyasu-sā) in 1881 in a rural village (Ono mura, Kamiina-gun) in Nagano prefecture. She was the eldest child in the family and had four younger sisters and three younger brothers, including the eldest son, Takeo (Masao), and Kanji (Teikichi). The Ozawa house was a branch family but a fairly prosperous one, with substantial holdings of land. In 1892, Kōzaburō sold much of his property and emigrated with his family to Tokyo, where he hoped to become a successful financial speculator. He failed after only a few years and returned to his home village in Nagano. His wife, Hama, and several other children were left dependent on his wife's relatives in Tokyo. The family was supported for a time by Hama's "aunt" (*oba-san,* actually her mother's cousin) Yashima Kinu, who managed a boardinghouse in the Yushima district of the Hongō ward. Kinu, a capable woman, was able to support her three sons—Kunitarō (Kikutarō), Kimimasa (Tadasu), and Morio (Hanzō)—through medical school. Sachi and her daughter Hama were next taken in by Sachi's brother Ozawa Toshikazu (Ozaki), a prosperous executive probably employed by Ishikawajima Shipbuilding Company or a smaller firm closely affiliated with it. Hama was essentially supported as a poor relation/maid by an extended family until she married a young restaurant owner in 1901. This marriage lasted less than a year, and she fled from her pathologically violent husband in 1902. By this time, Shūsei had hired Sachi as a live-in maid, and Hama began visiting her mother at the house Shūsei was renting in the Omote district.[27]

Ashiato is without doubt one of the most unusual novelistic structurings ever created. It is cited as one culmination of Shūsei's unique method of narration, a technique Noguchi Fujio has called "reverse narration" (*tōjo*), by which Shūsei gives the reader the conclusion of the story and then depends on his descriptive skill to hold the reader's interest.[28] In place of dramatic time, Shūsei gave primacy to the time of everyday life (*nichijō-teki na jikan*).[29] In digression within digression, Shūsei superimposed one story on another and merged intentions and voices in the overarching story of the heroine Oshō's life. Every word in this extraordinarily difficult and complex work belongs to Oshō, but she says next to nothing in the course of this rather long novel. Shūsei had to imagine the perspective of an eleven-year-old girl growing into womanhood in an environment of social disintegration over a period of ten years. As Shūsei recalled shortly after he finished writing the novel, he made up 80 percent of it.[30]

Ashiato is a wild and joyous celebration of the mystery and beauty of everyday *shomin* life. Shūsei was asserting the primacy and universality of the everyday not only for Oshō, the next-door maid, but for her class. The languages of the governmental, intellectual, and economic elites are simply irrelevant to the authentic, Japanese urban experiences of the majority, who aspire to mere common respectability.[31]

In fixing narrative perspective with Oshō in *Ashiato,* the first problem Shūsei had to resolve was Oshō as a child. He began the novel with a simple, declarative sentence: "Oshō and her family migrated to Tokyo when Oshō was just eleven or twelve" (3:249). He then digressed into a description of Oshō with her family in the rural village in Nagano, where she is helping her parents prepare to make the move to Tokyo. A wonderfully vivid description of the family's five-day journey to the nearest train station follows, but Oshō's perspective is not really differentiated from that of her family. This digression ends at the start of chapter 2 with the family's arrival at Tokyo's Ueno Station. Through the eyes of a newcomer to the city we sense the crowds and noise at the station and the dense, uniform neighborhoods the family's rickshas pass through. At the aunt's boardinghouse in Yushima, where the rickshas are bound, we are introduced to one of the few voices of wisdom that will impress the child Oshō. "Tokyo is different from the provinces," the aunt declares in a matter-of-fact Nagano dialect to Oshō's cowed mother, "Here there is not one single person living a life of comfort and leisure and doing nothing. I don't know if a man with no spirit and drive like your husband can make it in the city, but I do know that without extraordinary effort he won't make it here" (3:254).

The dwelling the family finds to rent is relatively respectable and spacious when compared to the closely packed tenements (*nagaya*) rented to the poor. It is an individual house separated from similar houses recently constructed in a tract to meet the needs of a seemingly endless stream of "respectable" immigrants to the city.[32] But Oshō's mother is uncomfortable and frightened in these living quarters, for in the country she was in charge of a huge house, which she seldom left, and now she has to do without servants, cook on her knees in a tiny kitchen, and obtain water from a common well with other unknown women in what by rural standards is a densely populated neighborhood.

In describing life in this neighborhood (chapters 5–7), Oshō's perspective becomes the central one of the novel. The "involution of time," in truth a range of literary techniques, is used to describe the gradual emergence of an individual consciousness. Chapter 5 opens with the passage of time: " 'Little hick, country witch, mumbo jumbo shaman bitch!'—by the time Oshō's provincial accent and dialect, which the neighborhood children teased so cruelly, had begun to disappear, her father still had not decided on a permanent occupation" (3:260). Then Oshō's moral education in common values is described through her reaction to her parents' quarrel and her growing rebellious awareness that her father is a monstrously selfish man. The involution of time next takes the concrete form of Oshō's memory of a rural economy gone insane:

When Oshō's father briefly rebuked his wife, she muttered some complaint in reply. He was sitting solemnly smoking, but he suddenly stood up, gathered together in both arms the children's garments and underskirts Oshō's mother had been working on, rolled them into a ball, took them over to the veranda, and threw them outside into the damp garden. The cries of insects were heard from the garden.

Oshō brought her wooden clogs over to the veranda and stepped down into the garden to retrieve the clothing, which she spread out on the veranda. Her father took out a broom and began to energetically sweep the room. Oshō's mother, with no work to do, departed for the kitchen. The children left the side of the hibachi and fidgeted around in the corner. Oshō scooped up the crying baby and, supporting him on her back with one hand, picked up an ear of roasted corn in the other, and she went out into the small, dark garden, where she walked back and forth, keeping a wary eye on the house. Her mother and father, working at different tasks, were quarreling in the kitchen.

In the dim light, Oshō sat down on the edge of the veranda. She felt sorry for her mother. A vague understanding had begun to form in her mind of the reasons for her rough, dissipated father's manner of doing business in the country and the course that had led to the start of her family's problems. For as long as she could remember, her father had almost never spent a day without seeking out pleasure. She had frequently been sent to bring her father home from the rooms of a middle-aged whore who had drifted to their village from the neighboring province of Gunma. The woman had tattoos on her arms. Dressed in a loose, short robe with a velvet collar, a garment which barely covered her, she would open the soot-covered shoji and come out to put coins in Oshō's hand or give her sweets. Thinking it over now, the actions of her father seemed those of a madman when he took in an Osaka-based, mother-and-daughter duo of *jōruri* ballad singers, set up a little stage in the largest room of their house, and invited people in to hear them perform. Oshō's mother, with other women from the village, attended dressed up in her best kimono. Oshō's father and some young men took the pretty young daughter into the shadows cast by candles on tall stands and played with her, fascinated by her beautiful eyes. Though she felt an uneasy embarrassment in doing so, Oshō learned snatches of ballads from the singers while they were living with her.

"Give me this child for four or five years, and I'll turn her into a performer you'll be proud of," the older woman proposed one day, and Oshō's father actually seemed to regret it when he replied, no, Oshō was too clumsy to ever become an artist.

When autumn winds came and the harvests were in, her father would bring a professional prayer-reciting couple into their home. These grimy beggars would sit beside the open hearth and chant legends about the great temples on Mount

Kōya or the romantic warrior Suzuki Mondo. Oshō's mother, dozing off in her seat, breathing through her mouth because her nose was clogged, listened entranced by their vulgar lyrics. As if he were the director, her father was proud to sit in the high seat of honor at the village's outdoor performances of ritual dramas to ensure fertile crops.[33]

During the season when everyone was busy raising silkworms, her father would invariably climb the pass that formed one of the borders of their village and walk the ten miles to the next town, where he would take up residence in a brothel. He wouldn't return until someone went to bring him back, and once he dragged the young man sent to fetch him into the brothel, wheedled the money sent to pay off his bill out of him, and then the two men spent several more days in a drunken stupor.

Oshō's father, his body and mind festering in wine, had returned with blazing red eyes on the evening at the height of the season, when every able person in the house was working through the night. He took up his place by the open hearth with his new friend and began drinking again, cooking food he had brought with him over the fire. His wild singing and laughter warned everyone in the family to stay clear of him.

Any number of times, Oshō had seen him beat her mother with pieces of firewood or kick her when the obstinate woman refused to withdraw. Once, when he threw a burning lamp at her mother, hitting her and cutting her cheek, Oshō too had fled, barefoot and clutching her mother's sleeve, as the woman ran out of the rear entrance into the night, dark blood gushing from the wound she tried to cover with her hand. On that occasion, Oshō had been terrified of her father.

While Oshō was remembering these incidents, her father was grilling a piece of salted fish and flavoring some boiled greens. He took a colored glass bottle down from the shelf.

"Oshō, will you go to the store and buy a little vinegar?" he said as he held the bottle up to the light.

"We run out of vinegar, we run out of sugar, it's all the same to her. Oh, the money . . ." He took out a coin and tossed it in Oshō's direction.

Oshō's mother, who was sitting near the lamp, turned and was about to say something, but she thought better of it and, with a vexed expression, remained silent. She was recalling anew the things that had been done to her by her husband.

"All right," Oshō replied in apparent good humor, and she obediently went out to wrap the bottle in a salt-patterned cloth hanging from the clothespole in back of the public water pump, but in her heart she resented being used by her father to run little errands. She thought him impudent. She knew that the girl who lived across the way from her, the one who got to take lessons from the teacher of *tokiwazu* ballads, and Oshō's friend, the daughter of the local used-clothes merchant, never once had to go out on this kind of stingy errand. If

Oshō played the slightest prank, say make her brother cry, her father would immediately pounce on her, wrap her up so tight in thick, countrified bedding she could hardly breathe, and put her in the corner of a dark closet, or he would lock her out of the house on cold, wet nights when sleet was falling and the cries of foxes resounded in the darkness while he snored loudly, warm and comfortable next to the brazier. It is not unnatural that a child would embrace a childlike spirit of defiance against such a father.

As Oshō walked through the neighborhood on her way to the alley which would lead her out to the main commercial street, she noticed in every house that a family had gathered around a table crowded with an assortment of foods. Coming out of the alley onto the lively evening street, Oshō avoided the brightly lit shops, where housewives from her neighborhood gathered, and instead walked alongside the ditch. She stopped at her usual place to listen to music drifting out from the ballad teacher's house. Someone was being instructed in the *shamisen* accompaniment to the ballad about the love affair between Okoma and Saiza. Holding the bottle, Oshō stood listening in the shadows for a while. Then she moved her arms in a quick little dance and dashed off. She looked around self-consciously to make certain that no one had seen her and then entered the wineshop.

When she arrived back home, Oshō found her frowning father heating rice wine beneath the light of the lamp. Her brothers and sisters were greedily grabbing at the food that had been laid out on the table.

Oshō's mother was crouched over the floor drain in the kitchen, where she was roughly washing rice. In the intervals when she strained the water from the rice, they could hear her grumbling. She's at it again, Oshō thought. Her father looked irritated and his face tensed when his wife's complaints were audible in the room.

By the time Oshō's mother had finished her chores and returned to her seat by the hibachi, Oshō's father was dead drunk and had fallen asleep. Oshō looked down on her father with revulsion. She was repelled by the high nose in the huge face, the receding hairline, and the long, bony white legs with hairy knees. Oshō sat down by her mother and began to eat dinner.

Oshō's mother continued her sputtering complaints. Her frightened, cowardly white eyes turned often to watch her sleeping husband. Oshō observed her mother as she began to noisily eat her dinner. She was a bosomy woman with a short, thick neck and teeth that she had ceased to apply black dye to and so appeared dirty. Remembering the face her father made when he cruelly imitated his wife disturbed Oshō. When she visualized the faces of the whore who used to give her money and the young ballad singer her father had taken into their home in the country, she felt convinced that her mother was not a good-looking woman. (3:263–68)

Drifting in and out of Oshō's memory against the background of a primeval, rural landscape, Oshō's father, the primary male actor in her imagination, appears as a potent demigod with the power to transgress any social convention. In Tokyo, her father is nothing. Once he is removed from the tight communal relations of his village, the only means he has to compel respect is physical violence. A man so irrational cannot hope to remain for long in the city, and he is soon reduced to a figure Oshō can safely ignore or even laugh at. When he disappears into the country, he more or less ceases to exist in Oshō's consciousness.

In this disintegrating social and familial situation in which sons of prosperous provincial families suddenly catch "Tokyo fever" and ruin themselves and the futures of their children in the naive search for success and pleasure in the city, the young Oshō is freed to pursue her own class aspirations in an atmosphere where rapid social mobility, up or down, is the rule. Oshō deeply resents being forced to go buy a small amount of vinegar. She lives in a neighborhood where most families buy foodstuffs in quantity, and she is sufficiently educated to the standards of common respectability to feel ashamed to appear before her neighbors on an errand to buy a daily amount of a commodity. And although she aspires to an ordinary life, she is also attracted to the arts traditionally associated with the demimonde and knows enough to feel uneasy about her desire to learn to perform popular music: it is not quite respectable.

Oshō is not a filial daughter who will allow herself to be sold into prostitution or semiprostitution for her father's benefit. She is far too "individualistic" to make such a stupid, melodramatic sacrifice. To obtain a loan, Oshō's father agrees to give Oshō up for adoption to a woman who operates a cosmetics shop in Asakusa. The details of this transaction are not clear because by this point the reader is generally informed only of what Oshō herself knows, and nobody tells her what is going on, but it seems certain that Oshō will not tolerate this arrangement. A year and some months after her arrival in the city, she has learned enough about the popular customs and manners of the Asakusa ward to sense danger in a man who suddenly appears as her "stepmother's" lover and calls her Oshō-chan with a familiarity that makes her skin crawl. She decides to flee from her stepmother:

In the evenings, the man first went out to the public neighborhood bath, came back with forehead and nose shining, and then departed again for the local theater or to shoot toy arrows at targets for prizes in the park. His lover [Oshō's stepmother] often scolded him for sleeping in during the mornings after his late-night adventures, but then as often as not the two of them were still in bed together after most people were up and working.

As was often the case, Oshō came down from her small room on the second floor to find herself alone, and she unlocked the kitchen entrance, went out to draw water, and started a fire under the cooking kettle. Her parents had been taken in by her uncle in Yokohama, where they had started a shop selling shirts, blankets, shawls, and the like, and so Oshō had no home to return to in Tokyo. With her sleeves tied and the hem of her kimono tucked up to do the housework, she sat down on the wooden floor and stared outside with heavy, dreamy eyes, a jumble of confused memories occupying her mind. It was the time of autumn when working with water left her fingers chilled, and the wind gave her an unpleasant sensation as it touched her white legs and the skin of her breast, still warm from sleep, through the opening under her raised sleeves.

She wrung out a cloth and began cleaning the corridor outside the couple's dimly lit room. She could hear the rhythmic hissing of their breath as they slept.

Lowering the hem of her kimono, she crept upstairs, removed her pocketbook from a drawer, tucked it in her red waistband, and then stole back downstairs. The man was awake and crouching in the kitchen. Still dressed in his nightclothes, he yawned and stretched. He was looking the other way. The sight of the man made her want to cringe away in disgust, but Oshō walked right around him, picked up a bucket, and went out to the public water pump. She was lost in thought as the gurgling water rose to the brim of the bucket, but she finally stopped pumping and, with no particular destination in mind, ran away. (3:275–77)

Oshō returns to her aunt's boardinghouse in Yushima and is repeatedly questioned by her aunt as to why she ran away from Asakusa. Oshō replies with monosyllables. She cannot offer one coherent reason for her action. Years of experience in descriptive writing are evident in this depiction of Oshō's inarticulate intelligence. Oshō's physical sensations suggest adolescence and the fastidiousness that accompanies it. Although she may not know for certain that on the nights the man hits the target with the toy arrow his prize is a prostitute, the environs of Asakusa have educated her to the fact that her stepmother's new lover is unsavory and perhaps dangerous. The passage suggests a young woman's justified fear of rape or other violation with an immediacy that overflows the text, much as the water overflows the full bucket: "explanation" is always implicit in "description."

Oshō's alternatives to the low-life cosmetics shop in Asakusa, however, are not very attractive either. Her perceptions of her family's living conditions in the *basue* ("on the edge of low-class urban districts") neighborhood in Yokohama reveal her distress on witnessing the pitiful condition of her family:

> The house [which contained the shop her father had started] was close to a lower-class neighborhood on the edge of a respectable one on the hill. A blue curtain bearing the shop's name was hung from low eaves, and inside, glass cases exposed to the sun contained a small inventory of fading knit undershirts, socks, aprons, and other such miscellaneous clothing.
>
> Oshō discovered her pathetic-looking brothers among the children from neighboring shops who were gathering around a big drum to watch the candy man perform.
>
> Her brothers had taken on the same color as the neighborhood, and their eyes seemed dull and listless.
>
> "Masa-chan," she called out to her brother and signaled with a wave of her hand that he should come over. But he just turned and stood staring at her.
>
> Entering the shop, Oshō immediately sensed an air of decline. Wearing the same type of plain, sleeveless overskirt as that worn by other housewives in the neighborhood, her mother was washing the children's clothes in the back of the house. Oshō noticed that her eyes were clouded and the skin of her face and hands was dry and cracked. (3:283–84)

This is a level of subsistence close to the shadowy, insubstantial world of the day laborer, registered in Oshō's eyes by her brothers' malnutrition and her mother's declining health. Perhaps the state of the déclassé poor is even more desperate than that of the laboring poor, for apparently Oshō's father regards working for wages as the ultimate disgrace for a provincial gentleman. Rather than actually work for a living, the father dissolves his family. The mother and younger children are cared for temporarily by the aunt at Yushima, the eldest brother is taken in by Oshō's uncle, another brother is led by his father back to his home village, and Oshō is sent into service into a prosperous merchant's house. There is never any question of Oshō's returning to the provinces. By this time, she has formed quite an active antipathy toward the country. Even when her family is in its most reduced circumstances, the city, through the members of Oshō's extended family who live in it, provides Oshō with exciting and liberating experiences. Her aunt in Yokohama introduces Oshō to her first contact with the West. Oshō gains entrance to the residence of a pink-skinned foreigner and his Japanese lover (*rasha*) and even rests for a moment on the couple's lavish bed. The aunt proposes to find Oshō a place in service with a foreign family, where the young woman will receive a Western education and better-than-average wages. But Oshō's mother refuses. It seems that Japanese poverty is preferable to strange and frightening foreigners.

The next corner of commoner experience that Oshō discovers is that of the older, slower-moving merchant world around Nihonbashi, a prospering holdover from the mercantile district of Edo. Oshō goes into service in the house of a traditional merchant family. Before the Meiji Restoration, merchants such as Oshō's employer, a pharmaceutical dealer, formed the foundation of Edo *shomin* culture. This older merchant culture is quite different from the rough, competitive immigrant merchant culture typified by the driven, lonely Shinkichi. The following description of Oshō going about her duties in the house in Nihonbashi reveals the more leisurely and comfortable attitude toward time in this older class milieu of Edo *shomin* culture:

Oshō spent almost the entire summer at Nihonbashi.

The house, with its outer walls heavily lacquered, extended far back from the street and was laid out so that the main rooms in its depths always seemed dark, while the thick skylights in the roof over the parlor, kitchen, and bath let in light even on rainy days. Much of Oshō's day was spent minding the fire under the kettle in a corner of the parlor.

Soon after she got up in the morning, Oshō tied up her sleeves with a red cord, revealing plump, white arms and hands dimpling at the knuckles, and she went to work cleaning the walls and dusting with a silk cloth the splendid tables and antiques such as the gold-lacquered inkstone case in a small, elegant set of shelves. Then she folded and put away her master's pale blue silk nightgown and his luxurious silk bedding.

Her master was an old man, about sixty, bald, with age spots on the dirty-looking skin of his face, and when he was naked, there was a noticeable lack of flesh along his bent spine and narrow pelvis; but then he seldom spent the night in his own house.

"He's just returned," Oshō had occasion to reply in answer to telephone calls from the mistress her master kept in the Mukōjima ward, and she would go to call the old man to the phone.

His wife was a tiny, refined-looking woman in her midfifties, and when she helped her husband on with his formal silk half-coat, she had to stand on tiptoe, a fact that made Oshō laugh when she recounted it later, drawing an angry glare from the middle-aged maid who was her superior. (3:300–301)

Photographs taken in the 1890s of the main commercial avenue through the Nihonbashi ward show rows of two-storied business/ residences similar to that described in the passage above.[34] These establishments had massive adobe walls painted over with lacquer to protect against fire, the inveterate scourge of Edo. In keeping with Tokugawa ordinances against extravagance, the fronts of these buildings were purposely kept small, and the prohibitions were circumvented by extending the business and house back behind the facade in large warehouselike structures that were distinctive to the merchants of Edo. Though the facades of these establishments would be transformed into Western-style fronts within the next few decades, the physical buildings and slower daily rhythms of this older *shomin* culture probably remained relatively stable until the national mobilizations for war in the mid-1930s. But the traditional apprenticeship system that provided this culture with cheap labor had begun to collapse as early as the mid-1890s.[35]

Of the dozens and dozens of characters that appear and disappear in the course of *Ashiato,* the elderly pharmaceutical merchant and his wife are the only ones who seem to have been born in Tokyo. Everyone else is a provincially born immigrant to the city. The rule in this immigrant *shomin* culture is social mobility in a valorized economy. The fifteen-year-old Oshō's duties in the house in Nihonbashi are not arduous, but she receives almost no money for her work. After some years of loyal service, she might receive some formal education and/or a portion of her trousseau from her mistress. As a young woman, she cannot even look forward to what *Arajotai*'s Shinkichi receives as the fruit of eleven years of apprenticeship: an independent business. The ethic of success of immigrant *shomin* life, which Oshō subscribes to as certainly as Shinkichi does, involves rising expectations. Oshō wants more than just stable, respectable subsistence. She rejects the traditional logic of her superior in service: "Be patient and stay on. They're not generous, but the old woman looks after her people. There's no easy house to serve in, no matter where you go" (3:305). Oshō is of fairly good family in the country, and she resents being treated like a servant. She is drawn to the happy-go-lucky, independent Oshima, a young woman who was hired after her, who puts the problem in a much simpler framework: "A respectable house is no fun at all. If you're going into service, do it in a place that serves food and wine" (3:306).

Oshima offers to find Oshō a position in Asakusa where she can hope to make enough money to support herself and her mother. Oshō is faced with the momentous choice of whether she will be educated as a stodgy young woman who is certified respectable by an established merchant or whether she will be educated in the popular, *shomin* culture of the latest fashions and songs of Asakusa. With her mother's grudging assent, Oshō chooses the latter, and she leaves Nihonbashi to work as a waitress/live-in maid in a teahouse (*hikite-jaya*). It is necessary to draw a fairly strict distinction between the older *shomin* culture Oshō rejects and the new one she embraces. In Shūsei's novels, the traditional world of the Edo commoner almost always appears as one gone crazily into decline, and it need not concern us further.[36]

The cultural milieu of immigrant *shomin* life is suffused with prostitution and semiprostitution. From the viewpoint of the present, there seems to be something disturbingly unrealistic about the all-pervasive presence of the demimonde in Shūsei's portrayals of *shomin* life. Was prostitution really all that common? An investigation of the historical record reveals that prostitution or semiprostitution must have been an integral part of everyday life. At the turn of the century, the Yoshiwara pleasure quarter alone was servicing well over a million guests a year. And Yoshiwara was only one of sixty-two pleasure quarters scattered throughout Tokyo and its suburbs. These contained over two thousand licensed houses of assignation and over three thousand establishments housing geisha. Official police statistics from 1922 state that almost 4 percent of Tokyo's total population was involved in licensed "stigmatized female trades" (geisha and legal prostitutes), but to form a realistic conception of the extent of prostitution in Tokyo, one should probably triple the official number. Perhaps up to 10 percent of Tokyo's adult female population below the age of forty was practicing some sort of prostitution. In addition to licensed pleasure quarters, whole districts of the city, Tamanoi and Kameido, for example, were famous as red-light districts specializing in illegal prostitution. Maids in houses of assignation and teahouses, waitresses in cafes, and, later, women dancers in dance halls were widely known to practice prostitution on the side. Keeping mistresses was also widespread among wealthy men.[37]

In contrast to the romantic and erotic allure of the demimonde in the Japanese literary tradition, the demimonde in Shūsei's novels of common life should be regarded in class terms. Women who work in the demimonde are a large, significant minority in the city. Their social position is analogous to that of the laboring classes. When women fall into the demimonde, they simply disappear from *shomin* life, as men do when they become day laborers, or as Oshō's father does when he returns to the provinces. Women are stigmatized not because of the morality of their sexual activities but because of their class status.

Oshō is worried that working as a maid in the teahouse in Asakusa will compromise her respectability. "Is it really a respectable house?" Oshō asks Oshima again and again. "Sure it's a respectable house," Oshima replies in a delightfully low urban dialect, "but it's a business where you have to appear before customers, so respectable there is something different from respectable here" (3:314). In the end, Oshō succumbs to the temptation of more money and the excitement of the culture of the demimonde. The teahouse in Asakusa is fairly respectable by the standards of the day, and Oshō is not expected to, nor does she, engage in prostitution. However, her dress, manners, and speech gradually become colored by the fashions and customs of the demimonde. This is a cause for great concern to her extended family in Tokyo, who are responsible to her provincial relatives for her conduct. Oshō's brother is sent to convince her to give up "the life" (*ashi o arau*). The brother makes clear his shame at being seen in the company of his gaudily dressed sister, and when Oshō returns to the teahouse, to a scolding by her employer, there is a new fear of corruption in her perceptions of the tawdriness and vulgarity around her:

"Where have you been the whole day? We've been busy while you've been out playing!" the woman employer screamed when Oshō came into the room. Her sharp eyes never missed a detail. As usual, this somewhat neurotic woman appeared to have been drinking. [After the stepchild she had subjected to constant abuse had been taken from her by an aunt] her elderly patron became the new object of her occasional fits of hysterical anger. During their fights, the woman would gulp down cupful after cupful of cold rice wine drawn straight from the cask.

Oshō laughed, made a brief apology, and walked past the woman.

Another woman, with the hem of her kimono tucked up revealing red undergarments, was cleaning the floor in the large reception room. Other women were gathered around the brazier and were trying to guess the prices of combs and hair ornaments bought the night before from the rows of stalls in front of Asakusa's Sensōji Temple.

"Was that your brother?" one asked Oshō.

"Yes," she nodded.

"Stands to reason, you look alike."

"Brothers and sisters don't always resemble each other."

"Of course not. Quite a few children don't even resemble their parents."

And amid vulgar laughter, the conversation turned to a discussion of facial features. Oshō, conscious of her low nose, frequently brought her fingers to her forehead. In a small adjacent room was a group that had been drinking since before Oshō had left that morning. Drunken songs and then loud clapping, a call for service, came from the room. "Damn," one of the women exclaimed, and she left, humming to herself, to see what they wanted. Oshō also went to work, pulling out dirty bedding in response to a request from a red-nosed customer who had just come in from the cold winds outside.

That night, Oshō received a postcard from her brother. She could not decipher many of the conceited misusages written in a poor hand, but she did get the strong sense that her brother was angry at her for working in a teahouse, and this made a deep impression on her. (3:322–23)

This is as close as Oshō comes to the self-obliteration that results from prolonged submergence in the demimonde. In response to her brother's admonitions, Oshō uses the first holiday available to her to visit her aunt in an unspoken plea for help. With the aunt's sale of her boardinghouse in Yushima and her move to a smaller residence in the same district, Oshō's family has once again disbanded, her mother and oldest brother taken in by her uncle Ozaki. Oshō's visit is not welcome, and, like the rebellious adolescent she is, Oshō rejects the sound advice offered by her aunt and cousin:

"You should go talk things over with your uncle Ozaki and get out of that place in Asakusa as quickly as you can, don't you think?" Oshō's cousin Tadasu suggested, but it was clear from his expression that he didn't want to become personally involved.

"That's what I'll do," Oshō said, and began putting away the combs she had been using to fix her hair.

"No one but Ozaki is going to look after you and your family," the aunt chimed in, "He's your closest relative. Go and explain your situation to him. They don't have any children, so he should help you."

The clock over the old chest of drawers struck five.

Oshō was reluctant to leave. She was irritated by the feeling that she had been done out of a chance to go to the theater. And her mind was filled with all the things she wanted to say to Tadasu. He cared about her, and she felt he best understood her feelings, how lost and confused she was without a family.

Oshō retied her obi and went upstairs to search for the handkerchief she had forgotten there. The cold wind of early evening rattled the ill-fitting shoji, but there was still a pale light coming through the window, which reflected off the table and walls. Oshō sat in the gloomy room and was absorbed in her thoughts for a time. Then she quietly arose and descended the stairs.

Her wooden clogs ringing on the frozen plank over a ditch, Oshō clattered briskly out of the alley. A harsh wind was blowing out on the street, which was almost empty now that the holidays were over. The shops on both sides of her seemed abandoned. Her eyes fastened on a small, darkened theater advertising board exposed to swirling dust.

She was not able to muster the courage to go to Tsukiji [to her uncle's house] alone. Even returning to Asakusa seemed preferable. But she stopped now and then on her way back and stood momentarily lost in thought.

She arrived at Asakusa at about eight o'clock. Alighting from the horse-drawn tram, she was attracted by the crowded shops running up to the main temple in Asakusa, the Sensōji, but her surroundings grew darker and darker as she wandered down the street.

Before she trudged wearily back to the teahouse, Oshō visited a fortune-teller seated that night on the main public avenue. Her fortune was not as bad as she had thought it would be. (3:328–30)

Ashiato represents a move away from extensive psychological analysis in favor of description.[38] Oshō's sense of insecurity concerning her social status, her growing independence as revealed by her reserve about her private affairs, the relief with which she escapes the cold gaze of her aunt, and her fears for the future assuaged in part by the fortune-teller are palpable in her perceptions of scenes. This passage is deeply embedded in a cultural milieu. There were two traditional holidays for servants, one on the sixteenth day of the first month, following the standard fifteen days of celebration to welcome the New Year, the other on the sixteenth day of the seventh month, following the three-day Bon Festival to welcome and see off the souls of the dead. On the sixteenth days of these two months, servants were allowed to return to their homes and celebrate these holidays with their families. In Asakusa, a ward known for its popular entertainments, however, these two days were good for business, and Oshō is allowed to return home only a day or two after the servants' New Year. Dressed in her brightest and most expensive clothing—garish attire in the conservative Yushima district—Oshō goes to celebrate her holiday with her aunt and her family, in the most stable environment she has known in the city. She is told frankly by her aunt, and more circumspectly by her cousin, however, that she has made a mistake in the choice of a "home" and that she should go live in her uncle's house, which she has never visited. In a holiday mood after the holidays are over, Oshō feels lost without a family and cheated out of an annual family celebration, which often included a visit to the theater. She soon recovers from this rejection, however, and briskly returns to Asakusa to search for a little fun during what remains of her day off.

The insecurity, individualism, and social mobility that characterize common life seem to cause the family to disintegrate, and yet somehow or other the extended family in the city holds together to protect its weakest members. The aunt has told Oshō before, when Oshō fled from the cosmetics shop, that she has no home left in Tokyo, but in the end it is this same aunt who takes Oshō and her mother in. This time, after Oshō defiantly breaks her promise to visit her uncle at Tsukiji, the aunt's son Tadasu badgers his cousin over the telephone (houses of assignation led other businesses in installing the new device) to force her to visit her uncle. It has been decided among the members of the extended family that if Oshō can be persuaded to swallow her pride sufficiently to merely face her uncle in person, he will help her.

The day Oshō goes to her uncle's house, she is immediately accorded a status somewhere between that of an adopted daughter and a live-in maid. In Uncle Ozaki, Oshō encounters one prototype of the present-day white-collar worker: the salaried employee who intentionally overextends himself to make himself work all the harder. She is attracted to Ozaki's urbane and easygoing household. On the night of Oshō's initial visit, Ozaki's wife takes Oshō into her confidence by frankly talking about her husband's economic situation. This story, in its telling, reveals as well the unspoken, shared assumption that Oshō is now a member of the family and will not be returning to Asakusa:

That night, Ozaki's wife spoke seriously to Oshō and her mother about the financial circumstances of her household. Ozaki had blundered badly several times before he gained the trust of his employers, and she was afraid he was neglecting his clerical duties at his company, which had good prospects if managed properly. But as soon as his buttocks got a little warm, he'd be up trying his hand at some other venture. He'd recently begun speculating in stocks and was also running around the country acting as a middleman in various mining deals. The profits he made in these transactions he spent on women in teahouses and small theaters.

"This is the start of his third year with the company, and if he can get through it without failing again . . . He invariably bungles things every third year. It's a strange weakness he has," Ozaki's wife concluded. (3:334)

Ozaki is obviously a man of considerable abilities, for to advance from the position of houseboy/student (*shosei*) to a white-collar position with a growing, prosperous firm was a rare success story that many young men would envy. This prototypical, mid-1890s "salary man," dressed in fine kimono, elegant white silk muffler, fashionable geta, and an imported panama hat, and carrying a Western-style leather portfolio, is a romantic and heroic figure. Oshō admires his speculative ethic of success and consumption. The years she spends with him in Tsukiji are the most comfortable and cultured she will experience in Tokyo, though the permissiveness of her upbringing— her smoking, drinking, gambling, growing fondness for the theater, and a love affair she has with a young student—is considered shocking by her relatives with more rural values. Toward the end of 1897, when Oshō is about sixteen and the Japanese economy begins sliding into recession after the boom years immediately following the Sino-Japanese War (3:357), Ozaki's complicated business ventures start to come unraveled, and he goes into financial and physical decline. He is ultimately ruined and disappears from Oshō's world and mind when he returns to the provinces.

Shortly before he departs, Oshō is married to the heir to a prosperous restaurant in the small town of Nakano, a short distance from Tokyo. Though the go-between, her father's cousin and a minor bureaucrat, has promised her that the match is a good one and will leave her in control of substantial resources, she encounters the following crazy situation at Nakano. Oshō's husband, Yoshitarō, a violent young alcoholic, is not related by blood to his stepmother or to his stepfather. Yoshitarō's real mother was driven out of the house by his real father, who then brought in his lover, a former Shinagawa geisha, as mistress of his restaurant. When Yoshitarō's real father died, this former geisha, Yoshitarō's so-called stepmother, brought in her lover, a man who was already married with children, to manage the business. Yoshitarō hates his stepmother, who raised him, only slightly less than he hates his stepfather. Oshō's new "mother-in-law" and "father-in-law" are plotting to get rid of their stepson Yoshitarō by adopting a new husband for their new daughter-in-law Oshō. Soon after the wedding ceremony,

Oshō begins scheming to leave Yoshitarō by convincing her own extended family in Tokyo that she is in a dangerous situation.

Oshō does not have psychological or sociological languages of pathology at her disposal, but she frequently reads the crime pages and can sense that the household she is in may explode into violent crime that might make the newspapers. She knows that she herself is the most obvious candidate for the role of victim. For most of her life, Oshō has witnessed domestic violence, and she has learned to recognize lethal forms of abuse. Her instincts are proven correct when Yoshitarō comes after her with a long, very sharp knife he used to cut sashimi during his training as a cook. Fortunately, he is restrained by two military officers who are customers in the restaurant at the time.

Oshō will not allow herself to become a passive victim, and she begins cunning preparations to flee from Yoshitarō. Dressed as a man, she escapes on a rainy night in the spring of 1902, and once again her aunt at Yushima takes her in. Oshō discovers that her mother has gone into service as a maid in the house of a young bachelor, an acquaintance of a friend of a friend of the aunt. The novel ends the next day with Oshō visiting her mother in the household in which she is working and talking with her there into the early evening. Oshō's mother's employer, a young man who is only mentioned and does not appear in *Ashiato*, corresponds to Tokuda Shūsei.

This study does not argue that Oshō represents a typical young Japanese woman growing up in the last decade of the nineteenth century (though if one is attracted to her, one wants to imagine that she was more typical than the stiff, severe "daughters of samurai" or the tragic geisha who dominate Western literature on Japan); rather, through Oshō we get some sense of the extraordinary diversity, richness, and sheer eclectic confusion that constituted the cultural milieu of the *shomin* within the borders and horizons outlined above. From country gentry to life in a crowded urban boardinghouse, to salesgirl in a small Asakusa cosmetics shop, to the edges of the subsistence, day-laboring class, to domestic in the house of old-fashioned merchants, to the edges of semiprostitution, to the comfortable and urbane house of a prototypical white-collar worker, to mistress of a prosperous restaurant with her own servants, to maid in the house of a marginalized intellectual—Shūsei's achievement in finding a novelistic way to exhibit all of these sociolinguistic registers, to represent this volatile social mobility, and to keep them unified in the consciousness of a young woman growing up cannot be evaluated highly enough.

Laughter, Darkness, and Laborsaving Devices

Oshō's laughter lingers in memory, ringing in one's ears. The young girl Oshō's raucous laughter on seeing her brother steal sweets, the embarrassed, reticent laughter of early adolescence, the hilarious laughter with her friend Oshima in the merchant's house, evasive and dismissive laughter in the demimonde, nervous laughter in tense situations, the stifled, cruel laughter of amusement on observing the pitiful condition of a relative, the therapeutic, renewing laughter at the absurd situations Oshō encounters at every turn, the shy laughter of infatuation, the gentle laughter of love—Oshō is always laughing, a streaming, anarchic affirmation of life.

And yet one can also agree with Takami Jun:

> *Ashiato* is dark. It is dark in the same way that Shimazaki Tōson's *Ie* [The Family, 1910], published in the same year, is dark. . . . Though the years immediately following victory in the Russo-Japanese War should have been years of national prosperity, these works speak to us of how dark it was within Japan. The darkness of *Ashiato,* which has to be counted among the greatest achievements of Japanese naturalism, is not so much the darkness of naturalism as such; rather it is the darkness of Japan's internal domestic situation at that time.[39]

Shomin life as portrayed in *Ashiato* is a social nightmare: tuberculosis, eye diseases, venereal diseases, and malnutrition are rampant; prostitution, gambling, alcoholism, and habitual physical abuse of women are a constant; housing is inadequate, prices are high, and no one seems care in the slightest about minimal standards of social welfare. Tōson's *Ie* and Shūsei's *Ashiato* both present darkly realistic visions of common life in the Meiji period. But the qualities of darkness in *Ie* and *Ashiato* are radically different. The following passage from *Ie* portrays Koizumi Minoru, who through unwise investments has brought his house to the verge of ruin, as he is about to leave his family in Tokyo to go to Manchuria, where he hopes to rebuild his fortune:

> Minoru clapped his hands in front of the family shrine and bade farewell to his ancestors.
>
> His wife, Okura, and his daughter, Otoshi, had prepared and laid out a meal on a tray by the hibachi. Dark tears ran down the cheeks of mother and daughter. Minoru gathered his family together and all drank a parting cup of tea.

"You mustn't come outside. Stay in the house," Minoru said, restraining the members of his family who were preparing to see him off in the street, and he walked alone out of the gate of his house. He could still rely on his powerful body and his courage, but he was over fifty. He had only enough money to enable him to make the journey to his brother-in-law's lodgings in Kobe. The plains of Manchuria were far away. And perhaps he did not expect to return alive. Still embracing heroic ambitions, he left the neighborhood where his wife and his children dwelled.[40]

It is a memorable passage in its original context, marking the end of a house of once proud, landowning gentry who are ruined by the capitalism of both rural and urban economies. Minoru, an ex-convict, may not be a model citizen, but he is granted the dignity and authority of his position as the patriarchal head of the Koizumi house.[41] Contrast this treatment with a similar situation involving Oshō's Uncle Ozaki in *Ashiato*. Ozaki and Minoru are of comparable common birth. After having exhausted his financial resources in unwise business deals, Ozaki leaves Tokyo for the provinces. Oshō and other members of her extended family see Ozaki off at the train station:

Oshō's uncle carried less baggage than he had when he first came to the city as a student. He had long since sold his watches and rings, and the only trace of his prosperous years as an entrepreneur in the Kyōbashi ward was a dirty panama hat. He had tried to sell even that to a friend of his nephew who had come to visit, but the price he had asked for it had provoked laughter, a response that had put him in a foul mood, and so he decided to leave wearing the hat.

As Ozaki climbed aboard the third-class coach of the train, Oshō and her brother were giggling behind his back at the sight of their uncle's gaunt, senile-looking figure, with that old-fashioned panama hat still perched on his head. (3:484–85)

Other than the fact that Shūsei was a more accomplished and original prose craftsman, the fundamental difference between these two realistic novelists was their respective attitudes to authority and language. Shūsei's realism was a matter of distancing language from himself. Oshō's uncle is in several respects a more admirable character than Minoru—he manages to stay out of prison, and at least he earned the wealth he squandered—but, from Oshō's perspective, once her uncle has failed in the city and is on the verge of disappearing into the provincial horizon, he becomes a pitiable, bathetic, and comical character lacking any authority. Legitimate authority is almost always negated in Shūsei's mature fiction: if Oshō's father says he will come home in the evening, he disappears for a week; if a foreign language is spoken authoritatively, Oshō laughs; if the state has any function, it is to start distant, inexplicable wars which are good for business but then leave the economy depressed six months or a year after they end; if a doctor solemnly declares that his patient will recover, the patient dies; if Oshō's uncle promises to provide her with a dowry, he soon goes bankrupt.

This is the rule of common life: no one is in control, no one knows what is going to happen next, and in this mysterious state of affairs, the predictions of fortune-tellers are about as dependable as any other pronouncement. It is the crazy unpredictability of this world that makes it so darkly humorous. The decline of the landowning, rural gentry at around the turn of the century undoubtedly provided ample justification for Shimazaki Tōson's abstract sentimentality. For Oshō, however, encompassed by the everyday realities of the city, the "tragedy" of the gradual eclipse of Japan's dominant rural class and its conservative ideology is welcomed as a source of mirth:

> They had recently come to understand that their father was not having as easy a time of it in his rural village as they had thought. He had involved himself in a difficult, last-ditch attempt at a settlement to save the stem house, now perilously close to collapsing after having failed to corner the stocks of a bankrupt company. Shortly after Oshō had married, the news had reached her family that the stem house had had its property attached by the bank, official wax stamps sealed the doors of its warehouses, and the young head of the house, pressured from all sides, had begun to go mad.
>
> Oshō and her brother laughed until their sides ached when they heard that the young master, now thoroughly unbalanced, had roughly slapped his doctor across the side of the head after the poor man had so kindly come all the way from the nearest town to examine his young patient. (3:467–68)

Oshō's world is dark; Oshō is always laughing. The lack of any legitimate moral or political authority leads to a sense of social disintegration, but, with easy laughter, Oshō always gets by. The darkness of the impoverished laboring class and the demimonde threatens, and yet there is a powerful economic energy at work, a growth of demand and the spread of consumer goods. Through *Ashiato,* it is not difficult to imagine the extraordinary transformations that occurred between 1892 and 1902 in the use of time. The duties of the next-door maid became infinitely easier. Oshō's perceptions reveal how important kerosene lamps were in lengthening the day for accomplishing basic women's work such as sewing. While the newly constructed housing Oshō lives in in the city is built on a smaller scale than houses in the provinces, it is also easier to take care of. Frequent references to metal buckets, which came into wide use in 1893, and public water pumps, part of the city water system completed in 1899, reflect how much less of a chore it has become for Oshō to provide a household with water. The large number of cheap rickshas and the small but growing network of telephones eliminate the need for Oshō to go out on many of the errands she would have had to do. The new public transportation system makes the errands Oshō must run seem pleasurable, like outings in the city. The following describes Oshō at about the age of sixteen, soon after she has gone to live with her uncle in Tsukiji:

Lifting the neighborhood child clinging to her skirts and supporting him on her back, Oshō set off in the evening to pay an installment into the mutual aid fund managed by the Konpira Shrine. Since it was some distance from Tsukiji to Toranomon, Oshō took the horse-drawn tram as far as it went, and then she sauntered on, rocking the child from side to side on her back. It was the night of the Ginza Jizō Festival. On her return, Oshō went out of her way to have a look, strolling down the crowded street, alternately carrying the little boy and leading him by the hand. Stifling close air, rank with smells of dirt, lamp soot, and human beings, was refreshed from time to time by a cool breeze. Her back and thighs drenched with sweat, she occasionally stopped to rest, shaking the drowsy child on her back awake to look at a phonograph or a stall selling wind chimes. Rough workmen in dirty cotton work clothes and straw sandals stared at her face as they passed. A group of men bumped into her, one exclaiming loudly, "Little young to have a kid, aren't you?" (3:343)

It has been the argument here that what Japanese critics refer to as *shomin* culture in Shūsei's novels was an immigrant culture coming into existence in the last decade of the nineteenth century. This culture was flexible enough to incorporate the latest laborsaving devices and technologies that were being imported and mass-produced in Japan. The transportation system, a grid of rails which will soon be transformed into an electrified streetcar system, allows mobs to gather from all parts of the city. Gas streetlights, for which the Ginza was famous until they were replaced by equally innovative electric ones, provide the light for workmen to ogle young women late into the evening. The latest inventions, such as Edison's phonograph, are on display to attract and startle the public.

Laborsaving devices enable Oshō to participate in any number of festivals at local shrines and temples: the festival of the fox deity, whose shrine is close to Ozaki's house in Tsukiji; the Otori festivals in November on the days that fall under the zodiacal sign of the bird, when symbolic rakes to pull in hoped-for profits are sold at the Otori Shrine in Asakusa; the regular festivals on the first, tenth, and fifteenth of each month at the Suitengū Shrine close to the Nihonbashi house where Oshō is in service. Oshō finds more private "festival moods" (*matsuri-kibun*) with friends and family in games of *hanafuda* (flower cards), in which Oshō gambles and usually wins small sums of money. There are frequent family outings to the numerous local theaters. The decline and death of Ozaki's wife provide a sustained period of release when everyone in the family feels justified in ordering out for food, eating in fine restaurants, and bickering over who will receive the poor deceased woman's clothing and personal effects. Then there are festivals of love and marriage that Oshō participates in.

Shomin life in *Ashiato* is dark, and yet there are also many leisurely pleasures for which the contemporary reader can feel great nostalgia or longing.[42]

Common Custom

Shūsei was virtually the last major writer associated with Japanese naturalism to write a full-length autobiographical novel. Tayama Katai had already completed his controversial *Futon* (The Bedding, 1907) and *Sei* (Life, 1908). Iwano Hōmei had published *Tandeki* (Dissipation, 1909), the humorous account of his debauched relations with a country prostitute. Tōson had finished *Haru* (Spring, 1908) and was releasing in installments his *Ie,* the second of the trilogy of his personal and family saga. Masamune Hakuchō, seven years Shūsei's junior, had caused an uproar with his "Doko e" (Where? 1908) and was publishing his confessional *Doro ningyō* (Earthen Doll, 1911). As Enomoto Takashi has argued, Shūsei was not in the least enthusiastic about portraying his strained relationship with his wife, but after *Ashiato* drew almost no critical attention, Shūsei felt he had to appeal to a public which seemed to have an insatiable appetite for sensational personal revelation.[43] To keep up with trends in the literary world, Shūsei wrote *Kabi* (Mold,

1911), his first sustained autobiographical novel. The work was commissioned for *Asahi Shinbun* by Natsume Sōseki, and he seemed satisfied with the novel Shūsei wrote for him. On August 1, 1911, Sōseki wrote to Komiya Toyotaka, "Shūsei's novel began [serialization] today. His style is tight and compact [*shimatte*]; it looks like we've got a new delicacy."[44] As Etō Jun has suggested, it is probably not a coincidence that when Sōseki portrayed the common people closest to himself, he chose much the same extremely fluid form pioneered by Shūsei in *Kabi*, suggesting that the cultural milieu of the *shomin*, which in *Michikusa* (Grass on the Wayside, 1915) has clearly spread to incorporate Sōseki's marginalized Edo-born relatives, required a new way of telling a story to account for new realities.[45]

Just as Shūsei's response to naturalism was a kind of antinaturalism, so his response to the genre of autobiographical fiction later called *watakushi-shōsetsu* was a kind of anti-*watakushi-shōsetsu* (anti–I-novel). It seems that at first Shūsei intended *Ashiato* to be his own story, but the material about his wife got away from him, and the novel developed into her story.[46] *Kabi* almost got away from Shūsei too. In 1912, Tayama Katai wrote of *Kabi*, "The description of the male protagonist's character and life is completely eclipsed by the description of the character and life of the woman protagonist."[47] In the same year, Shimazaki Tōson, who clearly had not read *Ashiato,* suggested that *Kabi* would have been a finer work of art had Shūsei cut the material about himself and concentrated only on the woman protagonist.[48] Almost every major review praised *Kabi* for the characterization of the woman protagonist, Ogin, and did not touch much on the male protagonist, Sasamura.[49] *Kabi* provides a detailed and accurate account of Shūsei's personal experiences during a period of just over five years, from the spring of 1902, when Shūsei was thirty, to the early summer of 1907. But once again, the woman character modeled on Tokuda Hama stole the novel away from the male author.

Kabi takes up Tokuda Hama's life at the point at which she meets Shūsei for the first time. Oshō becomes Ogin, the daughter of Sasamura's (Shūsei's) maid. Her mother is keeping house for Sasamura and another young novelist, Miyama (in real life, Mishima Sōsen). Having grown tired of boardinghouse life, these two aspiring writers have established an independent house in the Omote district of Koishikawa ward. Their landlord, K (in real life, Tanaka Chisato), is a friend of Sasamura's from his Kanazawa years. As in *Ashiato,* almost every character in *Kabi* is an immigrant to the city.

Shūsei had absolutely no interest in dramatizing his alter ego

Sasamura, and, in the breach, Ogin emerged as the more sympathetic and engaging character. *Kabi* can be read as a mere continuation of *Ashiato* as told from Sasamura's perspective.[50] But *Kabi* is an anti-*watakushi-shōsetsu* in a more fundamental existential sense. As he had done before, Shūsei adapted himself to a new definition of realism, confession, and took the form to its logical conclusion. Instinctively, as a professional novelist, he regarded theoretical debates about the philosophical status of the self as problems of descriptive narration. He went about grappling, in descriptive prose, with the issue Sōseki had articulated so lucidly in *Kōfu* (The Miner, 1908) three years before: "When the question of responsibility comes up and we are accused of breaking faith, why is it that none of us even thinks to reply, 'Well, that's because my personality is nothing but a bunch of memories. I'm just a mess inside'?"[51] Shūsei knew exactly what kind of confession would appeal to Sōseki. Sasamura is ordinary in every regard, and there is a universality in his ordinariness. As the critic Terada Tōru wrote in 1948: "We should not locate Shūsei's world next to ourselves in the [common] lives of people we are familiar with; rather we should discover it within ourselves. . . . I know of no literary work written since the end of the war that confronts us with as clearly an existential vision as Shūsei's *Kabi*."[52]

Sasamura is the same as "you or me" in that he knows that nothing will turn out as he intends. Volition is meaningless in his world, but nonetheless he is compelled to act. In Matsumoto Tōru's phrase, Sasamura is a "non-self" (*mushi*).[53] He is best understood not as a literary character but as a field of moods reacting hostilely to social obligations dictated by *shomin* life. *Kabi* opens with a flat declarative sentence describing Sasamura fulfilling a legal obligation: "Sasamura finally entered the name of his wife in his family register at about the same time he completed a similar procedure for the infant that had been born to them" (3:3). In reality, Shūsei registered his official intent to marry Ozawa Hama with the municipal ward office for Koishikawa on March 16, 1904. He officially recognized his son Kazuho as his own on March 22, 1904. It seems that Kazuho was actually born in July 1903.[54]

According to the Meiji Civil Code, Shūsei was under no legal compulsion to recognize his illegitimate son or marry Hama. Statutory law gave Japanese women almost no rights.[55] But in the unwritten law of the community, Ogin and her mother have strong rights, which they use against Sasamura. "Common law" might be an appropriate term to describe the body of precedent Ogin invokes. Unlike British law, however, Japanese "common law" is not interpreted by courts or lawyers. It is negotiated and enforced by neighborhoods, families, friends, villages, and so on. The first sentence gives away the result of the "legal" contest that will be waged between Sasamura and Ogin, and the reader is then taken back in associative digression within digression within digression describing how and why Sasamura loses the contest and Ogin wins. The work does not catch up with its narrative present—March of 1904—until chapter 39, about midway through the novel.[56] Even the Meiji critic Shimamura Hōgetsu, a highly educated reader, complained that he had difficulty following the action in *Kabi*.[57] The confusing quality of the work probably derives from Shūsei's attempt to mimic the associative properties of memory and consciousness.[58]

The battle for dominance between Sasamura and Ogin begins with neither having the moral high ground. Sasamura, a hack writer selling himself on the literary marketplace, has some claim to social superiority in his status as a man of letters (*bunshi*) and feels a certain moral contempt for Ogin's sexual generosity, but then he takes advantage of her generosity and feels a cowardly relief when she suggests that she will not hold him responsible for her future. (It is perhaps a sign of Sasamura's naiveté that he takes comfort in Ogin's suggestion.) Their long, contentious relationship begins as a study in pure ambivalence:

Ogin was prone to despair and self-abandon after her affair with Isotani had broken up. And Sasamura was not the sort of man to comfort her wounded feelings with gentle love. Even if he did decide to take her as his wife, he didn't feel much enthusiasm for reforming her or for making her reconsider her life.

"Don't worry, I won't tell anyone about us after I leave your house," she stated one evening as they were returning along a small dark path through a grassy field. They had gone out to eat before their separation. The woman had a toothpick in her mouth, and she was holding up the skirt of her kimono with both hands.

"But you mustn't tell my relatives in the country where I've gone after I've left."

Sasamura squatted down in the grass and stared appalled at the woman.

"You're really that desperate?"

"But everything is such a mess . . ." She sounded as though she had given up.

Sasamura's mood, subject to wild fluctuations during the previous days, had begun to calm. He was able to think quietly about what he had done to the woman. (3:33)

It is not clear at this point whether Ogin's self-abandon—her threat to fall into the demimonde—is calculated or not, but her appeal to

Sasamura's sympathies is not effective. Sasamura has quarreled with Miyama and suspects him of having slept with Ogin. In part to keep Ogin out of Miyama's hands, in part to counter ugly rumors about Ogin and himself spread by Miyama, Sasamura proposes marriage to Ogin, but he soon has second thoughts. A casual marriage proposal has no force according to custom, and it is of no use to Ogin in what might be her campaign to compel Sasamura to marry her. Sasamura's friends from Kanazawa—T (in real life, Shūsei's classmate Ōta Shirō), K (Tanaka Chisato), and B (Shūsei's old friend Kiryū Yūyū)—are already rallying around Sasamura to protect him from Ogin.

B offers his services as a man experienced in such matters to negotiate an end to the affair. Once Ogin is certain she is bearing Sasamura's child, however, she has a powerful claim on him. Of course, if an aristocrat, one of the high bourgeoisie, or an elite bureaucrat impregnated his maid, there would be no question of marriage. But class distinctions in common life are too murky to allow Sasamura to intimidate Ogin. There is not that much difference between the social statuses of the two: a previously married woman from a respectable rural family and a man of letters, a social position somewhere between an actor and a yellow journalist. Negotiations between Ogin, her mother, and Sasamura begin on fairly equal ground, with mother and daughter playing for time to make up for a slight disadvantage:

The three of them were lost in a serious discussion of the problem until one o'clock in the morning. Sasamura proposed that they end the affair in as amicable a way as possible. Both women readily agreed to this idea.

"If you say your reputation will be damaged, I guess we have no choice but to give up on the thought of marriage. I can see that this is causing you great concern, and I'm sorry," the mother said as she spread her sewing out in front of her. "As I'm sure you know by now, this daughter of mine will somehow survive on her own; they only problem is the burden she's carrying."

When it was decided that the issue was the pregnancy, Sasamura wanted Ogin to abort as soon as possible. There then ensued frightening, reckless talk carried on in hushed voices. Sasamura's eyes were gleaming wildly with excitement.

"I'll dispose of it. You can trust me in these matters." The mother's eyes were clear and determined.

"Let's not be too hasty about this," Ogin protested nervously, but then she returned to her own thoughts.

"There's almost never any danger," Sasamura declared.

On awakening the next morning, Sasamura's mood, so tense the night before, was listless again. His mind was painfully sluggish. What the mother so cheerfully agreed to the night before seemed almost preposterous today.

Sasamura couldn't work. He went over again in his mind the various options, and he arrived at the same conclusion they had reached last night.

With no change in her demeanor, Ogin was talking in good spirits with the landlord's wife in the back of the house. He caught her when she came in.

"I don't think I can bear looking at its face if it's born." He immediately launched into the subject of the night before. "It'll gain shape with every passing day you do nothing."

"You're right, but . . . ," Ogin just laughed. "I think I felt it moving this morning," she said with a teasing expression in her eyes, putting her hand on her stomach. "You shouldn't take things so seriously. You're one of those people who broods over problems." And she stared with wonder at him.

When Ogin was in low spirits, she would go play cards at the house of relatives in Shitaya.

"I'm going to earn my pocket money for today," she declared as she put on her makeup and set off from the house. (3:54–56)

Ogin, with her urbane sophistication and sense of humor, is so much more attractive than the grim, dour Sasamura. She is also more cunning. Playing on the ambiguities inherent in received custom, she gradually snares Sasamura and drags him into the innumerable petty obligations that constitute *shomin* life. Ogin and her mother have no intention of aborting the fetus. They delay and evade until abortion is no longer an acceptable possibility. Then mother and daughter make a "reasonable request." Sasamura is asked to support Ogin at a relative's house until she gives birth and the child can be given up for adoption. He agrees, but then the "relative's house option" never materializes. The "man of letters" Sasamura cannot throw an obviously pregnant woman out of his house, and he consents to allow Ogin and her mother to stay with him until the child is born. Through his friend B, he begins searching for suitable foster parents. He is finally forced out of his own house, and he rents a room in a boardinghouse where he can work in peace. When the child is born, Ogin refuses to give the healthy infant boy up for adoption, stating that she will raise the baby herself. After having paid the expenses for the birth, Sasamura is no longer able to maintain two separate households, and he asks B to negotiate a final end to the affair. The following is the account of B's negotiations with Ogin and her mother:

"I've known Sasamura for many years, and he's never had a problem like this before," Sasamura's friend said, opening the discussion on a frank note.

"Trust me," he continued, "After you leave him, if you want to start a business or something, I fully intend to be of as much help to you as I can. Of course, my resources are limited, but you needn't worry that you'll be left in a bad way."

Ogin listened in silence as B got that far in outlining his proposal.

Ogin began by seeking criticism from his friend concerning her own attitude and behavior toward Sasamura. She spoke of how difficult it had been when she came to his house, which at first did not have even one set of decent bedding, of Sasamura's terrifying moods, of how time and again she had dragged her heavy body to the pawnshop, of how she had frequently helped Sasamura out of financial difficulties with money she had raised herself.

Ogin's mother put in her say in a heavy halting tone: "Sasamura always says that I stay here only because I'm greedy, but if money was what I was after, even I could find a place to go where I'd be better off. I'm worried about my daughter. She's failed once, and if she's left with no place to go again, I won't be able to face my relatives." (3:101–2)

By this time, Ogin has built up sufficient precedent—daily domestic labor; pawning her primary resource, her clothing; bringing basic items of furniture into the house—to convince her family, the neighbors, and finally even Sasamura's friend B that she is entitled to be recognized as Sasamura's common-law wife. B returns and gloomily tells Sasamura that he should give up the idea of separating from Ogin: "What could I say when she started weeping as she stared down at the face of the infant feeding at her breast?" (3:100). In the late summer of 1903, Ogin and her mother, who still have no legal claim on Sasamura, are in complete control of his house and are in a positon to make demands which he must accept if he wishes to return. Ogin's father brings her registry from the country toward the end of 1903. Sasamura officially marries Ogin and recognizes her child as his own in the early spring of 1904. Once Ogin's name is registered in Sasamura's house, legal divorce becomes immeasurably more difficult than separation from a common-law wife. Nonetheless Sasamura continues his almost comical efforts to divorce his wife to the very end of the novel. He does not succeed. Ogin wins.

Sasamura does not want to marry. He suspects, without foundation, that Miyama is actually the father of Ogin's child. He does not believe his writing can support a family. At one point, it is hinted that Sasamura feels unfit for marriage because of a condition that sounds very similar to venereal disease. The principal reason Sasamura has for not marrying Ogin is that her reputation might make her seem an unsuitable wife for a respectable gentleman. But Sasamura is caught in a dilemma. He wants to use Ogin's past as a weapon against her, but he finds her lack of chastity to be an integral aspect of her erotic and literary attraction:

Sasamura came to feel that he was being unfair in his dealings with the woman. While trying to force her into the role of meek and obedient wife, he couldn't say that there was not also within him the rough impulse to treat her as an immoral, kept woman. It also occurred to him that perhaps he was thus filling his days with stimulation and excitement. (3:133)

Or again:

In hopes of finding even a scrap of a letter Isotani once sent to Ogin, Sasamura had searched through the drawers of her mirror stand. What he wanted to find above all else was something that would send his heart palpitating wildly when he read it. He enjoyed searching by himself through her mirror stand, chests of drawers, sewing box, and bag, with their scents of perfume and face powder. It gave him exactly the same feeling he had gotten as a child rummaging through his mother's moldy belongings in her personal letter box and chest in the dark closet of their provincial home. (3:229)

The central issue in *Kabi* is a legal one. Can Sasamura get rid of this technically respectable woman Ogin and her child? Common custom maintains that he must stay married to Ogin and support her and her child. The voyeuristic eroticism Sasamura at first experiences in his relationship with Ogin is transformed into pure rage at being manipulated by common custom, which is not some fixed code from the feudal past but a living structure constantly under negotiation and at which everyone is cheating. Does Sasamura solve the mystery of Ogin's identity at the bottom of his mother's box, or does he ultimately lose interest because Ogin is getting fat and starting to look like a duck (3:125)? Is the natural father of Ogin's child Sasamura or Miyama? Is Sasamura's jealousy justified, or is it merely an erotic obsession that is an excuse to write a novel? Is Ogin manipulating Sasamura, or is she a passive victim? Not one major question in the novel is resolved; not one conclusion is left uncontradicted. In this monstrously ambiguous atmosphere where no one's words can be believed, where there is no ground on which to base firm interpretation, a fragile stasis is maintained through shared custom. The last male prerogative left to Sasamura in common custom is violence. The author is reduced to inarticulate rage:

"I'm sorry I'm not good enough for you, and if we can reach an agreement on a way to separate, I don't see why you should have to keep me. But I really can't tell you I'll be leaving today or tomorrow," Ogin said.

Her usual flippant, teasing manner had disappeared in her occasional replies, but they both knew full well that they would not find a way to part.

"In any case, I think I'll liberate you. It has always had to be that way," Sasamura countered.

"Good! Why don't you go have a nice long talk with Miyama." He couldn't believe that these words were actually coming out of Ogin's mouth.

Sasamura didn't know how much more his enraged nerves could stand. There was a separate, other "self" quietly observing him as his blood rose furiously out of control, but this other self just looked on in fear. He cursed her with a string of abusive language, and when the tense Ogin, who was watching his every move warily, made the slightest protest, he trembled so violently that he felt as though the flesh of his body was leaping up independently of his will, a physical reaction which frightened and shamed even him. Sasamura was amazed that he had such violent blood within him.

"I'm no match for you!" Ogin said, smiling sadly as she shivered on the floor in front of him. Her face was pale with the fright of a wounded animal. Her hairstyle, subjected to blows from his bony, male hands, had collapsed at the center, and tears were running from her bleary eyes. Still, she made no attempt to flee.

"Such a strange temperament. You don't have to believe me, everyone says so!" she declared, supporting her hair with her hand as she gingerly shook her head.

Sasamura had beaten her about the head a number of times before. At night, he would gently remove her ornamental combs as she was sleeping and break them in half. The woman didn't mind being beaten so much as she regretted having her possessions destroyed. When she saw that his temper was rising, she kept a constant, vigilant eye on her mirror and chests, always keeping her body in a position to protect them.

Restrained by Ogin's mother, his weak heart beating wildly, Sasamura finally sat down. They hid his footwear and hats so he couldn't bolt out of the house.

Ogin and her mother had no choice but to wait until his nerves were exhausted by the force of time.

After spending several days away from the house, Sasamura returned to discover another Ogin he had never perceived before.

"I thought that time, for sure, I'd be driven out," she said.

When she saw that he was as gentle as a lamb, she became so familiar that he thought she would come over and put her head against his chest.

"Well, you were pretty awful, too," he replied, grinning broadly.

"You were being so unreasonable, I lost control and said what I did." She smiled, her cheek propped on her hand with her arm resting on the edge of the hibachi, in which she was preparing half-boiled eggs for a late-night meal.

"Even I can understand your position," she continued, "But for some reason, I exploded, I couldn't help it. I guess it's my lack of education." (3:186–88)

If one does not recognize the force of the rights Ogin possesses in common life, this passage is nearly incomprehensible. Ogin acknowledges that she was crueler than Sasamura. She confesses that *she* lost control (*sutekusare o itte yatta*) and *she* exploded (*nan da ka atama ga katto natte*), leaving Sasamura no alternative but violence. Both know that Sasamura's threat to "liberate" his wife is empty. Ogin states that she is no match for Sasamura, but she is referring merely to the physical contest. In the verbal battle, she turns Sasamura into a trembling bundle of enraged flesh. By requesting Miyama's mediation, she insinuates that even if Miyama is the natural father of her son, Sasamura is powerless to challenge her position. Later, she apologizes for the brutally frank way she confronted Sasamura with his own impotence.

After the birth of her second child in the summer of 1905 and her eldest child's bout with infantile dysentery in the summer of 1906, Ogin can safely ignore Sasamura's laughable demands for a divorce. Through Sasamura, she secures the common respectability to which she aspired. *Kabi* presents such a stark, unremitting negativity because Sasamura resents being defined by a common law that is so new no one is able to define it clearly, and yet he cannot imagine a life that does not follow the rules of common respectability. Sasamura personifies alienation.

Abandon and Death

When the patient grew tired of conversation, she let out a long sigh and twisted her heavy, numb-looking head on the steaming ice pack.

"I've suffered so long from domestic worries. To die like this is such a pity," she moaned to herself.

Oshō stared with loathing down at her aunt's face. (3:373)

The cruelty inherent in this passage is the cruelty of common life. As a result of her husband's compulsive use of prostitutes, Oshō's aunt has been infected by a venereal disease. This disease complicates the aunt's pregnancy and leads to a miscarriage late in the development of the fetus. The middle-aged woman is left emotionally and physically exhausted and goes into a long period of decline that culminates in death. Oshō, charged with caring for her aunt during the long months of her illness, resents her aunt's words because Oshō has been the woman managing the household. On another level, for Oshō, even the despair of impending death is no excuse for the banality of melodrama.

Melodrama is the psychotherapy of the masses, but it is terribly destructive. This is best illustrated by Shūsei's *Tadare* (Festering), which was serialized in *Kokumin Shinbun* from March to June of 1913. This novel concerns two highly motivated, intelligent people who survive in the city through cold calculation as they watch the people around them self-destruct in an orgy of theatricality. The protagonist of the work is a woman ex-prostitute named Omasu. Her lover, Asai, buys her out of the Yoshiwara brothel where she worked and sets her up as his mistress in her own house in a respectable neighborhood. One can confidently state that *Tadare* is one of Shūsei's novels of common life and not a work of the lesser genre *karyū shōsetsu* (novel of the demimonde) because it is a perceptive and subtle study of the psychology of a woman who aspires to and wins common respectability. The demimonde appears only as a vague dream. The following is a description of Omasu shortly after she has left the brothel and has moved into the small house rented for her by Asai:

It seemed that just as Omasu felt herself melting into sleep she was startled awake by the shrill voice of the old woman next door. Her troubled sleep had been occupied by rambling dreams, fragments woven together in an incoherent pattern: for some reason, Asai, whom she hadn't seen for several days, had suddenly appeared in a suit, looking as he did when he visited her in Yoshiwara, or she was in the dim light of the cage where she and the other women were exposed to the street, and a familiar customer, the head clerk of a hat wholesaling firm in Nihonbashi, passed by pretending he didn't notice her. She tried to call out to him, but an enormous hand seemed to press down on her chest, and she could not utter a sound.

Certain that the sharp voice was that of her girl attendant quarreling in the corridor outside her room in the brothel, Omasu opened her eyes to discover it was the old woman, screaming abuse at her aging, bald husband.

"They're at it again," Omasu thought and was at last clearly aware that she was sleeping alone in her own bed surrounded by mosquito netting in the house where Asai was keeping her. Shadows cast by the morning sun had already formed in the room, and she could tell that it was going to be hot again that day. From the common pump in the alley came the bustling sounds of splashing water and the metallic ringing of handles clanging against buckets.

The old woman's loud whining approached and receded as she went back and forth from the kitchen to the main room. The old man got in a word or two between her complaints. They frequently fought at night, and Omasu knew the reason why. Wives had fled one after another from the pale, morose old man.

"He's so stingy no woman'll stay with him long," Ochiyo, the neighborhood lady hired to help Omasu, had commented the other day, but it seemed to Omasu that there was more to it than that.

"I'll bet he's a nuisance at night," Omasu had added.

An odd expression had formed on Ochiyo's face. (3:511–12)

What an extraordinary craftsman of the novel Shūsei had become. With bits of dreams, a snatch of remembered conversation, and a few sounds, Shūsei created in Omasu a complex psychology at the level of physical sensations finely tuned in response to social situations which are in a constant state of flux. Omasu has spent her adult life in the city (she too is an immigrant) secluded in the Yoshiwara pleasure quarter. Of course, she was exploited there, but she was also protected. Everything in this ordinary neighborhood in Yushima is new and disconcerting for Omasu: the early hour at which people rise, the brightness of the morning light, the jarring sounds of busy housewives drawing water, and the shocked expression on Ochiyo's face at Omasu's reference to the old man's sexuality. Each of these perceptions suggests Omasu's insecurity as an outsider and her recognition that she must fundamentally change her daily schedule and manner of speech and dress if she is to adapt to common life.

Omasu is ambitious. She is determined to replace Asai's legal spouse, Oryū, as Asai's recognized wife. There are major obstacles to the success of Omasu's plan. It is widely known in the neighborhood that Asai's present financial prosperity owes a great deal to his legal wife's support of him through college. If Asai were an honorable man of some real social distinction, marriage to his mistress would be unthinkable. Fortunately for Omasu, Asai is a mere commoner, and class distinctions within *shomin* society are not so rigid as to preclude marriage between people of widely different backgrounds. Omasu's one great advantage is that she can maintain her household (*katei*) not as a part of a respectable business (*ie*) but as a sensual realm where Asai can have complete sexual control. In the following, Omasu attempts to induce Asai to spend the night with her instead of returning to his wife as he planned:

"I wonder if your wife's caught on to us yet," Omasu asked after she and Asai had returned from playing two rounds of cards at Ochiyo's house. She began opening sliding doors and windows to let air into the close humid room. She then called the maid across the way to bring over some live coals to relight the cold hibachi.

"Have you learned how to find your way around Tokyo a little?" A broad grin had formed on Asai's face.

"I was bored here alone, so I went to see my friend Oyuki in Asakusa." She had removed her red underdress, damp down the back with perspiration, and her white underskirt, and was spreading these out in front of the open doors to dry.

"Look, I'm covered with perspiration!" She was sitting there naked, cooling herself.

"Are you hungry?" she finally asked.

"Shall we go out for something?" Asai suggested.

"That doesn't sound like much fun."

After drying her body with a cloth in the kitchen, she changed into a yukata tied with a thin sash and went out to the corner ice shop to buy flavored ice and cold fruits. On her return, she firmly closed the wooden shutter over the front entrance.

Expecting consolation for the loneliness of the past several days, Omasu first folded Asai's clothing carefully and put it away with his personal belongings, and then she waited on him attentively, keeping the cup he sipped from filled with wine and methodically waving a fan to cool him. She felt moments of disappointment when she saw that he was concerned about the passing time.

Asai spent the night with Omasu and work up late the next morning. (3:527–28)

A skilled prostitute is also an actress, and Omasu's sexual abandon is clearly calculated. She will learn more conventional and cunning ways to manipulate Asai and her domestic situation. But in each new role Omasu learns, she maintains a calculated self-interest that prevents her from abandoning herself to it. In contrast, Asai's wife begins acting like a character out of a play. Asai wishes to rid himself of his asthmatic, disorderly wife, but common custom does not permit him to summarily divorce her. Oryū plays right into his hands. She abandons herself to the role of wronged wife, and her hysterical jealousy soon reduces her to the following condition:

Asai's wife, her hair wildly disheveled, was crouched on the floor weeping like a child.

Asai fled, but Oryū, barefoot, followed him outside, and he was obliged to return when he still couldn't lose her some distance from his house.

He heard conversations and saw lights from houses in the quiet, evening neighborhood.

"I'll follow you wherever you go," his wife declared, wheezing as she strained to keep up, walking beside him. She looked exhausted, and her lips were as colorless as those of a corpse. A cold wind blew her black hair across her face and neck.

As if she were an ill woman, Oryū did not leave her bed for several days after the incident.

"It's turned into a hateful situation," the pale Asai exclaimed when he made it back to Omasu's house. "She's gone insane," he continued.

"You have no alternative if it's like that," Omasu said with a frown. (3:548–49)

Custom recognizes Asai's right to keep a mistress if he can afford one. By giving in to the impulse to play the role of the betrayed wife, Oryū strengthens Asai's position against her. An incompetent, unstable wife who actively interferes with her husband's business is a liability. Asai can justify divorcing her as an economic necessity. He is cruel but not unreasonably so. He arranges for Oryū to return to her family in the provinces and pays her brother a large sum of money as a final settlement. Asai knows that Oryū will never see any of the money, but that is not his concern. He has lived up to his obligations to the community. Oryū, deceived by everyone around her, goes mad and dies.

Once Oryū is out of the way, Omasu goes about the task of learning how to be a proper wife to Asai. Soon, she becomes a model of the comfortable, attractive, almost ordinary housewife. Omasu's intelligence, her capacity to grow, and her sensitivity are qualities that save *Tadare* from the stereotypical form of melodrama. As she becomes more respectable, Omasu begins to feel guilt for her part in bringing about Oryū's downfall. For the reader, this guilt is mitigated by a brilliantly drawn secondary woman character, Oyuki, who represents what might have happened to Omasu had she not struggled to depose Oryū and escape from the demimonde. Oyuki is a beautiful and skilled woman of the demimonde who becomes Omasu's best friend during her years of prostitution in Yoshiwara. Before she turned to prostitution, Oyuki bore a child to a student who later became a prominent diplomat. She thus had an important claim on a potentially successful man who loved her. But Oyuki conformed to a popular dramatic role received from the Edo period: the young woman who allows herself to be victimized for the benefit of her family. She permitted her alcoholic mother to sell her into the Yoshiwara pleasure quarter, where she soon began exhibiting the sense of abandon and love of theatricality that accompanies the role of prostitute:

Oyuki's lover was a once well known actor associated with the new theater movement of the previous generation, and years before he had been active in the People's Rights movement. Omasu knew him well: he had a stern and handsome face with large almond-shaped eyes.

"Aoyagi's back again!"

Rumors about the man always reached Omasu's room first. He and Oyuki had fought and separated any number of times, and the man then usually left on a haphazard tour of provincial theaters, only to show up again in his lover's room, refusing to leave until Oyuki was called.

His trips to make money invariably left him as shabby as a vagrant, financially destitute, and with no place to go but to Oyuki's side, and although Oyuki repeatedly stated that it was over between them, at heart she was waiting for her lover to return. At that time, Oyuki, who was selling better than any other woman in the brothel, had begun to give in to fits of despair that she would never rid herself of her parasitical mother, who seemed intent on living for the rest of her life on the right she had to dispose of her daughter's body. Oyuki had taken to drinking heavily and would physically shove customers away when she didn't feel like entertaining. The affair between Oyuki and Aoyagi had degenerated to the point where they might have committed a love suicide had they been a little younger. Observing their relationship as an uninvolved outsider, Omasu saw many incidents which shocked and frightened her.

When she left the brothel, Oyuki had nothing. The chests that once contained her extensive wardrobe were empty. Of the various well-placed men who had patronized her, not one now came near her. With only the clothes she was wearing, she fled to the side of her lover. (3:514–15)

To Omasu, the traditional feminine values of the theater—sacrifice for the family, loyalty to one's man, a willingness to die for love—seem to be degenerate madness. Omasu's cruelty to Oryū is necessary for

Omasu's survival. The kind of self-sacrificing abandon Oyuki represents leads ineluctably to self-destruction. Omasu wants to live. She exerts considerable cunning in protecting her position. Omasu agrees to act as the guardian of a distant relative, Oima, who has come up from the provinces to study at a finishing school. When Omasu discovers that Oima and Asai are carrying on an affair, she reacts without histrionics, working quietly behind the scenes to marry Oima off to an appropriate young man. After successfully meeting this challenge, Omasu is next threatened by a relationship between Asai and another prostitute. In common life, men are usually crueler than women. The novel ends with Omasu attempting to affirm her status as Asai's wife. She feels that she is cursed by Oryū's ghost, but it seems certain that Asai will not separate from Omasu as easily as he did from Oryū.

Death is a constant in Shūsei's portrayal of common life in the Meiji period, and yet most of his common characters resolutely resist the impulse to abandon themselves to the theatrical roles that often seem to invite self-destruction. There is nothing heroic about death in most of Shūsei's mature fiction. It is almost always grim and frightening. Common people struggle against death to the very end, are terribly afraid, and deceive themselves that there is hope for recovery when there is none. Shūsei's controversial descriptions in *Kabi* of the long painful process of the death of his teacher Ozaki Kōyō caused Izumi Kyōka and Yanagawa Shun'yō to break off all association with Shūsei over what they saw as the defamation of the memory of their teacher.[59] Shūsei responded that he was merely touching on Kōyō's human side.[60] Kōyō died of stomach cancer in 1903. It was widely thought that Kōyō's preference for rich and delicious foods was the basic cause of his cancer. One of the most graphic passages in *Kabi* is the following account of Kōyō's death:

At the doctor's pronouncement late that night, messengers and telegrams were sent off to relatives and close friends.

People began trickling in, taking places around the sick man's bed.

"My god, what's happened?" exclaimed an artist with a bad heart as he came running in, pale and wheezing heavily.

The patient was awakened from his coma by his morning injection, and when his eyes suddenly opened wide, the faces of those crowded around were mirrored in them. A quietness, funereal but uncertain, filled the room. The footsteps of guests ascending and descending the stairs as quietly as possible added to the tension, giving the patient an awful intimation of what was to come.

As the fit of delirium gradually subsided, Sasamura's teacher was able to converse for short periods with members of his family. His voice then was fairly calm. Delirous, or perhaps enraged, his mind was pitifully disordered. Whether from being unable to bear the excruciating pain brought on by impending death or from a childish rage at the severity of the fate he could no longer hope to escape, he screamed all sorts of nonsense in a high whining voice.

When his suffering eased, he returned to his normal self. He even dozed off from time to time. In lucid moments, he made last requests that his wife be escorted to a hot spring resort to recover from the exhausting months of nursing him, or that his body be donated to medical science for autopsy.

"Death will at least mean an end to the pain," he observed with a sad smile.

"Bring your ugly faces here," he yelled and looked around with clouded eyes to pick out his students, who drew near.

"Eat awful-tasting food. I want you all to live as long as you can."

Muffled sobbing came from his wife and another woman, who were clinging to his hips.

The room upstairs, crowded with guests, suddenly grew silent, as if all had stopped breathing at once. Most of those behind the inner circle were standing. Sasamura's teacher drew his last breath late that night. (3:116–18)

To a writer such as Izumi Kyōka, who radically dismissed the entire project of literary realism, this description of Kōyō's death must have seemed irreverent to say the least. And yet through *Kabi,* one can gain a concrete impression of the personal qualities that made Kōyō such an admirable and compelling figure: his passion for life, his genuine and generous paternalistic concern for his family and the various odd young misfits he had taken under his protection, and his wonderful sense of humor, which he retained to the end. Death is never affirmed in Shūsei's mature fiction: his characters cling stubbornly to life for as long as they can, threats of suicide are transparently empty, and the process of physical decline is always drawn out and ugly. In a literary tradition in which suicide and honorable death are glorified, this aspect of Shūsei's negation of melodrama seems vital and refreshing; the bitter, pitiful struggle against death waged by most people is an affirmation of life.

4

Rough Living

I wonder if it is an exaggeration to say that since the time of
Futabatei Shimei and Tsubouchi Shōyō most people have quietly
acknowledged that literature is and should be the province of the
intelligentsia. At least the tendency for literary criticism and scholar-
ship to be activities engaged in by intellectuals is stronger today
than it ever has been. In this tradition, Shūsei is clearly a different
presence.

This difference is probably what makes it so difficult to appre-
hend Shūsei according to the conceptual frameworks we intellectuals have learned primarily from modern Western Europe.

The major hindrance in dealing with Shūsei is that he is not
accessible to the conceptual tools we have at hand, and this fact
should provide us with more than enough reasons to question our
methods. Of course, if our conceptual methodologies were adequate to come to terms with Shūsei, there would be no need to
question ourselves. And yet, as a practical matter, we have no other
choice but to use these same inadequate conceptual methodologies
to grapple with the challenge Shūsei poses.

—Matsumoto Tōru, *Tokuda Shūsei*

Shūsei's *Arakure* (Rough Living) concerns a seamstress named Oshima.
It was serialized in the newspaper *Yomiuri Shinbun* from January to
July of 1915 and was published as a book in September 1915. The
novel was almost universally praised as the most substantial work of
fiction of the year.[1] About the only significant negative criticism came
from Natsume Sōseki. Unfortunately, Sōseki's comments on *Arakure*
have been institutionalized in the secondary literature on Tokuda
Shūsei.

In October 1915, an unnamed newspaper reporter from *Osaka
Ashai Shinbun* visited Sōseki to gain Sōseki's views on the present state
of the Japanese literary world. Sōseki disliked such interviews. He saw
them as a weak substitute for the serious thought involved in writing
literary criticism, and he had seen his opinions distorted by careless
transcribers. But he felt an obligation to meet with the representatives
of publications he was affiliated with. He spoke at some length with

the reporter about Shūsei's *Arakure,* the major success of the literary season. One would like to think that the reporter misrepresented Sōseki's remarks, but the reporter's transcription evidently had Sōseki's approval, for it was reprinted in *Tokyo Asahi Shinbun* in November 1915.[2]

Sōseki was not exactly a disinterested critic. His own *Michikusa,* a masterpiece of the modern Japanese novel, had not received much critical attention while it was being serialized from June to September of 1915. It would be published as a book the day after his review of *Arakure* appeared in Osaka. It may have seemed to him that his own work would be ignored in the critical commotion surrounding *Arakure.*[3] Moreover, Sōseki had commissioned a novel from Shūsei, a work which was serialized in *Asahi Shinbun* from September 1915 to January 1916, and it was not turning out well. This novel, *Honryū* (The Torrent), which concerns a thirteen-year-old girl sold as a mistress to a corrupt, elderly, capitalist would-be politician, was a competent enough entertainment and was critically well received, but when compared to *Arakure,* which Shūsei wrote for Sōseki's rival newspaper *Yomiuri,* it was pulp fiction.[4] Sōseki had to write to Shūsei to request that the blatant eroticism of the work be toned down for a respectable audience.[5] *Arakure* had exhausted Shūsei, and he had little enthusiasm for *Honryū.* Sōseki's absurd assertion in the *Asahi Shinbun* interview that Shūsei seemed mediocre beside Mushanokōji Saneatsu sounds like a criticism of *Honryū,* which Sōseki, as *Asahi*'s literary editor, had to read.[6]

The tone of Sōseki's review of *Arakure* is negative. He states that he read *Arakure,* but there is no indication in his comments that he read the novel with any care. He deals with the work on a purely abstract level and addresses the basic theme of the novel, class origin, only in odd formulations.

The review begins by observing that *Arakure* is utterly realistic (*uso-rashiku nai*) and that it portrays the pain and corrupt, impure (*kegara-washii*) nature of the world. Then Sōseki stumbles. Well, maybe not the impurity of the world, he qualifies, but at least "what such young women as higher school students [*jogaku-sei*] mean when they use the phrase 'too much' [*zuibun ne*]. I will use their phrase: in short, in the sense that the world is too much, Shūsei does not tell us one lie."[7] In citing the collectivity of "nice young ladies" as a perspective on Shūsei's world, was Sōseki trying to be funny? Was he trying to establish an elevated position from which he could look down on the masses? He might as well have admitted that Shūsei's novel left him speechless. But he goes on:

> When one reads Shūsei's works, one is made to feel that *this* is the flavor of reality, but it is no more than that: one feels no sense of gratitude. After reading Shūsei, one is not allowed to feel deeply moved, to feel one is being led to a lofty, higher plane, to find some consolation, to feel a certain relief from the sadness . . . , to be moved to react against oppression, or to feel some joy opposed to the sorrow. "Yes, Shūsei, I think human existence is as you have portrayed it. You have quite accurately observed human existence and have portrayed it as it is. In that respect, your works have gone to the utmost. No matter who tries, no one will ever equal you in this regard." One can say this but only this. In short, one can concede, "Just so, you're quite right" [*gomottomo desu*], but one must stop there. One cannot proceed beyond that point.[8]

Sōseki is so uncharacteristically vague that one wonders if the reporter caught all of his words. What did Shūsei take to an extreme? Was it realism or was it an understanding of the human condition? In the next paragraph, Sōseki seems to be stating that Shūsei's penetrating vision put him at a disadvantage when compared to other Japanese writers.

Then comes a new paragraph and the line which has reverberated through the secondary literature on Shūsei from 1915 down to the present: "In short, Tokuda Shūsei's works portray reality as it is, but there is no philosophy [*fuirosofuī*] behind them."[9] Again, Sōseki's reasoning is difficult to understand. Perhaps he was arguing that the characters Shūsei portrayed were too unintelligent or uneducated to have a philosophy, that the 'individualism" of the neighborhood sake merchant did not count as *fuirosofuī*. Or perhaps he was contending that Shūsei himself did not have a philosophy, a position which upheld the notion that Japanese literature was the province of the intelligentsia, and Shūsei, who had not received a university education, was not qualified to belong among such elite "men of letters" as the aristocrat Mushanokōji Saneatsu.[10] In either case, Sōseki's words were a "cheap shot" but were effective in allowing intellectuals to get a class handle on Shūsei.

Sōseki's statement to the effect that Shūsei had got it right but that no one would thank him for having done so was simply not true. Nakamura Seiko expressed the general consensus of Japanese critical opinion when he wrote of *Arakure* in October 1915: "We owe a great debt of gratitude to the author [Shūsei] for his efforts in presenting this masterpiece [*Arakure*] to our literary world."[11]

But perhaps, from the perspective of "nice young ladies," Sōseki's professed lack of gratitude to Shūsei was not as irrelevant as it might seem. What intellectual could be pleased with a vision of the urban masses as "unimprovable" and as not desiring improvement? What progressive wanted to be confronted with urban masses so socially mobile that there was no hope of their ever forming a revolutionary class? What nationalist welcomed the contention that most people in the city were chiefly concerned with clinging to their own fractured families, with how much money was in their bank accounts, with clothes and fashions, and with having a good time? "Getting a handle" on Shūsei's vision of common life is like trying to rationally explain a feeling for time or a way of life.

Everyday life (*nichijō seikatsu*) is a class concept, but it is not quantifiable. It belongs to the city in the sense that it is experienced by the mass of nameless people we see all around us, any number of people like Shinkichi, the shopkeeper, or Oshō, the inarticulate next-door maid, or Omasu, the woman with the shady past who is struggling to remain in a respectable neighborhood, or Oshima, the seamstress in *Arakure*. The everyday is structured, remembered, and revealed by the stable, certain cycles of passing seasons: by the winter four years ago when Shinkichi took Osaku as his wife, by the young leaves of the willow, signs of early spring, by the cries of the evening cicadas at the end of summer, by cold metal buckets and public water pumps on autumn mornings, by the semiritualized changes in traditional clothing as the weather grows warmer or colder, decades marked by kerosene lamps giving way to electric lights on winter evenings.

The everyday belongs to the middle stratum of society in the city. The daily drudgery of the laborer, ricksha puller, or woman textile worker is repressed, a shadowy threat of what may befall those leading the far easier and more leisurely style of life of "ordinary people." The great themes of the intelligentsia, the symbols of the aristocracy, and the exhortations of the bureaucratic elites are absent or are laughable pretensions.

Like the everyday, Shūsei's *Arakure* escapes: escapes easy evaluation, escapes intellectual formulations, escapes the final, unequivocal judgment of canonization and legal codification. The everyday in *Arakure* is always on the verge of disintegration: families break up, businesses fail, social mobility is the rule. But somehow people "get by." *Arakure* is a celebration of the ambiguity and mystery of the everyday. Class consciousness is either class unconsciousness or prejudice directed outward. No miracle of class self-identification occurs to transform confusion into a clear and simple account of the world.[12]

Arakure was Shūsei's final vision of *shomin* life in the Meiji period. All of the features of common life enumerated in the previous chapter were incorporated into the work. Oshima, the heroine of *Arakure,* embodies the history of Meiji Japan at the level of the everyday. Embedded in the novel are the great structural transformations Japan underwent at about the turn of the century: industrialization, the decline of an older, landowning class, imperialistic expansion abroad, the Westernization of native customs and manners. But these are disassembled and reconstituted in Oshima's field of vision. Oshima rides each successive wave of change and exploits it. And yet "something" works inexorably to form Oshima, "something" in the end indefinable, for it exists in the everyday at the Pascalian point of intersection of innumerable systems and subsystems.

It seems clear that Shūsei was attracted to a new kind of human being he perceived in his contemporary society. In 1915, he wrote that he first intended to title *Arakure* "Like a Wild Beast" (*Yajū no gotoku*) and he wanted to portray a modern type who paid no heed to social conventions: "One does not often encounter such people in real life. But due to all the petty irritations I was experiencing at the time, I felt a great attraction to just such a person, and the woman who was the model for the protagonist of the novel was a person with some of the same tendencies as just such a character."[13] He recalls that he failed in his ambition because he was too faithful to reality. As is true of all of Shūsei's mature fiction, though narrative time advances fitfully, refracted backward and forward through flashbacks or descriptive seasonal imagery, and the reader is not provided with one explicit date, Shūsei's skill as a novelist and his tendency to rely on facts allow one to provide a temporal sequence in real life for the major incidents in the novel, which covers the years from 1883 to 1907.[14]

Suzuki Chiyo, the common-law wife of Shūsei's brother-in-law and the woman who was the model in real life for the heroine of *Arakure,* was evidently an extraordinary woman: fiercely independent, more capable than her various husbands, and sexually liberated.[15] But on the basis of his 1915 statement, Shūsei was mainly interested in Chiyo because she represented a new kind of common experience. He was interested in her only secondarily as a sexual being or as a liberated woman. Once again, Shūsei used an odd perspective—a woman in a man's business— to keep up with new developments in society and to project the experi-

ences of one woman as those of any number of men and women living
in the city.

Origins

Unwanted children who are abused by wicked stepmothers serve as an
almost universal plot device, and it is certainly a prominent generic
feature of the classical Japanese novel (*monogatari*). Embedded in
Arakure, this archetypical tale retains its power to portray the plight of an
abandoned child. Shūsei adopted a double strategy in maintaining the
tension between realistic history and *monogatari*.[16] On the one hand, the
reader is encompassed and swept along by Oshima's memory, the memory of an ordinary young woman who is not very well educated, works
harder in the fields than her male counterparts, and speaks a rough
vernacular dialect. On the other hand, the rhetoric of the narrative is
charged with and elevated by the most elemental images of labor, the
gods, and a dark, destructive natural order beneath the placid scene.
While Shūsei incorporated story elements of the *monogatari,* at the same
time he kept the form at arm's length with a series of reversals. Oshima's
true mother, who has formed an obsessive hatred for her daughter, fills
the archetypical role of the cruel, wicked stepmother. The threat of
child murder comes from Oshima's kindly, moral father. Oshima's foster
parents fill the roles of real parents by saving the life of the young heroine
at the last minute. Shūsei invested more care in the portrayal of Oshima
as a child than he invested in any other literary characterization of a childhood. What was at stake in his treatment of the child Oshima, her impotent father, and her confused parentage was the representation of the
formation of a class, the successive generations born free to emigrate and
fend for themselves in the city in the wake of the Meiji Restoration. In
the following, set in 1890, after suffering terrible abuse from her mother,
Oshima is led by her father to the bank of the Sumida River, where, it is
intimated, Oshima's father may intend to drown his daughter:

Oshima vividly remembered how, at the age of seven, she was adopted into
her present foster family. One evening, her stern, old-fashioned father took her
hand and led her out of the house to escape her mother's insane rage and a
savage beating, symptoms of the mother's obsessive hatred for her youngest
daughter. Father and daughter wandered aimlessly through wild fields. It must
have been toward the end of autumn, for red persimmons hung heavily from
the branches of trees clustered around many of the cheap food and tea stalls in

the neighboring impoverished districts through which they passed. Her father periodically stopped at wayside tea stalls to allow his child to rest her tired legs. He smoked and drank tea, and Oshima munched on rice crackers and persimmons peeled and brought to her by the serving girls. With timid eyes, she looked around at her unfamiliar surroundings. The flaming red sunset was gradually disappearing into darkness. A cold wind blew up from the empty fields. Evening's mist had begun to envelop isolated stands of trees here and there, houses in the shadow of the forest, yellow sheaves of rice hung out as offerings to the gods, and the dark earth of harvested fields. On the road outside, a workhorse, exhausted from the long day's labor, trudged wearily on. Oshima was moved to tears when she observed the wet, bleary eyes of that poor beast as it docilely pulled its large, heavy wagon by. Her father, who had fled from the violent rage of his wife and was now at a loss as to what to do with his daughter, also aroused her sympathy.

She remembered being led to the shore of a wide expanse of water. Perhaps they had come to the ferry crossing over the Sumida River at Ogu. Light from the still pearl-colored sky glinted on the surface of the slow-flowing, dark blue water, and several skiffs cast lonely, gliding shadows as they were oared silently by. Waves slapped the bank of the river, and the monstrous shadow of a huge tree looming above her swayed over the water. As Oshima gazed at this quiet scene, her child's being, from head to toe, was suddenly overcome by the physical sensations of both fear and peace, and in silence she clung single-mindedly to her father's thin hand.

Later on, considering what her father might have been planning that evening, Oshima could think of no reason why he had brought her to the edge of the river. Perhaps he had intended to take her across and leave her with an acquaintance living on the other side of the river. On that evening, however, her child's intuition had sensed something terrible, a cruel resolve, in the depths of her father's expression as he stood staring at the water. She was frightened. His eyes spoke of deep regret and agonized indecision.

Oshima had been sent away to be raised by close relatives soon after she was born, and when she was taken back in by her parents, she was already alienated from her strong-willed mother. On one occasion, irritated by Oshima's constant whimpering, the mother had pressed a pair of red-hot tongs against Oshima's tiny hand. With tears in her eyes, Oshima stared at the metal burning her flesh, but she obstinately made no move to pull her hand away. This only further aroused her mother's hatred.

"This stubborn little bitch!" The mother's rage only mounted, and she cursed her daughter.

Oshima's family, as village headmen, had formerly been charged by the shogunate with collecting district taxes, and during her childhood, her family was still greatly respected in the vicinity of Ōji. The fact that her grandfather had once offered his enormous garden as a resting station for the pleasure excursions of members of the Tokugawa house was an honor that lent a glorious light to their family's name and social standing in the area. That garden still exists as a public park for the local citizenry. As the heir to a long established house of gardeners, an honorable profession that entitled him to enter the homes of the wealthy and wellborn, her father had made one mistake that had damaged the reputation of his house: he had taken Oshima's mother, who was of low birth, as his second wife. She had been one of the women in a cheap, local restaurant he would occasionally visit to drink. After the marriage, the mother had secured a reputation as a hard worker, but no one spoke well of her deportment or moral character. (4:4–6)

The passage is permeated with the rhetoric of the classical Japanese literary tradition, but it portrays the emergence of an almost mythic individual consciousness that will come to represent as well a class unconsciousness. If not to "reality"—the biographical facts of Suzuki Chiyo's life—what can the ferry crossing over the Sumida River allude to but stories of kidnapping, enslavement, and killing of children, stories set on the banks of the Sumida and performed innumerable times in so many forms on the stages of the *nō, jōruri,* and kabuki?[17] The child Oshima emerges as a new type of individual born of an older primordial world of brute labor, violent expropriation, and primitive accumulation. She is a kind of foundling who retains connections with her blood family's common respectability while remaining independent of feudal obligations to it. To maintain this freedom, Oshima requires "something new": for now, call it capitalism.

By chance, her father meets a friend, Nishida, who acts as an intermediary to adopt Oshima out to a wealthy nearby family. Oshima's foster father is a papermarker who was almost driven out of business by the development of large-scale industries such as Ōji Paper Manufacturing (Ōji Seishisha). To survive, Oshima's foster parents diversified into moneylending and real estate investment. The money that enables the foster family to make this transition endows the family with a new, capitalistic origin. The account of this origin reveals that Oshima's education in *shomin* life is in part a gradual process of disillusionment with feudal fairy tales:

Oshima was introduced to her present foster family through an intermediary, her father's acquaintance who just happened to pass by the ferry crossing at Ogu on that evening. Oshima's new family had been eking out a bare subsistence with a papermaking mill, but at about the time of her adoption, her foster parents were blessed with a miraculous windfall. Their wealth increased dramatically, and they began buying local properties one after another. Oshima learned of the wondrous event from pieces of conversation she overheard from her new parents, and it seemed to her like something out of a fairy tale [*tsukuri-monogatari*]. One winter evening, a wandering Buddhist monk, bearing an altar on his back and exhausted from his long pilgrimage, arrived at the foster father's door and begged for a night's lodging. At dawn, as the monk departed, he foretold that good fortune would bless his host's house. A very large sum of gold coins was found in the monk's wake several days later in a pile of harvested paper mulberry bushes. In part to search for the wandering monk, in part to give thanks to the surrounding Shinto gods and Buddhist deities for their blessing, the foster father, some time later, set off on a pilgrimage of his own, but he encountered no one who resembled the monk. Be that as it may, from then on only prosperity visited Oshima's foster family. Her new mother and father began lending moderate sums of money to people in the town, and the couple watched in delight as their wealth increased.

"I wonder who on earth that monk really was, the one who brought us such good fortune years ago?" her foster father would exclaim after contributing generously to the rare mendicant monk who came to their gate. On such occasions, he recounted for Oshima what he remembered of the miraculous event. Oshima had little interest in the subject.

Oshima had only infrequent opportunities to see her real parents and brothers and sisters since she had come to her foster family's house.

As time went on, however, the truth of the matter gradually took form in Oshima's mind. According to information she picked up almost involuntarily on this occasion and that from the talk of friends at school who had knowledge of the origin of her foster family, Oshima determined that on that night so many years ago the wandering monk had suffered a sudden attack of illness and had died in her foster father's house. Tucked under the clothing, tied by a cord around the neck of the dead monk, was a purse heavy with gold coins. Oshima's foster parents took all of the money and kept it as their own property. Oshima found this version of the story more convincing, and it left her with an unpleasant feeling.

"Let them say what they please. When someone makes a little money, people will talk such nonsense," her foster mother replied with a forced laugh after Oshima discreetly questioned her. But Oshima felt that the confidence she had placed in her foster parents was gradually being betrayed. She even felt that her hopes for happiness had been stained by a dark stigma. She did her best to avoid touching on her foster parents' secret and to be considerate and protective of their wounded feelings, but she could not help but experience as well a new strain and estrangement in her dealings with them.

Oshima had to pass through the isolated room containing the family Buddhist altar, the room where the monk was said to have slept, on her way to the toilet at night. It was a relatively large room, its floor was covered with old, warped matting, and light did not penetrate into its interior even during the day. . . . When Oshima passed through the room at night, the outstretched body of the pale monk still grasping his purse appeared vividly before her eyes, and at times her heart raced and she shivered in fear. Was it not, she wondered, the vengeful spirit of the poor dead monk that haunted the dreams of her foster father, causing him to call out and groan in his sleep after he took to his bed early every evening? His moaning awakened Oshima in the night. (4:6–9)

Arakure is a description of the disintegration of the class order of a previous generation and the bitter resentments this engendered. Old stories—the glory of having members of the Tokugawa house stop to rest in Oshima's grandfather's enormous garden, now mortgaged—are superseded by a new story, the origin of the prosperity of Oshima's family in the face of industrial capital's mass production of paper. Did Oshima's foster father murder the monk? New wealth always invites antagonism in Japanese society, often taking the form of fox-possession (*kitsune-tsuki*) legends, similar to the ghost's haunting of the foster family. But according to the axiom "Above all, know greed, or you'll be at a disadvantage for the whole of your life" (4:48), which Nishida, the man who acted as the intermediary in Oshima's adoption, teaches the young Oshima, the stories about the origin of the foster family's wealth are irrelevant.

The adolescent Oshima plots to gain control of her foster family's wealth, and a ghost is not going to deter her. But "Know Thee Greed" is not the most important ideological aspect of Oshima's nature. Shūsei was portraying the rise of humankind from slavery, the emergence of a consciousness or a manner of self-definition born of the elemental images of labor but opposed to the despicable mentality of the slave (*iyashige na dorei konjō*, 4:39), a passive submissiveness and lack of pride which are antithetical to the ethics and principles of common life.

Oshima's foster mother and father, who are childless, promise that Oshima will inherit their wealth if she marries the father's nephew Sakutarō. Time and again Oshima refuses this match. To the foster father, who is a blood relation to Sakutarō, there is perhaps little difference in the social standings of Oshima and Sakutarō: both were abandoned by their parents and were adopted and raised together to provide free labor for the family enterprises. But class orientation seems to be fixed at an early age, and, from Oshima's perspective, the respective childhood experiences of Sakutarō and herself create an unbridgeable gap between them. Oshima's social origin allows her to become an ordinary, free individual. Sakutarō's social origin condemns him to slavery, to a set of feudal relations that are an anathema to Oshima:

When she was a child, Oshima was often taken to and from school by Sakutarō, her foster father's nephew. He was a young man who for years had been sent to work in the paper factory with numerous young women laborers, and he was also driven hard at fieldwork and at arduous tasks during the silkworm season. Nonetheless, Otora, the strong-willed foster mother, would constantly scold Sakutarō severely, and Oshima, for her part, loathed Sakutarō as if he were a pig. Exhausted from the ceaseless hard work, Sakutarō would sometimes sleep late in the morning with the excuse that he wasn't feeling well. Otora would not allow it and would begin cursing him.

"What kind of lazy bastard is still in bed while we're so busy! Think about where you came from!"

As she peered into the dirty, closetlike room where Sakutarō had hidden to sleep, Otora screamed the usual insults she always reproached him with. Her shrill voice seemed to ring in the depths of his mind. Sakutarō was the offspring of his foster father's elder brother, a criminal [*yakuza*], and a wandering performer/prostitute, who came from no one knew where. Sakutarō's real father had squandered his inheritance on gambling and women and had been living as a burden on his younger brother when, relying on a relative, he suddenly left for Gunma prefecture to earn money. There he was snared by that woman, and his circumstances were soon reduced to those of a beggar. The two of them came straggling back. The woman, pregnant with Sakutarō when she arrived, gave birth, left the infant with her brother-in-law, and set off alone on a journey for parts unknown. Two or three years later, news that the father had died came from Kisarazu, a place famous for its criminal elements.

Oshima often heard Otora admonish Sakutarō with the circumstances of his birth. How Otora loved repeating for Sakutarō the description of his parents crawling back home, both of them exhausted and with no money for train fare, their emaciated faced burned dark and hard by the hot sun of summer and the harsh winds off the wild fields. On the occasions when Sakutarō was even a little lazy or sly, Otora would bring up once again the story of his parents' homecoming.

"If you'd stayed with that gang, mark my words, you'd be a beggar today! Yearn for your real mother. Go to her, see where it gets you!"

There were times when tears would run down Sakutarō's cheeks as he listened to Otora's story about his parents, but in the end he invariably laughed obsequiously and remained silent.

He was not really a homely person; rather his skin color and tone were poor, and his eyes, even from his adolescence, were dull and dry, products of a stunted upbringing and a lack of proper nutrition brought about by being worked constantly at arduous labor during the crucial period of his physical development. (4:10–12)

Arakure is a catalog of prejudices and resentments current in Meiji society and based on differing familial or economic origins: mutual resentment between proud older families and the nouveau riche, and prejudice on the part of everyone against those such as Sakutarō born into the feudal netherworld of crime and prostitution. Ugly stereotypes and social fears are a prominent part of Oshima's world: revulsion for the lepers who lurk ominously near shrines and temples (4:17, 190); distrust of the valiant soldiers who fought in the Russo-Japanese War and who are now dissatisfied with common life and peacetime professions (4:169); utter contempt for prostitutes and kept women, who are referred to as *daruma-san,* tumbler dolls who lie down at a slight push and spring right back up again to a standing position (4:120–23); aversion to citizens of Nagoya, who are reputed to be slow, stingy, and insensitive (4:163–64); antipathy toward poor peasants (4:185–86); suspicion by provincials of *okyan,* strong-willed, boisterous women associated with Edo (4:187–88); and the torture of the insane (4:260).

The following exchange between Oshima and her second husband, Onoda, whom she marries in 1904, illustrates the pure hostility between people of differing classes and regional origins that distinguishes common life:

"You're going to end your life as a mere workman, just another wage slave. I suppose that's a little better than your peasant father slogging around in the mud of his rice paddies," Oshima declared.

"So you know everything! Your parents are so superior! Doesn't your father make a living by fiddling around in the dirt?"

"Who went to those same parents and begged to marry me? My father may not look like much now, but he was born well. He used to lord it over the district as the village headman. Still, I've never bragged about my family."

"Because you're an unfilial daughter and your parents won't let you near them. There's no profit in your pride. Go home, bow and apologize a little, and figure out a way to get some money out of them."

Onoda repeated what he had been urging Oshima to do for some time.

"Don't ask me to act like a cowardly hypocrite! Even in death I won't approach my family until I have my own respectable shop in broad sunlight facing the street."

"See, as I've always said, you don't have the instinct to succeed in business," Onoda countered. (4:205)

In spite of the vagueness in the terms expressing class consciousness in the cultural milieu called *shomin* life, Oshima's life perhaps personifies the birth of modern Japan in the sense that the fragility of common life after the Restoration allows for only negative class identification. The sense of confidence in origin, no matter how fictional, may be strong in relation to the other—the origin of everyone's status is fairly murky anyway—but inwardly there is little class solidarity. And what of the notion of "Japaneseness" once the notion of "foreignness" is abolished? Shūsei, the master at portraying social disintegration, was concomitantly the master at creating and then undercutting myths of origin.

A Mysterious Economy

The assumptions and values of capitalism are so pervasive in *Arakure* that capitalism has ceased to exist as a distinct, indentifiable category. The economy manifests itself as the will of the gods or fate. The everyday is constituted by the relative congruence or incongruence of two cycles of time in the city. Japan's economy in the first decade of the twentieth century still appears to be dependent on cyclical, seasonal fluctuations in supply and demand. And yet there is a tendency for something like a mysterious business cycle to dominate, at times, the seasonal textures of the everyday. An aesthetic of the scene, a leisurely pace of life, and a feeling of being confined or trapped are often characteristics of the natural, seasonal cycle. When the business cycle of time dominates, so does an aesthetic of the awesome and mysterious, a sense of liberation, and the feeling of shock and anxiety that things are moving too fast, that the seasons have come loose from their moorings in nature and are spinning madly out of control.

Alienated from her foster parents because of her obstinate refusal to marry Sakutarō, Oshima's options as a young woman of seventeen or eighteen at the turn of the century are fairly limited: return to her true parents, go into the demimonde, or be exploited in unsponsored apprenticeship. Oshima has an adolescent fantasy of escape to the United States, but this too is still securely rooted within the framework of a seasonal economy (4:46–47). She continues to consider her dilemma in the context provided by a fairly traditional system of employment.

However, Oshima's natural adolescent impulse to escape is gradually denaturalized. She comes to have contempt for her foster family's old-fashioned way of doing business, for accumulating profit slowly by collecting small sums of interest (4:31). She determines early on that the best way to establish herself on respectable, independent ground is to gamble on rapidly changing political circumstances in the hope of making a large fortune quickly. In the following passage, Oshima has returned to her true parents' house, to which she fled after she became convinced that her foster parents were seriously attempting to marry her to Sakutarō:

At dusk, Oshima put her tools away in the storage shed and at last went in to dinner. Sitting next to the brazier, her father, looking harassed, had begun drinking the measured amount of wine he indulged in every evening. Outside, the colors of night were spreading slowly, and the lowing of cattle was heard from a nearby pasture. The children who had been playing detective on the road had disappeared. The light of the stars had softened, suggesting the arrival of spring.

"Let Oshima stay here for a month or two. Once we find her a place to go into service, she'll be able to take care of herself," her father stated in an attempt to mollify his wife, who was complaining about her daughter's presence. Pricking up her ears, but not listening too obviously, Oshima was taking her eating utensils out to the kitchen.

"Wait and see! I'll accomplish something that will make your eyes pop out of your head!" Controlling the resentment welling up within her against her mother, Oshima left the room with a composed expression on her face. She thought she might like to try her hand at the business the old man Nishida was involved in. Nishida had recently started supplying feed for the horses of the Imperial Army. (4:35–36)

The unnatural desire, for a young woman, to speculate and succeed in business in a big way has to be suppressed as long as Oshima is confined to the traditional economy. Her chance to escape occurs suddenly midway through the novel, but while Oshima remains rooted in the tradi-

tional economic order, she discovers more pleasure, comfort, and leisure in her life than she finds later when she has an opportunity to act
out her desire to succeed.

In 1902, Oshima is married to the widower Tsuru-san, a merchant of
canned goods, and she moves to his shop in the Kanda ward. The marriage is soon on shaky grounds due to Tsuru-san's various adulteries.
Toward the end of the year, Oshima returns to her home in Ōji to give
birth to Tsuru-san's child, but she suffers a miscarriage after a violent
physical fight with her mother. With the loss of the child, her marriage to
Tsuru-san ends in divorce.

There is much to feel nostalgia for in the slow-moving, sociable
world of eccentric, pleasure-seeking merchants in Kanda, to which
Oshima tries to become accustomed in her role as the respectable wife
of Tsuru-san. After the breakup of her marriage to Tsuru-san and her
move to the house of Uegen to work as a live-in servant, Oshima has
less social status but still a comfortable, easygoing life. There are lovely
scenes of a traditional economic order in synchrony with seasonal
change, an order so forgiving that it allows everyone the time for a nap
in the heat of a summer day (4:96–97). The rhythms of the passing
seasons also govern life during Oshima's nine- or ten-month sojourn in
the Shiobara region of Tochigi prefecture, the most pleasurable period
of Oshima's life (4:124–40). Much of the political significance of
Shūsei's work for the present lies in his beautiful and evocative descriptions of the wonders of a way of life that has long-since disappeared, at
least in the city.

But Shūsei also recognized that there was a "new type" of individual
in Japanese society who was not satisfied with this natural, traditional
economic order. The major transformation in Oshima's perception of
the world comes in 1904 while she is working as a seamstress in the
house of an elderly aunt in Shitaya. War breaks out with Russia, and
though this event is only briefly mentioned, it has immense ramifica-
tions for Oshima. Almost overnight, mysteriously, an economic cycle
relatively distinct from seasonal associations comes into dominance, and
Oshima has her first chance to realize her long-held ambition to become
independent and, by her own efforts, ride the rough seas of a new
economic order:

At the start of the war with a foreign country, a war producing varied, new
employment for many busy people, Oshima resolved for the first time to devote
herself to work in which she could invest all of her purpose of mind and physical

strength. She did so in partnership with a tailor named Onoda, a young man who occasionally brought customers' orders for sewing simple garments of serge or flannel to Oshima's aunt, with whom he was on friendly terms. From time to time, Onoda would come over to Oshima's cutting board and stretch out to chat and joke.

At about the time Hamaya had returned to his mountain home after a brief visit to Tokyo, Oshima had come to realize that up until then she had been forced to survive by blind reaction or submission to authority, a way of life that left her close to slavery. How she longed for once to work solely for herself. . . .

Onoda had brought in a bundle of garments intended for the troops on the battlefront overseas, now faced with the onset of frigid weather. "How would you like to help me out with this job?" he had asked.

Onoda was employed at a workshop which, until the outbreak of the war, had manufactured ready-made clothing, but when the new orders that began flooding in proved too much for his fellow workers, Onoda began taking work out of his company, which held the contract, for the final stages of production, and he was now busy making the rounds of people who might subcontract some of the work from him.

"You can have as much to do as you want. I can't keep up with it now as it is," Onoda declared as he brought in a load of "blankets" on his back. He then began teaching Oshima what tasks she had to perform on this order, which she had agreed to try her hand at.

What Onoda referred to as blankets were overcoats to protect against the cold; they were reddish-brown garments the soldiers put over their heads. Oshima soon educated her quick fingers to sew on the buttons and hooks and darn the buttonholes of the blankets, which were already finished to a stage suitable to be worked on by a woman.

"Each one you finish is worth thirteen sen," Onoda had told her. In one day, Oshima completed thirteen or fourteen overcoats, four or five times the amount of work done by the average woman.

The busy Onoda arrived to collect what Oshima had finished, but he was soon nodding off in a doze by her side as she kept up her rapid pace of sewing.

Oshima had little trouble making about two yen a day, and the purse tucked in her obi was always filled and rustling with the money that seemed to spin from her fingers.

"No worries about spending money if I could get this woman as my lover." Onoda had woken from his nap and sat staring at Oshima as she busily darned a buttonhole. He was amazed at how intensely she labored.

"Take me as your lover and you'll find out," Oshima replied laughing.

"Fine with me!" Onoda said as he gathered up the finished garments. He took these back with him on his bicycle.

As Oshima grew used to sewing on hooks and darning buttonholes, these tasks became unbearably tedious.

Toward the end of the year, she learned how to operate the sewing machine at the workshop where Onoda was employed, the place that held the contract for the work she was doing. She was soon able to sew quite proficiently even difficult officers' uniforms on the machine.

"What are all these frills for? Men are such sissies," Oshima exclaimed, making the slow bunch on the factory floor laugh.

It often happened that on hauling the finished products to the government office at Tameike that was functioning as a temporary depot for the Bureau of Clothing, ill-tempered officials there criticized the workmanship and were reluctant to accept the garments.

"If you won't take these, what will you accept?" Oshima declared when she went in place of the men to deliver the clothing. The fast-talking Oshima easily won over the bureaucrat, who at first pushed the garments away, complaining that the sewing machine had missed stitches or that the quality of the cloth was inferior. (4:147–51)

For Oshima, the war has nothing to do with ideology. She has no qualms about sending defective or inferior uniforms to the poor soldiers fighting on the freezing fronts at Port Arthur or on the Liaotung Peninsula. In common society, patriotism is viewed as something to be taken advantage of. The wonderful thing about the war for Oshima is that it creates an economic subsystem which she can exploit with no property and only a small amount of capital.

The Seinan War (1877), the Sino-Japanese War (1894–95), the Russo-Japanese War (1904–5), and World War I (which provided enormous stimulus to Japan's domestic wool-producing industry)—it is probably not an exaggeration to say that war established the domestic Western-style clothing industry in Japan, providing tailors with large profits. Oshima's wage of fifty or sixty yen a month was a great deal of money even by the standards of male wages.[18]

Oshima and Onoda borrow heavily and wager everything on the wartime boom. They form a common-law marriage and open a tailor shop in the Tamachi district of the Shiba ward. At the height of the war effort the shop prospers, with Oshima working desperately around the clock to pay off her debts before the end of the year. With the coming of the warmer weather of spring, which alleviates the pressing need for winter clothing on the front, the orders from the government dry up as suddenly as they appeared. For Oshima and Onoda, the war boom is

over by April of 1905. This business cycle lasted a mere three and a half
months. In the winter of 1905, Oshima, Onoda, and their hapless
employee Kimura are forced to move to a smaller shop in the less
prestigious neighborhood of Tsukishima. The war is over. Japan is in
recession. There is an inversion in the descriptions of nature. Whereas
former scenes speak of a landscape exploited appropriately in accord
with the passing seasons, at this point on Oshima's career, her perceptions of nature reflect the depression of the Japanese economy. Nature,
distinct from the passing season, has become a function of the economic
cycle. Left with nothing to do to keep herself occupied, Oshima feels
her own biological cycle plunge her into new depths of wretchedness
and pain. Tsukishima as a whole reflects the decline of shipbuilding, the
major industry in the district. The environment, lacking standard seasonal associations, is stark, mechanistic, and frightening. However, if
the economic cycle has become so all-pervasive that it is a god, it is not
purely a malevolent one. It rewards speculation, mysteriously and seemingly at random. In the following passage, Kimura, the employee who
has stayed with Oshima and Onoda only because the police may be
searching for him as a deserter, returns to Oshima and Onoda's shop to
find it in a state of chaos:

Having gained nothing from his two-day search for employment but the certain
knowledge that ugly rumors about his sudden moral corruption were circulat-
ing around tailor shops throughout the city, Kimura crossed over to the island
on the cold, windswept ferry and walked to the neighborhood where Oshima
had her shop. He intended to ask Oshima to keep him on a little longer. Oshima
was nowhere to be seen. Onoda was hard at work mopping up water that had
inundated the small room off the kitchen.

Timid but sturdily built, with thick lips, a prominent nose, and tanned skin,
Kimura stood at the entrance of the room and stared in shocked amazement at
the room's condition. Shoji, fusuma, and tatami were soaking wet.

"What's happened? Did a small fire break out while I was gone?"

"Oshima's been up to her tricks again. The woman's a monster," Onoda
replied laughing.

Since the evening of the previous day, Oshima, her eyes bloodshot, had
stayed in bed. She complained of a headache. Her hair was a fright and the
rough skin of her face was as tense and chiseled as a rock. She occasionally
groaned in pain.

The couple had recently been reduced to buying staples such as rice and soy sauce in small daily quantities. Oshima had barely eaten since morning and lay covered by the bedding she had miraculously held onto from the time of her marriage to Tsuru.

Onoda, doing the cooking and shopping himself, was irritated by the disorder he encountered everywhere in the household, functioning as it was without a woman's guiding hand, but, at the same time, he was worried by the severity of Oshima's menstrual pain, which was evident from her moaning.

"The bones in my lower back are about to crack and break apart," Oshima exclaimed, moving to cling to Onoda's arm. Watery eyes stared up at him.

Onoda spoke some comforting, gentle phrases and began massaging Oshima's lower back.

"I wonder if there is something physically wrong with me. I've never experienced this pain before. Perhaps my body is different. Do all women suffer like this?" As her back was being rubbed by Onoda, Oshima expressed some of the doubts that were troubling her. She went on to voice her concern that perhaps there was a defect in her sexual constitution or in Onoda's.

She felt apologetic toward Onoda, but, on the other hand, she had never imagined that marriage to him would inflict such pain on her. The bedding recalled Tsura to her mind and led her to bring up details of her physical relations with her former husband. This put Onoda in a bad humor. Resisting Onoda's advances, Oshima's hand suddenly whipped across his hot cheek.

The ferocious Oshima fled to the water tap and frantically turned the hose on Onoda to defend herself against his vengeance.

The instant Onoda flinched and drew back, Oshima was out of the house. Her legs moving like the pistons of some wonderfully invigorated machine, Oshima strode rapidly through one neighborhood after another until she found herself moving in the direction of the waterfront.

Wherever she looked, the long broad street, monotonous and ugly, was depressingly empty, and yet, in that winter evening, a tremendous racket had insinuated itself in the deserted surroundings. Dark, vacant faces of men and women appeared in the occasional dim shop. Dispirited-looking factory workers streamed past her, and bicycle bells dampened by the wet air from the sea rang dully in her ears. Invisible white sand blown up from the broad street struck her face hard enough to hurt her eyes and her cheeks, which were wet with tears.

The road brought her to a bridge, and she wandered back and forth in front of it as if she were a vagrant woman searching for a place to die, but from time to time she walked out onto the structure to lean against the rail, resting there, breathing in deeply to restore her body so tired from combat. Cold wind from the sea stung, seeming to penetrate her white skin.

Colors of dusk steadily approached, spreading over the expanse of water before her. When she was calm and was leaving, severe pain again wracked her lower back.

On her return, the neighborhood was dark, and she discovered an old man she'd never met before waiting at the entrance of her shop.

After exchanging a few words with this stranger, Oshima realized that he was informing her that she had won the clandestine lottery she had recently bought into on an impulse, drawn to play by her love of speculation.

"You're sure to win," Kimura had insisted, "your aura is remarkable and will bring good luck."

Oshima, nerves worn thin by worry over how to settle the shop's debts by the end of the year, was persuaded to make the gamble by her young employee, who was very knowledgeable about such matters. He was even acquainted with a local house that was secretly taking bets.

"No! I won't lower myself . . ." She was tempted, but at first she refused.

"Don't be so certain. Life is taking a chance. But don't make a habit of it either. Once you've won, stop," Kimura urged.

"What should I bet on?"

"Whatever appeals to you. Something you've seen or heard. . . . Or better yet, if a dream can guide you."

Oshima had seen a dragon in her dream the night before, so she decided to put her money on the dragon.

Out of the blue, the old man had brought her two hundred yen, a completely unexpected windfall.

Secret joy filled the hearts of Oshima, Onoda, and Kimura, who had all been badly frightened by their economic situation.

"Something eery in this, isn't there?" Oshima whispered to Onoda as she clapped her hands in prayer before the household altar, upon which she had placed the money after the old man departed.

As if they had completely forgotten the fight earlier, their eyes flashing with a shared excitement, Oshima, Onoda, and Kimura sat together in the illumination cast by a lantern burning red hot. Oshima thought that perhaps her fate was a rare and wonderful one indeed. Light seemed to rise from the dark depths of her mind. (4:171–76)

This is one of the darker passages in *Arakure*. Oshima is reduced to a pitiable condition by forces beyond her control. But even in this darkness there is light. Money cures all of Oshima's ills, physical, mental, and marital, and yet it is a manifestation of "something" else: fate revealed by the subconscious, the benefice of the gods, or perhaps the capricious work of a business cycle that comes around again in the nick of time to save those who believe in the "system." The light of joy, self-confidence, or knowledge comes from the depths of the mind, not from the heavens or learning or self-analysis. It illuminates only briefly. Everyday existence is, for the most part, a matter of blundering around in the darkness.

This revolution in the business cycle ends in March 1906, when Onoda and Oshima fold up their shop and set off for Shanghai, which in Oshima's imagination has taken the place of the United States as the foreign land where she can fulfill her ambitions. The couple get stuck in Nagoya, Onoda's birthplace. In Tokyo, Oshima's aggressive selling tactics, her fast talk, and free spending are appreciated as aspects of an urban aesthetic which values strong women and the eroticism of gender reversal. In Nagoya, Oshima's style of doing business is unpopular: "The self-assertive Oshima was snubbed and treated as an offensive outcast wherever she went in Nagoya, a city of gentle manners but suspicious of strangers. She was despised as a troublemaker in the shop where Onoda worked, and her careless talk and her loose management of personal affairs caused the people around Onoda's sister to avoid Oshima as if she were a ruffian female swindler" (4:187–88).

On their return to Tokyo, Oshima and Onoda find jobs with their former boss, Kawanishi, employment they soon lose because Oshima refuses Kawanishi's sexual advances. They move to a six- by nine-foot room in Atago. They were formerly dependent on a business cycle determined by indecipherable events abroad; now they are dependent on a force even more nebulous and difficult to read: fashion.

Onoda and Oshima are tailors (*yōfukuya*) of men's Western-style clothing. By the time Oshima and Onoda started their business, the market was already being supplied by a variety of clothing manufacturers. In 1897, the Tokyo Federation of Tailors of Western Clothing (Tokyo Yōsai Hōgyō Kumiai) had 953 members. By 1908, the membership of a similar organization, the Commercial and Industrial Association of Western Clothiers (Tokyo Yōfuku Shōkō Kumiai), had increased by more than 50 percent to 1,560 members. This increased capacity to manufacture Western-style clothing undoubtedly came about because of the literal "uniforming" of Japanese society at around the time of the Russo-Japanese War: military uniforms for officers and soldiers; uniforms for postmen, railroad conductors, and policemen; court dress fashioned according to rank and modeled on the clothing of European aristocracy; tuxedos and morning coats worn at upper-class events and entertainments; and frock coats worn by politicians, educators, and doctors. At least in Tokyo, the bifurcation in men's clothing between public and private wear—Western-style clothing for official occasions and government employment, Japanese-style clothing at home and for personal ceremonies—appears to have been well established in the years after the Russo-Japanese War.[19] For most people, however, uniforms or claims to social distinction through Western-style clothing were not very important. The majority of the population continued to dress in Japanese-style fashions.

In the years immediately before and after the Russo-Japanese War, Japan's domestic production of the materials used to make Western-style men's garments, principally wool cloth, was negligible, and most of Oshima and Onoda's small capital is tied up in expensive, imported cloth obtained through their indirect connection with the West, the wool wholesaler. Onoda buys cloth, either on credit or outright, from the wool wholesaler, then he or Oshima goes out with samples to attempt to gain orders from prospective customers. The critical problem with this manner of doing business is, as the employee Kimura puts it, "the capital of a tailor shop [yōfukuya] is always asleep. There's not much chance a small operation can make a go of it" (4:177). When the audacious Oshima manages to gain a huge order from a company in Ōji for new uniforms for its employees, she has to decline it, for her small shop has no access to the large quantity of wool the job would require (4:167).

Toward the end of 1906, something happens. Within five or six months, working out of their small room in Atago, Oshima and Onoda manage to earn two thousand yen (4:213). It is not clear how the couple makes this immense sum. Throughout *Arakure*, the economy, when not grounded in season, is presented as a mysterious, inexplicable force. Onoda and Oshima simply get lucky. However, there are hints earlier in the work that the preference for Western-style clothing is drifting down from the elites and is insinuating itself in the desires of common people. In Oshima's eyes, Western clothing is symbolic of vigor and strength while traditional clothing is effeminate:

Onoda was tall and had beautiful hair, and when he dressed in a suit, his sternly dignified, well-built figure somehow made Oshima feel secure. At times, she spoke without reserve to the stolid, taciturn Onoda: "You're the homeliest man I have ever met!"

Onoda merely chuckled in reply.

"But at least you don't look like a tailor. Don't government officials usually dress like that?"

Having come to find something wanting in the soft, pliant Tsuru, always dressed in his shopkeeper's apron, and the young inn owner Hamaya, who was merely beautiful, as delicately featured as a waxwork doll, Oshima found herself attracted to Onoda's stern bearing and manner.

"I'm going to take Onoda out of that workshop and make him a man with my very own hands," she resolved. (4:152–53)

The large amount of money Onoda and Oshima earn in such a short period of time may well indicate that Western-style men's clothing was becoming popular among commoners. The couple move to more spacious quarters in the Nezu district of the Hongō ward in hopes of profiting from the government-sponsored Exhibition of Industry and Commerce of 1907. At first, this festival celebrating technical innovation (it is the same affair whose neon lights amaze the ignorant crowds in Sōseki's *Gubijinsō*) stimulates business, but it also provides Oshima and Onoda an opportunity for release, which by the end of the exhibition leaves them once again on the brink of ruin. They have exhausted their resources entertaining friends and relatives who flocked to Tokyo from the provinces to witness the wonders of modernity. When the Nezu district once again becomes a sleepy residential district at the end of the exhibition, the couple move their shop to a new location. This cycle from boom to bust has lasted approximately eight or nine months.

The process by which Onoda and Oshima establish their fourth shop "over the hill" from Nezu on one of the main commercial avenues in Hongō, close to Tokyo Imperial University, can be read as a textbook study on how to start a small business on almost nothing. Oshima has learned how to obtain the free use of sewing machines. The number of these once rare machines has increased markedly from about the turn of the century, and inducements must be offered in order to sell them. She acquires a machine for a trial period, complains that the machine is defective, and returns it just before payment is due, then receives another machine for yet another trial period (4:204). Onoda stocks the shop by making the rounds of wool wholesalers to collect samples and materials on consignment, thus eliminating the need to purchase the expensive imported cloth. The traditional close tie between gardeners and carpenters provides Oshima, through her father, with a connection to a carpenter who defers payment for his own labor remodeling the shop and who obtains lumber for the job on credit from a friendly dealer. Lacking even the cash to buy nails, Oshima opens a line of credit with a local hardware shop. She declares that she intends to buy so much merchandise that paying for each item individually would be too much bother. Oshima makes frequent trips to the pawnbroker to exchange her clothing for money, this time even the bedding she has had since her marriage to Tsuru.

A subsystem of production has formed that allows Onoda and Oshima to survive by informal agreements. They have almost no capital and a dubious grasp of their trade, but they have mastered the more important skill of negotiating and forming alliances with the local business community. Oshima's reckless generosity is repaid in kind: the tailor shop, started on a string and a prayer, succeeds. Oshima, in some ways so emotionally fragile, is totally assured in guiding this fourth fledgling business to solid ground. The couple invents a successful promotional technique for selling uniforms to middle-school students. Onoda and Oshima are still tied to a kind of seasonal economy, but it is an institutionalized season: the beginning and end of the school term.

Once the shop is well established and Oshima has attained the success she has long desired, however, she announces that she is thinking of leaving Onoda and setting up yet another business with an employee in her shop. The novel ends with Oshima again considering a recklessly speculative move. At issue is not wealth. Oshima is comfortably off in her marriage with Onoda. She is searching for something else: "From the tales of romance she had heard from the various women she met in the course of searching for business connections—women such as herself who were active in a trade, independent women, wives—Oshima had received the sure intimation that she too was a woman, and she had occasion to lose herself in secret longings and fantasies. At times, she felt that even her remarkable energy could not help her attain her shadowy desires" (4:215). Oshima continues to strive for success, but she recognizes that it will not bring her pleasure, contentment, or peace. She personifies an aggressively independent entrepreneurial spirit that has filled every corner of Japan's domestic market: small businesses started on almost nothing and surviving by alliances and mutual dependencies.

The Modern

Tsuru and Oshima went out together for the first time. Tsuru strode on ahead through the neighborhood and after walking half a block turned and looked over his shoulder. Oshima was hurrying to catch up, each long, reaching step revealing a flash of underskirt. She had spread her cream-colored parasol to protect her from the sun. A warm spring breeze lightly swirled up sand from the street, and willow branches bent gracefully under the weight of young leaves that had appeared suddenly, as if by magic. Oshima's heart was dancing with excitement. She was jubilant over her debut in this bright new society, but her happiness was clouded by moments of self-doubt and sadness, for she knew she had not yet fathomed the depths of her husband's heart. Oshima's kindness and benevolence to others had been remarkable enough to occasion criticism from her foster mother and foster father, and she herself took pride and satisfaction in her own generosity, and yet she had never before felt she could love a person with her whole heart. No one had ever truly loved her either. She wanted to love Tsuru, but it seemed to her that the ghost of Tsuru's dead wife still occupied his heart. (4:72)

One has to believe that Shūsei's words are appropriate to a young woman of Oshima's education, age, and social status in 1902 and that Oshima would conceive of her situation in terms of a desire for love (*ai*). Of all the women discussed until now in this study—*Arajotai*'s Osaku, *Ashiato*'s Oshō, *Kabi*'s Ogin, and *Tadare*'s Omasu—only Oshima, at this point in her life, is permitted the desire for love. The love Oshima yearns for is not romanticism's "high love" (*ren'ai*) advocated by the intellectuals Iwamoto Zenji and Kitamura Tōkoku in the 1890s. Nor is it merely the "low love" (*koi, iro*) of sensuality and eroticism.[20] Because Oshima has been so emotionally deprived all her life, her longing for love covers the widest spectrum of what the term *ai* had come to mean at about the turn of the century. She wants the love of a father, the love of a mother, the pleasure of physical love, and the security of the love of a faithful spouse. But she is betrayed in every personal and familial relationship she becomes involved in.

Oshima is a thoroughly modern type who has come to expect betrayal and disappointment in her personal affairs. And yet she never abandons her search for love. While of all Shūsei's women characters Oshima is most like an "economic animal," she is also the most willing to make economic sacrifices for love. She is the least inclined to use male sexual desires to her own advantage. She is sexually generous and liberated.

For many readers, Oshima's honesty about her emotional and sexual needs must have seemed shockingly modern.[21] However, in the cultural milieu of common life, modernity does not remain remarkable for long. New ways of thinking become natural very quickly. Modernity filters down and covers everything.[22] It is electricity, telephones, record players, irons, sewing machines, trams, public water systems, neon lights, magazines, and Western-style clothing.

In contrast, the effect on common life of another aspect of the modern is conspicuous in *Arakure*. This is the modern as cheap imitation, a means for the safe domestication of foreign eroticism for internal consumption. From her teens, Oshima longed to go overseas and was attracted to the foreign. Onoda manipulates this desire and persuades Oshima to project it onto the domestic market. He comes up with the idea of having Oshima dress in Western-style women's clothing (*metōfuku*) to commission orders for middle-school uniforms from students. In 1907, it was extremely rare for Japanese women in common life to wear Western-style clothing, and Onoda's ploy works. The costume, which Oshima obtains from a special seamstress in Yokohama, transforms Oshima into a grotesquely erotic advertisement:

For the first time, Oshima wore a white summer dress and a large straw bonnet with a light-blue ribbon around its high crown when she made the rounds of her best customers. . . .

"How do I look?" Oshima asked as she left her full-length mirror and came over to stand before Onoda and Kimura. The corset binding her substantial torso was so painfully tight she could scarcely breath. To cover blemishes on her skin, she had applied a thick coat of white makeup, and her face was ghastly and beautifully pale.

"You look ridiculously young. At least you'll pass for a magician just back from Hawaii or somewhere," Kimura commented and laughed.[23]

On her way to take orders from a dentist and a lawyer, two long-standing customers, Oshima met a group of students she was acquainted with.

"Here we thought it was a Western beauty from a foreign land, and all the while it was you!" one exclaimed, his eyes wide in amazement at Oshima's strange appearance.

"Come to our school in that outfit," said another, and he stepped forward and shook Oshima's soft, plump hand.

"The clothes were a huge success," Oshima declared on her return that evening. She immediately had Onoda help her out of the tight corset. When it was off, Oshima felt that her plump, pinkish body had at last been returned to her. (4:240–41)

Acting was perfectly acceptable in common life so long as the objective was rationally calculated and one did not get carried away in one's role. In *Arakure*, Oshima's dressing up is very profitable. Especially after Oshima learns to ride a bicycle, a shocking practice for women of the day, she becomes a well-known and sensational presence on school grounds in Tokyo. Orders for school uniforms flood her shop. The audacity of Oshima and Onoda's avant-garde advertising methods earns them a niche in the developing economy of Western fashion. And yet there is a strange ambivalence in Oshima's attitude to Western women's clothing. On the one hand, she regards the West with almost as much contempt as she regards Nagoya, and she refers to the clothing she wears as *metōfuku*. *Metō* is a derogatory term for Caucasian women corresponding to *ketō* for men. On the other hand, Western women's clothing provides her with a sense of liberation that is at once erotic and alienating, the kind of thrill obtained from dressing in drag. The language of the body makes palpable the strange feel of Western-style garments against her skin. Oshima, however, does not allow herself to be carried away by this sense of liberation. She has a right to wear Western-style garments because she is the wife of a tailor. They are a part of her business, and her role-playing goes no further than her work:

While Onoda and the employees were sleeping, Oshima left her bed and went to her mirror to apply her makeup. She then nimbly got into her corset and put on the petticoats she had finally grown used to. The way the dress fit, biting into her skin, and the way the corset tightly squeezed her ample flesh gave her a pleasurable sensation. When she slipped her high-heeled shoes on her tiny, graceful feet, a marvelous resiliency came naturally to her limbs; her stride seemed as light as air. She felt not the least shame or hesitation in leaping into places and situations she would never have dreamed of entering dressed in flowing, heavy Japanese robes and cumbersome traditional hairstyle.

On waking in the morning, her listless body craved the buoyancy provided by Western-style clothing. Dressing seemed to wonderfully invigorate her. If she did not appear wearing Western-style clothing on the dew-covered street early in the morning, she did not feel well for the rest of the day.

Once Onoda, who was making deliveries, drew up alongside her as he pushed his bicycle.

"It's a pity you're so short," he declared and stared at Oshima's broad figure.

"These are my work clothes. I'm not concerned about how I look," Oshima replied. (4:243–44)

The modern, which is so prevalent in common life as to be unnoticed, is grotesquely erotic when it becomes conspicuous. This will be made clearer in the discussion of Shūsei's *Kasō jinbutsu* (In Disguise, 1935–38). In contrast to Yōko, the late-1920s heroine of that novel, however,

Oshima has a strong enough sense of identity to allow her to resist becoming enraptured with the role of the Western beauty.

Oshima is certainly the most amusing of all the heroines Shūsei created. Several critics have perceived in *Arakure* a shift in Shūsei's attitude from pessimism to optimism.[24] The situation is probably never so unequivocal in Shūsei's best fiction. In *Arakure* as well, one is beyond such oppositions. Rough living takes a toll. A scene toward the end of the novel quite vividly describes what Oshima loses in her transition from a seasonal to a far more abstract economy. Onoda takes a lover. This rival is physically driven away by Oshima, and the unfortunate woman loses her mind:

The woman, who had fallen into absolute nymphomania, became all the more insane once Onoda departed for the provinces to visit his father. She was discovered in the back of Oshima's shop trying to set fire to the place by lighting a pile of plane shavings and scraps of wood she had collected from a nearby construction site.

The woman was arrested and led away by the police at the petition of the neighbors. Oshima as well witnessed one of the several occasions when the police strung the woman upside down from a beam in the police station and threw water from buckets at her face.

"You see! Even when we douse her with water, she doesn't shut her eyes. That's certain proof she's mad," the officer in charge said laughing. They were in a room whose walls were lined with instruments of torture. (4:260–61)

At the age of seven or eight, Oshima is moved to tears by the sight of an exhausted workhorse's large bleary eyes. Some twenty years later, she is unaffected by the unblinking eyes of a woman being tortured. The child Oshima, born out of feudalism, has grown up and has been deprived of a certain natural capacity for compassion.

In an October 1915 interview, Shūsei stated that if he were so inclined, he could write two or three more novels like *Tadare* or *Arakure,* but that he was tired of "that kind of thing," and he did not intend to write other works like them.[25] He was true to his word. *Arakure* marked the abrupt end to the phase of Shūsei's career that began in 1907. In a sense, it is curious that Shūsei would declare so forthrightly that he was going to change the direction of his writing, for when one reviews the criticism of Shūsei from 1913 to 1915, one finds that *Tadare* and *Arakure* had raised his reputation as a novelist to new heights. In 1913, the house critic for *Shinchō* observed that with *Tadare,* Shūsei had attained a state of intellectual transcendence by which "problems" were simply not problems (*mondai ga mondai ni naranu shinkyō ni tasshite iru*) and that consequently *Tadare* was the greatest work of Japanese natural- ism.[26] A critic for *Bunshō Sekai* called Shūsei the finest realistic writer in Japan at that time.[27] In the October 1915 issue of *Waseda Bungaku,* an anonymous critic recommended *Arakure* without reservation, praising it as the most brilliant work to appear on the literary scene in recent years.[28] Sōma Gyofū, Nogami Shirogawa, and Nakamura Seiko evalu- ated *Arakure* in high terms in *Shinchō.*[29] Writing in a 1916 issue of *Bunshō Sekai,* Chikamatsu Shūkō assessed *Arakure* as the most substan- tial work of fiction published during the previous year.[30]

Given the fact that the overwhelming majority of the reviews of *Tadare* and *Arakure* were very favorable indeed, why did Shūsei sud- denly declare that he was no longer interested in writing "the kind of thing" that had established him as a major literary figure? By the end of 1915, Shūsei must have been exhausted. He was forty-three years old and had been supporting himself, a wife, and up to six children almost solely by writing fiction for fifteen years. During the approximately seven years from October 1908 until July 1915, he had written five major novels that were critically well received when they appeared as independent volumes and which have since been acclaimed as master- pieces of Japanese naturalism. In addition, during the same period, Shūsei wrote about 125 short stories, which earned him the reputation of being a fine short story writer, and some 20 serialized novels for a popular audience. Two of these, *Nijū-shi-go* (Twenty-four or Twenty- five, 1909) and *Honryū,* were well received when they appeared.[31] It would be wrong to underestimate the sheer linguistic labor and effort to remain original Shūsei expended in maintaining his literary career from the turn of the century to 1915.

Hirotsu Kazuo has characterized Shūsei as a *hirasakka,* "just a novel- ist," meaning that most Meiji novelists who continued writing were not only novelists: Nagai Kafū and Masamune Hakuchō had independent incomes, Sōseki and Tayama Katai were editors, Ōgai was employed by the state, and so on.[32] Masamune Hakuchō has suggested that Shūsei changed directions in his literary career because he wanted an easier way to make a living.[33] As a major literary figure (*taika*), Shūsei could get away with writing less demanding works. There is perhaps some truth in this observation, though as we shall see in the next chapter, Shūsei probably had more artistic integrity than Hakuchō was willing to give him credit for.

Another reason Shūsei's writing changed so radically after 1915 was that literary fashions were changing. *Arakure* and *Michikusa*, both published in 1915, represented the artistic culmination of the antinovelistic novel, the non-storylike story (*shōsetsu-rashiku nai shōsetsu*), or the tendency toward fiction with no resolution (*mikaiketsu no mama*), which was in part a reaction against the melodrama of the European novel and which became manifest in 1908 with Sōseki's *Kōfu* and Shūsei's *Arajotai*. Both men's reactions to naturalism as a national literary movement resulted in attempts to create a realism truer to Japanese experience, and these attempts left both men exhausted by 1916. Among a new generation of writers—the young Shiga Naoya, Akutagawa Ryūnosuke, Tanizaki Jun'ichirō, Satō Haruo, Satomi Ton, Mushanokōji Saneatsu—the tendency was toward allegory.

A final reason for Shūsei's decision to stop creating the kinds of novels he had been writing may have been that the common life he saw around him was undergoing transformation. Most of the characters in the novels discussed so far were born in the 1880s. Perhaps Shūsei sensed in 1915 that the common life of the Meiji period was gradually giving way to the mass culture of the Taishō period, to better education and nutrition and more cultural and social homogenization.

Since Shūsei was not given to expanding in print his views on literature, it is difficult to say anything more definitive about why he stopped writing "that kind of thing" so suddenly in 1915, but one can state more precisely what "that kind of thing" was. If a distinctive feeling for place and time in the novel can be said to define genre, then it is probably compelling to consider the five novels that have been discussed here as constituting a genre.[34] This genre, the novel of Meiji common life, was the product of a unique confluence of historical circumstances. Education in the Meiji period was a literary education to an extent almost inconceivable today. This genre was born of the People's Rights movement of the 1880s and was nurtured by succeeding generational demands for Japanese realism and a series of literary movements that militantly advocated a break with the literary traditions of the past. The editors and audience who bought Shūsei's fiction were as literate and open to literary experiment as any in the history of the world. Finally, the institution of literary apprenticeship that allowed Shūsei to master the craft of the novel by writing fiction for money will probably never exist again.

Time in this genre is the time of everyday consciousness: digression, memory, and association. Narrative perspective is almost always fixed with common, ordinary characters: narrative does not drift to the position of the outside observer, of a presence providing psychological analysis, or of the storyteller. Written for serialization, all of these works are episodic, a series of short stories given overriding unity by the life of a character modeled on a living person.

In all of these novels, the voice of the author is refracted through enormous language diversity: highly original sound symbolism (conventionally held to be not literary), the representation of regional and urban dialects, nonstandard pseudoclassical narrative forms, beautiful seasonal imagery, and dialogue in mixed dialects. This extraordinary linguistic diversity is, in all of the novels discussed, woven into extremely dense configurations of common voices.

The four years from Shinkichi's life, the ten years from Oshō's life, the approximately six years from Sasamura's life, the two or three years from Omasu's life, the twenty-odd years from Oshima's life: time in all of these novels belongs to the class-cultural milieu of *shomin* life. They are about ordinary people from somewhere else, immigrants to the city, who are being educated to the norms of common respectability and who are seeing the city and its new economy from odd perspectives and with fresh eyes. All of these novels speak of extreme social mobility within the social boundaries outlined above and of ethics of success quite different from those officially sanctioned by the state.

Whether it be Shinkichi's "individualism," the metal buckets and public transportation system Oshō utilizes, Sasamura's desire for a wife he can love, Omasu's *katei,* or independent domestic unit, or the Western-style men's clothing that Oshima manufactures, the modern is quickly assimilated in common life, and if it is not, it appears as grotesquely erotic. In all of these novels, social prejudice against "peasants," "workingmen," the diseased, *eta,* prostitutes, and others who have fallen out of the commonly respectable is pervasive. Social origin is important in these novels, but given the fluidity of the social situation and the fact that almost everyone is born somewhere else, most characters are insecure about their own origins, which are rather murky. As for larger social and economic movements of history, these are portrayed as mysterious and unpredictable.

As Isoda Kōichi observed in 1977, there have been no writers in the postwar period to carry on the form of realism that Shūsei pioneered, though some have tried, notably Nakagami Kenji in his own *Arakure*.[35] The genre Shūsei developed, the novel of common life in the Meiji period, died out after he lost interest in it in 1915.

5
In Disguise, 1915–1938

> As she grew up, Mizuko's skin became whiter and softer. A resemblance to her mother's father became apparent in the way the corners of her eyes rose slightly. She probably inherited her well-formed mouth as well from her maternal grandfather's side of the family. At two or three, her chest was broad and strong, her cheeks plump, and her limbs chubby and round. She just grew up on her own, without causing me too much trouble, without my paying too much attention to her, without my loving her. I can't go on writing like this now without weeping.
>
> "Her nose looks like a pig's snout," I used to say, laughing at her nose when she was a baby.
>
> —Tokuda Shūsei, "Giseisha" (The Martyr)

No objective assessment of Tokuda Shūsei's literary career can avoid addressing the reality that he is not much read today. His works have been more or less excluded from the canon of literature assigned to secondary school students, a canon that was established by academic critics who write literary histories. As Funabashi Seiichi noted as early as 1941, academics tend to dislike Shūsei because his works contain no ideals or concepts that require scholarly elucidation.[1] If literary historians had been able to ignore Shūsei, his reputation in the post–World War II period would probably have fared better; unfortunately, they were not able to.

During the height of literary naturalism, Shūsei was consistently acclaimed as Japan's most realistic writer. On November 23, 1920, Japan's prospering Taishō literary establishment displayed unprecedented unity in organizing a gala affair called the Tayama Katai Tokuda Shūsei seitan gojūnen shukugakai (Celebration of the Fiftieth Anniversary of the Births of Tayama Katai and Tokuda Shūsei). This celebration was as large scale, festive, and complex an event as had ever been organized by writers, critics, editors, and publishers.[2] By 1927, in connection with his sensational love affair with his literary disciple Yamada Junko, Shūsei's name had become a household word even among those who did not read novels. His career went into eclipse from 1929 to 1932, but he made a "miraculous comeback" in 1933, and with the appearance of his *Kasō jinbutsu* (In Disguise, 1935–38) in 1936, he was praised in the kind of extravagant terms cited earlier. In the late 1930s and early 1940s, Tokuda Shūsei was the preeminent representative of Japanese realism. Writers formed study groups to read his novels, a literary journal was established and named after one of his novels, *Arakure,* and he was said to personify the "Spirit of Prose Literature" (*sanbun seishin*), a slogan used to defend realism against the attacks of rightist intellectuals. His importance was symbolically recognized when he was chosen as the head of the novelists' division of the Japanese Literature Patriotic Association during World War II. For at least three decades, Shūsei was a *taika,* or an eminent, sometimes preeminent, figure in the Japanese literary world.[3]

Postwar academics, in definitive literary histories, could not ignore Shūsei, but they could not engage him either, for to do so would have contradicted various postwar shibboleths.[4] As a result of this impasse, Shūsei and his work were integrated into a theory of the distorted development of Japanese literary realism which was at the same time a theory of the distorted development of Japanese personality and society. Perhaps the earliest formulation of this theory was created by Tanigawa Tetsuzō in 1931. In his writing, one can perceive the clear influence of orthodox Japanese Marxism in the 1920s and 1930s:

A unique characteristic of Japanese society and culture is that the hegemony of the bourgeoisie did not result in the full realization of liberalism and individualism, and of course Japanese naturalism reflects this unique characteristic.

The literature of naturalism is very weak in its criticism of society and the social challenges it raises. Naturalism's doctrines of "nonclosure" [*mikaiketsu*] and "anti-idealism" are signs of the movement's surrender and submission, often to feudal values. The result was that naturalism came to be seen as representing lethargy, lack of purpose, and passivity—lethargy in particular. Shūsei's naturalism is representative of this lethargy and passivity. . . . Shūsei alone perfected Japanese naturalism by pushing its method in a Japanese direction. Shūsei's life is the manifestation of the most Japanese tendencies.[5]

Tanigawa's argument was remarkably similar to that employed by intellectuals associated with the Communist party who believed that Japan's historical development deviated from the norm established in the West and that contemporary Japanese society was stagnating in a semifeudal condition under the total domination of an absolute-emperor system. It was the function of the vanguard of the proletariat to advance a true bourgeois revolution, which would witness the emergence of a firm bourgeois sense of self, democracy, and individualism. Substitute Tanigawa's "lethargic Shūsei" for orthodox Marxism's "stagnant, semifeudal Japan" and one has essentially the same argument.[6]

This theory of Japanese society and personality gained wide popularity among academics in the years following World War II. Defeat in war could be laid at the feet of the "lethargic" masses who did not rise in struggle to win that abstraction, a bourgeois society of equal citizens. Kataoka Yoshikazu, Itō Sei, Ara Masahito, Hirano Ken, Nakamura Mitsuo—one critic after another adopted the strategy for dealing with Shūsei that Tanigawa had pioneered. Yes, it was quickly agreed, Tokuda Shūsei was the greatest novelist of Japanese naturalism, but Japanese naturalism resulted in defeat: the trivialization of literature by the autobiographical novel (*watakushi-shōsetsu*) and mentalstate fiction (*shinkyō-shōsetsu*). The oppressive conditions of Japanese society, it was argued, did not allow Japanese novelists to develop the scientific and positivist spirit of Zola's naturalism and to grasp Japanese society as a totality, revealing all of its inherent contradictions; instead, Japanese writers were slaves fleeing from their oppressive society, and they escaped into the narrow confines of Japan's literary world, where they indulged in the mundane practice of writing about their own lives. Since Shūsei was the quintessential author of naturalism, and historically Japanese naturalism resulted in the deviation of the Japanese novel from its proper course and led it down the mistaken path of personal fiction, Shūsei of necessity must have been primarily a writer of personal fiction. This is the dominant mode of argument about Shūsei among a generation of older progressive academics.[7] A variation of it can be found in a 1983 English-language study of naturalism by Homma Kenshiro:

Naturalism found the justification for its existence as defining society and emancipating the individual from ages of exploitation, deprivation, and subservience. Japanese naturalism, however, was far from paying attention to social problems and science. Instead, it took an observant attitude of life, introducing *watakushi-shōsetsu* (autobiographical fiction) and *shinkyō-shōsetsu* (mental state fiction). . . . Shūsei was wanting in a sophisticated and passionate quality with which to cope adroitly with the outside world. Rather he lay in melancholy at the bottom of a human valley into which it was impossible for outside stimuli to penetrate, his eyes shining like a reptile's, a true characteristic of his literature.[8]

Tokuda Kazuho attempted to defend his father's reputation with a few facts and a little common sense, writing as follows in 1975:

Arajotai, Ashiato, Kabi, Tadare, Arakure, of these major novels only *Kabi* is an I-novel. Shūsei has been accused of having adversely influenced Japanese literature through his I-novels and stories about his personal affairs. Shūsei did write I-novels, but most of his writing was objective fiction. And, in discussing the autobiographical fiction he did write, it should be remembered that his autobiographical fiction was unique to him. It is simply unthinkable that these works could have affected Japanese literature adversely. In the case of science, one builds on the work of one's predecessors, but in the case of the arts, one must ceaselessly begin again, starting over, taking the first step. "Following in the footsteps," "imitation," have no meaning in the arts. Shūsei continued writing I-novels, and he attained a harmony of objective and subjective perspectives. Shūsei's novels are unique to him. (18:446–47)

Even during the Taishō period, when personal fiction dominated the literary world, most of Shūsei's writing was pure fiction. Labeling Shūsei as primarily a writer of confessional or autobiographical fiction, as several literary historians have done, is the function of postwar literary theory which posited the devolution of Japanese naturalism. This postwar theoretical hysteria, which Shinoda Hajime termed "literary masochism," was not kind to Shūsei's reputation.[9]

In recent years, however, young academics and critics have begun to challenge the notion that to appreciate Shūsei's literature is to be feudalistic or reactionary. In 1982, Kanai Keiko wrote as follows:

For my generation, the literary histories of Nakamura Mitsuo and Hirano Ken were a priori truths. They were not "theory" but "common sense" and had already become the textbooks for our literary education. . . . If individuals of Shinoda Hajime's generation experienced "shame at not understanding" a particular author or work, members of my generation were made to feel "shame for being fond" of certain writers and works. We were taught that certain areas were taboo or off-limits.[10]

What were the taboos of the postwar period that Shūsei's works violated? Progressive academics, in the face of the horrors of the immediate postwar period, which were ascribed to an all-powerful imperial institution, saw as their function the creation of a new orthodoxy which held that prewar modern life was impoverished both for the masses and for writers. Shūsei's career and works contradict many of the basic assumptions of this orthodoxy on various levels. Shūsei frequently complained about the poverty and the hardships involved in leading a literary life, but, on reflection, in the twentieth century there were few nations before World War II that had publishing industries vital enough to allow novelists to continue to portray their contemporary society and make a living—support a family of seven, buy a house, and so on— almost solely by writing fiction, without affiliation with or salary from a political party or state or religious institution. In the light of the freedom Shūsei enjoyed and the horror stories of the suppression of writers in the twentieth century in Europe and in the colonized nations, Shūsei's career challenges the notion that Japanese society was particularly oppressive toward writers, or makes such arguments seem naive.

On another level, Shūsei's literature highlights the extent to which common life in the postwar period has become impoverished. In terms of clothing, living space, public spaces, leisure, and culture, postwar Japanese society often does not compare favorably with the world Shūsei projected as the norm in prewar, modern society. In short, there is a sense of security, place, and sovereignty in Shūsei's literature that seems to be lacking in the literature of the postwar period. Finally, the social sciences and humanities in postwar Japan have been vitally concerned with postulating and promoting theories, both universal and particular, of the Japanese masses. In contrast to "ideological fiction," Shūsei's novels and short stories present no unitary, programmatic conceptualization of the urban masses and so have been difficult to incorporate into the curricula of pedagogues. On all of these levels, then, Shūsei's career and works violate some of the basic assumptions of postwar intellectual life, and so they have been dismissed by many academic critics.

Eulogy

Shūsei was not primarily a writer of personal fiction, but it is undeniable that some of his most memorable writing was done in the so-called *watakushi-shōsetsu* or *shinkyō-shōsetsu* modes. Indeed, Donald Keene has called Shūsei's *Kasō jinbutsu* perhaps Japan's finest autobiographical novel.[11] It was argued above that at about the time he was creating *Kabi* in 1911 or so, Shūsei was uncomfortable with writing about his own personal affairs, and he did so only because it was the literary fashion of the day. In 1916 with his "Giseisha," he became willing to write short stories whose protagonists are clearly identifiable with himself, and he was probably motivated by his desire to eulogize and memorialize common people of no particular social distinction whom he cared for greatly.

"Giseisha" ranks rather low on the list of Shūsei's works that should be translated, but it occupies a crucial place in his oeuvre, for it marks his transition to yet another kind of realism, less intense and less obviously brilliant than the great novels he wrote from 1908 to 1915 but equally serious and full of insights. With "Giseisha," he abandoned all of his "tricks"—the lovely impressionism, the humor, the sound symbolism, the funny slang, the experimentation with time, the eroticism—and exposed himself in a way he never had before.

One Shūsei in the story is the first-person narrator, recounting how and wondering why his daughter Mizuko died. This "I" objectively describes the arrival of tainted noodles sent as a gift for Shūsei's having acted as an intermediary in the adoption of an infant, how he prepares and serves them to his children, the first symptoms of Mizuko's illness, which her mother does not think are serious enough to warrant calling the doctor, and then the panicked realization that Mizuko is becoming very ill. Three doctors are called in. The first two make a wrong diagnosis of Mizuko's ailment, and her condition grows worse. The third doctor correctly diagnoses the illness as infantile dysentery but then washes his hands of the case. It only occurs to the father later that his daughter was already beyond help. The first two doctors continue their ugly and painful treatments, Mizuko becomes delirious, bursting into a school song, coma ensues, and she dies. The other children begin showing similar symptoms and are quickly hospitalized. Who was to blame for Mizuko's death? The people who, with good intentions, sent the tainted noodles? Shūsei's wife, Hama, whose very life was her children? The two doctors who are so ignorant? Though there is clearly enough blame to go around, the final moral responsibility for the child's death lies with the father:

Blankly, I went over in my mind the events of the miserable day and night from the onset of the infection to her death. If I or my wife had been as sensitive as we usually were to the illnesses of our children, and if I had doubted as deeply as I had in the past the abilities and intelligence of those doctors, perhaps I would have recognized something that would have enabled me to save her life. But a combination of unfortunate circumstances, my lack of concentration, and my lack of love for my innocent child blinded me to the things I should have seen. What had I been thinking of, what had I been doing during that crucial twenty-four hours which would never be returned to me? After I lost her, I finally realized I should have treasured her precious life. All of those qualities I had willfully ignored in myself, pretending they weren't there for so many years—my fatuity, shallowness, and arrogance—had come together before my eyes to create this enormous rupture in our lives. (5:212–13)

And yet there are other voices in this short story which appear to disrupt the voice of the first-person narrator. One is the "I" in the passage quoted at the beginning of this chapter, the "I" that declares directly to the reader that he cannot go on without breaking into tears, tears which seem to flow from the text, washing away the ink, allowing Shūsei to return to the silence and privacy of his personal grief.

Another voice becomes manifest in that moment of self-realization and confession when we are told that Shūsei has something to gain from the death of his daughter (5:213), which, of course, is the story we are reading. This is the cold clinical author, composing himself in front of his writing desk and staring down at his dead daughter. Shūsei the professional writer knew that this new experience of grief would enable him to write yet another story, which would perhaps bring in enough money to help pay for the funeral.[12]

A fourth image of Shūsei emerges from the novelist Satomi Ton's violent objection to "Giseisha."[13] Satomi Ton asks why the reader is being exposed to this awful story, which is so frightening because, given the circumstances, it could happen to anyone: a little less care than usual in preparing a meal, a little late in calling the doctor, a wrong diagnosis, and within twenty-four hours, a child is dead. How many millions of children have died under similar conditions, martyred to circumstances and negligence? But what was Mizuko martyred for? As Satomi Ton points out, nothing. This brings us to the Shūsei who wanted desperately to eulogize his daughter. That her death was so senseless makes her life indescribably precious. Given her careless, shallow father, her loving but illiterate mother, and the atmosphere of scarcity she has been brought up in, Mizuko is a far finer person than anyone has a right to expect her to be. She emerges as the most innately accomplished, intelligent, and beautiful member of Shūsei's household. Shūsei, then, can be seen to have been sacrificing his first-person narrator to Mizuko.

One senses as well in the work a certain clumsiness, revealing the strain of this attempt to use prose narrative to perform a function formerly reserved for such genres as Chinese poetry, classical Japanese poetry, or the formal, pseudoclassical eulogy. "Giseisha" is a failed experiment, one that the author himself expressed dissatisfaction with, but it is only Shūsei's first attempt to articulate the central thematic concern of much of his best personal fiction written over the next nineteen years from 1916 through 1934: coming to terms in narrative with the deaths of people close to him, hardly a trivial theme unless one has adopted the elitist assumption that the deaths of ordinary people are trivial. To write these unconventional, realistic eulogies, Shūsei started over again as a stylist, making his writing simpler, more reflective, and more responsive to subtle changes in human relationships. This new commitment to a more personal realism came years before Shūsei had even heard of such a term as *shinkyō shōsetsu*.[14]

In "Kanashimi no nochi" (After the Mourning, 1917), Shūsei again took up the subject of his daughter Mizuko's death. In "Yakō ressha" (Night Train, 1917) and "Kinoko" (Mushrooms, 1925), Shūsei attempted to memorialize his mother, who died in a cholera epidemic three months after Mizuko. His experimentation with this subgenre of personal fiction reached fruition in his beautiful and moving "Kanshō-teki no koto" (A Sentimental Story, 1921), a tribute to Take, his mother. Perhaps Shūsei was influenced by the simpler, contemplative prose of the writers associated with the *Shirakaba* group, but, for whatever reason, when compared to "Giseisha," Shūsei's writing in this story has a new certainty and confidence reflected by the title: despite the fact that the short story is an enormously moving portrait of Take, there is not one sentimental moment in it. The work concerns an elderly woman and her adult son who have naturally grown apart and who have nothing much in common any longer. Once again Shūsei "sacrifices" the narrating "I," this time to emphasize his mother's devotion and self-sacrifice. "Kanshō-teki no koto" concludes as follows, with the son preparing to return to Tokyo:

I left Kanazawa early in the morning. My mother, in consternation, was fidgeting around the house. While I was packing, she came to my side to see what I was doing, and as I locked my bag, two large tears, about the size of raindrops, fell from her eyes.

But she showed me only a few tears.

"The next time you come, don't worry about the gifts, just bring yourself," she declared and began making preparations in good spirits, as if she did not want me to regret leaving.

Three rickshas left my sister's house.

My mother's small, delicate body seemed on the verge of tumbling to the ground as she ran alongside my ricksha as it picked up speed.

"Stop! It's dangerous!" I yelled nervously.

Regretting I had come so late in her life and was leaving after so short a visit, I abandoned her to her eternal loneliness.

It was the last time I saw my mother alive. (6:425)

As we have seen, early in his career, Shūsei tried to memorialize his elder half brother Naomatsu, and he wrote three short stories which deal with the circumstances of Naomatsu's death in 1921: "Shotō no kibun" (Feelings at the Start of Winter, 1923), "Shikii" (The Threshold, 1925), and "Gakkō o denai otoko" (The Man Who Didn't Graduate from School, date unknown). Shūsei's main efforts to eulogize Naomatsu, however, centered on his "memoirs"—*Mudamichi* (The Wasted Journey, 1923), *Omoideru mama* (As I Remember, 1934), and *Hikari o ōte*—works in which Shūsei returned almost obsessively to his memories of Naomatsu's kindness and generosity while Shūsei was growing up in Kanazawa and during his time in Osaka in 1892 and 1893.

Shūsei lost his wife, Hama, in 1926. The woman who had served as the model for so much of Shūsei's best fiction died quite suddenly of a stroke at the age of forty-four. Shūsei mourns her passing in such short works as "Orikaban" (The Portfolio, 1926) and "Sugiyuku hi" (The Passing Days, 1926) and in the long novel *Kasō jinbutsu,* where she appears as an almost saintly presence.

Until the end of his career, Shūsei would continue to memorialize the dead and dying through the short story. "Shi ni shitashimu" (Growing Accustomed to Death, 1933) is a tribute to Shūsei's personal physician, a man who affirmed life and faced death with composure and dignity. When he heard that his old friend Mishima Sōsen was dying of cancer, he wrote "Shiroi tabi no omoide" (Memories of White *Tabi,* 1933), an affectionately humorous short story based on incidents from three months in 1901 when Shūsei lived with Sōsen and his three sisters. Shūsei's last short story to be published, "Kuwareta geijutsu" (A Body of Art Consumed, 1941) concerns the death of Ozaki Kōyō and the straitened circumstances this left his family in.[15]

This imperative to eulogize naturally evolved into "journey home," or travelogue (*kikō-bungaku*). "Machi no odoriba" (The Town's Dance Hall, 1933) is based on a trip Shūsei made to Kanazawa in 1932 to attend the funeral of his half sister Ōta Kin. The critical success of this short story signaled Shūsei's "miraculous comeback" to the literary world after several years of relative silence. In 1933, Kawabata Yasunari praised this story using religious metaphors: "In reading this work, one feels the pleasure of a state of mind at play in a realm emancipated [*gedatsu*] from human concerns."[16] Paradoxically, this subtle mood of freedom and transcendence is achieved through the language of corporeality, the whole effect of the story coming from the utter refusal to go beyond the physical sensations of the body. The short story opens with the "I" deciding what he will wear to his sister's deathbed in Kanazawa:

> It was summer, so I wanted to wear light, cool clothing, but I dislike formal crested kimono, and, as a rule, I go to funerals in Western-style clothing. Crested kimono somehow remind me of lances, bows and arrows, and feudal ancestors. Japanese clothing is simply too much trouble; it hangs from the body so sloppily, even one's mood becomes loose.
>
> But when it came to putting together a matching suit of Western-style clothing, I couldn't manage that either. I had an old-fashioned morning coat, but the trousers that went with it were too tight and uncomfortable. What I finally decided on was a cashmere suit coat with a new pair of winter trousers I had had made in the spring, and, to serve as changes in clothing, I stuffed the morning coat and the kimono in my old suitcase. (8:157)

In "Machi no odoriba," the "I" is a field of physical sensations: feet hurting at the funeral, hunger for a type of fish called *ayu* instead of the vegetarian fare served in observance of his sister's death, the body's craving to flee the incense-laden house crowded with believers and find some suitable physical exercise, the pleasant tiredness after an evening of dancing with the provincial "moderns" at a local dance hall. Even the memory of his sister is a matter of pure physical sensation. While the head of the corpse is being shaved (a tonsuring symbolic of reaching Buddhist salvation), the "I" suddenly remembers being embraced by his older sister when he was a child, the smell of her pure white skin, and the slightly sweetish scent of her underarms.

Shūsei wrote a great deal during the twenty years from 1916 to 1936, and although most of his writing was pure fiction, "Kanshō-teki no koto," "Sōwa" (An Episode, 1925), "Machi no odoriba," and "Shi ni shitashimu," born of the fundamental human need to eulogize and commemorate people and memories, attain the sublime. Shūsei's short stories represent some of the finest moments of the modern Japanese literary tradition in the sense that they could not have been created without the sustained support of the modern Japanese literary world (*bundan*) as an institution. Shūsei would begin the process of creation by hacking out a subgenre of personal fiction, the short story as eulogy, for example, and then he tenaciously kept working in these subgenres year after year until he brought them to polished perfection. His publishers and readers supported him in his laborious endeavors. Shūsei the short story writer is yet another literary figure who deserves a separate book-length study. One of the last works that Shūsei wrote was an unfinished short story entitled "Furusato no yuki" (The Snows of Home), in which once again Shūsei's persona is boarding a train to return to Kanazawa.[17]

Morality and Social Manners and Customs

Shūsei came to write *Kasō jinbutsu* (In Disguise, 1935–38) in much the same way he came to write his best short personal fiction. He started by creating a subgenre of personal fiction in which he dramatized his affair with his literary disciple Yamada Junko. "Shichimotsu" (Pawned Goods, 1926), "Ko o tori ni" (Come to Take the Child, 1926), "Futari no byōnin" (Two Sick People, 1926), "Nigeta kotori" (The Little Bird That Fled, 1926), "Moto no eda e" (Returning to the Branch, 1926), "Atsusa ni aegu" (Panting in the Heat, 1926), "Hikkoshi" (The Move, 1926), "Ma" (The Interval, 1926), "Haka" (The Grave, 1927), "Haori" (The Half-Coat, 1927), "Shiromokuren no saku koro" (When the White Magnolia Blooms, 1927), "Urikai" (Selling and Buying, 1927), "Mizugiwa no ie" (The House by the River, 1927), "Haru kuru" (Spring Comes, 1927), "Joryū sakka" (The Authoress, 1927), "Kiku to take" (Chrysanthemum and Bamboo, 1927), "Kosame furu" (Light Rain Falls, 1927), "Aru yoru" (A Certain Night, 1927), "Anya" (A Dark Night, 1927), "Nagomu" (Calm, 1927), "Kusaikire" (The Smell of Grass, 1927), "Inu o ou" (Chasing the Dogs, 1927), "Wakare" (Separation, 1928), "Ha-Ita" (Toothache, 1928), "Bishō no uzu" (Her Smile, 1928), "Samayoeru" (Wandering, 1928), and "Hi wa terasedo" (Though the Sun Shines, 1928) are referred to collectively as Junko-mono, or stories that feature a barely disguised Yamada Junko.[18] He came back to this material from 1935 to 1938, when he used these short stories as the foundation for rewriting his love affair as social critique in *Kasō jinbutsu*.

The major difference between the method of creation of the "short story as eulogy" subgenre of Shūsei's personal fiction, for example, and the subgenre Junko-mono is that Shūsei produced the latter at a terrific pace with seeming disregard for the craft of the short story: the works grew more journalistic and less literary. The public and the literary establishment, with some justification, would not allow Shūsei to get away with simply recording the events of his love affair. "Shūsei is becoming hysterical," Uno Kōji wrote in February of 1927.[19] It was obvious that Shūsei was using the drama of his love affair with Yamada Junko to keep up with developments on the literary scene.

It made him a public personality in the same way other literarily "incestuous" love affairs—Satō Haruo's affair with Tanizaki Jun'ichirō's wife, Nakatogawa Kichiji's affair with Satomi Ton's sister—turned other writers into public figures. In the mass media, Shūsei became a household name. The following headline appeared in the April 25, 1927, issue of *Asahi Shinbun:*

Yamada Junko going from one man to the next / As if jumping from one stepping-stone to another / She suddenly betrays her lover Shūsei / Promises marriage to a student at Keiō University / A hateful woman, a pitiable woman, a poison flower, Shūsei states.[20]

When Shūsei and Yamada Junko appeared in the provinces, crowds of young people gathered to cheer the couple. At roundtable discussions, writers and critics asked Shūsei intimate questions about his relations with Junko. He was interviewed in women's magazines concerning the moral instruction of his children during the course of his love affair. To dispel rumors that Junko was only after his money, Shūsei appeared in a weekly magazine to reveal the amount of his personal assets, thus proving that he had few resources that she could take from him. Shūsei, the famous man of letters in the press, and Shūsei's literary persona were drawing perilously close to each other as, in one tedious short story after another, Shūsei's hero demonstrated his love for the young authoress, hobnobbed with movie personalities and other famous writers, and visited elegant resorts, hotels, and houses of the demimonde.[21]

For a writer whose nature contained a strong element of negative phototropism, the bright light of self-exposure and celebrity was too much, and Shūsei fell into silence. In 1936 he wrote, "From the end of the Taishō era through the first years of Shōwa, I wrote almost nothing. It was the first time in my literary career that such a thing happened. It is true that during this period I really was not driven by any great desire to write. Nonetheless, it was quite painful for me to abandon my pen for four or five years" (18:514).

The period Shūsei remembers as the time of his greatest lack of productivity was in fact the years he was active creating the subgenre known as Junko-mono. Perhaps, as his son Tokuda Kazuho has suggested, Shūsei wanted to erase those twenty-seven short stories from his memory. The years Shūsei actually stopped writing were well into the early Shōwa period: one short serialized novella and seven short stories in 1929, two short stories in 1930, one short story and one long serialized novel in 1931, and no works of fiction in 1932. It would not be an exaggeration to say, however, that Shūsei wrote nothing of significance for almost seven years, from April 1926 ("Orikaban," "Sugiyuku hi") until his "miraculous comeback" in March 1933 with "Machi no odoriba."[22]

The disintegration of Shūsei's literature, his subsequent silence, and his vindication through the success of *Kasō jinbutsu* can only be understood in the context of historical developments on the Taishō literary scene. Takami Jun in his *Shōwa bungaku seisuishi* (History of the Rise and Decline of Shōwa Literature, 1958) argued that the Celebration of the Fiftieth Anniversary of the Births of Katai and Shūsei in 1920 was the last hurrah of the Taishō literary establishment, and there can be no question that the 1920s took a terrible toll on Japanese writers.[23]

By 1931, Tayama Katai was dying and Shūsei had fallen into silence. The two brightest young fiction writers and theoreticians of the Taishō period, Akutagawa Ryūnosuke and Arishima Takeo, had committed suicide. Uno Kōji and Kasai Zenzō had taken autobiographical fiction to a logical extreme, sacrificing themselves to their respective personae and falling into despair, nervous collapse, and, in Zenzō's case, death. Shimada Seijirō, the "genius" who, in 1918 and 1919, at the age of twenty, had set an all-time record for the sale of a novel with his *Chijō* (On This Earth), died in 1930 after a prolonged stay in a mental institution. Fujimori Seikichi, Ogawa Mimei, Eguchi Kan, and Hosoda Tamiki had become a part of the left-wing literary movement. Kume Masao, who in 1924 had proclaimed the moral and philosophical superiority of Japanese personal fiction, had turned to writing popular fiction for a mass audience. The literary establishment that had met on November 23, 1920, to honor Katai and Shūsei had utterly collapsed. *Kasō jinbutsu* is, in some senses, the story of the disintegration of the Taishō *bundan*. Takami Jun argues that "ideas" destroyed the Taishō literary establishment, the same ideas positively evaluated in Kobayashi Hideo's famous statement that the proletariat literary movement brought "ideas" to Japanese literature for the first time.[24]

What did the left-wing literary movement mean for Shūsei's literature? We have seen that, beginning in 1908 with *Arajotai,* the "content" of Shūsei's writing remained constant, but the "form" of his novels changed radically. Once the detached, outside narrator disappeared and perspective was brought down to *shomin* characters, the "masses" as a unitary concept began to stratify into a bewildering number of conflicting groups and subgroups. In his writing after naturalism, one can discern at least five different images of the masses, and these are quite often contradictory. First, there was Shūsei's reaction to the leftist idea of the masses allegorized as a progressive political force awaiting the leadership of the proletariat vanguard. Second, there was the image of the masses as consumers of popular literature—melodramas, tales of chivalry, romances. Then there was the image of the masses we have isolated here from Shūsei's great novels of common urban life. The fourth image of the masses concerns Shūsei's own identification with ordinary people as revealed in his autobiographical fiction. Finally, in *Kasō jinbutsu,* there is a critique of the modern from the perspective of the masses.

In 1923, Shūsei wrote that he had lived most of his life as a member of the propertyless classes and that he thought all writers should imbue their works with what he called the revolutionary spirit, a position essentially no different from those he had taken in 1895 and 1906.[25] As leftist literary figures began uncritically importing Stalinist doctrine on the arts, however, it became clear that no rapprochement between Shūsei and the orthodox Left, dominated by the Communist party, would be possible. In 1927, Shūsei wrote that as an individual he identified more with the proletariat than with any other class, but, at the same time, he insisted that literature was a far freer discourse than Darwinism or Marxism and that he could not conceive of a Marxist literary movement.[26] Shūsei continued to hold fairly progressive political views, even resolving to run for the Diet in 1930 on the platform of the Social Democratic party (Shakai Minshūtō), but, as we shall see, he tended to dismiss the leftist literary movement as a mere passing fancy among the intelligentsia.[27]

Another concept of the masses threatening to Shūsei was the one implicit in the notion of a "mass consumer society" represented by the growth of a mass readership for popular literature in the 1920s. During this time, the Japanese publishing industry underwent a boom as dramatic as the one it experienced at the turn of the century. By 1928, monthly sales for *King* (or *Kingu*), "the national park of magazines," a popular-entertainment periodical founded by Noma Seiji of Kōdansha, were approaching 1,200,000. Other major publishing houses followed with their own monthlies designed to attract a mass readership: *Heibon* (Heibonsha, 1928), *Asahi* (Kakubunkan, 1929), *Hinode* (Shinchōsha, 1932), *Hanashi* (Bungei Shunjūsha, 1933), and *Yūoma Kurabu* (Shun'-yōdō, 1937). The twenties also saw the birth of several of the weekly entertainment magazines that exist even today, *Sandē Mainichi* and *Shūkan Ashai*, for instance. A host of women's magazines carried fiction, including Shūsei's: *Fujin no Tomo, Fujin Kōron, Fujin no Kuni, Josei, Akai Tori.*

The *"enpon* wars" of the late twenties and early thirties provided an impetus to the mass publication and distribution of modern Japanese literature on an unprecedented scale. In November 1926, the publishing house Kaizō, under the leadership of Yamamoto Sanehiko, announced that it would issue a thirty-eight–volume series entitled Collected Works of Modern Japanese Literature, each volume costing one yen (hence the name *enpon,* or "one-yen book"), a half to a third of the price of a single volume bought independently of the series. The number of subscribers to the series rose rapidly to 230,000 and ultimately totaled 400,000 or 500,000. Shun'yōdō entered the competition in May 1927 with its fifty-volume Collected Literature of Meiji and Taishō. Shinchōsha, in February 1928, came out with a twenty-four–volume Collection of Modern Novels. And so it went into the early 1930s.[28]

On the one hand, this publishing boom benefited Shūsei greatly. He made a small fortune off the *enpon* wars, though he spent most of it in an extravagant search for pleasure. On the other hand, Shūsei feared that the rise of this new popular culture based on the mass consumption of the printed page would lead to the homogenization of Japanese literature and the drying up of publications carrying serious literature. He foresaw that editors would tend to pick potential bestsellers and popular fiction over serious works of literature. Though Shūsei continued to write fiction for a popular audience, at one point in 1925 even declaring that he planned to concentrate on popular fiction, his heart was never in it. He also denounced popular literature as "having a tendency to fall in with the cheapest grade of journalism in pandering to the masses."[29] Shūsei's son Kazuho remembers his father's frustration over having to waste so much time on rubbish for a popular audience.

With Ozaki Kōyō, Shūsei had undergone his apprenticeship in writing popular works for the masses, and one suspects he resented having to return to the earlier clichés and stereotypes of melodrama, especially during an age when he thought the modern world was making the daily experiences of most people more complex; nonetheless, he continued to write popular fiction for money. Shūsei believed simply that serious fiction was the discovery within oneself of "something" which satisfied an artistic need and the conveying of this "something" to a "refined" (*kōkyū*) readership.[30] It seems clear the Shūsei never expected the masses to appreciate his best work. In 1935 he wrote, "The spirit of the gambler! Traditionally, among the masses, this has been an important Japanese spirit. Just as the warrior class had its *bushidō* [way of the warrior], the masses had their gambling spirit. It is advertised as chivalry, but essentially it's the business of the gang" (15:261).

The fifth image of the masses comes to the fore in Shūsei's *Kasō jinbutsu,* which, as noted above, portrays the stormy love affair between Shūsei and his beautiful literary disciple Yamada Junko. Etō Jun has elucidated this image in a perceptive manner, and it is profitable to quote him at some length:

[W]hen intellectual chaos came to the literary world [in the late 1920s], Shūsei, perhaps for the first time in his career, attempted to rise socially in the world. Supported by new income from payments of copyrights for the *enpon* series and by his love affair with the new woman Yamada Junko, Shūsei finally exposed himself to the "modern," the modernity that had always eluded him before. Or perhaps one can say that the "modern," which had formerly belonged only to the intelligentsia or the elite, people who had received "higher education," had at last filtered down to the "mildewed" [*kabi no haeta*] homes of the masses [*shomin*]. *Kasō jinbutsu* is the record of the allergic reaction that occurred when the "modern" and the "masses" came into contact. . . .

In the background, of course, there was the historical transition Japanese society underwent in the years following the Great Kantō Earthquake of 1923. On the one hand, there was the collapse of the Meiji worldview formed by the fusion of Confucianism and Social Darwinism, and on the other hand, there was the rise of Marxism, which replaced Social Darwinism in giving the intelligentsia a new means of interpreting reality. The "modernity" of this period represented the disintegration of the Meiji "modernity," which Natsume Sōseki had portrayed, and the rise of the "fourth class" [the proletariat]. It was natural that Shūsei, who had missed the opportunity to come in contact with Meiji "modernity," wanted to grasp the "modern" in this new age of transition. But, for Shūsei, who was not an intellectual, "modernity" could not be Marxism; . . . rather it could only be the "mood" created by the "beautiful, licentious young harlot" Yamada Junko.

But why did Shūsei long so for this "modernity"? Unlike the modernity of the Meiji period, there was no idealism involved in this new degeneracy, nor did it provide a means for interpreting the world. Leaving aside for the moment the natural inclination of a novelist not to be left behind by fashion, Shūsei's desire for the "modern" was simply a physical desire corresponding to what he called "an attraction to the other sex." This was the unsurpassable limitation of the "modern for the masses." Any "modernity" that can only be realized at the level of physical sensation must of necessity be a "modernity" that is "in disguise." The value of Shūsei's *Kasō jinbutsu* is that all of this is remorselessly portrayed not from the perspective of the "modern" but from the perspective of "Japan," that is to say from the perspective of the damp house off a narrow street where "dazzling light" does not penetrate. In this regard, there has never been another novel like it.

For "commoners" [*shomin*], the arrival of "modernity" was the arrival of chaos, and there has never been another writer who has portrayed as realistically as Shūsei how people disintegrated in the midst of this chaos.[31]

Kasō jinbutsu, then, is a critique of modernism from the perspective of the masses. It describes the disintegration of the Taishō *bundan* from the perspective of common life. The achievement of this novel in the history of Japanese letters is that the *watakushi-shōsetsu* (also called *shishōsetsu*), or autobiographical novel, had been developed by Shūsei into a critique of popular customs, manners, and fashions, a novel about poses in social contexts. Kobayashi Hideo has put it expressively as follows: "The author [of *Kasō jinbutsu*], after years of self-analysis, has penetrated to his innermost being, and he can declare, without hesitation, I am the monster [*bakemono*] you see before you." *Bakemono* is used by Kobayashi as a high form of praise: a superhuman being capable of changing visage and voice at will. Kobayashi goes on to write:

Shūsei's *shishōsetsu* has transcended the literature of everyday experience. The "self" in everyday life is merely a disguise. Moreover, the most intimate "self" is only manifested in disguise; it cannot be grasped. The road of Shūsei's personal fiction has led to this polished, refined temperament of the pure novelist.

What I would like to make clear is that *Kasō jinbutsu* is not a masterpiece of the so-called *shishōsetsu* genre. The human (some might say all too human) wisdom of the author is universal. What the author calls the temperament of the novelist is of course a fiction. In truth, it is the wisdom shared by people who have undergone intensely painful experiences and have subsequently come to terms with their situations in life.

The light of this wisdom, which is not ideological or academic or commonsensical, is the poetry and beauty of this novel.[32]

Kanai Keiko is yet another critic who views *Kasō jinbutsu* primarily as a social novel rather than as a confessional novel. She employs an intelligent strategy in defending Shūsei against the reductionary theories of academic critics. By linking *Kasō jinbutsu* to the writings of Tosaka Jun, Kanai appeals to an alternative Marxist tradition and historicizes the novel at a point in the mid-1930s.[33] It was Tosaka Jun's insistence on maintaining a distinction between the categories "individual" and "self" that perhaps led to his arrest as a thought criminal in 1938. In 1936, he wrote:

The individual is a sociological concept. It can be taken care of by historical materialism. The self, in contrast, is a literary representation. It possesses infinite literary and moral nuances and flexibility. The systematization of the individual is the splendid science called sociology. The systematization of the self may be literary, but it is not scientific—positivist, technological, and so on— theory.[34]

Much of what Tosaka called the "Japanese ideology" in the field of literature consisted of readings which conflated these two categories (in a different sense, postwar academic criticism performed the same operation) to establish the essential Japaneseness of the narrating Japanese subject. Tosaka maintained to the end that abstractions such as the "Japanese spirit" were simply meaningless in discussions about literature, which provided a "moral mirror" through which the self (*jibun*) was perceived, and, given the rightward politicalization of Japanese society in the thirties, this intellectual integrity was dangerous. He died in prison in 1945.[35]

For Tosaka, the bridge between the two categories of individual and self was "morality," but a morality that was certainly not the pronouncement of moralists. Rather it was morality socially contextualized as popular manners and customs, the morality of the masses, which, as we have seen, was always under negotiation. As Tosaka wrote in 1936:

If we truly believe in an idea, it becomes integral to our tastes. It becomes a part of our consciousness, conscience, and morality. When a great many people living in the same society at the same time have the same tastes, this constitutes popular customs and manners [*füzoku*]. . . . An idea can possess a corporeal reality in society only when it takes the form of popular customs and manners. Popular customs and manners correspond to society's skin.[36]

He wrote again in 1936:

The aesthetic, material, and secretionary manifestation of morality is popular customs and manners. As one aspect of literary criticism, I must stress the importance of depicting popular manners and customs. Whether the morality of a work is persuasive or not, whether characters have individual personalities, whether the work is realistic, whether it is popular, whether it is "interesting," all of these questions are, I think, related directly or indirectly to whether popular manners and customs are explored and portrayed in depth. The most conspicuous area mediated by popular customs and manners is the sexual.[37]

Kanai Keiko employs Tosaka Jun's literary theory to derail the post-war "textbook" critic and literary historian Nakamura Mitsuo, who argued that Japan's aesthetic realism was unable to give "flesh" to "ideas" (*shisō*) and instead degenerated into the "mere" depiction of popular customs and manners. Her choice of *Kasō jinbutsu* was appropriate to embody Tosaka's theory and illustrate that the "flesh" of morality and ideas in society is indeed popular customs and manners.[38] In Shūsei's novel, also written in the mid-1930s, the "ideas" which helped to bring chaos to the Taishō literary world are dealt with as fashions, and clashing moralities concerning sexual affairs are portrayed as popular manners and customs in conflict. Examining these conflicting moralities, however, first requires a look at the facts of Tokuda Shūsei's love affair with Yamada Junko. The style Shūsei developed for *Kasō jinbutsu* is extremely complex—Keene compares it to Proust's—and without a firm grasp of the order of events, one tends to bring false chronologies to bear on the work.[39] (In the following discussion, the names of fictional characters in the work appear in parentheses after the names of the real-life people they correspond to.)

Of Shūsei's serious novels, *Kasō jinbutsu* is the longest in terms of number of pages but the shortest in terms of the period of time it covers. It took the longest time to write: three years from July 1935 to August 1938, with interruptions for illness, notably in April 1936 when Shūsei collapsed from carotid artery mesoangiitis.

In March of 1924, Shūsei (Inamura Yōzō) and his wife, Hama

(Kayoko), received a visit from Yamada Junko (Kozue Yōko), then Masukawa Junko (Matsukawa Yōko), and her husband, Masukawa Saikichi (Matsukawa). The couple had come to request Shūsei's help in getting Junko's novel published.

Yamada Junko was born Yamada Yuki on June 25, 1901, in the town of Honjō in Akita prefecture to a relatively wealthy family of ship-owners. She graduated from Akita Women's Higher School in 1919. The next year, at the age of nineteen, she married Masukawa Saikichi, a graduate of Tokyo Imperial University, and she crossed over to his home in Otaru, Hokkaido. She soon became the society darling of the provincial elite in Otaru. In April of 1924, the local newspaper reported Junko's departure for Tokyo and her stated intention of visiting Shūsei and gaining his help in having her 1,500-page novel published. It seems she had a letter of introduction to Shūsei from a local newspaper editor who had bought Shūsei's popular novels for serialization.[40]

In Tokyo, Shūsei frankly told Junko that she should give up her ambitions of publishing her novel and of establishing herself as an author. He pointed out that it was difficult to publish because of in-creased competition and costs and that Junko had basic problems in her mastery of the grammar and punctuation of the written language. Junko, however, persisted in her request that Shūsei help her, citing the people in the provinces who had great expectations for her. Shūsei agreed to do what he could. Masukawa Junko returned to Otaru and gave birth to her third child. She was subsequently diagnosed as having breast cancer and underwent a mastectomy.

Perhaps the decisive event in Yamada Junko's life was the bankruptcy of her husband. Masukawa Saikichi had been employed by Mitsui in Hokkaido but quit to oversee various enterprises he had started. Japan was undergoing financial crisis, and his business failed. During her first visit to Shūsei, Junko was still able to maintain the pretense that she was a fairly wealthy woman, dabbling in the arts as a hobby. On her second visit to Shūsei in the fall of 1924, it was clear that Junko and her husband were moving to Tokyo to escape their hopeless economic situa-tion in the provinces. With Shūsei's help, Junko met Kume Masao (C), who introduced her to prospective employers at a movie studio. She finally found work as a waitress in the Cafe Printemps (Purantan), her primary qualification for the position being her great beauty. Saikichi and Junko agreed to a divorce late in 1924 so that Junko would not be burdened by Saikichi's enormous debt. (When Junko was living with Shūsei, Saikichi's creditors attempted to confiscate Shūsei's furniture.) Saikichi immediately married Junko's maid, left two of his children with

Shūsei and his sons and daughters in 1935.
Left to right: Momoko, Masahiko, Kazuho, Shūsei, Jōji, and Kiyoko

his new wife, and later fled to Shanghai to escape his creditors. Junko kept her daughter Yoshiko (Rumiko) with her for as long as she could.

In 1925, through Shūsei's introduction, Yamada Junko met Adachi Kin'ichi (Isshiki), the owner of the publishing house Shūhōkaku. She was soon carrying on a love affair with Adachi, who published her novel *Nagareru mama ni* (Swept Away) in the same year. She thus became a certified member of the Taishō *bundan*. It was also in 1925 that Junko fell in love with Takehisa Yumeji (Yamaji Kusaba), the famous artist whose work was popular among young women. Takehisa did the illustrations for Junko's book, and they lived together for a month or so until Junko discovered that Takehisa had no intention of marrying her. Disappointed, she returned to her mother's home in Akita.

Shūsei's wife, Hama, died on January 2, 1926, and Yamada Junko came back to Tokyo ostensibly to pay her respects on January 8. She found lodging in a boardinghouse, the Onoya Ryokan, close to Shūsei's home in Morikawa district. According to Yamada Junko's account of the affair, Shūsei forced himself on her in her lodgings in February 1926, while according to *Kasō jinbutsu*, Junko seduced Shūsei at about the same time. Whatever the truth of the matter, Junko and Shūsei were soon living together. The April 17, 1926, issue of *Asahi Shinbun* reported that Shūsei had given Junko permission to live in his house as a literary apprentice, which meant that he had taken formal responsibility for her conduct. It was well known, however, that the fifty-four-year-old Shūsei was carrying on a love affair with a twenty-five-year-old woman, and both Shūsei and Junko were subjected to much criticism and even expressions of disgust.

Shūsei felt deep regret over the pain the affair brought his family. Kazuho (Yōtarō) resented Junko. Shūsei's eldest daughter, Kiyoko (Eiko), was forced to withdraw from high school for a time as a result of the scandal. Momoko (Sakiko) developed a fondness for Junko and was hurt by the frequent quarrels between her father and "new mother."

From the start of her love affair with Shūsei, Yamada Junko continued seeing and sleeping with other men. There was the poet and wealthy politician, an Akita prefectural assemblyman, Murata Kōretsu (Akimoto). He continued through 1926 as Junko's patron, sending her money on a regular basis. There was talk in Akita of her marrying the assemblyman. Toward the end of 1926 and the beginning of 1927, she carried on a liaison with the surgeon Yashiro Toyō (K Hakase), who operated on her to remove chronic hemorrhoids. In Zushi, a seaside resort where Junko moved in the spring of 1927 to write and establish her own literary salon, she fell in love with Imoto Takeo (Sonoda), a wealthy young Marxist who, after World War II, was to translate Mark J. Gayn's *Japan Diary*. Motivated by jealousy, Shūsei made some indiscreet remarks to a journalist, and the result was the headline in *Asahi Shinbun* quoted earlier. Imoto's family moved to break up the match, and Junko, enraged by Shūsei's betrayal, demanded that he act as an intermediary for her in getting the proposed marriage back on track. Shūsei failed.

In the early summer of 1927, Junko was again living with Shūsei. They soon fought, however, and Shūsei threw her out of his house. Through a lawyer, she demanded one thousand yen as a final settlement, and Shūsei paid her the money. Junko traveled to Akita but quarreled with her mother there and returned to Tokyo almost immediately. She joined Shūsei on a trip to Hakone, where they spent much of the settlement money together. A short-lived reconciliation followed. On August 4, 1927, the press reported that Shūsei and Junko would marry. Junko became angered and indignant over Kazuho's insistence that her name not be officially entered into the family register. The final break came on the eve of 1928. After a quarrel provoked by Shūsei,

Junko left and moved in with a new lover, the brilliant young literary critic Katsumoto Seiichirō (Kiyokawa), who would later represent Japan's orthodox Communist literary movement (Nippona Proleta Artista Federacio in Esperanto) at the 1930 Kharkov Conference of the International Union of Revolutionary Writers. Shūsei sent the couple a large sum of money as a final settlement.

By the early summer of 1928, Junko was fed up with the life of the proletariat. She forced the issue in the autumn of 1928 by having her brother come from Akita to confront Katsumoto concerning his intentions about marriage. Katsumoto refused to marry Junko. She turned once again to Shūsei for help. He found her an apartment, paid three months' rent in advance, and encouraged her in her attempts to write. Under a pseudonym, she submitted a novel to a literary competition held by a women's magazine, a contest which Shūsei was judging. He gave her novel, which was based loosely on her love affair with him, the second-place prize, thus dashing her hopes for reviving her literary career. She suddenly disappeared. Shūsei later learned that she had opened a bookshop in Shibuya, obviously with the support of new lovers.

During the three years from 1926 through 1928, on the frequent occasions when Shūsei was separated from Junko, he often visited Tsuge Soyo (Sayama Sayoko) at her "house by the river," and *Kasō jinbutsu* contains extensive descriptions of her relations with various men: a German aristocrat, Shūsei himself, the popular writer Mikami Otokichi, and even Shūsei's son Kazuho. Tsuge Soyo was twenty-eight or twenty-nine when Shūsei met her in 1926. She was the daughter of a mistress of a gentleman of distinguished birth, and her illegitimacy apparently led her early to antisocial behavior. At school she became the leader of a gang of delinquent girls and in 1911 or so graduated to the "water trade." She became one of the "seven beauties" of the Cafe Lion, the Meiji-era cafe which pioneered in the development of the "modern demimonde," later to flourish in the Taishō and Shōwa periods. She later became a conventional geisha in the pleasure district at Shinbashi and even descended into straight prostitution in Yoshiwara. In about 1918 or so, a German aristocrat, who was living in Japan in order to sell armaments in the Far East, took Soyo as his mistress (*rasha*). Presumably, it was the money she received from this arms merchant on separation that enabled her to buy a house of assignation (*machiai*) by the Sumida River close to the Kiyosu Bridge in the Nakazu district of the Nihonbashi ward.[41]

There are several literary and journalistic sources other than *Kasō jinbutsu* which provide different perspectives on Shūsei's love affair with Yamada Junko. A rather self-defensive interview given by Katsumoto Seiichirō after World War II reveals that in addition to Junko's lovers described in *Kasō jinbutsu*—Masukawa Saikichi (Matsukawa), Adachi Kin'ichi (Isshiki), Takehisa Yumeji (Yamaji Kusaba), Shūsei (Yōzō), Murata Kōretsu (Akimoto), Yashiro Toyō (K Hakase), Imoto Takeo (Sonoda), and Katsumoto himself (Kiyokawa)—Yamada Junko slept with several other prominent literary figures. He describes her as a literary groupie and, excepting himself and Shūsei, condemns the Taishō literary establishment for its cruelty to her.[42]

Junko's own account of her affair with Shūsei, *Onna deshi* (The Woman Apprentice, 1954), is an angry, bitter denunciation of the "old fox" whose "nature revealed itself in so many different aspects that he was impossible to understand." In her own defense, Yamada Junko wrote that she was forced into affairs with other men because of Shūsei's stinginess.[43] Shūsei admits to this in several places, but, as we shall see, from the perspective of ordinary life, his use of money was sheer extravagance. By the end of the affair, he had gone through thousands of yen, exhausting the substantial profits he had earned from the publication of the *enpon* series.

Perhaps the most enlightening aspect of Yamada Junko's *Onna deshi* is that it illustrates how difficult it is to write about one's personal experience and how much skill was brought to this project in *Kasō jinbutsu*. Of all of Shūsei's major women characters—Osaku, Oshō, Omasu, Oyuki, Oshima, and Ginko of *Shukuzu*—Kozue Yōko/Yamada Junko was the most distinguished and talented. She was the most beautiful, a woman who seems to have stepped out of a painting by Takehisa Yumeji. She was raised in the most comfortable and cultured of circumstances and was educated to the standard of the provincial elite. She was the most intelligent and articulate, and her amazing, striking metaphors and wild flights of fantasy enabled her, however briefly, to make a name for herself as an author.[44]

She was also the most tragic of Shūsei's heroines. Once her position as the wife of one of the provincial elite was taken from her, society left her nothing to fall back on but her body, and that was flawed, tortured, and cut. Perhaps, in the end, Yamada Junko was enraged by *Kasō jinbutsu* because it reflected yet another aspect of Shūsei she did not know, a Shūsei capable of pitying her profoundly, of robbing her of even her fictions.

The Feminist Intellectual and the Geisha

Kasō jinbutsu opens as follows:

> After it was finished, Yōzō, through a chance acquaintance, took up social dancing at dance halls, and on several occasions, he also attended club rehearsals for a costumed Christmas dance party, where he was chosen, against his personal preference, to put on the Santa Claus suit; embarrassed, wanting to smoke, he jutted his chin out of the mask and struck a match to light his cigarette: the cotton beard caught fire and, in an instant, disappeared in flames. On that occasion as now, here prepared to beat from the folds of his heart the dusty, sweet dreams and old, bitter grounds of memory, he was forced to recall himself, unseen by others, as a solemn buffoon, so pretentiously costumed, so distorted, he had to chuckle wryly, or perhaps that was his real image, and he was suddenly embarrassed by his inability to distinguish one from the other. Telling the story, describing himself so caught up in the affair, would bring back no pleasant memories, nor would it have a material effect on the life he was leading now, and so perhaps it would be best to put it away softly in the back corner of a drawer, but, to be truthful, he somehow regretted leaving it at that. He had met her again, by chance, some time ago at a dance hall and had led her around the floor once in a foxtrot: "Isn't this fun?" she exclaimed, but Yōzō felt nothing at all, and he envied her capacity to pity him. An old wound, long since healed, was being probed, and it flinched painfully. She had gone downhill—become a woman of the streets—and it utterly depressed him to have to drag her now flabby body around the dance floor. (17:3)

As is true of much of Shūsei's fiction, we are given the ultimate conclusion of the story at the story's beginning. The narrative present is 1935 with the aging novelist Inamura Yōzō determining to write about his love affair with Kozue Yōko. The reader is then taken back to a Christmas party in the early thirties and to another occasion, by which time "the woman," Yōko, had sunk into prostitution (*sukkari chimata no onna ni narikitte shimatta*)—and had become for Yōzō an inconsequential person. The novel ends in 1930 or so, at a point when Yōko's "career was taking the opposite direction of that of her heroine Colette's, and she seemed headed toward making a living on the street" (*chimata no seikatsu ga hatten shisō ni mieta*) (17:302).

The work, then, never catches up with its opening lines, and the scene at the Christmas party, which is unrelated to the action of the rest of the novel, and the title *Kasō jinbutsu* have invited a number of critics to read the novel as a meditation on the nature of fiction.[45] It is the view here that every major character in the novel is "in disguise," using appearances, popular manners and customs, and fashions to manipulate and exploit. Shūsei was the mediator between these fictions, and he was a remarkably objective and fair one. One of the major clashes in terms of fashion and morality in the work is between Sayama Sayoko (Tsuge Soyo), the geisha, and Kozue Yōko (Yamada Junko), the feminist intellectual. Sayama Sayoko is an often present reminder that promiscuity pays as long as women retain control over their own stories. She highlights the view that the fatal moral flaw in Kozue Yōko's character is not her lack of chastity but her class pride.

Kozue Yōko and Sayama Sayoko both manipulate Yōzō to use his position as an eminent novelist to the advantage of their own social standings. Sayoko encourages Yōzō to visit her at her house of assignation by the Sumida River not because she needs the relatively small amounts he spends there but because "she wanted to attract his associates" (17:72). Her plan to utilize Yōzō to bring in a better, or at least a new, type of customer succeeds: "As Sayoko became acquainted with an increasing number of writers, artists, and journalists, her old clientele— stockbrokers, wholesalers, and the like—began to seem vulgar to her, and she grew bored with the type of connoisseur who knew and loved the moods and pursuits of the traditional demimonde" (17:200–201).

Always in Sayoko's "tastes" in terms of customs and manners there is a calculation which keeps her one step ahead of fashion and allows her to maintain self-control. With Japan sliding into a severe economic depression in the late twenties, Sayoko moves to exploit the only estate—journalism and publishing—which will continue to prosper. During the late Meiji and Taishō periods, she played both sides of the money-for-pleasure game, first participating in the "formless consumerization" of eroticism represented by the success of the Cafe Lion (and other cheap Westernizations of sexual mores and manners) and then learning the eroticism of "form" in the traditional geisha world around Shinbashi.

There was, of course, nothing new about *rashamen* (a derogatory term for Japanese women who became the mistresses of Caucasians) in Japanese society—we have seen such a woman before through Oshō's eyes in Yokohama—but arms merchants in Japan had made vast profits during and after the First World War, and Sayoko's choice of the German aristocrat as a patron and her timing in breaking with him and starting her own business are signs of her sensitivity to socioeconomic trends:

The German aristocrat named Kurube had prospered enormously by dealing in new types of weaponry, but he had invested nearly all of his capital in merchandise and transportation in a plan to sell arms to state authorities in China. Just when all the arrangements had been made, he heard that a direct contract had been signed between German governmental circles and the Chinese. The project on which he had expended all of his wealth and power burst like a bubble. He collapsed in the lobby of the Fujiya Hotel when he read the telegram informing him of the contract. (17:69)

In this uneasy period of transition and uncertain economic circumstances, Sayoko's "taste in men" remains flexible and reflects financial fortunes shifting from preparation for war to a boom in the publishing industry. Her preferences in fashion are equally eclectic. In the following, Sayoko and Yōzō go shopping at a famous clothing store:

Yōzō accompanied Sayoko, who for some time had been longing to dress in the latest Western-style fashion, to the Hitsujiya to look at cloth. Sayoko already had an expensive suit of Chinese clothing, usually worn by well-bred women, and, as the German's mistress, she was expected to attend dances held at hotels, and so she possessed formal and casual dresses, though these were out of fashion.
"I'd forget about the Western-style dresses if I were you. The Chinese dress would look nice though," Yōzō suggested.
"The German felt much the same way. He used to say, why should Japanese women throw away their kimono for dresses. Still, I'd love to try on the newest fashions." (17:200)

Once again we are in a world where the standard opposition Western/modern versus Japanese/traditional has little meaning. In some senses, due to her long association with foreigners, Sayoko knows more about the West than any other character in the novel. Women such as Oshima in her bonnet and dress are no longer remarkable. Even the mistress (kami-san) of a traditional machiai can be expected to own a formal or casual older-style Western dress. Sayoko's every instinct strains to keep up with the fashions of contemporary Tokyo society, but she is growing older, and, unlike Yōko, she cannot adapt to the clothing styles of the "flapper age" of the twenties, Western fashion so different from that of the previous decade. It is the general rule in the novel that women who approach middle age, such as the former geisha and teacher of classical

Japanese dance, Yukie (in real life Uchida Yai, also known as Fujikage Shizue, Nagai Kafū's ex-wife and Katsumoto's patroness from whom Yamada Junko "stole" Katsumoto, 17:218), wear Chinese dresses when they want to appear exotic and alluring. One of the essential ideas behind the modes of fashion which differentiate Sayoko from Yōko is a professional, conservative morality. It is palpable in the description of Sayoko during one of her early meetings with Yōzō:

> Yōzō suddenly became aware of what a mysterious and wonderful presence Sayoko indeed was: dark hair coursing across her white delicate wrist, the magnificent diamond gleaming on her finger, large pearl and coral rings worn in profusion on her other fingers, two giant keys to her safe peeking out from the folds of her loosely tied, gaudy obi, and the huge man's purse she carried. And yet, gradually, as he was talking with her over dinner, he sensed in the flicker of an expression or a movement that she had once been a geisha. She inquired about Yōzō's age and his family circumstances, but of herself she merely said, "Well, a great deal has happened, but I suppose it all started when I answered an ad for waitresses at the Cafe Lion, which had just opened, and they hired me." She looked up at the ceiling and said no more. (17:18)

The huge purse, the expensive rings, and the keys to the safe (we are later told it was one of the two largest imported from Germany and required twenty-five men to move) constitute an eroticism which whispers of Sayoko's possession of hundreds of romantic tales about the rich and well-connected men she had known. But she also emits the moral certainty that these stories will never be told and the men will never be identified. In contrast to Yōko, who is constantly talking, compelled to define and redefine herself as the romantic heroine or seductress in tales of passion, Sayoko generally lets symbols of wealth and power speak of a mystery which is morally sound. When she does fall into a mad love affair with a writer, it is with a writer of popular fiction (in real life Mikami Otokichi, author of the immensely popular *Yuki no jō henge*), who works only in genres that will not compromise her privacy. Once again, in her choice of a lover, Sayoko demonstrates her brilliant ability to foresee social trends, for many of the troop of popular writers who subsequently "occupy" her *machiai* (17:287) will soon come to call their reconstituted traditionalism "fascism."[46]

For all of her intelligence and beauty, Sayoko is never a serious rival to Yōko for Yōzō's love:

Yōzō followed the instructions Sayoko gave him and went down the hall to the bath. The bath chamber had a high ceiling. One removed one's clothing in a dressing area furnished with a variety of toiletries and then went down two or three steps to the bath. Yōzō had gotten out of the water and was shaving when Sayoko came in. Accustomed as she was to manipulating men, sharing the bath with him differed not the least from sharing a taxi.

She soon left the water and was combing her hair by the heater. The way she gathered her hair with both hands at the nape of her neck as she knelt there on one knee, the graceful slope of her shoulders, the symmetry of her arms and legs, hers was the exact form of one of the beauties painted by Suzuki Harunobu. And yet even at that moment, he could not forget the beautiful vision of Yōko. Perhaps Sayoko personified a certain type of beauty, but Yōko possessed naturalness. (17:74)

Yōko is missing a breast and cannot claim Sayoko's almost perfect physical symmetry, and yet throughout most of the work, Yōko is described as being a stunningly beautiful woman. Photographs of Yamada Junko taken in the late 1920s reveal that this portrayal of her was not an exaggeration. She is remembered as one of the great beauties of the Taishō period. Perhaps there are kinds of physical human beauty which crystallize in moments of history and can never be re-created. One views a painting of a woman by Takehisa Yumeji entitled *Kuro-funeya no musume* (Daughter of the House of Black Ships), and one realizes that this is an aesthetic of the Taishō period whose "parts" will never be put together again.[47] Her clothing is a Japanese kimono worn slightly askew, with the white of her shoulder visible. The obi is worn loosely, this not suggesting prostitution, rather comfort and freedom. Her hair is traditionally Japanese, very long, jet black, and straight, and yet it is done up in a free, individual way, with long combs supporting it. This tall, slim woman, who is seated on a chest and is holding a black cat, seems completely self-assured. Her eyes are enormous black pools, reflecting innocence from an almond-shaped face of pure white complexion. This painting could be a portrait of Yōko. Shūsei's treatment of her stresses the fragility of her beauty.

Freedom, reflecting the liberalism of Taishō democracy, is of decisive importance to the "naturalness" of Yōko's aesthetic. Her independence is a kind of feminism and is largely dependent on her status as an author. Yōko's family background and education allow her to be an intellectual and a feminist in a way that Sayoko can never hope to be. The first time Yōko and Sayoko meet at Sayoko's house of assignation, it is clear that Yōko intends to use "her writing" as a weapon to establish her superiority:

"I want to write. Can we stay here tonight?" Yōko asked Yōzō.

The fact that she had received commissions from several publications seemed to make her feel superior, and when Yōzō nodded his head, she immediately went to the telephone at the entrance, contacted her maid through a boarding-house in Yōzō's neighborhood, and ordered that her new *haori,* recently tailored for the New Year, and writing paper be brought to her by car.

After the parcel, wrapped in elegant white dotted silk crepe, arrived, and Yōko had put on her new *haori* and was in the mood to frolic, Yōzō called a maid and told her that he and Yōko wished to stay the night. The maid finally returned and announced, "I'm sorry, but I'm afraid we are a little too busy this evening."

Yōzō and Yōko stared at each other in disbelief at this act of rudeness. (17:133–34)

The author requires more than pen and paper to write; she must have a new *haori,* dyed with patterns of the most recent fashion, one that contrasts with the splendid but older *haori* the geisha Sayoko wears (17:133). Yōko's standing as a woman intellectual entitles her to adopt fashion trends associated with feminism, from which Sayoko is excluded, and, in resentment, Sayoko drives Yōko from her house. *Kasō jinbutsu* describes how this mode of fashion forces Yōko to ever more radical, self-destructive positions.

During the spring of 1926, Yōko's dress code is still acceptable according to the standards of the Taishō cultural establishment. Her hair, for example, is long enough to permit her to draw on favors and income from various sources: her writing, the publisher Isshiki, the potential husband Akimoto, and her formal protector Yōzō. This is a period, however, when the consensus and solidarity of the literary world were being challenged by "ideas," and Yōko is tempted to desert her former patrons in favor of new fashions and literary trends. As Yōzō himself concedes, this move is in part necessary for Yōko to remain in the public eye. But the "new freedom" she obtains in matters of fashion actually constricts her options in life. She transforms herself into a "modern girl" (*moga*), a feminine mode of fashion which caused great controversy in the late twenties. The scene is the summer of 1927. Yōko is trying to establish her literary salon at the popular seaside resort of Zushi. She announces that she must go to Tokyo to consult with the editors of a

popular women's magazine, and Yōzō waits for her return in her rented
house at Zushi:

> Eight o'clock passed and then nine, and Yōko still had not returned.
> The honking of the horns of the automobiles escorting guests to the hotel
> often reverberated through the small resort town, and when it had grown quite
> dark, he thought that at last he heard the sound of the engine of a car pulling up
> in front. It was Yōko returning, her gleaming black hair set in the latest wave at
> the beauty salon of May Ushiyama, her brows, eyes, and lips highlighted promi-
> nently with heavy powder, eye shadow, and other new types of makeup. She
> radiated a beauty that adhered to a kind of form. Her black *haori* with patterns
> of flying plovers, some embroidered in silver thread, made her face seem all the
> more expressionless, as if it had been cast in plaster. (17:178)

The "modern" seen from "Japan" is this eery mood of beautiful gro-
tesqueness. May Ushiyama's salon is still in business and her successor
frequently appears on television as a member of the fashion establishment, but what is presently the dominant form of hairstyling was, in the
late twenties, radical indeed. Women intellectuals with short, permanent-
waved hair proclaimed themselves to be Westward-looking freethinkers.
And yet in Yōzō's eyes, Yōko is losing her spontaneity and is coming to
be governed by a system (*kata ni hamatta yō na utsukushisa,* 17:178).
Once Yōko wholeheartedly adopts the fashion of feminism, she seems
compelled to take a Marxist lover. New customs and manners are forced
to represent new ideas. In Japanese society, Marxism takes corporeal form
as a fashionable object of desire:

> [A]t Yōko's salon, Yōzō had an opportunity to glimpse the Marxist boy who
> was his son's classmate. It was late in the evening. The young man, whose name
> was Sonoda, had been playing billiards at the hotel when Yōtarō had intro-
> duced him to Yōko, and the two had gotten on well from the start. She had
> dragged him back to her house after they left the hotel. . . .
> Yōzō was immediately struck by the beauty and youthful vigor of the shy
> young man, and while a sixth sense gave him an intimation that something was
> to come, this was more an objective feeling of admiration for the boy's illusion
> of beauty; if a contemptible jealousy did arise within him, he was able to repress
> it with his intellect. He felt he had no need to worry that an incident would
> occur: not even Yōko would stoop to corrupting that pure young man.
> (17:192–93)

Yōko does corrupt the young leftist, who succumbs quite readily to her seduction. Thus the vanguard of the proletariat and the vanguard of fashion are united. The Marxist boy (*marukusu boi,* 17:192) spends his summer at a resort town where he plays billiards and carries on a scandalous affair with a well-known author. When the press loudly reports that the young student intends to marry the older Yōko, the Sonoda family moves to break up the affair. A sinister uncle with powerful connections to the political world is soon manipulating events in the background, and Yōko must give up her ambitions to marry the boy and remain content with a final cash settlement.

Yōko's next conquest is another Marxist: Kiyokawa, the lover of Rumiko's dance teacher, Yukie. This new affair is also marked by a transformation in Yōko's style. To maintain a position as one of Japan's leading woman "intellectuals" by attracting one of the brightest young men of the rising Left and, concomitantly, to keep up with the fashion of feminism, she abandons Japanese dress for Western-style clothing:

Yōzō at times suffered from doubts that the relationship between Kiyokawa and Yōko was more than friendship, but at other times his suspicions disappeared. After all, though Yukie was getting older, she did have a great deal of experience manipulating men, and no matter how much passion there was on Yōko's part, she probably would not transgress the relationship of disciple and teacher between her daughter Rumiko and Yukie. Neither would the young Marxist Kiyokawa give in easily in Yōko's seduction. The reasons for Yōzō's insouciance were admittedly shallow, but he preferred not to face the possibility of yet another incident.

At about that time, Yōko was in the habit of borrowing popular American magazines from the beautician May Harumi and choosing designs from them she thought suited her. She found one that particularly appealed to her, and, like a child, she begged Yōzō to buy her cloth and buttons. She had no training in Western tailoring, but somehow she managed to cut the pattern. The material was orange satin, and it could be said that the garment's unique feature was the numerous narrow pleats in the skirt. As she was sewing, Yōko was probably taking pleasure in imagining how she would look for Kiyokawa, but Yōzō had no way of knowing that at the time. Although he thought the style and color were odd, he remained silent. She had left him no room to criticize. (17:269–70)

Yōko's affair with Kiyokawa does not turn out happily. Kiyokawa refuses to hire a maid but does not help with household chores, is stingy about the purchase of food, is cruel to Yōko's daughter Rumiko, and perhaps continues an affair with another woman (17:285–89). The ultimate insult is that after she perseveres with him, Kiyokawa blames her for his inability to write and refuses to marry her (17:288): " 'I guess Kiyokawa told my brother that he couldn't study while I was around,' Yōko explained, chuckling nervously as if she were being tickled, but her pride and sense of self-worth had been stripped from her. She was like a bouquet of flowers that Kiyokawa had crushed and then cruelly thrown down by the side of the road" (17:296).

Kiyokawa theoretically subscribes to the most feminist ideals current in Japanese society in the late twenties, but he treats women abominably. Transcendental, political morality is a function of fashion with as much intrinsic value as Yōko's orange satin skirt. Kiyokawa and Yōko use the latest foreign fashions and intellectual trends to distinguish themselves from the masses, but since their actions are governed by foreign abstractions which rob them of their capacities to contextualize their behavior in concrete Japanese social situations, they are moral children. The following scene, which takes place during her affair with Kiyokawa, is a metaphor for what Yōko has lost by her embrace of foreign values: "When she disrobed in the dressing room outside the bath, Yōzō saw that her chemise was dirty and the heels of her silk stockings were worn thin" (17:288). Women have rights to property in common life, and these are often manifest through traditional women's silk clothing, which has long-lasting economic value. For "romance" and "ideas," Yōko gives up these rights and is left with worthless garments originally produced for foreign markets.

Every major character in *Kasō jinbutsu* is in disguise, and it is the nature of disguise to change according to circumstance. Sayoko, it will be remembered, is a sound and stable person, not inclined to reveal much about her personal history or feelings. In the following, she appears in different aspect:

Sayoko was obviously drunk and in a dramatic mood when she was shown into Yōzō's study, and his son, in the company of a friend, a young writer, came in to have a look. She was rambling incoherently as she pounded her fist on his sandalwood desk.

"I'm thirty-three!" was all he could make out of her nonsensical babbling. She soon staggered to her feet.

"Will you see her home?" Yōzō requested of his son.

As Yōzō saw her off at the door, she turned and kissed him full on the lips, but the act was an instinctive impulse; she was not aware of whom she was kissing.

Forty minutes later Yōtarō returned.

"She's a fascinating woman!"

"What happened?"

"She insisted she had to see the German, so we went with her in the taxi, but the door of his house was locked. She rang and rang the bell and pounded on the door, but no one answered, so she broke a window. Then a splendid, bald-headed German opened the door, and she tried to force her way into his house, but he kept pushing her back. He looked at me and said, 'You're a gentleman, please take this drunk home. Her hanging around my house this late is bad for my reputation.' Well, I managed to calm her down and get her into the taxi, but on the way to her house, she wouldn't stop kissing me. . . . There was blood running from her hand. I wrapped my handkerchief around the wound, though. He must have done something to make her angry. But even so, that German was a handsome old gentleman."

Yōzō listened in silence. (17:136–37)

This is the other face of Sayoko: out of control, self-destructive, exploding with rage. In her confession that she is thirty-three, one realizes how fully she is aware, despite her beauty and financial resources, that fifteen or sixteen years spent in the demimonde is a sad, corrupt way to have wasted a life. Yet she is also mature enough to know that she has no choice but to continue as she has. There is something moving about the way she uses her belief in Buddhism and popular customs to regain control:

Sayoko learned from her indiscretion and stopped drinking alcohol altogether. Not only that, she gave up eating meat and chicken as well. She also abstained from drinking tea. Perhaps she was merely following a superstitious custom popular among women of the demimonde, or perhaps it was motivated by a deeper desire for atonement, but Yōzō could only conclude that this sudden abstinence by Sayoko, who represented something newer than the traditional demimonde and something older than the "modern girl," meant that she had shut and locked the entrance to the depths of her heart. (17:145)

As Yōko becomes the personification of the modern girl, she loses the capacity for this kind of self-discipline, and, in part, this is due to the class determinations of her childhood. Feminism is not Yōko's only disguise. She is also a full-fledged member of the provincial elite. She was born and educated to deal with servants and others who do not know their proper places. In the following, Yōzō has accompanied Yōko on a trip to her hometown in Akita, where she meets her former maid, the present wife of her ex-husband Matsukawa, the legal guardian of Yōko's children:

> Yōko had a slight fever and looked drawn, but when it came to her children, she turned as ferocious as a cat protecting her kittens, and she rushed out of the room to confront Matsukawa's new wife.
>
> Certain there would be a scene, Yōzō strained to hear; Yōko's resounding, dramatic voice, as usual blazing away like a flame put to oiled paper, drifted in on the wind, but her words were disconnected, and he could only make out the gist of what was being said. The stepmother of her children had once been Yōko's trusted personal maid, and so, apparently, Yōko had nothing but contempt for her; it was not as if she were talking over a matter with Matsukawa's new wife but as if she were still the mistress scolding her servant; and since there was not the slightest trace of malice or rebellion in the stepmother's attitude— she merely sat meekly with downcast eyes—there was no possibility that a real fight would occur; the two young men the stepmother had brought with her simply laughed off Yōko's insults with the observation, "She's at it again!" Yōko's Tokyo dialect, which she used so fluently in the city, in conversations often sounding like a character from a romantic novel, had given way to an utterly rural dialect, and vulgar language streamed from her mouth, one string of curses leading to another of even greater intensity. Yōzō heard a scraping sound and turned to see several faces peering over the wooden fence in the shade of a leafy pomegranate tree. Nothing obstructed the neighbors' view of Yōzō. He left the room and went to see what had happened to Yōko. Perched on one knee, she was holding forth as though the poor woman in front of her were still her domestic.
>
> "I suppose you think Matsukawa loves you. He couldn't possibly love a bitch like you! If I wave my little finger, he'll come crawling back to me. I'll show you how it's done one of these days." (17:86–87)

Only a woman with complete confidence in her social superiority would use such harsh language in scolding an inferior. The other guise of the feminist, or modern woman, then is the "tyrant" (17:224). When Yōko feels she has been slighted by the elderly writer Yōzō, she displays nothing but contempt for him. Yōko bitterly resents Yōzō for having spoken about her in disparaging terms to a newspaper reporter, and she takes her revenge as follows:

Though it was a little early for autumn colors, one afternoon Yōzō and Yōko paid an ambling visit to the Park of the Hundred Flowers in the Mukōjima district, and after contributing haiku to the hundreds of selections hung there by previous generations of poets, they went for something to eat at the nearby Torikane. This famous establishment was older than Yōzō and had been built in a comfortable, old-fashioned design with gardens and corridors arranged to protect the privacy of guests; it was an inn that could have been from a kabuki play of the Edo period. They had stayed there once before on an autumn night when the moon shone brightly down on the nearby Sumida River, and Yōko, who loved expanses of water, had urged him to hire a car for a drive along the bank of the river to the Shirahige Bridge; on that occasion, in their dim room with its low, dark, sooty ceiling, a space invoking the ghosts and monsters of the traditional Japanese theater, Yōko had let her long, black hair down to cover her face, and, in imitation of the vengeful spirit of a wronged, dead woman, loomed over Yōzō as he lay in his bed. But this time, Yōko had experienced too much suffering over her two failed love affairs, and Yōzō as well had been forced to drink bitter dregs—there had been too many hurtful words exchanged between them—for a reconciliation and merging of moods in play to be possible.

They dined on the specialties of the inn—its famous shellfish soup, sweet potatoes boiled in soy sauce, the choicest white meat of chicken eaten raw— and, as Yōko sipped the rice wine she almost never touched, her eyes reddening slightly, her irrepressible resentment came out in asides during the otherwise respectful conversation, but finally she began a stinging criticism of the remarks he had made to the journalist, and he could only respond to her complaints with self-serving excuses.

After they had taken a bath together, Yōzō lay down in the gloomy room for a brief rest, but he soon felt Yōko leaning over him, and there was something in her eyes that said she wasn't joking as she wrapped a thin rope around his neck.

"Murder is too good for you, but I may kill you anyway," she said as she slowly tightened the rope.

Yōzō stared steadily up into her face, and his expression became a contortion of a grimace and a smile.

"You have my permission. Kill me if you must!"

Yōko sat on his chest as if riding a horse, and she alternately loosened and tightened the rope even harder. At last it became difficult to breathe, and he tried to snatch the rope from her. A brief struggle, half in earnest, half in play, ensued, but she finally sprang off of him and let go of the rope. He sat up and felt the swollen skin around his windpipe. There was a little pain at his touch and when he swallowed.

In Yōko's eyes, there was a despicable, sly old man sitting in front of her, somewhat shamefully rubbing his neck. (17:233–34)

Kozue Yōko, in almost every situation, is convinced of her own social superiority. The reader may like and admire Sayoko more, but one knows that she, like Omasu, Ogin, Oshima, and the other remarkable women Shūsei portrayed, will get by. One is never certain that Yōko will survive the loss of her social position. By the end of the novel, she is "sleepwalking through life" (17:259), and she has been terribly victimized by fictions: by her romantic aspiration to become an author, by Yōzō's stern realism, and by a host of social trends—Marxism, modernism, feminism—which are little more than transient fashions. Yōko's pride, social background, addiction to romance, and fall into prostitution are the stuff of tragedy.

The Temperament of the Novelist

Of course, Inamura Yōzō, the aging author, is also in disguise: "Yōzō could not escape appearing as a costumed character in the drama" (17:20–21). This signifies that Yōzō is as manipulative and calculating as any other character in the work. There is almost no self-justification in Shūsei's portrayal of Yōzō. Yōzō uses Yōko sexually to reinvigorate himself. But this motivation is a disguise for his desire to use her economically, in terms of both the income he earns from writing about her and his helping her spend money she obtains from other sources. This, in turn, is a disguise for Yōzō's use of Yōko to keep up with new literary and cultural trends, a disguise enabling Yōzō to explore the city anew in the company of Yōko or in search of her.

When Yōzō suddenly lost his wife, Kayoko, he felt "as if a pillar upon which he had long leaned had collapsed," or as if "his left arm had been wrenched from him," and yet, at the same time, he felt he had "regained the freedom of his youth" (17:14). Through sexual relations with Yōko, Yōzō hopes to find salvation from the stale, boring realities of everyday "Japanese" existence (including the so-called *cha-no-ma shō-setsu,* "fiction of ordinary life") and achieve rejuvenescence:

For the first time, youth seemed to bloom in the inadequate vessel of Yōzō's desiccated heart and in his tired, failing flesh; as he remembered the night before with Yōko, a vague, unconscious passion, which had been in long winter hibernation, awakened within him, and with it came an almost unbearable loneliness driving him to an agony of intense, cruel desire. The soft skin of her glowing white hand, her thin, pouting lower lip, the color and shape of the petal of a red flower, her beautiful eyes like black diamonds framed by gracefully arching eyebrows, the infernal coquetry of the curve from the corner of her mouth to her cheek—her features flowed licentiously into his dry veins, while her youthful spirit ate its way into his heart. Yōzō even came to curse his long, unfortunate life without her. (17:22)

In Yōko's company, Yōzō's life becomes a search for pleasure, a succession of trips to fashionable hotels, inns, Western-style restaurants, the movies, kabuki plays, concerts of classical music, and fashionable bars serving cocktails. From the start of the affair, the city naturally divides itself into modern spaces, where Yōko is in her element, and traditional spaces, in which Yōzō is comfortable. The Ginza is Yōko's territory, and at first Yōzō does not feel at home there: "For twenty or thirty years, Yōzō had been afflicted by a chronic nervous disorder, and when he went out, the noise and racket of the streets resonated in his ears as clamor from the depths of hell; on the infrequent occasions he paid visits to the Ginza, all of the excitement only made him dizzy" (17:54). However, his affair with Yōko forces Yōzō to venture into unexplored modern territory because the more traditional neighborhood around his house in Morikawa rejects Yōko:

In the neighborhood where Yōzō and his wife often took evening walks, the merchants in the shops at which Kayoko frequently stopped to buy Yōzō's bread and the contents of her children's lunch boxes or footwear or cooking and eating utensils usually paid their respects by bowing to her as she passed by, but when he took Yōko with him to buy footwear or tofu, the shopkeepers reacted unpleasantly. Yōzō found it difficult to continue frequenting the shops around his house. When Yōko and he went out for their walk, they almost invariably passed through the old neighborhood to the intersection and then turned left, walking along the street that was crowded with the bookshops they often paused to peer into. At times, they continued their walk down to the bottom of the hill and did their shopping at the department store there or at the prosperous, crowded food stalls that narrowed the once broad avenue. On rare occasions, when they were so inclined, they paid for admission to the local vaudeville theater. Far more often, almost every time the movie billing changed, they would take the tram to the Cinema Palace, but whenever Yōko and he entered the cafe in the theater, students stared brazenly at them, and at times he heard Yōko's name being whispered, so he felt constrained from talking. Together they saw such silent films as *Light in the Darkness* and *Resurrection*. She also read a great many translated novels, and, for Yōzō, who found reading tiresome, a particularly interesting part of his daily routine was listening to her highly colored explications of the plots of these works, performed with her usual verbal fluency. (17:55)

These activities represent the healthier aspects of the modernism that flourished in the years of reconstruction after the Great Kantō Earthquake. Now Yōzō seldom attends the traditional Japanese vaudeville, which his wife enjoyed, and, with Yōko, he is exposed to and develops a taste for culturally uplifting pursuits. In addition to department stores, imported movies, and new novels, Yōzō learns to appreciate classical music performed by famous European musicians, who come to Japan because of the impoverishment of Europe after World War I. Yōko introduces Yōzō to Colette and Proust. Under Yōko's influence, he buys the latest recordings for his new record player. It is also through Yōko that Yōzō experiences the "cheap modernism" of the urban masses. In pursuit of Yōko, who has fled from his house after one of their fights in the summer of 1926, Yōzō encounters the rather disconcerting changes that have transformed the Tokyo of his youth:

The next morning, following up on the same impulse of the previous evening, Yōzō visited boardinghouses in the Surugadai district on the chance that he might find Yōko.

He remembered a friend who years before had pursued his unfaithful wife and had feverishly investigated the registers of every inn in the Nikkō region until he discovered the name of his wife's lover, and he then tracked the couple down in their room; at the time, Yōzō had been appalled by the love-crazed antics of his friend, but now he was in no position to laugh. Given his present situation, he felt capable of performing similar acts of foolishness.

On the first narrow side street he came to, he discovered several small boardinghouses, and he inquired at them about Yōko. It was the time of morning when the maids were tying up their sleeves to do the cleaning. At one house, he felt he was being viewed as a police detective. Nests of Chinese students were scattered through that squalid back street.

He soon gave up and moved on, emerging from that neighborhood onto a broad street, where he inquired at two inns and a large Western-style apartment house: it was no use. He wandered aimlessly until he came to a broad avenue where the tram ran, close to the Ogawa station, and he followed it in the direction of the Jinbō district. Usually, when he passed through this part of the city, he was oblivious to his surroundings, but today, he paid close attention, and he seemed to catch the scent of his carefree youth spent in boardinghouses and the mood of this neighborhood when he used to walk its streets every evening. Depressed and alone in his room by the canal, he would invite an artist friend who lived nearby, and together they would go to eat pineapple or drink cocoa at one of the first, what might be called, cafes, a strange mixture of a milk hall and a fruit parlor. One night he went to hear the famous raconteur Enzō, who kept up a rapid-fire narration of traditional comic stories. As he was listening, Yōzō suffered a severe attack of gastric atony.

"How many years ago was that?" he wondered.

He turned.

Walking up the bustling, crowded street of shops in the Jinbō district, Yōzō, on an impulse, suddenly entered a narrow alley by the side of a huge bookstore. He was astonished by the transformation in the street that lay before him at the back of the building. The entertainment district he had known in his youth had been replaced by two long expanses of cheap bars and cafes. Shielding his eyes from the sun, he could see in the distance, on the edge of the jumble, a large red and white flag bearing the words "Inn of Spring Light." He climbed the stone steps of the shabbily constructed barracklike structure and peered inside the entrance. There was Yōko's distinctive hairstyle. She sat primly, dressed in a serge kimono in front of an open fusuma in the first room off the back of the stairs. Relieved, he called to her. She was startled and blushed. (17:62–63)

Yōzō's pursuit of the "modern girl" has opened his eyes to the significance of changing urban topology. Despite the minimal reference to place-names, this passage is very geographically specific. With the help of a 1946 map of Tokyo, one can trace Yōzō's walk on a 1986 map. He descends the present-day Hongō-dōri in the neighborhood of Ochanomizu, turns right at Ogawa onto what is now called Yasukuni-dōri, proceeds along the street until remembrance causes him to change direction and walk north, probably up the present-day Hakusan-dōri, before he takes a left into the alley and heads west to his ultimate destination, the inn (in reality the Kōeikan) located close to Senshō Daigaku in the tenth block of the Jinbō district of the Kanda ward. The main arteries of public transportation—the broad avenues and tramlines—remain unchanged in Yōzō's memory of the Meiji period, in the late Taishō period, and even today in the 1990s. Off the principal thoroughfares, down the alleyways and back streets, Yōzō experiences the shock of dislocation between past and present. In the reconstruction of large expanses of Tokyo destroyed in the earthquake of 1923, "cheap modernism" has come to prevail, and a combination of instinct and memory of a time before he was burdened with the responsibility of a family guides Yōzō to Yōko. The insubstantial, flimsy construction of the Inn of Spring Light, where the well-known socialist Diet member Yamamoto Senji was assassinated in 1929, recalls Yōko's lamp, which appears on several occasions as a symbol of cheap modernism: "the mood of a foreign whorehouse created by Yōko's French lampstand, with two light bulbs forming the breasts of a woman and a lampshade of heavily embroidered silk" (17:262–63).[48]

Vulgar fashion is cheap in the sense of being artificial and insubstantial but is very expensive both economically and in the toll it takes on normal, "Japanese" life. In the following, from the early autumn of 1926, Yōko is living with Yōzō and is recovering from a failed surgical operation to cure her hemorrhoid problem:

Sometimes Yōzō slept under a narrow, constricting mosquito net with his children in the small back room. He did not feel at ease in his own house. Yōko was supposed to be managing the household, but the direct supervision of children and maids was left to him. She often looked on those who entered her room as intruders. There was no reason to expect that relations between the two families would be harmonious. He would tend to become disgruntled and come rushing out of the children's room. His study did not calm him. Once, without warning, he even slapped Yōko across her white cheek as she was lying down under her mosquito netting. She merely gaped at him in appalled disbelief.

On other occasions, Yōzō returned to find that she had gone out, and either the maids had been left alone in the house or all of the entrances were locked.

At about that time, Yōzō began to accompany Yōko on her shopping trips. They would hire a car and set off for the Ginza or Kanda with Yōko seated on Yōzō's lap. She would purchase a grandfather clock or have a new ring made or buy cosmetics. They got into the habit of eating out, and they would frequently take a taxi to first-rate restaurants. One reason was that Yōzō's kitchen, left in the charge of two maids, was in terrible disorder. Vegetables bought in too great a quantity were rotting under the sink, perfectly usable tableware had been thrown away and overpriced inferior-quality crockery bought in its place, deep-sea fish was boiled in a soy sauce syrup so sweet Yōzō found it inedible, and the pickled vegetables fermenting in a bucket had begun to smell like a sewage ditch. On top of all this, things kept disappearing, and the sums he handed over for household expenses were used for other purposes. But at a time when maids were in scarce supply, Yōzō's only recourse was to ignore the incompetence and petty crimes.

Yōzō, however, did not always pay the bill at the restaurants. More often than not, Yōko took her purse out and announced with a flourish that she would pay. She seemed to have an inexhaustible source of wealth.

Cool breezes came at last. Yōko moved to the second floor of a house directly across from Yōzō's. She began work on a serialized novel for a women's magazine, a commission she had obtained with his help, but the hemorrhoidal pain she had been relieved of returned. The gynecological surgeon's scalpel had not cut far enough. Yōzō considered introducing her to a well-known doctor, but after the coarse treatments she had received in the provinces, she had had enough of orthodox medicine.

"I'd rather go for treatments at a hot spring," she declared one day. "What do you think of Yugawara hot spring?"

"I don't know," he replied.

"I have money. It won't inconvenience you. Four hundred yen should be enough for the two of us for two weeks, don't you think?"

Yōzō gathered a sum of money, and they boarded the train in the afternoon of the next day. (17:102–4)

The amount of labor necessary in the 1920s to keep a respectable household functioning normally was beyond the capacity of a single woman, and certainly Yōko was not interested in the job. Yōzō must make a choice. If he continues to eat out, stay at hotels, and travel to resorts, his normal living standard and his family life will disintegrate. If he expends the effort and money necessary to maintain his house, he will lose Yōko. A part of Yōzō is fascinated by Yōko and the new culture she represents, but another part of him finds the expense, extravagance, and ostentation of this new culture morally offensive. Shortly after Yōzō gives his critical comments about Yōko to a journalist in the spring of 1927, his infatuation turns into a moral allergic reaction against the extravagance she symbolizes:

If Yōzō was not a novelist—that is to say, if it was not his professional inclination to habitually explore human relationships and to maintain a more than passing interest in the events of society, if he were a normal person who valued first and foremost an orderly, ordinary life—he probably would not have worked so tenaciously to keep informed concerning the developments of the affair between Yōko and her young lover, Sonoda, and while he had foreseen that his love affair with Yōko would reach a denouement about then, and he knew that this was a good time in terms of his image to return to his own life, and while he had been able to bring 80 percent of his feelings for her under control, in the end he could not quite free himself from her lingering scent, a faint love that remained, and this, as well, incited his curiosity in tracking her in her pursuit of one new lover after another. At one point, he locked his heart, and liberated from his daily, boring obsession, he would go out into the garden and care for the flowers or cut down the weeds or read a book, but as he was enjoying these leisurely pursuits, he was often assaulted by the impotent sentimentality of a man who had been left alone: memories of his dead wife and, then, transcending these in the depths of his mind, vague, ghostly images of his beloved daughter and the circumstances of her death brought melodramatic tears. Sometimes, at night in his bed, pressure coming to his chest, he would wake up remembering his beloved daughter and her death, and he would dissolve into sick tears, which flowed down his cheeks and formed little rivers on the pillow. Drowning in his own weakness, he next longed for forgiveness from his dead mother, whom he had ignored to the end. As for his wife, he felt he had loved her fully while she was living, and he need not feel guilt now.

Yōzō often spread his bedding and dozed in the afternoon, but he was disturbed that day by his son's friend Gondō, who arrived in a state of great indignation over the fact that Yōko was betraying Yōzō, and he accepted the young man's offer to arrange a meeting, but after he had passed the settlement money over to her at the famous restaurant at Ueno, specializing in skewered chicken, he felt that she had become quite distant, and while he was suddenly freed from a malevolent spirit which had possessed him, he also felt a great emptiness. He wondered if he could pray for Yōko's happiness in marriage, and he realized that secretly he was hoping that her personality would not allow her to adjust to a normal, serious household, that her licentious passion might impel her into a new affair but that it would soon break up; and as he came to understand that even if he were to meet her again, he could never feel for her as he had before, a kind of reactionary hatred chilled his entire body, and, at the same time, he found forming within himself the diabolically decadent impulse to take revenge by playing with her for as long as he could. (17:204–5)

This is a crucial point in the novel when the deep structure of the everyday reasserts itself through the memory of dead women: the wife, daughter, and mother, who represent the feminine quotidian, the collectivity of decent, hardworking women. Yōzō's revenge is their revenge. From the perspective of "Japan," Yōko's conspicuous consumption is immoral because it is such a waste of resources. Yōzō the author is more than capable of articulating this Japanese point of view, and his talent as a realistic writer frightens Yōko:

Yōzō agreed to Yōko's persistent demand that he put a promise in writing. It was not a vow to the gods of eternal love or of marriage or something erotic like that, but a promise that he would never again portray her in his literature. "If I write about you, Kozue Yōko, in any form, I will pay, without complaint, an indemnity of one thousand yen."

In a coarse hand, Yōzō hurriedly wrote on manuscript paper exactly what she told him to write.

"Is this what you want?"

"Thank you."

Yōko appeared to find some peace of mind in that child prank of a contract, and the shadow of a smile replaced the bitter, hard expression on her face as she put the piece of paper in her handbag, but her fears concerning what and when he might write about her were not altogether allayed. Ever since the appearance of the newspaper article, she had perceived that his was a multilayered character. While she didn't see him as a villain, she was no longer certain that he was her kind protector. She had been shocked by his blind passion, but always in his love-crazed infatuation, which now was an annoyance to her and which she feared might bring her unhappiness, there was in the depths of his mind something; it was different from playing at love or an icy critical stance, call it the repressed temperament of the novelist, which she had vaguely begun to discern. Yōzō was just an ordinary person, and he knew nothing of the tricks or logic of love, and yet his sheer tenacity of will had pulled her to him time and again— that there would be a by-product created from his experience was already part of the equation. Yōko invariably looked at reality through a beautiful, thin veil, and her vision of herself was always a reflection of the flames of longing and admiration for her in the eyes of men. When she discovered that beneath his cold surface she had ignited the flames of passion, be that passion mere lust, be it calculated, or be it somewhat sincere, she experienced a secret, ticklish elation at what she had done to an unfortunate, elderly novelist, who had previously closed himself up in his small, cramped house, who knew only one woman, her hair done in the traditional matronly style, and who was coldly indifferent to the love scandals that delighted the public—that his passion should return to take vengeance on her was something she didn't expect.

Yōzō felt somewhat unpleasant about having been forced to write that silly contract. Written promise or no, if he wanted to write about something, he'd write about it—that was purely a matter of his own free will—but the feeling that his written word was of no more significance than a scrap of wastepaper depressed his occupational state of mind. Even though her action was tentative and informal and was done on the spur of the moment, still, he didn't consider her attempt to bind him by threat of payment to be cute.

Their temporary reconciliation was soon disrupted over a slight matter, and the two of them were once again fighting like monkey and dog. Rumiko started crying and came over and began beating Yōzō with her tiny fists.

Scooping up the odds and ends scattered on his desk, Yōzō stuffed them into his portfolio and rushed out of the house. In straw sandals, he walked in the rain to the nearby ricksha station.

After he had boarded the train, he remembered how cruel he had been during their fierce battle. He recalled how she dragged Rumiko off of him, hugged the child to her breast, and exclaimed in torment, "The insects of passion are devouring my body!"

Tears were streaming down her cheeks. (17:235–37)

One comes to this novel, which is clearly based on incidents Shūsei experienced in real life, expecting to discover what Shūsei actually felt about Yamada Junko, and instead, in long, complicated sentences which seem to represent a stream of consciousness, which force the reader to pay close attention or lose the thread of narrative continuity, one finds this strangely philosophical meditation on fiction. In the context of the novel, languages which express the certainty of the law, of contract, of authority, or of "genuine feelings" are mere superstitions.

Shūsei was chronicling the end of an intellectual era, which Kozue Yōko personified. As he was writing *Kasō jinbutsu,* overt discussion of Marxism had been proscribed by censors and the educational bureaucracy, the dance halls he frequented were being shut down by the police, and women with short hair and dressed in Western-style clothing were becoming more and more the objects of public ridicule. Shūsei vocally opposed this narrow-mindedness. As president of the League of Academic and Artistic Freedom (Gakugei Jiyū Dōmei), perhaps the only organized opposition to the stricter censorship of the early 1930s, and in several essays, Shūsei criticized what he and other intellectuals perceived to be fascism.[49] And yet if one comes to *Kasō jinbutsu* with the expectation of finding "literary opposition to fascism," one will be disappointed. On the contrary, through Shūsei's alter ego, Yōzō, one understands that the progressive intelligentsia, who claimed to represent the future, were radically out of touch with the realities of Japanese society in the 1920s. As Yōko loses contact with "Japan," she is devoured by the "insects of passion." Yōzō reacts against the vanity of Yōko's modernism and is saved by the ghosts of "decent" women from his past.

Yamada Junko suffered a great deal of ridicule during her life, and the critical consensus is that she enjoyed pretending to be a famous author but that she had little talent for writing.[50] Shūsei's Kozue Yōko, however, is certainly not a ridiculous figure. Perhaps Shūsei took Yamada Junko seriously because he recognized in her many of the aspirations of her generation. One wonders if he imagined to what extent many aspects of her cheap modernism would come to dominate Japan's future cities, though of course young women today need not turn to semi-prostitution to pay for their cosmetics, Western-style clothing, rent, or trips to hot springs. Indeed, the final urban space Yōko occupies in the novel is the prototype of the dwellings of the vast majority of independent young women in Japanese cities today:

Her apartment was in the first apartment building put up in the third block of the main avenue of Hongō in the years immediately following the Great Kantō Earthquake. The city as a whole was still on the road to reconstruction, but at least the fronts of the buildings facing the major thoroughfares had been, by and large, rebuilt in a new manner. The apartment building was sturdily constructed of reinforced concrete, there was a pharmacy on the ground floor, and though the building occupied only a narrow expanse of land, the rooms on the fourth floor had balconies, which provided wonderful views; the second and third floors each contained four or five apartments with tatami, tokonoma, traditional shelving, and nicely crafted latticework. A certain distinguished educator's son and the owner of the pharmacy had formed a partnership and had built the apartment building with an investment of ten thousand yen. Yōko contracted for a fourth-floor apartment with approximately one hundred and fifty square feet of space and gas but not water. At night, on parting the curtains and opening the large window, covered with a heavy metal screen, the blue and red characters of the department store's neon sign were visible, glowing alone in the midair darkness, and directly below were the lights from the numerous cafes that had been encroaching into that backstreet for some years. When the window was open, one could hear the record players blaring from the cafes below, but the noise from the main street in front didn't reach her apartment, and since voices from the neighboring apartments were seldom heard, her room was generally as silent as if she had been confined to the tower of a castle.

"I'm writing again. I'd like you to look at it when it's finished. I'm really revving up the horsepower on this one."

Yōko had hinted before that she was working on a project, and she wanted to close herself up in the apartment to complete it. She intended to submit her novel to the literary competition held by the newspaper *Kokumin Shinbun* in the hope that it would allow her to revive her failing literary career. She was putting her life's blood into the work.

Knocked down and abandoned by Kiyokawa, she was struggling to regain her feet, and Yōzō couldn't bring himself to ignore her plea for help. He paid the three months' rent required as a security deposit, acted as her guarantor, and visited her almost every day. (17:296–97)

Yōzō is the judge of the competition to which Yōko submits her novel, and, in the end, his disguise as a novelist with artistic integrity takes priority over his role as her friend and teacher. He awards her novel the second-place prize, which means it will remain unpublished. A week or so later he visits her apartment and discovers that she has moved away. Perhaps the ultimate irony of this great novel is that for a few years in the late twenties, Kozue Yōko, the most pitiable and tragic of Shūsei's heroines, really did represent the future. As for Yamada Junko, in the postwar period she became an evangelist for Buddhism and died of cancer in 1961.[51]

6
Social Realism

[A]t about the time of the Russo-Japanese War, the nation's citizens entered a whole new stage of self-awareness, and the new literary trends dominated as a surging tide. It was not limited to naturalism, for which Tayama Katai and others propagandized so passionately; by reacting critically to naturalism, other writers as well helped to create the new literature. I do not know whether the naturalism of Tayama Katai and the others was truly grounded in French naturalism, but whether it was or not, as realism it represented enormous progress in the way people were perceived and portrayed when compared to the so-called *shajitsu* form of realism which preceded it. . . . It was during this period that the Japanese people, who for generations had been kept subservient, cast off their fetters and awakened to their humanity. . . .

Since naturalism, various "isms" have arisen in the Japanese literary world. . . . However, upon reflection, just beneath the surface of this literature which is ostensibly based on foreign models, one discovers that works written by Japanese people are Japanese literature; it couldn't be any other way, and it shouldn't be.

—Tokuda Shūsei, preface to *Meiji bungaku sakka ron*
(Discourse on the Novelists of the Meiji Period)

During the years from 1935 through 1941, Shūsei was respected, even venerated, by a broad spectrum of the literary world as Japan's most important novelist.[1] This was true for four closely related reasons:

1. Shūsei was one of the few active professional writers who had survived repeated calls in the modern period for a genuine Japanese realism: the *shajitsu* movement of the 1880s, Kitamura Tōkoku's Christian romanticism in the 1890s, the *shaseibun* movement at the turn of the century, Zolaism in the first years of the twentieth century, naturalism immediately after the Russo-Japanese War, the more personal, sincere realism called for by writers associated with the *Shirakaba* group, and social realism in the 1920s. Shūsei's survival as a realistic novelist portraying his contemporary society gave him the authority to define naturalism, Japan's most important literary movement.

2. Shūsei was famous for his generosity to younger writers, in the

181

manner of Ozaki Kōyō but without the paternalism. He thus carried on a tradition of mutual aid and support among writers that had existed from at least the middle of the Meiji period. In part out of a sense of gratitude to Shūsei, young writers, Shūsei's "disciples," gathered around to support their "teacher" a year after the death of Tokuda Hama. This school or coterie which formed around Shūsei took on a life of its own, serving as a rallying point for a kind of cosmopolitanism in the face of the rise of the dogmatic literary Left.[2]

3. After the suppression of the orthodox Left in the early thirties, progressive writers, critics, and literary theorists realized Shūsei's importance because they discovered that for years he had been writing the type of fiction they were now advocating.

4. From 1935 on, Shūsei ceased producing popular fiction and devoted himself to serious writing. In terms of the quantity and quality of the serious fiction he produced, the seven years from 1935 to 1941 are second in importance in Shūsei's career only to the period from 1908 to 1915.

These four points will be dealt with in more detail below before proceeding to a discussion of Shūsei's last major novel, *Shukuzu* (A Microcosm, 1941).

As was argued in previous chapters of this study, Shūsei was not one of the propagandists of naturalism, and during the period in his career when he came to his unique brand of realism in the novel (the years from 1908 to 1911, which saw the creation of *Arajotai, Ashiato,* and *Kabi*), he was supported, by and large, by Takahama Kyoshi and Natsume Sōseki, literary figures opposed to naturalism. In later statements such as "Shinkyō kara kyakukan e" (From Objectivity to Subjectivity, 1926) and "Bungei zakkan: Masamune-shi e onegai" (Thoughts on the Literary Arts: A request of Masamune Hakuchō, 1934), Shūsei maintained a posture of skepticism, as he had during the height of naturalism, concerning the validity of the subjectivity/objectivity opposition essential to naturalism, and he particularly objected to the use of these terms by Masamune Hakuchō, the most influential remaining critic associated with "nihilistic" naturalism.[3]

Nonetheless, as the years passed and Shūsei became more and more identified in the public mind with naturalism, he was placed in the enviable position of being able to define this most important literary movement from the detached perspective of a writer who had not taken part in the emotional, divisive debate in the years immediately following the Russo-Japanese War. Shūsei came to identify himself wholeheartedly with naturalism some twenty years after the movement had died.

What did Shūsei mean by his strange 1934 expression "the grandeur of naturalism?"[4] Shūsei defined naturalism as an antiauthoritarian, nationalistic movement which discovered, for the first time, the humanity of common characters. He felt that the primary defect in the Japanese literary tradition was its tendency toward abstraction, either the artificial, mannered pose of the wandering poet or the use of literary characters as stand-ins for concepts. Naturalism was an attempt to bring literature down to a human scale, and this meant a rejection of literary models of the past. Shūsei did not care to speculate on how much foreign literature influenced Japanese naturalism, but in the case of his own work, he was convinced that a true Japanese realism, based as it was in form and content on the incorporation of extraliterary dialects into narrative, had to differ fundamentally from foreign models.

According to Shūsei, Japanese naturalism was born of Japanese nationalism. And yet this nationalism was profoundly antiauthoritarian, for the project of the realist was to wrench the concept of "the Japanese masses" away from the state and give it concrete life in a realm where political slogans had no currency. Shūsei may not have been as radical as his old friend Kiryū Yūyū, in whose company he had first traveled to Tokyo in 1892, and who, in 1941, on the verge of death, wrote as follows: "I welcome the fact that I will soon disappear from the face of this earth, which is degenerating into a hell occupied by beasts. My only regret is that I won't be here to witness the vast disarmament of the Japanese military after the war."[5] Shūsei was not an expert on Japanese politics and the military, as was Kiryū, and he undoubtedly hoped for Japan's victory in war, but he shared with his boyhood friend a profound distrust of those in positions of official authority. In 1942, addressing the war effort, he wrote, "What we must never forget or ignore is the individual human being. All of us must live first and foremost as human beings."[6] The "grandeur of naturalism" was a realistic, native humanism, and the fact that Shūsei personified this tradition was one of the reasons he was so respected late in his life.

In 1927, one year to the day after the death of Shūsei's wife, Hama, a group of Shūsei's "disciples" formed a club called the Society of the Second (Futsuka-kai), which met regularly on the second day of each month to commemorate Hama's death and to console Shūsei. Members included Uno Chiyo, Ozaki Shirō, Okada Saburō, Ono Michiko, Kano Sakujirō, Kamitsukasa Shōken, Kawasaki Chōtaro, Kitami Shiho, Sata Ineko, Kubokawa Tsurujirō, Koganei Kimiko, Kodera Kikuko, Sakakiyama Jun, Narasaki Tsutomu, Mitsugi Teiko, Morita Tama, Yasunari Jirō, Yoshiya Nobuko, Yamada Junko, Nakamura Murao, Murō Saisei, and Chikamatsu Shūkō. Though not a member of this coterie, Kasai Zenzō was another well-known disciple of Shūsei. This group eventually evolved into the Arakure Society, with the following additional membership: Abe Tomoji, Ibuse Masuji, Tanabe Moichi, Tokuda Kazuho, Nakamura Murao, Narasaki Tsutomu, Noguchi Fujio, Funabashi Seiichi, and Mikami Hidekichi. With the financial backing of Tanabe Moichi, the founder of the famous bookstore Kinokuniya, the Arakure Society published a monthly literary journal entitled *Arakure*.[7]

Tokuda Shūsei had become an institution representing generosity in the literary world, but he did not behave like an institution. Ozaki Shirō recalls Shūsei's circumstances as follows:

> According to popular opinion, it was and is very important whether a novelist, in the public eye, lives a first-class life or a second-class life. Shūsei didn't care in the least about such distinctions. Among the eminent novelists of the day, Shūsei would have been the most satisfied with a mere second-class lifestyle. He didn't care if he lived like a second-rate writer, but in his writing he could only be first-rate. Shūsei did not adopt a single pose to identify himself in the public mind as a first-rate literary figure, and yet he was a man who was fated to be a first-rate novelist.[8]

So many younger writers—Kawabata Yasunari, Noguchi Fujio, Funabashi Seiichi, Hayashi Fumiko, Sata Ineko, Yoshiya Nobuko— remember Shūsei fondly as a major literary figure who lacked any trace of pretension or vanity.[9] Given Shūsei's generosity to young writers, especially women writers, it is not surprising that when he experienced financial difficulty in the early 1930s, the literary world organized and came to his aid.[10]

In 1930, Shūsei met the geisha Kobayashi Masako and was attracted to her. She moved in with Shūsei in 1932. Shūsei probably financed the construction of the apartment in back of his residence in Morikawa-chō with the remnants of his profits from the *enpon* series and with the sale of a former land investment in the Shibuya area. By the summer of 1933, after he had gotten his household back on some kind of firm economic footing, he invested in what would become the Tomita geisha house in the nearby Hakusan pleasure quarter, a business which Kobayashi Masako wanted to run. Shūsei became a semi-permanent resident of this house and helped Masako manage her trade, which of course was based in part on illegal prostitution. Shūsei most certainly knew but did not care that connoisseurs of the demimonde such as

Satomi Ton and Izumi Kyōka looked upon a geisha of Masako's status and working-class background as a third-rate whore; nor did he feel it was demeaning to actually work in the demimonde, become a part of it, and describe it from the inside.[11] As he wrote in 1936, this last phase of his career was a time when he felt at home with the lower classes.

After 1935 or so, Shūsei spent more time in the Hakusan geisha house than he did at home, and young writers seemed to enjoy associating with him in this demimonde setting. Kawabata Yasunari describes how comfortable and at peace Shūsei seemed in that house. Hayashi Fumiko recalls Shūsei keeping the books of the establishment with an abacus and taking messages for the women living there. Toward the end of 1936, Yoshiya Nobuko lent Kobayashi Masako a thousand yen to enable her to remain in business and later forgave half the debt.[12]

Shūsei, then, came to personify not only the literary tradition of Japanese realism but also the spirit of mutual support that was a characteristic of the Japanese literary world from at least the time of Ozaki Kōyō.

The third reason Shūsei was such an important presence on the literary scene in the thirties was that critics and literary theorists finally "caught up" with what Shūsei was doing. After the suppression of the orthodox Left in the early thirties, progressive intellectuals, in line with foreign developments, called for a popular front to oppose what was widely perceived to be the rise of fascism. Young intellectuals who had been imprisoned in the mass arrests of the early thirties and had promised to desist from political activities as a condition for release— anarchists, syndicalists, and unorthodox Marxists—began to rethink what might constitute a progressive literature. The writings of Tosaka Jun were merely one manifestation of this new thinking. As the well-known, orthodox Marxist Nakano Shigeharu would argue in 1937, it was an age for writers to give up their attempts to delineate "ideas" or "political movements" and instead turn to "the description of everyday scenes from the life of the masses." Or again, "It is undeniable that there are ideas in literary descriptions that have abandoned ideas."[13] This, of course, was exactly what Shūsei had been doing since the Meiji period, when he abandoned melodramatic concepts about the lower classes.

In opposition to the nationalistic aesthetic of death being formulated by such "new Japanese romantics" as Yasuda Yojūrō, Hayashi Fusao, and Kamei Katsuichirō, a diverse group of former leftists led by Takeda Rintarō and Takami Jun founded the journal *Jinmin Bunko* (People's Library) in 1936. Their theoretical banner was "The Spirit of Prose Literature" (*sanbun seishin*), a phrase which originated in a 1924 debate between Arishima Takeo, who argued that artists who devoted themselves wholly to their art were superior to those who were distracted by the petty matters of life, and Hirotsu Kazuo, who countered that the "spirit of prose literature" was the highest form of art precisely because it was the most common, immediate, and relevant to human existence. By the midthirties, what had been a debate over aesthetics became, for the major participants Takami Jun and Yasuda Yojūrō, politicized: prose narrative open to extraliterary diversity was held to be democratic (and thus, according to Yasuda, unaesthetic), while high poetic art forms were symbols of the nation's beauty (and thus, according to Takami, reactionary). For young progressive intellectuals, Shūsei came to symbolize this "spirit of prose literature."[14]

One cannot help but feel that the state suppression in the late thirties of the first serious efforts by literary theorists associated with social realism to come to terms with Shūsei's work greatly impoverished the critical discourse on modern Japanese literature not only in the thirties but in the postwar period as well.

The primary reason Shūsei was held in such high regard during the last decade of his life was the quality and quantity of his writing. During this period, he created the masterpiece *Kasō jinbutsu*, for which he was awarded the first Kikuchi Kan Literary Prize in 1939. He was serializing his two substantial memoirs *Omoideru mama ni* (As I Remember, 1934–36) and *Hikari o ōte* (In Pursuit of Light, 1938–40). He wrote a number of essays, some of which were collected in the volume *Haizara* (Ashtray, 1938). And throughout this period, he produced fine short stories, many of which were based on his relationship with Kobayashi Masako. One of the collections of these short stories, *Kunshō,* was awarded the Bungei Konwakai (Literary Chat Society) Literary Prize in 1936.[15] "Hitotsu no konomi" (A Certain Preference, 1934), "Hitokuki no hana" (A Single Stemmed Flower, 1934), "Inazuma" (A Flash of Lightning, 1934), "Kanojo-tachi no mi no ue" (The Women's Circumstances, 1935), "Heya kaishō" (Solving the Problem of the Room, 1935), "Futatsu no genshō" (Two Phenomena, 1935), "Chibi no tamashii" (The Child's Soul, 1935), "Razō" (A Nude Figure, 1935), "Ikita bonnō" (Earthly Desires, 1937), and "Noramono" (The Lazy Person, 1937) constitute a subgenre of short story generally called Shōko-mono, following the *on* reading of the character corresponding to the *masa* of Kobayashi Masako's name.[16]

With Japan's rapid industrialization in the Taishō and Shōwa periods, there was a major expansion of the propertyless working classes, and perhaps there was some merit in the criticism by leftist critics that

Shūsei's brand of naturalism ignored this growing reality. On reading Shūsei's "Shashō fufu no shi" (The Death of a Tram Conductor and His Wife, 1924) and comparing it to Nakano Shigeharu's "Kisha no kamataki" (The Stoker on the Locomotive, 1937), one realizes that Shūsei probably did not understand in any depth the indignities and regimentation working-class people were being subjected to in the twenties and thirties.[17] Kobayashi Masako and the so-called Shōko-mono served as the means by which Shūsei explored the new realities of working-class life for those of Masako's generation.

As Shūsei had done so often in the past with other subgenres of the short story, he worked with the Shōko-mono type of story for some years and then transformed it into a major novel: *Shukuzu* (A Microcosm, 1941). This last novel was serialized from June to September of 1941 in the *Miyako Shinbun*. Shūsei ended serialization of the work in midsentence when the Cabinet Information Bureau ordered major revisions. The novel remains unfinished. The state finally managed to suppress the "Japanese naturalism" that Shūsei had devoted almost fifty years of linguistic labor to develop, and it did so at a point when Shūsei was moving in the direction of social realism.[18]

A Microcosm

I have argued elsewhere that the original political impulse of Shūsei's realism was the ideology of the People's Rights movement of the 1880s and that, in time, this concern was translated into a problem of narrative perspective: that of allowing common characters to speak.[19] After almost fifty years of grappling with the incorporation of extraliterary dialects into narrative, Shūsei created perhaps his most complexly structured fiction around the lowest class character he would treat in a serious, full-length novel. With its interweaving of historical perspective, memory, and characterization, *Shukuzu* is a highly hybridized, difficult work. Based on the life of Kobayashi Masako, a prostitute of working-class background and Shūsei's lover, the heroine of *Shukuzu*, Ono Ginko, is Shūsei's final interpretation of Japanese naturalism as the representation of common humanity.

It is extraordinarily simplistic to read this work, as several critics have done, as an autobiographical novel and criticize Shūsei for his failure to condemn prostitution.[20] The male protagonist of *Shukuzu*, Mimura Kinpei, lives with Ono Ginko in her house in the Hakusan pleasure quarter, but he is some fifteen years younger than Shūsei. Kinpei is the product of an elite education, probably the Law Department of Tokyo

Imperial University, and he has married into an extremely wealthy family. *Shukuzu* is basically different from Shūsei's other serious novels in that it truly constitutes a "microcosm" of Japanese society, from the educated bureaucratic elite, to the high bourgeoisie, to powerful politicians, to the utterly impoverished. Shūsei places Ginko in a wider social context to relativize her corruption in the greater corruption of other classes and to demonstrate her worthiness. The novel opens in 1941, in the midst of Japan's total mobilization for war, with Mimura Kinpei and Ono Ginko dining together at the famous French restaurant Fūgetsu on the second floor of the Shiseidō building overlooking the Ginza:

It was the fifth year of the war with China, and while there were shortages in basic materials, and while there were a number of irresponsible businesses that took advantage of the strictly controlled prices and wartime prosperity to fill their shops with inferior products, nonetheless, it is undeniable that the public had unprecedented purchasing power.

When the bread and soup were brought to them, Kinpei, who had been absorbed in smoking and staring out the window, balanced his cigarette on the lip of the ashtray and reached for a slab of butter with the butter knife. The weather was unseasonably cool for the end of May, and the moist air penetrated to his throat; he sneezed as he was breaking off a piece of bread and had to pause to wipe his nose with his napkin.

"We'll be lucky if there isn't a crop failure this year," Kinpei said.

Ginko, who retained a certain simplicity and innocence, was not a person to indulge in needless worry about issues beyond her control. She was an unfortunate woman who had been oppressed since childhood, but though at times she was moody when the weather suddenly changed for the worse, she never became melancholy or depressed. Kinpei was anxious by nature, and when he fell into depression, he discovered within her a means to cheer himself up. One couldn't say that she lacked altogether a darker aspect to her nature, but she didn't regret the past or grieve over the present. She read the newspapers every day, but in contrast to Kinpei, who often denied reality by imagining how incidents would play out, she didn't complain about the difficulties of doing business in a wartime economy totally mobilized and regulated by the state.

"At the end of the Edo period, there was a famine that lasted for two years. They say people wore warm undergarments into June."

With no means to reply, Ginko continued to eat her bread in silence.

Until the waiter brought the next dish, Kinpei gazed at the street below.

Suddenly, three rickshas and a car hurtled into the crowded Ginza traffic in an attempt to cross. Then another ricksha dashed across the broad avenue.

This trickle turned into a wave of vehicles carrying women dressed in brightly colored kimono. As were restaurants, houses of the demimonde were forced by government regulation to open only after 5:00 P.M., and since it was now close to six, there was a flood of rickshas pouring across the street, traffic backing up on all sides in the rush. It was not the first time Kinpei had witnessed such a scene, but it continued for such a long time during his meal that he was struck by a sense of incongruity as he watched from the window.

Since the Meiji period, this area had been the birthplace and focal point of Japan's modernization and new cultural awareness; during Kinpei's boyhood, the main street had already been paved with red bricks, and horses pulled trams down rails laid in the middle. Almost all of the major newspapers had offices in this neighborhood, and all were united in their support of the People's Rights movement. Shops carrying the latest imported fashions from abroad, Western-style accessory shops, tailor shops, Western-style bakeries, and imported food shops were first opened in this pioneering district. The Fūgetsu, where they were eating, was part of a business founded to sell Western-style cosmetics, and, even today, only a small portion of the building was given over to the male waiters dressed in striped cotton jackets hurrying to serve soda water or take orders for the French food businessmen crowded in to eat. It didn't seem so long ago that the Cafe Lion, with its squads of seven beauties, was opened on the corner of Owari-chō to delight the Keiō University boys from wealthy families and young aristocrats. At about that time, the electrified rail system had spread to almost every district of the city, shrinking time and space, the grassy fields of the mansions abandoned by the gentry in the Marunouchi district had been covered by brick buildings, and, with the rapid development of capitalism in the years following the Russo-Japanese War, there was the attempt to remake the face of the city in the manner of European culture. Soon there were places serving delicious coffee and wonderful cakes, and the second floors of old-fashioned bazaars were turned into ultramodern cabarets. At last, department stores began to take customers away from the older, once crowded merchant streets, and modern entertainments and pleasures seemed fated to absorb this city's ever expanding masses.

In the small back streets behind the substantial buildings facing the main street, the world of the traditional demimonde rode on successive waves of changing fashion. When the modernism of the post–World War I period reigned supreme and Western-style women's clothing and the permanent wave became the dominant fashion, the refined customs and manners and the traditional hairstyles of the geisha were in eclipse, and a geisha walking on the Ginza in the daytime even made one feel the humor and shabbiness of an anachronism. The geisha as an institution, however, had been brought up in easy circumstances as the spoiled child of the Meiji period's economic and political elites, and as such its existence was deeply rooted. The geisha was acclaimed even by foreigners, together with Mount Fuji, cherry blossoms, and the kabuki, as the pride of Japan, and now, with the revival of interest in "things Japanese," as the economy boomed under total mobilization for war, geisha were celebrated at the banquets of the upper classes and had regained, at least temporarily, their former prominence. Undoubtedly, Kinpei thought, there was an inevitable relation between the prosperity of the geisha and the present-day structure of society and condition of the nation.

"Looks like there'll be a huge banquet tonight," Kinpei murmured as he stirred his coffee.

Ginko, who could be abrupt at times, said nothing. She was paying attention to what the women, sitting up straight and proud in their rickshas, were wearing, the colors, fabrics, and designs. Ginko was the mistress of her own house of geisha, though her business was in a lower-class neighborhood, and while she didn't care about her own makeup or clothing, she spent relatively large sums on the clothing that her girls wore when they appeared before customers. She didn't have a mind for buying good-quality clothing at cut-rate prices or buying used clothing and dyeing it a new color; rather, she purchased clothing in a businesslike manner in quantity, usually following the clothier's advice as to what to buy. But she wanted to keep informed about the lastest fashions in the demimonde.

"This pleasure quarter is quite distant from its patrons. It isn't in a convenient location," Kinpei muttered as he gazed absently out at the scene, which was taking on the colors of gathering dusk. (17:306–9)

Kinpei's perception of this beautiful spectacle—waves of high-class geisha in their colorful kimono streaming across the broad avenue—is as close as the novel comes to romanticizing the Japanese demimonde, and the scene speaks of the military-industrial complex that has come into existence in the late thirties and early forties, an alliance of the right-wing "new bureaucrats," reform military leaders, and nouveau riche war profiteers, an alliance which can throw a party of extraordinary extravagance and lavishness. There is also something very artificial and corrupt about this rise of cultural "Japanism" that accompanies the growing power of the Right. Kinpei is an old-fashioned Meiji intellectual, and the clarity and precision of his perspective implicitly raise certain questions about social equality. In the first half of the novel, Kinpei's view of the world testifies how living standards have improved substantially for a great many people since the Meiji period. In fact, one might say that a new middle class is coming into shape with employed businessmen, white-collar workers, and their wives now able to eat in restaurants that were once the preserve of the intellectual elite or the wealthy. To some extent, this prosperity has trickled down. Farmers can afford to eat rice instead of corn or millet (17:328), government regulations concerning the treatment of women of the demimonde have improved markedly (17:322), and the radio and its culture of propaganda are widely available (17:334–35). On the other hand, the basic condition that allows the geisha to continue to exist as the "spoiled child" of the conservative economic and political elites has remained unchanged: the hunger and deprivation that provide the demimonde with a constant source of young women. The following is Kinpei's clear, intellectual view of the demimonde from the inside of a lower-class house of geisha that he occupies with Ginko:

For the girls in Ginko's house, the meals provided were grand feasts. Ginko herself had often been hungry when she worked for others, and so she made certain her girls had enough to eat to feel satisfied, even if it was sometimes poor-quality food. When the manager from the local restaurant sent Ginko a gift of food for a favor, Ginko readily shared it with all the girls, no matter how expensive or delicious it was. After a month or so in Ginko's house of wolfing down their meals, even the palest, hungriest-looking children began to eat more slowly, as if they felt assured that food would be regularly available. Some of the girls were malnourished as children living with their parents. In the public schools in the poor neighborhoods in Komatsugawa, Yotsugi, and Sunamura, free bread and butter was distributed to children who didn't bring lunch from home. The schools in the Koishikawa ward didn't have such a compassionate policy. One of the young girls, before she had come to Ginko's as an apprentice geisha, would say at school that she was going home for lunch and then wander the city streets, for there was nothing to eat at home. Another, when she had first arrived, sat before the only bowl of warm rice she had seen for weeks, and she appeared to ascend to heaven on the fragrance. These two girls and two others, who were now learning the arts of the demimonde, had come from families in the Ichikawa area, and so their families generally survived on cheap, leftover rice the soldiers at the nearby military base didn't eat the day before. One girl had so many brothers and sisters that she had to be satisfied with a mere three-fourths of a bowl of rice if her younger sisters were to have any at all. At mealtimes at Ginko's, every girl had similar stories, and when these were told at the table, there were always sympathetic listeners and, quite often, laughter which masked tears. Of course, Ginko had had similar experiences herself. (17:320–21)

Indeed, we later learn that one of Ginko's five younger sisters may have died of an illness brought on by malnutrition (17:507). Kinpei is still enough of a Meiji moralist to feel a certain outrage over the gap between the rising living standards of the middle classes and nouveau riche and the lowest class, whose condition has not changed markedly since the Meiji period.[21] The contrast between the lavish banquet of the elites and the meals of those who serve at the banquet is implicit and shocking, revealing the ultimate bankruptcy of the social welfare legislation which accompanied war mobilization. (And perhaps it was just this contrast between hungry children roaming the streets and upper-level military, political, and bureaucratic figures buying geisha that led censors to order major revisions in the novel.) It is relevant here to examine some popular conceptions of the geisha as an institution in the light of the world of the demimonde portrayed by Shūsei.

"Geisha" was a legal definition of a kind of female entertainer who performed for public and private parties, a definition formed and supported by the economic, political, academic, and military elites during the Meiji period. The Hakusan pleasure quarter was officially established in the late Meiji period with the sponsorship of the powerful politician Hatoyama Kazuo (1856–1911), the Yale-educated father of the postwar prime minister Hatoyama Ichirō.[22] It existed in an area famous for illegal prostitution, an area that was the setting for Higuchi Ichiyō's masterpiece *Nigorie* (The Muddied Inlet, 1895). The quarter consisted of the standard "three trades," the *machiai chaya* (house of assignation), *ryōtei* (restaurant), and *geisha okiya* (house of geisha), each of which was licensed by the state. To purchase a *geisha okiya,* one had to buy the license from its owner. Generally, to become geisha, women and those legally responsible for them signed contracts of indenture, for which they, most often the parents, received a lump sum of capital from the owner of the house. The woman's official registry was kept by the owner until portions of the geisha's earnings retired the debt she owed the house. Most of the income earned by the geisha was taken by the owner, but the percentage that went to paying off the debt varied greatly from one establishment to another. All houses were responsible for meeting the basic needs of their "girls/children" (*ko*), but many got around this provision by charging fees for "extra services," which came to include bedding and clothing. Geisha had to be affiliated with a house to work legally, and even women who were not indentured and owed nothing to the owner had to "borrow a signboard" (*kanban o kariru*) (that is, pay a fee for affiliation with a house) to ply their trade.[23]

The legal conception of the geisha was the one acclaimed, together with "Mount Fuji, cherry blossoms, and the kabuki," as representing the best of Japanese culture: a woman so beautiful, accomplished in the arts, and charming that she would be hired, at high rates per set periods of time, purely for her personal talents and attributes. There were undoubtedly "star" geisha, who were educated in the traditional performing arts from an early age, who at the height of their beauty were sought after in the higher-class demimonde districts of Shinbashi, Kyōbashi, Yanagibashi, Ginza, or Yoshiwara, who later retired to be supported by a wealthy patron or work as a teacher of the traditional arts, and who generally lived up to the chaste image of the ideal geisha. In reality, however, most geisha, especially those of Ginko's class, were involved at some level in illegal prostitution. As we shall see, perhaps as many as one-third of Ginko's engagements were with customers she slept with. Perhaps someone such as Sayama Sayoko in *Kasō jinbutsu,* who was born and bred in demimonde settings and was related by blood (albeit an illegitimate relation) to wellborn, powerful people, could hope to receive training from an early age from expert teachers of the *shamisen* (a stringed instrument), traditional genres of narrative and song, and traditional dance to entertain a discriminating audience. In contrast, plucked out of a shoe factory at the age of fourteen or fifteen, given a hasty course in the *shamisen* and a couple of songs, and sent to perform as a full-fledged geisha at about the age of sixteen, Ginko had to use the promise of sexual relations to attract patrons. It was understood that after calling a geisha of Ginko's status to entertain a number of times and that if the geisha and the customer got along well together, a physical love affair would ensue. This illegal (*kage,* 17:372) prostitution, based as it was on conducting only a few affairs at any given time and retaining some sense of romance, was probably easier than legal prostitution and was certainly far less degrading than being sold overseas, where women had no legal protection at all. Nonetheless, to Kinpei, prostitution is prostitution and is inherently corrupt and exploitive:

Ginko took in one girl who was not very attractive but who had the advantage of being healthy. As it turned out, though, her father was a garbage scavenger with an ugly temper who repeatedly forced his way into Ginko's house and refused to leave until he had extorted money from her. Ginko had seen much of life, and she was sometimes forced to deal with gangsters and small-time crooks. She also knew bloodsucking monsters who wanted to live off their daughters or lovers. These kinds of people thought they could take advantage of Ginko, and so she had occasion to call Kinpei down from his room upstairs. As often as not, though, Kinpei tended to come out on the short end of the deal too.

"This is an ugly business," Kinpei once declared.

"That's true. Shall I quit?" Ginko offered.

"This is your livelihood. Those raised in the mud have to go on living in the mud. There are people who actually succeed in this business." (17:319)

About the closest thing to true villains one finds in Shūsei's serious fiction are these "bloodsucking monsters" who selfishly sacrifice their daughters: the father in one of Shūsei's short stories, for example, who failed at business and sold his daughter into indenture as a geisha, failed again and attempted to force his adolescent daughter to agree, in the name of "filial piety," to being sold to a foreign brothel. Fortunately, the characters corresponding to Kobayashi Masako and Shūsei manage to persuade the young woman to refuse her father's demand and to go to the police and have her father formally rebuked for illegally harassing her to sign a contract against her will.[24]

Kinpei, with typical moral and intellectual certainty, is fully aware of the immorality of prostitution, but in the context of a microcosm of Japanese society, this immorality is relativized:

Some ten years ago, at about the age of forty, Kinpei went through a period of moral disintegration, when in search of neon lights, he immersed himself in the pleasures of the cafes, then at the height of their popularity. He started drinking too much, and he and his drinking buddies would go on long night drives on the newly opened Keihin highway to booze and dance in Yokohama's Westernized Honmaku district. In those days, he still held a great deal of stock in his wife's family's shipping company, stock he had been given after his marriage, and for a time, he was able to put on quite a gaudy show of his wealth, but his present situation was utterly changed. It seemed like a dream now, the world of that time. With no productive abilities of his own, he had succumbed to self-abandon, had fallen into a spiraling descent, and had lost sight of his true self. His life derailed, the brakes no longer worked, and he slid into the dreamlike addiction of searching for pleasure. On the verge of awakening from his drunken stupor, he was shocked by something like cold fear, and his body would ache when he heard reports concerning the progress of the men he went to school with. Drinking and carousing ceased to interest him. On rainy nights in particular, he would remember his son and daughter, whom he had left in the care of his wife's family, and he was overcome by tears of regret. But the coldly indifferent attitudes and actions of his in-laws turned his normal amiability into frantic resentment.

He had awakened from the nightmare some time ago, but on awakening, he discovered that he had exhausted his resources. Still, if he had not sold his stock so whimsically, he might have been able to keep the house his father-in-law had built for him and his wife as a wedding present.

The world was changing then. Profligate economic policies had resulted in widespread bankruptcy, and financial panic swept the business world. Politicians cried for drastic cuts in government expenditures, and the national defense budget was cut to the bone. On graduating from the university, Kinpei immediately entered the provincial bureaucracy of a governor appointed directly by the minister of internal affairs. As a consequence, he had more than a passing interest in political matters, and he paid close attention to trends in the imperial Diet and in the press, though of course these did not materially affect his present life. At the beginning of his career in the bureaucracy, Kinpei had quarreled with his superior, a man whose sympathies were deeply colored in favor of one of the political parties. He handed in his resignation in an angry protest of his ministry's blatant interference in legally free elections. He didn't like the life of a bureaucrat anyway. Kinpei briefly joined the political desk of a major newspaper, but his youthful rashness led him to reject the kinds of personal compromises and negotiations necessary to becoming a first-rate journalist, and he soon quit. He finally found long-term employment at a paper-manufacturing company with the help of the husband of one of the daughters of the Mimura house, a man who was on the board of directors. Kinpei didn't feel comfortable in this position, but his aging mother in the provinces was worried that he would never succeed at anything, and she had asked a student of his father's in classical Chinese poetry to assist her in finding him a suitable job. Kinpei was ashamed that he had caused his mother to worry, and he determined, as a matter of personal pride, to persevere at the paper company. This decision ultimately led to his marriage to the third daughter of the Mimura house, his adoption into her family, and his taking the Mimura name. He became the legal head of a Mimura branch family.

Finding himself thrust into the midst of Mimura's complicated family situation was hardly a welcome development for Kinpei. He was born into a house of several generations of Confucian scholars, and his early education in the traditional learning left him out of step with the age of capitalism. On the other hand, neither could he fully accept the self-defensive hypocrisy of Confucianism's independence and pride in loneliness. Kinpei became self-aware during his boyhood and adolescence under the progressive thought of the mid–Meiji period. The spirit of rebellion was an integral part of his nature, arousing within him the desire to oppose or escape from the fate his upbringing held in store. Thus when he graduated and entered the bureaucracy and was suddenly confronted with the realities of the world, his expectations were completely confounded, and his superiors and fellow workers could only seem to him to be deceitful, fawning opportunists. But after working at one job after another, and observing for several years how society actually functioned, he came to an understanding of human nature and was able to affirm a way he could live in human society; some of his idealistic edges were worn smooth. With his growing worldliness, however, came the sudden realization that his own standing in society was insecure, and this led him to agree to marry a daughter of the Mimura family, with the stipulation that he would be the adopted head of her branch house. This decision, however, was to be the origin of his own inner tragedy. (17:309–11)

In *Shukuzu,* Shūsei, for the first time, created in Mimura Kinpei an intellectual of the type created years before by Natsume Sōseki: isolated, alienated individuals who are articulate in their reflections on the morality of their actions in highly ambiguous moral circumstances. Kinpei differs most markedly from the young intellectual of the Meiji period in that he himself has become a prostitute of sorts and is in no position to make a moral judgment on the way the women around him lead their lives. The world is corrupt. At the top, we see the immorality of Kinpei's father-in-law, the great capitalist vulgarian, Mimura the Elder, the founder of a shipping empire based on renting defective ships to the government during the Russo-Japanese War, a man who now delights in the prospect of a world war because his investments will increase in value (17:332). At the bottom, there is the intellectual Kinpei, who has been offered every opportunity to join the bureaucratic, journalistic, and economic elites and who has become a shabby old pimp. Shūsei, however, was not interested in the tragedy of Kinpei's life. Kinpei is an appealing character only because he has the capacity to perceive the common humanity of Ginko. Shūsei used Kinpei to ease the reader into Ginko's world, but once this was accomplished from the intellectual's perspective, Shūsei dismissed him. *Shukuzu* reveals Shūsei's long-held conviction that it was the function of the novelist to give narrative voice to those segments of Japanese society that were normally voiceless. Shūsei's sympathy was reserved for Ginko.

The second quarter of *Shukuzu,* with its mix of narrative present and memory, serves as a transition during which Kinpei becomes more of a listener to Ginko's stories than an active observer of the demimonde. Then, in the last half of the novel, the narrative present and Kinpei disappear, and the reader is encompassed in Ginko's past. There comes a point beyond which Kinpei is not able to penetrate, a darker class realm that cannot be clarified by intellectuality. The viewpoint of the alienated individual suddenly gives way to a harsh, brutal communality, first appearing in the account of the origins of Ginko's parents and of Ginko's birth in 1904:

Orphaned at the age of three, taken in by the stem line of her family, Ginko's mother had grown up on a hard regime of fieldwork too difficult for a child and on the rhythmic movement of the shuttle over the loom she was made to operate for long periods at a time, and as she grew, she gradually became aware of the pain of not being loved as much or treated as well as her stepsisters. Tired of her every move being coldly supervised, she resolved at the age of fifteen to join a group of young people escaping from the village.

In this materially impoverished, isolated village, where there was one oil producer, a shop manufacturing tofu, and only three in ten were involved in agriculture, the other 70 percent eking out a living from looms, young men and women could only look forward to backbreaking labor for the rest of their lives at almost no wages, and so in the spring and autumn, young people would gather secretly, pool the few coins they had managed to save over the years, and form bands to flee from the village and emigrate to other provinces. Ginko's mother's group consisted of twelve individuals and a leader who organized such young people for a living. The emigrants were aged from fifteen to twenty-five. Whispering among themselves, they fled into deserted areas of the mountains as if they were breaking out of prison. They slept during the day, and at night made their way across rough terrain lacking any semblance of a road. After five days and nights, they at last emerged at the pass at Mikuni on the border between Niigata prefecture and Gunma prefecture, and they proceeded from there along a well-traveled road into Gunma, but Ginko's mother remembered how her heart thumped in her little chest when the party came upon a rough woodsman's camp one night deep in the mountains. Their guide had arranged for balls of cooked rice mixed with miso to be prepared at regular stations along the route, and so they did not starve during their journey. Once they entered Gunma prefecture, everyone was much relieved, and when they arrived in Maebashi, the provincial capital and an old castle town, the guide asked each of the youths their preference, and depending on their replies, either turned them over to local labor contractors or took them on to Ueno Station in Toyko.

Ginko's mother hoped for a position in a respectable house where she would be paid a wage in real currency, and thus she was quite satisfied when, in the end, she was indentured to a family of floss silk producers. She was born with a strong personality and enjoyed the freedom of the anonymity of being a stranger in a foreign land. She no longer needed to maintain the pretense of good communal relations in a small village, relations which invariably placed her in a position to be pitied: for the first time in her life, she felt there was a purpose to her hard work.

The production of floss silk involved boiling the silk cocoon to a pulp in soda water, separating out the ends of the threads, plunging the cocoon into cold water and taking out the chrysalis, and finally unwinding and ironing the threads out on a wooden board. Without learning one song or embracing a single youthful dream, she worked hard at these tasks through the changing seasons which visited the mountains until she was twenty-three. Her body was plump and firm, her skin white, and her chubby cheeks were as red as an apple.

Ginko's father was a former *yakuza* [criminal] who quit his gang to make a new life for himself by learning the trade of shoemaker from another *yakuza* who had had the foresight to establish a factory to mass-produce shoes for export to the Ruskies. Her father eventually returned to his home in the provinces to start his own shop. His sister-in-law owned the floss silk business, and impressed by the diligence of Ginko's mother, she arranged the marriage between her employee and her brother-in-law in the hope that it would domesticate him.

The marriage, however, was not a happy one. Within six months, ugly rumors about his criminal past had spread about the town, and then his former lover, a prostitute from Ibaragi, arrived to extort money from him. It took most of the mother's savings, accumulated over ten years, to buy the woman off. Ginko's mother realized the marriage was a terrible mistake and resolved to leave the man, but, by then, it was too late, for she discovered she was pregnant with Ginko.

Five months after Ginko first opened her eyes to the light of the world, her father closed his shop and moved with his wife and child to Tokyo. Soon he was making regular visits to a commercial export firm located in the Kudanzaka area of the Kōji-machi district. With money obtained from the sale of some rice fields he had inherited, he started a small shop in the Yanagiwara district of the Honjo ward. When Ginko turned fourteen, at about the time she began to commute to a shop in the Kuramae district in Asakusa to learn the craft of shoemaker, Ginko's father, who now had many children to support, suffered an injury in an accident, and soon his shop in Yanagiwara, which had once employed four or five workmen, went into decline.

Ginko had an aversion to geisha, and she went to the large Kuramae shop as a live-in apprentice with the intention of learning a trade. The shop was well known for pioneering the most recent styles in shoes. It was owned by a former samurai of the Sakura domain, many of whose retainers had gone into shoemaking after the Restoration, and his wife was a Christian graduate of a famous women's college in Yokohama. The couple took Ginko in because they thought it would be interesting to train a woman in the trade.

Ginko was given moral discipline and instruction in manners in this Christian household, she associated with the numerous other apprentices, learned the basics of cutting and sewing leather, and was soon skilled enough to earn a wage, which she contributed almost entirely to her family. In the end, however, her frail arms could not support them all, her mother, father, and sisters.

The hands calloused by the leather-cutting knife and the thick sewing needle were soon trained to take up the pick of the *shamisen* and the stick of the big drum and to beat the shoulder drum, and she was made to learn simple dances, such as "Plum Blossoms of Spring" and "Maiden of the Wisteria," all to display a minimum level of competence in performing at engagements for paying customers. She wasn't tall, but she had developed into a beautiful young woman. (17:388–90)

Of all of Shūsei's heroines, Ginko is clearly the lowest born and brought up in the most impoverished and disadvantaged circumstances. Ginko's mother (in real life, Koshimaki Miyo) was born in a mountain village in Niigata, which was once "a tribe" (17:386) consisting almost solely of the Koshimaki clan. Ginko's grandmother lost her husband and son to tuberculosis and died of burns she suffered when the lamp oil she was selling accidently caught fire. As an orphan in a village so poor people seldom saw a yen of paper currency (17:387), Ginko's mother is worked from childhood for bare subsistence, a condition from which she flees. Ginko's father (in real life, Kobayashi Tōhei) is the "human refuse" of Japanese society. Even his legitimate trade, working with leather, is stigmatized. To support her family, Ginko agrees to be sold into the demimonde of Hasuike in Chiba for a loan of two hundred yen, of course paid to her parents. For the rest of her youth, Ginko remains the principal support of her parents and five younger sisters. She despises being sexually used by the elderly owner of the house in Hasuike, and she briefly returns to live with her family in Tokyo in 1920 or so, but despite her intention not to resume prostitution, her family's situation requires that she sacrifice herself once again:

Ginko resolved never to return to the demimonde and once again took up the trade of shoemaker where she had left it a year before. She washed off the white face powder and the red lip-paint and picked up the leather-cutting knife. Her father spent much of each day trying to collect orders.

"Fools aren't cured till they die," she said to herself, and yet she was certain that making shoes, no matter how hard, was far preferable to wearing beautiful clothing and feeling constantly compelled to flatter and please men. She worked at her trade as if she had been reborn, as if working with her whole heart would redeem her for the months she had spent in corruption and degradation. She did the easier work, and her father did the work that was beyond the capability of a woman. They made an odd father-and-child pair of craftsmen, and they urged each other on and worked together very diligently.

The father did his best, but he was still plagued by the chronic effects of the accident he had not fully recovered from, and after two days of labor, he had to recuperate for three. A sister who had been sent out to work had damaged her health and had returned home to rest. The money Ginko earned was not sufficient to meet household expenses. When autumn winds blew white across the great Sumida River, Ginko began to feel acutely the economic pressures bearing down on her family, and she understood, even more clearly than before, the reasons why a decent, ordinary life was beyond her reach.

"On Ginko's and father's earnings, we can barely pay for our rice. Where will the rest of our food come from?" her mother said time and time again.

Talk of separation repeatedly came up. When it was decided that the father would take three children and return to Gunma and the mother would take the rest of the children and return to Niigata, Ginko went to Asakusa to consult with a procurer for the demimonde.

"I'm going back into the business, but I want a little money this time. Do you know anyone looking for girls?" Ginko asked when she visited the procurer at the end of the year. She had thought about it and determined that she would have to give up making shoes because she couldn't earn a living for her family no matter how hard she worked, and she desired a considerable sum to buy the rights to a shop in a neighborhood better for her father's trade.

"How much do you need?" the procurer asked.

"Twelve hundred, thirteen hundred yen."

"How about the house in Yoshi-chō? The woman owner was asking what had become of you the other day. You'll probably get a little more money from her."

"Well," Ginko paused.

A thousand yen was a good deal of money in those days, but as she had frequently heard in the provinces, girls in Tokyo were worked the hardest and often their bodies didn't bear up. For lower-class parents such as hers, people who out of the necessity to survive had to weigh the relative values of love of a husband for a wife, love of a wife for a husband, or love of parents for their children, the class of people who saw nothing unnatural in selling their children to buy food, questions of preference—did she want to stay in Tokyo, did she dislike the provinces—were irrelevant; since she alone had been chosen to shoulder her family's hard and painful burdens, she alone decided that she would go to the house that paid the most with the easiest working conditions. Of course, considerations of where her status as a geisha might be improved or where her performing skills would become more polished were not important to her.

"How about Sendai? My daughter has a house there. I'd be able to hire you here on the spot," the procurer said.

It seemed to Ginko that she would be at a disadvantage if she had a conflict with the procurer's daughter.

"No, I think I'd rather go somewhere I'm not known."

"Then it'll be a little further away. There's a house that's been asking me for a girl. It's rustic, but on the other hand they're easygoing out there, and they probably won't work you too hard. They'll come immediately when they receive my telegram." (17:426–29)

Ginko sells herself into a pleasure district in the city of Ishinomaki in Miyagi prefecture. Her motives are the traditional ones: those of the filial daughter who agrees to prostitution for the benefit of her family. This is predictably tragic. Noguchi Fujio describes what distinguishes *Shukuzu* from other novels of the demimonde genre (*karyū shōsetsu*): "[I]n the prewar period, a geisha was generally thought of merely as a plaything for men, but Shūsei conceived of Ginko as a living human being. *Shukuzu* was, first and most important, a chronicle of Japan's lower classes during the dark, prewar period when there was no notion of social welfare. The lower classes are personified by this single, nameless woman who survives entirely by her own strength. This was the reason that during the war the authorities hated the work so much."[25]

It is important to stress, however, that Ginko, this woman of close-to-outcast birth who practices a stigmatized profession for most of her adult life, can aspire to and retain values of common humanity and decency. This is unthinkable in the case of the "lower classes" in Shūsei's works set in the Meiji period, works in which people who remain in stigmatized subcultures, such as prostitution, *yakuza* gangs, or the theater, are so damaged they become one-dimensional oddities or stereotypes. This never happens to Ginko. There is still malnutrition, terrible disease, and want in Ginko's world, but an essential element of common life, a sense of individual self-worth, has extended down to even the lowest classes. This is clear in the account of Ginko's love affair in Ishinomaki with Kuramochi Shingo, a young provincial landowner of fairly good birth:[26]

In May, when the cherry trees bloomed, plum and peach blossoms were out briefly at the same time, and the myriad young leaves on branches and the grasses reemerging from the dark earth gave the warming air the heavy smell of life, arousing in Ginko, who suffered all winter from the cold, the joyful sense of being able finally to stretch her limbs and grow. The gulls flying over the somber, dark sea seemed like lonely phantasms, and the sound of whistles from steamboats on the river, which woke her from sleep, and the whistles of passenger trains echoing sadly in the sky invited her to set off on a journey. It was not pleasant for her to see Kuramochi off at the station when he boarded the train for Tokyo. Having been brought up in Tokyo and having suffered from poverty all her life, Ginko didn't fall into the sentimentality that many countrywomen, with their sensitivity to nature, succumbed to when seasons changed, but at times, seemingly on currents of wind, the pain of being enslaved by confederates in a strange land would come over her heart, and she was seized by the impulse to flee, to fly away somewhere.

But she also had the sense that she had come all this way and was about to pull off a major coup, and she wanted to see how the play she had set in motion turned out; with the idea of protecting what good fortune might be in store for her, she resolved to exploit her charms and the situation to the utmost. She agreed to keep Kuramochi's ring, which she wrapped in soft paper and put away gently in a drawer of her mirror chest. Kuramochi seemed all the more enamored of her and would engage her for four or five days straight, forgetting his responsibilities at home. . . .

"For a time, anyway, I'd like to set you up in a house of your own, and I'd come to visit you there. If we could do that, my mother would surely consent to our marriage. Everyone will recognize you as my wife. You see, I'll almost never be home, and my family and those who depend on me will be worried. They don't know what to do without me. I'll use that as a lever—'Well, why don't you let me marry her then?'—and I'll keep up the pressure to make them accept you," Kuramochi argued.

Because Kuramochi was the only heir who could carry on the bloodline of his family and was a future source of support his mother could depend on, the success of his plan seemed plausible to Ginko, but it made her feel uncomfortable.

"You're just turning me into your mistress, that's what you're doing."

"That's not my intention. It's a different route to marriage."

"I don't care about your family's wealth or connections. I won't become your mistress. You'll keep me and then marry a respectable young lady. That's the way it'll turn out, whether you intend it to or not. I won't have any part of it."

"So you don't trust me," Kuramochi declared, scratching his head, and he didn't mention the matter again.

Though Ginko knew nothing of society as a whole, she nonetheless worried about the difference in social status between herself and Kuramochi, a difference hinted at by the woman who held her contract. Still, people raised in circumstances such as hers had little opportunity or means to learn complex class distinctions, and while she was not jealous or spiteful toward those born better than herself, neither did she feel particularly humble or inferior. She had seen men come into sudden wealth and spend limitless sums, and she knew that a ring of glass shines brighter than a diamond worth a thousand yen. (17:442–45)

Of course, there are class distinctions in Japanese society, and, in the end, Kuramochi's mother manages to break up the affair. As Ginko predicted, Kuramochi marries a "respectable young lady," though Ginko learns of it in the newspapers, and, in chagrin, she transfers her contract to the Yoshi-chō geisha house in Tokyo. The important point, however, is that she thinks that there is a strong possibility that Kuramochi actually will take her as his legal wife. While others may discriminate against Ginko on the basis of her birth or occupation, Ginko does not judge herself in the same class terms. She does not act like a geisha. In her eyes, Kuramochi's mother is a silly, rural woman acting on backward, unfounded prejudice.

Shūsei acutely perceived that the modernization of common urban manners and customs provided the lowest classes with transcendent cultural values which enabled even a person of Ginko's mean social status to maintain a sense of self-worth. The common respectability Shūsei described as it came into existence in the years around the Russo-Japanese War had, by the 1920s, extended down to the lowest classes. Of course, Ginko despises her occupation and vows that her sisters will never become geisha (17:409), but a new cultural identity allows her the confidence that she is far more than her occupation. Also, above and beyond the traditional ideological assurance that she is a filial geisha (kōkō geisha), prostituting herself for the good of her family, Ginko gains consolation and dignity from her ability to read.

Most of the heroines—Ogin, Oshō, Omasu—of Shūsei's novels of common life are illiterate or barely literate. That Ginko, who is of lower social status than these characters, enjoys reading reflects the enormous strides made in the expansion of cultural standards. While she is in the

demimonde at Ishinomaki, a greengrocer who regularly visits her house
to make deliveries befriends Ginko by introducing her to the novel:

"If you don't read while you're stuck in a place like this, you'll become an
idiot. I'm just a greengrocer, but reading gives me reason to live. When you're
feeling sad or lonely, read a book. You'll be saved," the pale young man stated
and left a well-thumbed, translated novel for Ginko to read.

This first work was Kuroiwa Ruikō's translation of Victor Hugo's *Les miséra-
bles*. . . . Most owners disapproved of their girls reading and attempted to prevent it. Even today, in Tokyo, there are a number of houses which prohibit their
girls from going to the movies. Many girls don't have much time in the late
morning and afternoon. They have to clean their rooms and those of their
owners, do the laundry, attend regular lessons in the traditional performing arts,
wait their turn for the always busy hairdresser, or go to the public baths, and
sometimes the girls were late for their first engagement because they hadn't yet
put on their makeup. One ostensible reason for the prohibition of reading was
that if the girls got lost in novels, their daily schedules would go awry, but, in
truth, most of the owners of these places were afraid their own ignorance would
be exposed. They were generally ignorant people. The men had vulgar tastes.
Perhaps they knew a few popular songs, but they had no ear certainly for
Western classical music and most often not for kabuki or classical Japanese
music either. Their lack of cultivation led them to strictly forbid reading. During the time the Salvation Army took the law into its own hands by leading
near-riots against prostitution, the owners were so frightened that they tried to
prevent their girls from reading even newspapers. Women had had no protection under the law for such a long period, and they were often taken advantage
of by immoral procurers, but it was the kind of business that militated against
self-pity. While everyone appeared to be living in harmony, behind the scenes
parents were living off their children, and husbands off their wives, and so it was
a world occupied in part by a strain of bacteria feeding on pollution, or parasites
who went through life sucking the blood of women; perhaps all of this was
covered with a veneer of mutual kindness and regard, but beneath the surface
cordiality, there was an unremitting struggle to survive.

Because Ginko too was poor, she was taken advantage of at every turn. She
was one of the women who sacrificed their bodies so their parents and siblings
would have food. Consciously or unconsciously, perhaps it was not fortuitous
that the young greengrocer gave Ginko the story of Jean Valjean to read.

Stealing time from her duties, Ginko read through the novel at a terrific pace.

"I wonder if all of that could happen over a simple piece of bread."

Although she didn't understand the theme, she was fascinated by the plot.

Curled up in bed, she continued reading through the night until the break of dawn. She returned the book to the greengrocer after four or five days.

"I read the whole thing. It was very interesting," she told him.

"Did you understand it?"

"Yes, I did," she replied.

"I'll bring you another book tomorrow."

The next day he brought her a translation of Alexandre Dumas's *The Count of Monte Cristo* and he also left a copy of the progressive women's monthly *Fujin Kōron*. (17:438–40)

The modernization of common customs, manners, and fashions in the twenties has a substantial effect on Ginko's life. It provides her with an alternative set of values to those of the demimonde. It enables her to think in terms of lines taken from a novel: "As long as one is in the business, one's body will be sullied, but one can maintain the chastity of the pure spirit, which no amount of money can buy" (17:426). Margaret Mitchell's *Gone with the Wind*, Pearl Buck's *The Good Earth*, *The Biography of Marie Curie* (17:313), movie versions of Dumas's *La dame aux camélias*, *Antony and Cleopatra*, and Oscar Wilde's *Salomé* (17:418)—these fictions about heroic women or tragic love affairs allow Ginko to give her own circumstances the dignity of tragedy:

The evening Ginko saw the movie *Jeanne d'Arc*, she was enormously moved by the heroic image of the young, French countrywoman who was about her own age. She felt deep emotions stirring within her. She realized that she had no great religious faith or burning patriotism, and yet the moment she saw Jeanne d'Arc on the screen, she experienced a shared purity and heroism, and she cursed her present despicable status. (17:425)

It is this movie which inspires Ginko to break with the old lecher in Hasuike, Chiba, and return to the honest trade of shoemaking (17:416).

But Ginko is not really a victim either. The reader learns early on in the novel that, with Kinpei's support, Ginko bought the license formerly held by her master (in reality, Nagashima Nobuhide, d. 1931) and opened her own house in 1933.[27] Not only does Ginko survive the years of illegal prostitution, she thrives on the system. She becomes an "exploiter" of women generally younger than herself. Managing a house of geisha is a creative balancing act between the display of extravagance and observing every economy, and Ginko's success speaks of her intelligence. The difficulties of staying in the geisha business are clear in the description of Ginko's living and working conditions in 1921 or so, when Ginko transfers her contract from Ishinomaki to a house in Tokyo:

The geisha house Haruyoshi was located in a narrow alley off the Daimon-dōri [Great Gate Avenue] in the Yoshi district of the Nihonbashi ward. . . . Haruyoshi was not a strongly felt presence among the almost three hundred geisha houses in the area, and the house itself was as small and crowded as a chicken coop.

The house shared a kitchen with a shop selling footwear, which occupied most of the first floor and fronted on the main avenue. One went down an alley and entered at the side of the building to find a small room in front of a staircase leading up to the second floor. Upstairs, there was a 55-square-foot room and a 110-square-foot room. There was a corridor behind the staircase, and the kitchen was off that corridor. The shop was separated from the geisha house by a flimsy wall of thin wooden boards. The shopkeeper, his wife, child, and an apprentice lived on the other side of the wall. Due to the zoning laws which limited the demimonde to back streets in certain areas of the city, it was difficult for this house to expand or find more spacious quarters.

This small geisha house was originally a branch of one of the district's largest houses whose owners were very influential in the self-government of the demi-monde, and at first it was managed off the license of the main house, but the speculative nature of its mistress, Yoshimura Tamiko, created problems for the main house, and they removed their license. The present Haruyoshi was a young enterprise based on Yoshimura Tamiko's purchase of a new license. There were two telephones in the house, one for Tamiko's personal use on the second floor and one in the corridor. Though the house was very small, its front entrance was extravagantly decorated.

Now that she had her own house, Ginko frequently remembered her former mistress Tamiko, and she thought she finally understood the woman's reckless spending and ceaseless manipulations. Drawn from the earnings of independents who paid a fee to borrow her license, apprentice geisha, and more than ten indentured girls, a monthly income of over ten thousand yen was not sufficient to pay her debts, and after exhausting a variety of shrewd strategies, she had to sell her business and flee to Osaka in the night. Tamiko's career seemed a strange and particularly adventurous one to Ginko.

Tamiko was born the daughter of a small landowner in Urawa, and much of her youth was spent in strict service in the house of Gotō Shinpei, the hero of the age, colonizer of Taiwan and Manchuria, promoter of the invasion of Siberia, and mayor of Tokyo. Because she was clever, Gotō grew quite fond of her, and they kept her in service until she was eighteen, when they married her into an ex-samurai family of former merchants. Tamiko moved to the Bakurō district of the Nihonbashi ward. The new family she joined there led a comfortable, leisurely life on rents from lands and houses. Tamiko's husband had received military training in college, and upon graduation was granted a commission as a second lieutenant in the army reserves. . . . In the second year of the marriage, the Russo-Japanese War broke out, and Tamiko's husband was called to the front, where he was killed. The moment that Tamiko, who was nine months pregnant, heard the news that her husband had died in battle, she received such a tremendous shock that she fainted, fell to the floor, and lost consciousness. She was carried to the hospital, where she miscarried. Committed to a mental hospital, she remained in a state of mental collapse for almost three years, and when her sanity returned to her, her formerly shy, reserved nature had changed completely.

A source of pride for Tamiko was the high regard she had been accorded at Gotō Shinpei's residence, and she frequently told stories to her girls about Gotō's daily activities, but it would appear that the atmosphere of the household where she spent her youth in service had an adverse effect on her later life. Her pride in having associated with such a distinguished person began to emerge as she recovered from her mental collapse, and resolving that she would capture for herself a remarkable man as a partner, she took her first position as a geisha in the demimonde at Shinbashi.

The men regarded as the great successes of the Meiji period, whether in politics or in business, invariably had connections with either the Shinbashi or the Yanagibashi pleasure quarters. The demimonde is indispensable to the social life of the upper classes, as it was in the flowery pasts of the political parties, and there is no end to the great banquets engaging geisha from Shinbashi and Yanagibashi. It seems that what glory there is to be had for lower-class women is generally found in or develops out of these two areas. After losing her husband and child and returning to consciousness, there was no doubt a certain logic in Tamiko's decision to cast herself into the demimonde at Shinbashi: she had been infected by the air breathed by the upper classes.

But, of course, not every woman who manages to become a geisha in Shinbashi or Yanagibashi realizes her dreams of glory. The class order has become fairly stable in the present world: women either become the mistresses of wealthy or important men or they buy their own restaurants or houses of assignation; if they are unfortunate, their careers take the opposite course, and if they are lucky, they spend most of the rest of their lives paying high interest rates dictated by the holders of their loans; much farther down the scale are the women overwhelmed by enormous debts and forced to sell themselves into

foreign brothels, where they have no legal protection and cannot defend themselves from being worked to the bone. Rare is the girl who returns alive.

Tamiko was one of the women who did not realize her dreams in the pleasure
quarter around Shinbashi, and from there her life of abandon began.

She was of delicate build, thin, tall, and graceful, but with a rather unpleasant
long face and unbalanced features: narrow eyes, a low nose, and a large mouth.

She had mastered a few of the basics of the traditional arts, but given the
number of beautiful and talented women in Shinbashi, she had little reason to
expect that her performances would be well received. When she saw that her
debt would only increase, she fled to Hokkaido, where she worked her way
around the southwest of the island, a year or two in a house in Hakodate, a year
or two in Otaru, and then a year or two in Muroran. She next jumped north,
across the sea, to the Japanese colony in Sakhalin, where she practiced her trade
out of the famous Flower House in Vladimirovska, about two hours by train
from Korsakov. By the time she made her way back to Tokyo, to appear suddenly in Yoshi-chō, she was thirty, an old woman by the standards of the trade,
but working out of the Haruyoshi, she managed to ensnare an elderly gentleman who had made something of a reputation speculating in foodstuffs in
Kakigara-chō. This person, named Hanamura, had recently lost his wife, and in
his loneliness was susceptible to Tamiko's seductions. She was able to get a large
sum of money out of him with the promise that she would invest it in a house,
and this was the capital she used to start her new Haruyoshi. . . .

The first evening Ginko visited the Haruyoshi, she was led upstairs to a seat
in front of Tamiko and was made to listen to her new mistress hold forth on the
customs of the quarter and what would be expected of her the next day, when
she would be ceremoniously introduced to the restaurants and houses of assignation in the area. That night Tamiko rested in her own luxuriant bedding, using
her accounts box as a pillow. Four girls sharing two sets of bedding joined her
in the 110-square-foot room. In the 55-square-foot room, six women slept,
sharing three sets of bedding. In a tiny room off the entrance on the first floor,
the maid and cook—a Nara-born old woman blind in one eye and Tamiko's
adopted daughter Natsuko—slept back to back under one set of bedding. . . .

Ginko took the name Kiyoko and went through with the ceremony of introduction. She signed a standard contract which accorded her 30 percent of her
earnings. But because the cost of her *shamisen*, silk underrobes, and other
clothing was deducted from her percentage, and because Tamiko kept the books
in an obfuscatory manner to her own benefit, in the end, Ginko's "30 percent"
amounted to almost nothing. When Ginko needed money, she often had to
borrow three or five yen from Tamiko. And when these small sums accumulated, Ginko was forced to fix her seal to yet another bond of debt, on which she
agreed to pay 3 percent interest. In this pleasure quarter, first engagements

involving prostitution cost fifty to one hundred yen. All of this money went to the owner. Engagements which monopolized a geisha for the full period of her working day but which didn't involve prostitution cost only a third of those that did, but prostitution was not limited to engagements which occupied a geisha all day and night. With more than ten girls working for her, figuring conservatively that thirty out of a hundred engagements involved prostitution, and estimating again conservatively that each of these brought in fifty yen, every girl was regularly earning Yoshimura Tamiko fifteen hundred yen for every hundred engagements. And, of course, she was also paid the traditional commissions legally due to her from the customer for the girl's affiliation with her house, whether or not the girl was actually indentured to her. . . .

Judging the economics of running a geisha house solely in terms of the income it generated, one would have to conclude that, during the course of her lifetime, Yoshimura Tamiko should have been able to create capital of hundreds of thousands of yen. In reality, however, the situation was not that simple. It was inevitable in this business that owners could not avoid borrowing large sums of money at high rates of interest from rapacious moneylenders, and one also had to subtract the seemingly countless illogical expenditures involved in maintaining status and fulfilling customary obligations in the demimonde, and even after subtracting these costs from the equation, by far the greatest losses came in the form of problems with the girls: having to support girls who weren't earning their keep or girls who reneged on their contracts and disappeared. Clever young women would take the initiative, decide to get out of the business, and flee into the underground subculture of the cafes or run away to become mistresses of salaried businessmen and live in their own apartments. When establishments with little capital sustained these kinds of losses, they were driven to the wall and often collapsed.

At Haruyoshi, there were at times more than ten girls. The eldest was Fukutarō, the daughter of a Buddhist monk at Ueno, followed by Haruji, the daughter of a skilled plasterer in Kanda. There was the beautiful Koine, the daughter of a craftsman who specialized in a unique, boat-shaped fan associated with the Awa region. The epileptic Inaji transferred her contract to Haruyoshi from a house close to the Karasumori Shrine in Shinbashi. She was popular because she was very coquettish. Umefuku was one of Tamiko's adopted daughters, taken in during her Hokkaido days. Although Kofuku was the daughter of a sumo wrestler, she was a tiny girl, albeit with a sharp wit. Another adopted daughter was Isoyakko, whose name Tamiko had put in her family registry in Vladimirovska. She had left the girl in the Flower House, but Isoyakko had bolted before serving out her contract and fled Sakhalin to join her "mother" in Tokyo. And there was Umechiyo, an elegant girl who came from Shinbashi and was said to have delighted her patrons at every engagement. Tamiko preferred beautiful women to such an extent that she was reputed to enjoy a sickeningly sweet candied fruit named after Benzai-ten, goddess of feminine good looks. With little regard for the expense, she tried to maintain as beautiful a stable as she could, but the only women who served out the full length of their contracts were the aging ones: unsold goods. The contracts of the attractive women were often bought out by lovers or transferred to other houses. When Tamiko discovered that Inaji was an epileptic, she feared a calamity and sold her contract to a house in Nagano, at a great financial loss to herself. In her place, she brought in Somefuku, who was born in Sakhalin, but this girl, who claimed to be a graduate of a women's college, had been influenced by leftist thought. One night after drinking heavily, she got into a fierce quarrel with Ginko over a customer and fell out of a window on the third floor of a house of assignation in Hama-chō. Her injuries appeared to be serious. She lost consciousness and was groaning as she was carried into the hospital. When they went to visit her the next day, however, they found she had absconded, leaving Tamiko to write off her seventeen or eighteen hundred yen debt. The sumo wrestler's daughter wasn't being hired for many engagements and was thus embarrassed every evening. Leaving a sizable portion of her debt unpaid, she finally ran off to take up a position as a live-in maid in a house of assignation. Tamiko had a violent temper, but there was simply nothing she could do to prevent these disasters. (17:474–80)

The front of Tamiko's establishment is decorated in an expensive, gaudy manner, but inside, women are living in unconscionably crowded conditions. Tamiko spent a great deal to obtain beautiful women but then did not feed them adequately: "The meal at night consisted of two or three pieces of pickled radish and rice. On rare occasions they were served half a slice of cooked salmon, about the quantity of fish that would satisfy a kitten, but that was a special treat. In the mornings they had to settle for cold miso soup and perhaps some deep-fried tofu. As for rice, they were only allowed child-sized bowls, and more than two refills was strictly forbidden. If a girl asked for a third refill, Tamiko glared at her coldly and declared, 'Geisha aren't supposed to eat enough to feel full' " (17:482).

Clearly, in the balance struck between showing an extravagant, prosperous face to the public and being frugal in the management of one's personal household, Tamiko goes to extremes. The result is that her women either flee or become ill. Ginko comes down with acute pneumonia and almost dies (17:504). Years later, when Ginko is in a similar position of running a geisha house, she faces many of the same problems—women who run off, become ill, or want to transfer their contracts—but she solves them in a far more maternalistic way. Rather than try to maintain a second-class house to compete with the more fashionable districts of Shinbashi and Yanagibashi, Ginko remains content to run a third-class establishment, taking in women who are not remarkably beautiful or talented, women Tamiko would never consider. There is the implication that, in Ginko's business, there is more prostitution at cheaper prices for a local clientele of students, bureaucrats, lawyers, scholars, and others living around Tokyo Imperial University who wanted "a more private place to play" (17:354). On the other hand, Ginko makes certain that the women in her charge are adequately fed, clothed, and housed and have some access to medical care. She thus avoids some of the disastrous losses that Tamiko incurred due to her frugality. The balance Ginko strikes appears to be more successful and humane than the one struck by Tamiko.

Shūsei began his literary career in 1896 with the success of his short story "Yabukōji" (The Spearflower), a work in which he attempted to present a sympathetic portrait of a woman outcast (*eta*) who is driven to madness by her "environment." Some forty-five years later, he presented, in Ono Ginko, a woman of the lowest class who survives a demeaning, stigmatized life in prostitution to graduate to the successful management of a competitive and distasteful business. Everything in Ginko's upbringing and background should have worked to create a mean, petty person, but, on the contrary, she emerges as a sympathetic, dignified individual who symbolizes the common humanity that naturalism had come to signify for Shūsei at the end of his career.

Tokuda Shūsei and the Postwar Canon

In 1953, the noted literary critic and scholar Kuwabara Takeo proposed a "canon of national literature," from which the works of Tokuda Shūsei were to be excluded. An unknown provincial higher-school teacher, Imura Shōkai, wrote an impassioned protest of this exclusion. Imura's polemical essay is of interest because of its honesty and because, at a crucial point in the 1950s when Shūsei's reputation was about to go into a severe decline, Imura clearly articulated that the reason many academics objected to Shūsei was a disinclination to come to terms with real class divisions within Japanese society:

Of course, we are now in the postwar period, but the vast majority of the Japanese people still live in the world inhabited by Ginko and Oshima. To put it bluntly, if Japanese literature develops along lines which ignore Shūsei, it will, regrettably, have no relation to the enormous energies of the Japanese people. . . .

It would be ridiculous for me to argue that Shūsei's *Shukuzu* should serve as the model and standard for [Kuwabara's] canon of national literature. On the other hand, I utterly disagree with the claim that Shūsei's literature should have no relation to the canon, or the claim that it is an error to even consider the question of what relation Shūsei's work should have to the canon. I have no faith in the canon of Japanese literature which springs from the impulse to exclude Tokuda Shūsei. . . .

I believe we should recognize Shūsei's efforts in having explored, to a greater depth than any other author, the lives of common [*shomin*] women, and I would think that we should want to retain the legacy he has left us. . . . Even in situations in which despair seems the only recourse, not only do Oshima and Ginko go on living, but they do so retaining a vital, youthful beauty. That Shūsei was able to discover this strength, which really transcends words like "strength," and moreover that he was able to discover it in ordinary women provide the Japanese quality of his work. Today, the great majority of Japanese women inhabit worlds not so distant from those of Ginko and Oshima.[28]

Imura Shōkai's fears that Shūsei would not be included in the canon of modern Japanese literature have probably been realized. Forty years ago, when he wrote his polemic, Japan was still under occupation, and the living standards of the working classes were far worse than they are today. Perhaps *Shukuzu* no longer accurately reflects the realities of lower-class life in Japan. Even if it does not, the novel and the literary career that produced it deserve a consideration they are not receiving in the present, if only because they testify powerfully to the sacrifices of countless people who were integral to the economic development of modern Japan.

According to Kobayashi Masako's own account of her love affair with Shūsei, the year after he died, authorities forced her to close her house in the Hakusan pleasure quarter, and they put her to work, with four of the women indentured to her, in an aircraft parts factory. She maintains that the wages paid to her were not sufficient to survive on, and she had to use her savings to support herself and the women she felt responsible for. Toward the end of the war, she found places for some of these women in one of the few remaining pleasure quarters in Ikebukuro. The police called her in, accused her of being "a liberal," and threatened reprisals if she did not persuade the women to return to the factory. She refused. As of 1967, Kobayashi Masako was still working, managing a small bar in Ikebukuro.[29]

Epilogue

For much of his life, Tokuda Shūsei was plagued by a variety of physical ailments: he was tubercular, probably had some sort of venereal disease, suffered from painful hemorrhoids and ulcers, and later in his life was diagnosed as having diabetes. In 1936, it was feared he would die after he collapsed from an attack of carotid artery mesoangiitis. On recovering, he wrote the following haiku:

> Still alive,
>   Summer grasses green,
> How pleasurable to the eye.[1]

Shūsei was a small, physically frail person whose constant concern about his health was probably symptomatic of his desire to continue writing. In mid-August of 1942, he coughed blood shortly after composing the following afterword to a volume of his writings:

I do not believe that my literary career is at an end, but even if I were to live on for a number of years, I cannot imagine that this body could produce a work worthy of being passed on to later generations. Night and day, I am lost in thought, but I am certain that no grand project, one written in capital letters, one suitable to the times, will come to me from out of the air. Scientists do not recognize miracles, and I myself was born with a nature disinclined to search for miracles or great leaps forward. . . . Literatures have their own destinies too. A literature fated to follow course A cannot follow course B, and a course B literature cannot follow course A. Perhaps, through study, one can develop beyond such limitations, but, like my handwriting, my literature cannot transcend myself. The only alternative, then, is to work to expand my outlook as much as possible. I feel an aversion to my literature, which has developed as it has, but I have yet to learn from past experience, and in grappling with a new literary work, I feel the pleasure of being alive.[2]

213

In the face of an intensifying Pacific war, Shūsei declared that he planned to continue writing and that he could not and would not write propaganda. In this determination, one senses how completely life and writing had become synonymous for him. Even in his weakened physical condition, the force of will that enabled him to survive for so many decades as a professional novelist is evident. It is the same quality of character that led him to maintain his independence and make the transition in 1899 to a new literary language while he was an apprentice under Ozaki Kōyō, to retain the conviction that he was Japan's realistic writer in his reaction to the challenge of naturalism in 1907 and 1908, to change the direction of his literary career in 1916 in the midst of his greatest success, to defy public opinion in the twenties by continuing his love affair with Yamada Junko, to effect the "miraculous comeback" in his literary career in 1933, to ignore social convention by helping to manage a business based on illegal prostitution when he was over sixty, to adopt elements of social realism in his *Shukuzu* over the strenuous objections of state censors, and to defiantly stop serialization of his novel in midsentence rather than comply with alterations ordered by the authorities. His literary career was extraordinary. As a person inextricably tied to his image as a novelist, surviving decade after decade on his fictions, Shūsei was an unfathomably complex human being.

And yet, for all his independence, cunning, and strength of will, Shūsei's declared intention in mid-August of 1942 to expand his outlook and make yet another transition to a new form of realism was not in the cards. The seventy-one-year-old Shūsei was too ill. In the company of his son Kazuho, he could manage visits to his physician, Ōhori Taiichirō, or a short trip to a hot spring in Chiba prefecture, but he continued to cough blood. On July 11, 1943, he told Kazuho that he did not expect to live to see the end of the war, and that night he began bleeding from the nose, a condition that continued for three days and left him exhausted and confined to his bed. Toward the end of August, Ōhori suspected his patient was suffering from cancer of the pleura and had Shūsei hospitalized for tests at the nearby Tokyo Imperial University. Ōhori's diagnosis of lung cancer was confirmed. As was standard Japanese medical practice, Shūsei was not informed that his illness was terminal. He was sent home to die surrounded by his family. Confined to his bed in the study of his house in Morikawa-chō, he lingered for several months.[3]

According to Tokuda Kazuho, Shūsei's last words were "The novel is such a difficult thing, isn't it?" (*shōsetsu wa muzukashii mono da ne*). Noguchi Fujio remembers that as death approached, Shūsei's arm was

Shūsei toward the end of his life

extended out of the covers and his hand was clinging tightly to the leg of his writing desk. Shūsei died in his study at 4:25 A.M. on the morning of November 18, 1943. The cause of death was cancer of the pleura.[4]

The funeral was held with the support of numerous government-controlled cultural organizations and was, considering the wartime conditions, a fairly elaborate and well-attended affair. Beginning with a representative from the Ministry of Education, followed by a number of representatives from cultural organizations, one cultural functionary after another mounted a stage surrounded by wreaths of flowers to give their prepared speeches in praise of the memory of the "eminent man of letters" they had obviously either not read or not understood.

Funayama Kaoru, a member of one of Shūsei's coteries, remembers with some bitterness the hypocrisy of the banal platitudes spoken by those associated with the Cabinet Information Bureau, which had so systematically suppressed the aging author's writing less than two years earlier. How the bureaucrats actually regarded Shūsei can be judged from the fact that he did not receive, in life or posthumously, any of the imperial institution's numerous awards for cultural achievement, honors granted almost every other major novelist of Shūsei's generation: Sōseki, Ōgai, Tōson, Hakuchō, Kyōka, Kafū, and so on.

Noguchi Fujio remembers Shūsei's funeral as a cold, boring ceremony, remarkable only for the deep grief displayed by Tokuda Michiko, the daughter of Shūsei's old friend Chikamatsu (Tokuda) Shūkō, and for Masamune Hakuchō's brief eulogy, which stated, in part:

> Shūsei, your literature developed along an even course without the least sensationalism, and though you portrayed common society, you were able to invest it with infinite human nuances. The enduring feature of your literature is that the more carefully and appreciatively one reads your works, the more delicate and subtle pleasures one will discover.[5]

Tokuda Shūsei should be remembered first as a master stylist of the modern Japanese novel. This reputation rests on seven major novels— *Arajotai, Ashiato, Kabi, Tadare, Arakure, Kasō jinbutsu,* and *Shukuzu*— and a handful of relatively short personal fictions, including "Kanshō-teki no koto," "Sōwa," "Sugiyuku hi," "Machi no odoriba," and "Shi ni shitashimu." It also owes much to a score or so of finely crafted short stories, some purely fiction and some based on Shūsei's experience, including "Zetsubō" (Despair, 1907), "Nirōba" (Two Old Women, 1908), "Oi" (The Nephew, 1908), "Hokkoku umare" (Born in the North, 1908), "Tabi no soko" (At the Bottom of His Tabi, 1913), "Oshina to Oshima no tachiba" (The Positions of Oshina and Oshima, 1923), "Fuaiya gan" (Fire Gun, 1923), "Shiroi tabi no omoide" (1933), "Kanojo-tachi no mi no ue" (1935), "Razō" (1935), and "Senji fūkei" (Scenes from Wartime, 1937).

This body of work constitutes a wonderfully realistic, frequently humorous, and beautiful aesthetic of common experience in Meiji, Taishō, and Shōwa Japan. It was unique to Tokuda Shūsei and to Japan and reveals few identifiable influences from Western literatures. As this study has attempted to show, Shūsei's literature was the product of an extremely varied mixture of stylistic influences current from 1895 to 1941, the repeated theoretical calls for a Japanese realism from 1885 to the mid-1930s, and Shūsei's literary sophistication, acquired over decades of writing hundreds and hundreds of fictions, many of which do not make for easy or pleasant reading today. Given the present state of Japanese literary education, it seems unlikely that an aesthetic similar to Shūsei's will ever be created again.

Shimazaki Tōson, Tayama Katai, and Nagatsuka Takashi have left moving portraits of the provincial gentry and rural poor. Kobayashi Takiji, Nakano Shigeharu, and Miyamoto Yuriko, at great personal sacrifice, described the brutal sufferings and regimentation experienced by the working poor. Natsume Sōseki, Shiga Naoya, and Tanizaki Jun'ichirō, in brilliant and different ways, chronicled the rise and fall of the prewar middle class, a small minority which has so influenced the mores, fashions, and ideology of the postwar middle class. To my knowledge, only Shūsei managed to portray that confused realm of urban immigrants, each with his or her individual ethic of success not sanctioned by the state, that protean middle stratum of fairly heterogeneous origin, which *actually became* the new middle class in the postwar period. The cultural milieu of *shomin* life that Shūsei described in changing aspect for over forty years was in many ways quite dark: there was malnutrition, a great deal of disease, and much violence against and exploitation of women. But there was also much laughter and beauty and leisurely textures of time, which seem to be disappearing today. Surely Shūsei's complex portrayals of the unconscious nature of mass class identification with the commonly respectable are as universally relevant and true today as they were before the end of World War II.

Notes

Introduction

1. Tokuda Shūsei, "Shin no shakai shōsetsu," *Bunshō Sekai,* Nov. 1906, pp. 16–17.

2. As translated and quoted in Jay Rubin, *Injurious to Public Morals: Writers and the Meiji State* (Seattle: University of Washington Press, 1984), p. 253.

3. Tokuda Shūsei, "Jo ni kaete," in *Kunshō* (Chūō Kōronsha, 1936), pp. 2–3.

4. Edward Fowler, *The Rhetoric of Confession: Shishōsetsu in Early Twentieth-Century Japanese Fiction* (University of California Press, 1988), pp. 62 and 128–30.

5. Kawabata Yasunari, "Kaisetsu," in *Tokuda Shūsei,* vol. 9 of *Nihon no bungaku* (Chūō Kōronsha, 1973), 1:519–20.

6. Tatsuo Arima, *The Failure of Freedom* (Harvard University Press, 1969).

7. Fowler, *Rhetoric of Confession,* p. 6.

Chapter 1. Born into Kanazawa's Decline

1. Donald Keene, for example, writes, "Shūsei was born in Kanazawa of low-ranking samurai stock" (Keene, *Dawn to the West* [New York: Holt, Rinehart, and Winston, 1984], 1:271). In contrast, Shūsei's biographer, Noguchi Fujio, argues:

The Tokuda house was not a direct retainer to the Maeda *daimyō* of the Kaga domain but was the retainer of the third most important retainer to the Maeda, the Yokoyama, who had a stipend of 30,000 *koku* and was one of the eight senior advisers [*hakka,* the eight families] in the Kaga domain. From the perspective of the Maeda, the Tokuda house was a rear vassal [*baishin*], and although the Tokuda stipend of 70 *koku* (reduced from 90 *koku*) was not high, the family was firmly in the middle rank of the rear vassals. It is not appropriate to look upon the Tokuda family as lower-class *bushi* [*kakyū bushi*]. For example, Watanabe Kazan's father, Ichirōbei, was the senior adviser [*karō*] of the small Tawara domain (12,000 *koku*), and he had a *koku* income of 100 *koku* 4 *fuchi*. The Watanabe family and the Tokuda family were not all that different in status. The reason people tend to look on the Tokuda family as low-ranking samurai is that the Kaga domain, with its 1,000,000 *koku,* was so enormous. (Noguchi Fujio, *Tokuda Shūsei no bungaku* [Chikuma Shobō, 1979], p. 367)

The *koku* measure (1 *koku* = about 5 bushels) was based on the average annual consumption of rice by one person and was the standard unit of measure of individual and domainal income up until the 1870s.

2. James L. McClain, *Kanazawa: A Seventeenth-Century Japanese Castle Town* (Yale University Press, 1982), p. 77.

3. This description of Kanazawa before and after the Restoration is drawn from McClain, *Kanazawa*, pp. 32–46, 74–85, and 124–33; Noguchi Fujio, *Tokuda Shūsei den* (Chikuma Shobō, 1965), pp. 1–70; Wakabayashi Kisaburō, ed., *Ishikawa-ken no rekishi* (Kanazawa: Hokkoku Shuppansha, 1970), pp. 197–99 and 214; and Takazawa Yūichi, ed., *Kyōdoshi jiten Ishikawa-ken* (Shōheisha, 1980), pp. 150–53. On the decline in Kanazawa's population, see Kanazawa Shishi Hensan Shingi Iinkai, ed., *Kanazawa shishi: gendai-hen* (Kanazawa-shi, 1969), 2:8.

4. The question of Shūsei's date of birth is dealt with in Noguchi Fujio, *Tokuda Shūsei den,* pp. 3 and 549; Noguchi Fujio, *Tokuda Shūsei nōto* (Chūō Daigaku Shuppanbu, 1972), pp. 83–86; and Noguchi Fujio, *Tokuda Shūsei no bungaku,* p. 463. See also Uchida Masao, *Nihon rekijitsu genten* (Yūsankaku Shuppan, 1975), p. 490; and Nihon Shiseki Kyōkai, ed., *In'yō-reki taishōhyō* (1940; reprint, Tokyo Daigaku Shuppankai, 1978), p. 172.

February 1, 1872, the date of birth given for Shūsei here, contradicts all other English-language sources. Shūsei's father legitimized Shūsei's birth by registering it with the just recently prefectural (not domainal) authorities, and undoubtedly he and the authorities followed the traditional lunar calendar in recording the date. It was not until December 9, 1872, that the Meiji emperor declared that the third day of the twelfth month of the fifth year of Meiji would become the first day of the sixth year of Meiji, consistent with January 1, 1873, of the Gregorian calendar. On the correct date of Shūsei's birth according to the Gregorian calendar, see also Matsumoto Tōru, "Tokuda Shūsei no ichisokumen: sakusō suru jikan, 2," *Gakutō* 4, no. 7 (1985): 44.

It is definitely not an exaggeration to say that a study of this kind could not have been written without the definitive research done on Shūsei's life by the novelist, critic, and essayist Noguchi Fujio. Because the primary sources concerning the date of Shūsei's birth were not available to me, I wrote to Noguchi Fujio seeking confirmation of the February 1, 1872, date. Though he was quite busy, he graciously took the time to answer in great detail and at length this and other questions I had about Shūsei's life. He confirmed the February 1, 1872, date (letter received from Noguchi Fujio, 3 June 1987).

Henceforth, in the notes, Noguchi Fujio's *Tokuda Shūsei den* will be abbreviated *Shūsei den,* his *Tokuda Shūsei nōto* will be abbreviated *Shūsei nōto,* and his *Tokuda Shūsei no bungaku* will be abbreviated *Shūsei bungaku.* I have attempted to cite primary sources as often as possible, but in matters concerning Shūsei's life and the people close to him, I was frequently guided to the primary source and influenced in my understanding of it by Noguchi's works.

5. Noguchi, *Shūsei den,* pp. 4–27. See also Matsumoto Sachiko, "Tokuda Shūsei kakei nenpu," in Nihon Bungaku Kenkyū Shiryō Kankōkai, ed., *Shizenshugi bungaku,* Nihon Bungaku Kenkyū Shiryō Sōsho series (Yūseidō, 1975), pp. 217–20.

6. Tōda Yasutaka, "Tokuda Shūsei: hito to bungaku," in Ishikawa Gendai Bungaku no Kai, ed., *Furusato to bungaku tanbō: Kyōka, Shūsei, Saisei* (Kanazawa: Noto Insatsu Shuppanbu, 1985), pp. 115–16.

7. Tetsuo Najita, *Japan,* Modern Nations in Historical Perspective (Englewood Cliffs, N.J.: Prentice-Hall, 1974), pp. 94–95.

8. Parenthetical citations in the text refer to Tokuda Shūsei, *Shūsei zenshū,* 18 vols. (Kyoto: Rinsen Shoten, 1974–75; reprint, 1989–91), by volume number and page number(s). The original *Shūsei zenshū* was published by the company Hibonkaku in 1936 and 1937. Shūsei was still living and writing, and thus these original fifteen volumes did not include some of his most important work written later in his life. The publishing company Sekkasha undertook the project of bringing out a more complete edition of Shūsei's work in 1961 and 1962, but this house ran into financial problems and ceased publication after only six volumes. About ten years later, the publisher Rinsen Shoten purchased the rights to both the Hibonkaku *Shūsei zenshū* and the Sekkasha *Shūsei zenshū* and reproduced the fifteen volumes from the 1930s edition and added three volumes from the Sekkasha *Shūsei zenshū.* The Rinsen Shoten *Shūsei zenshū* is considered the definitive one.

A true "complete works" for Shūsei would probably be very difficult to compile. Shūsei wrote a great deal and works bearing his name come to light regularly. Shūsei's son Tokuda Masahiko has informed me that negotiations are under way to publish a diary Shūsei kept for many years, a work essential to an edition claiming to be a complete works. At present, it seems highly unlikely that a complete works including this diary will ever be published.

As noted above, parenthetical citations in the text refer to the Rinsen Shoten *Shūsei zenshū,* which will henceforth be abbreviated SZ in the notes. The Sekkasha *Shūsei zenshū* will be abbreviated SSZ. For further information on the bibliographical problems created by Shūsei's complete works, see Richard Torrance, "Tokuda Shūsei and the Representation of *Shomin* Life" (Ph.D. diss., Yale University, 1989), nn. 3 and 4, pp. 485–88.

9. Shūsei wrote that *Hikari o ōte* was "like a memoir" (*jijoden no yō na mono*) and that he had intentionally avoided using literary techniques in writing it (Tokuda Shūsei, "Atogaki," in *Sandai meisaku zenshū: Tokuda Shūsei shū* [Kawade Shobō, 1942], p. 404). The same remarks are quoted in full in Tokuda Kazuho, "Kaisetsu," in *Tokuda Shūsei shū,* vol. 11 of *Shōwa bungaku zenshū* (Kadokawa Shoten, 1953), p. 388.

10. Noguchi, *Shūsei den,* pp. 15–16.

11. Noguchi cites a report written by a regional bureaucrat to the central government describing such scenes of deprivation. Apparently government offi-

cials were monitoring the situation out of the fear that yet another armed revolt would break out as they had in Hagi and during the Seinan War (ibid., pp. 19–20). Similar scenes of destitution are described in Kanazawa Shishi Hensan Iinkai, ed., *Kōhon Kanazawa shishi: seiji hen,* in *Kōhon Kanazawa shishi* (Meicho Shuppan, 1973), 13:304–5. According to another history of Ishikawa prefecture, Shūsei's memory was correct in regard to the saying "Cops are Kanazawa's special regional products." So many young people of samurai birth emigrated to take up low-paying or stigmatized jobs in other parts of the country that policemen, elementary-school teachers, and prostitutes were said to be Kanazawa's specialty products (see Hashimoto Tetsuya and Hayashi Yūichi, *Ishikawa-ken no hyaku-nen* [Yamakawa Shuppansha, 1987], pp. 14–15). James L. McClain describes the advent of capitalism in Ishikawa prefecture in far more positive terms in his "Failed Expectations: Kaga Domain on the Eve of the Meiji Restoration," *Journal of Japanese Studies* 14, no. 2 (Summer 1988): 403–47.

12. Some of these prohibitions are described in McClain, *Kanazawa,* pp. 112–14 and 142–44.

13. Shūsei wrote, "I am addicted to traditional Japanese music and the theater as an alcoholic is addicted to wine" (Tokuda Shūsei, "Morikawa-chō yori," *Shinchō* 16, no. 3 [Mar. 1912]: 7). A history of Kanazawa confirms that many ex-samurai with no financial sense squandered their newly gained money on "degenerate" pleasures and entertainments (Kanazawa Shishi Hensan Iinkai, ed., *Kōhon Kanazawa shishi,* 13:303).

14. Noguchi, *Shūsei den,* pp. 44–47; Noguchi, *Shūsei bungaku,* pp. 400–403; and Matsumoto, "Tokuda Shūsei no kakei nenpu," pp. 220 and 224–25.

15. McClain, "Failed Expectations," p. 442; and Hashimoto and Hayashi, *Ishikawa-ken no hyaku-nen,* pp. 17–20.

16. As quoted in Maekawa Ryūnosuke, "Kyōka to Kanazawa," in Ishikawa Gendai Bungaku no Kai, ed., *Furusato to bungaku tanbō,* p. 21.

17. Shūsei was apparently unaware that his mother, Take, was his father's fourth wife. Unpei was married to yet another unfortunate woman, who died young and childless (Noguchi, *Shūsei bungaku,* pp. 358–64; letter received from Noguchi Fujio, 3 June 1987; and Matsumoto Tōru, *Tokuda Shūsei* [Kasama Shoin, 1988], p. 17).

18. Two of these novels have been translated by Edwin McClellan as *Grass on the Wayside* (University of Chicago Press, 1969) and *A Dark Night's Passing* (Kodansha International, 1976). Donald Keene has translated Dazai's novel as *No Longer Human* (Norfolk: New Directions, 1958).

19. Robert Rolf ("Tokuda Shūsei," in *Kodansha Encyclopedia of Japan* [Kodansha, 1983]) states that Shūsei had "a somewhat drunken father" (p. 45). There seems to be a bit of blaming the victim going on in this statement. To my knowledge, Shūsei mentioned his father's drinking habits only once in his memoirs and autobiographical fiction: "In the evenings, when he had a chance, his father would drink five *shaku* of rice wine" (SZ, 2:515). Five *shaku* of rice

wine is about one-half of a cup. In fact, Shūsei's father appears to have disapproved of heavy drinking (SZ, 18:210).

20. The work is contained in Tokuda Shūsei, *Kyōmanji* (Shinseisha, 1902). It is discussed in Tomita Hitoshi, "Tokuda Shūsei to Arufuonsu Dōdē: *Kyōmanji* to *Ru Puchi Shōzu*," *Hikaku Bungaku Nenshi* 9 (1973): 1–24.

21. "Namakemono" (The Lazy One, 1899, SZ, 1:295–362), "Shikkoku" (Fetters, 1903, SZ, 1:453–534), and "Gisei" (Self-sacrifice, 1907, SZ, 2:280–300) are three relatively available and readable works of a number that express this theme.

22. Tokuda Shūsei, "Ware we ikani shite shōsetsuka to narishi ka," *Shinko Bunrin* 3, no. 1 (1907): 56–57; Tokuda Shūsei, "Yo ga jōkyō tōji," *Waseda Bungaku*, July 1908, p. 69; Tokuda Shūsei, "Watakushi to yū ningen," *Waseda Bungaku*, Mar. 1917, p. 41; and Tokuda Shūsei, "Yū'utsu narishi koro," *Bunshō Kurabu* 14 (Mar. 1929): 116–17. The fact that Shūsei gave so many reasons for dropping out of school probably indicates that it was one of the most important decisions in his life.

23. This description of the educational system in Kanazawa is taken from Noguchi, *Shūsei den,* pp. 31–69, with supplementary information from Donald Roden, *Schooldays in Imperial Japan: A Study in the Culture of a Student Elite* (University of California Press, 1980), pp. 7–44. Shūsei's grades seemed to fluctuate with the state of his health. At times he did quite well, once placing seventh out of 132 examinees. On his grades, see Iwanaga Yutaka, "*Shūsei roku Muchoan nikki* ni tsuite: Tokuda Shūsei kenkyū shiryō," *Kokugo to Kokubungaku* 31, no. 365 (Sept. 1954): 40; and Noguchi, *Shūsei den,* p. 550.

24. Shūsei worked for the fiery People's Rights politician Shibuya Mokuan (Noguchi, *Shūsei den,* pp. 106–10). One of the first of many eulogies Shūsei would write was for Mokuan (Tokuda Shūsei, "Fugū no kishi Mokuan-kyō o itamu," *Uzue* 2, no. 4 [1904]).

25. Iwanaga argues that two short pieces Shūsei wrote in 1893 and 1894 reflect a deep commitment to liberalism ("*Shūsei roku Muchoan nikki* ni tsuite"). Noguchi counters that these documents should be ignored because of the lack of sophistication of the ideas presented (Noguchi, *Shūsei den,* pp. 106–8). These early short essays do not contradict the picture Shūsei presents of himself in his memoirs. He apparently was a lonely, intense, and often sad young man whose pen name, "Voice of Autumn," which he began using in *Shūsei roku,* was romantically appropriate. It is probably an error to use later political categories such as liberalism to describe his political inclinations at this time. As Noguchi observes, many other young men of samurai birth expressed wild admiration for both the "liberal" Itagaki Taisuke and the "reactionary" Saigō Takamori.

26. Carol Gluck, *Japan's Modern Myths: Ideology in the Late Meiji Period* (Princeton University Press, 1985).

27. Tokuda Shūsei, "Yo no isshō o shihai suru hodo no ōkinaru eikyō o ataeshi hito, jiken, oyobi shisō," *Chūō Kōron,* Feb. 1923, p. 101.

28. Hasuda Ichigorō (1833–61) was one of the most skilled of the Mito and Satsuma assassins who killed Ii Naosuke (1815–60), the senior adviser to the Tokugawa Bakufu. Hasuda's letter to his mother was written while he was awaiting execution. The letter from Yamagata Aritomo to Saigō Takamori is a moving document in which Yamagata advises his old friend to commit suicide on being defeated in the Seinan War. For a copy of the letter, see Mitarai Tatsuo, *Yamagata Aritomo* (1958; reprint, Jiji Tsūshinsha, 1985), pp. 124–29.

29. Suehiro Tetchō's *Setchūbai* (Plum Blossoms Opening in the Snow, 1886) was an enormously popular political allegory set one hundred and fifty years in the future. It recounts the oppression suffered and the love that developed between the hero and heroine in their struggle to bring democracy to the politically barren soil of Japan so many years before. Tōkai Sanshi's *Kajin no kigū* (The Coincidental Meeting of Superior Persons, 1885–97) was a political novel in which the hero meets revolutionaries from Spain, Ireland, and China. Reflecting the author's own bitter disappointment over defeat in the fight for independence of the Aizu domain, the work chronicles the evils of the great powers' imperialism and the aspirations of weaker nations—China, Egypt, India, Poland—for independence. *Kuzuya no kago* (The Junkman's Basket, 1887) was a satire of Japan's "enlightenment" written by Nishimura Tenshū, a scholar of classical Japanese literature. Shūsei mistook Hattori Bushō, a prominent journalist who satirically portrayed the customs and manners of his contemporary Tokyo society, for the work's author.

30. Shūsei probably meant quite literally that at first he could not understand the new colloquial style being hammered out by Futabatei Shimei and others. Several years after entering college, he had become a supporter of the new literary language (SZ, 18:60).

31. The plays of Kawatake Mokuami (1816–93) served as an important transition from the popular theater of the Edo period to that of the Meiji period. Aeba Kōson's *Muratake* (Bamboo Growing in Profusion, 1889–90) is a twenty-volume work combining fiction and travel essays.

32. Tokuda Shūsei, "Gaikoku bungaku no ishokusha," *Shinshōsetsu: rinji sōkan* 27, no. 8 (Aug. 1922):31–32, special edition commemorating Mori Ōgai shortly after his death.

33. Carol Gluck, *Japan's Modern Myths,* pp. 12 and 171–73; Suzuki Toshio, *Shuppan: kōfukyōka kōbō no isseiki* (Shuppan Nyūsusha, 1970), pp. 118–26.

34. Though Shūsei portrayed himself as being naive in going up to Tokyo to gain Kōyō's support (SZ, 18:78–79), within a year of leaving home, he was publishing a serialized novel in a newspaper in Osaka.

35. Kiryū Yūyū's account of his trip to Tokyo with Shūsei is found in Kiryū Yūyū, *Omoideru mama,* in Ōta Masao, ed., *Kiryū Yūyū jiden* (Gendai Jyānarizumu Shuppankai, 1973), pp. 3–11. Kiryū led the kind of fascinating, varied, and tragic life that is very attractive to biographers, and at least three books on his life have been written: Maeda Yūji, *Pen wa shinazu* (Jiji Tsūshinsha, 1964); Ide Magoroku, *Teikō no shinbunjin Kiryū Yūyū* (Iwanami

Shoten, 1980); Ōta Masao, *Hyōden Kiryū Yūyū: senjika teikō no jyānarisuto* (Fuji Shuppan, 1987). In addition to portraying Kiryū in his memoirs, Shūsei also portrayed him in *Kabi* (Mold, 1911) and "Taoreta kabin" (The Fallen Flower Vase, 1926).

36. Noguchi, *Shūsei den*, pp. 72–242. Keene, *Dawn to the West*, 1:271–72, has a brief but accurate summary of this period in Shūsei's life.

37. Noguchi, *Shūsei den*, pp. 142–43.

38. Due to inflation during the forty-odd years Shūsei worked as a professional writer, it is difficult to determine how his income compared with those of other professions. When he had established himself as an independent literary presence but was still associated with Kōyō's guild (see chap. 2), he earned 90 sen per manuscript page (Matsuura Sōzō, ed., *Genkōryō no kenkyū: sakka jyānarisuto no keizaigaku* [Nihon Jyānarisuto Senmon Gakuin Shuppanbu, 1978], p. 50). When Shūsei serialized a successful novel such as *Shōkazoku* (The Minor Aristocrat, Dec. 1904–Apr. 1905), he was earning at least 70–100 yen a month. Shūsei certainly did not earn as much as Natsume Sōseki did as the literary editor of *Asahi Shinbun* (200 yen a month) or the prime minister (1,000 yen a month), but his monthly earnings were a great deal more than the average salary for a writer-journalist (Ishikawa Takuboku earned 35 yen a month). Though he frequently complained of poverty, Shūsei did not have to endure the role of the starving artist, as Shimazaki Tōson did in 1904 when he survived on the equivalent of a skilled carpenter's wage (ibid., p. 81). As an established, professional novelist in 1933, he could command 10 yen or more per page, which placed him in the top rank of writers, together with Tanizaki Jun'ichirō, Shiga Naoya, and Shimazaki Tōson. He was infinitely better paid than, say, a laborer in 1930 (ibid., pp. 117–18).

39. Masamune Hakuchō, *Shizenshugi seisuishi*, in *Masamune Hakuchō shū*, vol. 16 of *Gendai Nihon bungaku taikei* (Chikuma Shobō, 1969), p. 265. In contrast, Tayama Katai recalled that Shūsei "had a comparatively good mind. He had only to hear a story and he could go right to the heart of the matter" (Tayama Katai, *Kindai no shōsetsu*, in *Kindai bungaku kaisō shū*, vol. 60 of *Nihon kindai bungaku taikei* [Kadokawa Shoten, 1973], p. 154).

40. For a convenient listing of Shūsei's self-deprecating remarks lovingly collected by a critic who has little understanding or sympathy for Shūsei, see Sakamoto Hiroshi, "Tokuda Shūsei ron," *Hyōron* 1, no. 9 (1934): 10.

41. Noguchi, *Shūsei nōto*, p. 17.

42. Tokuda Shūsei, "Atogaki," in *Sandai meisaku zenshū: Tokuda Shūsei shū*, p. 404.

43. Nakamura Akira, *Hiyu hyōgen jiten* (Kadokawa Shoten, 1977), items 2152 (pp. 216–17), 2549 (p. 235), 4193 (p. 305), and 5233 (p. 356). See also Yasuda Yojūrō as quoted in Izumi Aki, *Nihon roman-ha hihan* (Shinseidō, 1968), p. 109.

44. A convenient listing of some of this high praise for Shūsei is found in Kōno Toshirō, ed., *Ronkō Toduka Shūsei* (Ōfūsha, 1983), pp. 245–58.

Chapter 2. Popular Entertainment, 1895–1908

1. Enomoto Takashi, "Nenpu," in Toduka Shūsei, *Tokuda Shūsei shū,* vol. 21 of *Nihon kindai bungaku taikei* (Kadokawa Shoten, 1973), p. 472. My discussion of Shūsei's literary career and works during the period 1895–1908 is informed by Yoshida Seiichi, *Shizenshugi no kenkyū* (Tokyodō Shuppan, 1955), 1:421–52; Yoshida Seiichi, *Katai Shūsei,* vol. 8 of *Yoshida Seiichi chosaku shū* (Ōfūsha, 1980), pp. 229–76; Wada Kingo, *Shizenshugi bungaku* (Shibundō, 1966), pp. 287–97 and 314–37; Ikari Akira, *Ken'yūsha to Shizenshugi kenkyū* (Ōfūsha, 1975), pp. 194–209; Iwanaga, "*Shūsei roku Muchoan nikki* ni tsuite"; Enomoto Takashi, "Jōkyō tōji no Tokuda Shūsei," *Kokubungaku Kenkyū* 14 (1956): 114–26; Enomoto Takashi, "Shūsei no shoki no hito-kōsatsu: Kōyō to no kankei o chūshin ni," *Bungaku Gogaku* 12 (1958): 103–13; Enomoto Takashi, "Shūsei nōto 2: Seiyō bungaku juyō," *Waseda Daigaku Kyōiku Gakubu Gakujutsu Kenkyū Kokugo Kokubungaku Hen* 28 (1979): 41–50; Enomoto Takashi, "Shūsei nōto 3: 'Yabukōji' 'Namakemono,' " *Waseda Daigaku Kyōiku Gakubu Gakujutsu Kenkyū Kokugo Kokubungaku Hen* 29 (1980): 29–41; Matsumoto Tōru, "Meiji sanjūni, sannen no Shūsei: *Kawanami, Shiokeburi, Kumo no yukue,*" *Kinki Daigaku Kyōyōbu Kenkyū Kiyō* 14, no. 2 (1982): 11–22; Matsumoto Tōru, "Tokuda Shūsei no shajitsu: *Arajotai* o chūshin ni," *Kinki Daigaku Kyōyōbu Kenkyū Kiyō* 15, no. 1 (1983): 1–14; Yamamoto Yoshio, "*Seinenbun* ni okeru Shūsei," *Komazawa Kokubun* 1, no. 1, pp. 61–70; Kataoka Tsutomu, "Tokuda Shūsei Meiji sanjū nendai no shōsetsu," *Komazawa Kokubun* 16, pp. 15–32; Kataoka Tsutomu, "*Shūsei shū Naraku:* Shūsei no shōsetsu, 2," *Komazawa Kokubun* 17, pp. 73–91; Sasaki Tōru, "Tokuda Shūsei ron," in Nihon Bungaku Kenkyū Shiryō Kankōkai, ed., *Shizenshugi bungaku,* pp. 227–51; and Tomita, "Tokuda Shūsei to Arufuonsu Dōdē."

2. Enomoto Takashi, "Nenpu," in Tokuda Shūsei, *Tokuda Shūsei shū,* vol. 21 of *Nihon kindai bungaku taikei,* p. 472; Matsumoto Tōru, *Tokuda Shūsei,* pp. 32 and 107–15. It seems that when Shūsei became a fairly prominent literary figure in 1904–5, he used the works of friends and other professional writers under his own name without attribution and shared the profit. Writers who wrote for publication under Shūsei's name included Okamoto Reika, Nakamura Murao, Arima Chōrai, Mishima Sōsen, Mayama Seika, Takahashi Yamakaze, and Kojima Masajirō (Matsumoto Tōru, *Tokuda Shūsei,* p. 36; see also Noguchi, *Shūsei den,* pp. 285–86; and Noguchi, *Shūsei nōto,* pp. 150–57).

3. Matsumoto Tōru, *Tokuda Shūsei,* pp. 415–25.

4. Ibid., 415–17. On Kōyō's dominance of the literary world, see Rubin, *Injurious to Public Morals,* pp. 40–41.

5. Noguchi, *Shūsei nōto,* pp. 19–20. It has been reported in English-language sources that Shūsei was a member of the Ken'yūsha (e.g., Keene, *Dawn to the West,* p. 272). This is not correct. In a short piece he wrote in 1937, Shūsei stated that he was not a member of the Ken'yūsha and knew little about it. He was a member of the Sōsha, a different Kōyō guild formally

established in 1902 (Noguchi, *Shūsei den,* p. 132; Matsumoto Tōru, *Tokuda Shūsei,* p. 393).

6. See chap. 1, n. 38.

7. The most straightforward and amusing account Shūsei provides of his years in Kōyō's school, the Tochimandō-juku or Shiseidō-juku, and his relations with Kōyō and other young writers who made up the Sōsha is in a series of articles covering his career from his first job at Hakubunkan in 1894 to the formation of the Ryūdokai, an association of writers connected with naturalism organized in the first years of the twentieth century: Tokuda Shūsei, "Waga bundan seikatsu no sanjūnen," *Shinchō* 23, nos. 1, 3–6 (1926): 11–21, 24–33, 19–29, 33–39, and 26–40. Tokuda Shūsei, "Yo ga jōkyō tōji," pp. 68–72, provides a concise account of Shūsei's failed first attempt to become established in Tokyo. Chapters 2–4 of Noguchi, *Shūsei den,* give an exhaustively comprehensive and reliable sifting of evidence concerning the biographical facts of Shūsei's life during the years 1892–1908. Noguchi's comparison of Shūsei's *Kabi* with nonliterary sources allows one to confidently read this novel as a personal history of Shūsei's life from 1902 to 1908 or so (Noguchi, *Shūsei bungaku,* pp. 4–216).

8. Noguchi, *Shūsei den,* p. 30.

9. The school which holds that Shūsei's apprenticeship to Kōyō was a betrayal of Shūsei's personal inclinations is represented by Sasaki, "Tokuda Shūsei ron," p. 241. The opposing view, that Shūsei benefited from his complex relationship with Kōyō, is found in Ikari, *Ken'yūsha to Shizenshugi kenkyū,* pp. 194–209. For Shūsei's words, see Tokuda Shūsei, "Katai-shi," *Chūō Kōron,* May 1908, pp. 82–83. It should be noted that Shūsei's remarks were made in praise of Tayama Katai for not selling out.

10. Richard Torrance, "Tokuda Shūsei and the Representation of *Shomin* Life" (Ph. D. diss., Yale University, 1989), pp. 68–75.

11. Matsumoto Tōru, *Tokuda Shūsei,* p. 35.

12. By temperament and style unsuited to the sophisticated, urbane atmosphere of Kōyō's school, Shūsei was the most politically serious and intense member of the guild (Yoshida, *Shizenshugi no kenkyū,* 1:431–33 and 438–39). Something of the despair Shūsei was prone to while living independently as a member of the guild can be judged from Shūsei's *Kabi* (SZ, 3:3–246).

13. Yoshida, *Shizenshugi no kenkyū,* 1:433.

14. Noguchi, *Shūsei den,* pp. 142–43.

15. Ibid.; and SZ, 3:77–78, 15:551, 18:161.

16. Tokuda Shūsei, "Waga bundan seikatsu no sanjūnen, II," *Shinchō* 23, no. 3 (1926): 31–33; Noguchi, *Shūsei den,* pp. 174–75 and 557.

17. Tokuda Shūsei, "Waga bundan seikatsu no sanjūnen," *Shinchō* 23, no. 5 (1926): 33–35. Osada's original translation, probably done in part by his apprentice or students, was incomprehensible, and Shūsei had to retranslate large portions of it.

18. For a description of the cartoon, see Matsumoto Tōru, "Tokuda Shūsei no ichisokumen: kore mo seiō taiken, 1" *Gakutō* 4, no. 6 (1985): 44–45.

19. The information about plagiarism comes from Matsumoto Tōru, *Tokuda Shūsei,* pp. 32–33.

20. Noguchi, *Shūsei den,* pp. 285–86 and 368–72.

21. On early Western literary influence on Shūsei, see Enomoto, "Shūsei nōto 2: Seiyō bungaku juyō," pp. 41–50; and Matsumoto Tōru, *Tokuda Shūsei,* p. 34.

22. SZ, 17:238.

23. Tokuda Shūsei, "Waga bundan seikatsu no sanjūnen," *Shinchō* 23, no. 1 (1926): 19.

24. Tokuda Shūsei, "Kōyō Sensei no juku," *Bunshō Sekai* 2, no. 2 (Feb. 1907): 23.

25. Tokuda Shūsei, "Waga bundan seikatsu no sanjūnen," *Shinchō* 23, no. 1 (1926): 20.

26. Ibid., pp. 17–18.

27. Torrance, "Tokuda Shūsei and the Representation of *Shomin* Life," pp. 82–90.

28. Tokuda Shūsei, "Tansu-chō no juku," *Bunshō Sekai* 7, no. 14 (Oct. 1912): 62; Tokuda Shūsei, "Sōsaku seikatsu no nijūgonen," *Shinchō* 33, no. 5 (Nov. 1920): 6. Kōyō even tried to restrict and censor what his students read. He seems to have thought that authors do not read, they write (Tokuda Shūsei, "Waga bundan seikatsu no sanjūnen," *Shinchō* 23, no 1 [1926]: 19). For a realistic and reasoned summary of the personal relationship between Shūsei and Kōyō, see Enomoto Takashi's excellent notes to *Kabi:* "Hochū," in *Tokuda Shūsei shū,* vol. 21 of *Nihon kindai bungaku taikei,* nn. 27, 34–41, and 43–45, pp. 433–37.

29. Torrance, "Tokuda Shūsei and the Representation of *Shomin* Life," pp. 68–128.

30. This is true of other Japanese novels of the period; see David Blaylock, "Industrialization and Image of the Merchant in Meiji Japan" (Ph.D. diss., Ohio State University, 1992).

31. Peter Brooks, *The Melodramatic Imagination: Balzac, Henry James, Melodrama, and the Mode of Excess* (1976; reprint, Columbia University Press, 1985), p. 205.

32. Ibid., p. 44.

33. As reported in Yoshida Seiichi, roundtable discussion, "Tayama Katai to Tokuda Shūsei: shizenshugi bungaku, III," *Bungaku* 28, no. 4 (1960): 59 (p. 405). An interview with Shūsei, "Tokuda Shūsei-shi to bungaku to shumi o kataru: sakka to kisha no ichimon ittō roku 13," *Shinchō* 43, no. 6 (Dec. 1925): 35–36, tends to confirm Yoshida Seiichi's memory.

34. Matsumoto Tōru, *Tokuda Shūsei,* pp. 52–56.

35. On the condition of Shūsei's health at the time he wrote *Kumo no yukue,* see Tokuda Shūsei, "Waga bundan seikatsu no sanjūnen," *Shinchō* 23, no. 4 (1926): 19–20.

36. This work is discussed at length in Torrance, "Tokuda Shūsei and the Representation of *Shomin* Life," pp. 105–11.

37. Yoshida, *Shizenshugi no kenkyū*, 1:446; Matsumoto Tōru, *Tokuda Shūsei,* pp. 61–64.

38. Shūsei probably did not have a very clear notion of what a Nietzschean character was. Nietzsche, Henrik Ibsen, and others had gotten mixed up in the flood of imported late nineteenth-century European literature (Matsumoto Tōru, *Tokuda Shūsei,* pp. 77–79).

39. SZ, 15:537; Noguchi, *Shūsei den,* pp. 316–17.

40. Tokuda Shūsei, "Jijo," in *Shōkazoku* (Shun'yōdō, 1905), first two pages, unpaginated.

41. For a list and the summary of the plots of a number of the melodramas Shūsei continued writing into the Taishō period for a provincial audience, see Wada Kingo, *Shizenshugi bungaku,* pp. 314–37.

42. Several critics have argued that *Arajotai* (1908) established Shūsei's reputation (see, e.g., Keene, *Dawn to the West,* p. 273).

43. "Useikai," in Nihon Kindai Bungakukan, ed., *Nihon kindai bungaku daijiten* (Kōdansha, 1977).

44. The photograph is reproduced in the front of Nakamura Mitsuo, *Meiji bungakushi,* Chikuma Sōsho, vol. 9 (Chikuma Shobō, 1963).

45. Rubin, *Injurious to Public Morals,* p. 112.

46. Matsuura, *Genkōryō no kenkyū,* p. 36.

47. Tokuda Shūsei, "Shajitsu-ha," *Waseda Bungaku,* Nov. 1895; and see Torrance, "Tokuda Shūsei and the Representation of *Shomin* Life," pp. 68–71.

48. Karatani Kōjin, *Nihon kindai bungaku no kigen* (Kōdansha, 1980), pp. 47–113, esp. pp. 97–106 for the process of Christianization, which Shūsei did not undergo.

49. Torrance, "Tokuda Shūsei and the Representation of *Shomin* Life," pp. 126–32.

50. Wada Kingo, *Byōsha no jidai: hitotsu no Shizenshugi bungaku ron* (Sapporo: Hokkaidō Daigaku Tosho Kankōkai, 1975), pp. 7–8.

51. Masamune, *Shizenshugi seisuishi,* in *Masamune Hakuchō shū,* p. 262; Hirotsu Kazuo, "Shūsei to Hakuchō," in *Hirotsu Kazuo zenshū* (Chūō Kōronsha, 1974), 9:360.

52. Rubin, *Injurious to Public Morals,* p. 60; Katagami Tengen, "Sakka no saikin no inshō," *Shumi* 3, no. 10 (Oct 1908): 62.

53. Until about the time of the Russo-Japanese War (1904–5), Shūsei was known as a writer relatively well versed in Western literature, but with the coming of naturalism, he distanced himself from foreign letters. After naturalism, Shūsei explicitly stated on a number of occasions that he had received little influence from Western literature. As early as 1906, he mapped out a reading program that was basically nationalistic. In order to become a writer, he argued, one should read one's own national literature. First, read one's contemporary literature, for it mirrors one's most personal concerns and motives. Next, read one's national classical literature, for this will allow one to judge the transience of the present. Finally, one should read foreign literature but always with the

awareness that literature in Europe is as subject to changing fashion as any other ("Shōsetsu to shūchiku," in Nihon Bunshōgaku, ed., *Shōsetsu sahō* [Shinchōsha, 1906], pp. 45–50).

In 1910 he declared, "I confess that we are all following in the footsteps of Western literature. Though I once had occasion to be touched by the mood created by foreign literature in Japan, I had few opportunities to come into direct contact with it. Still, of the few works of Western literature I have read, none have really surprised me" ("Taika no honyaku yori wa wakai hito no honyaku," *Bunshō Sekai* [sōkan], Aug. 1910, p. 36).

In 1925 he stated in an interview, "I haven't read that many things from the West. Well, I've read some. When I was at school, I studied Shakespeare with a friend and read a little English literature, and when I first came to Tokyo, I regularly read some things. But comparatively I haven't received much influence" ("Tokuda Shūsei-shi to bungaku to shumi o kataru, p. 30).

In 1932 he wrote, "Now, on the rare occasions when I read a foreign work, I can absorb it, but in the past, I didn't receive such works without resistance, and I didn't understand them" ("Baruzakku-kata to Hadēi-kata," *Bungei Shunjū*, Aug. 1932, p. 34).

Let us turn to critical reception. In 1912 Morita Sōhei wrote of Shūsei's *Kabi*, "The first thing one notices about *Kabi* is that there is no novel of this form in the West" ("*Kabi* no hihyō," *Shinchō*, Feb. 1912, reprinted in Inagaki Tatsurō et al., eds., *Kindai bungaku hyōron taikei* [Kadokawa Shoten, 1972], 3:445). Masamune Hakuchō wrote, "One will almost certainly not find a novelistic style like Shūsei's in a foreign work" ("Tayama Tokuda ryō-shi ni tsuite," *Bunshō Sekai* 15, no. 11 [Nov. 1920]: 126). In the same issue of this journal, Nakamura Seiko observed that Shūsei was unique to Japan ("Katai Shūsei ryō-shi ni tsuite," p. 135).

54. The prosecuted short story, "Baikaisha" (The Mediator, 1909), truly is smutty in an adolescent sense. Shūsei seldom descended to this low quality of writing, and Noguchi concludes that the work was a *daisaku* (ghostwritten work), not actually written by Shūsei but published under his name (Noguchi, *Shūsei den*, p. 368). The story is conveniently found in Odagiri Hideo, ed., *Hakkin sakuhin shū* (Hokushindō, 1957).

On Shūsei's relations and affinities with Takahama Kyoshi and Natsume Sōseki, see Etō Jun, "Kaisetsu," in *Tokuda Shūsei*, vol. 10 of *Nihon no bungaku* (Chūō Kōronsha, 1973), 2:516–20; and Sōma Tsuneo, *Nihon Shizenshugi saikō* (Yagi Shoten, 1981), pp. 176–202. On the difficulties Shūsei encountered in selling *Ashiato*, see Wada Kingo, *Shizenshugi bungaku*, pp. 297–314.

55. Haten Kōshi, "Ken'yūsha tsui ni horobu," *Shinsei*, Apr. 1907, pp. 19–20; Yobidashiya, "Bundan hyakunin: Tokuda Shūsei-shi," *Shinsei*, Apr. 1907, p. 85.

56. Gyofū-sei, "Shūsei no *Honoo*," *Waseda Bungaku*, Mar. 1908, p. 24.

57. Sōma Gyofū, "Shinsho zakkan," *Waseda Bungaku*, Nov. 1908, pp. 70–71.

58. Kisha, *"Shūsei shū,"* *Chūō Kōron,* Oct. 1908, p. 150.

59. Choin-sei, "Boshin bundan gaikan," *Chūō Kōron,* Jan. 1909, pp. 14–15.

60. Matsubara Shibun, "Tokuda Shūsei ron," *Shinchō,* Nov. 1908, pp. 31–32.

61. Tokuda Shūsei, "Mienu tokoro wakaranu oku," *Waseda Bungaku,* Mar. 1908, p. 85.

62. Tokuda Shūsei, "Shōsetsu keishiki ron," *Shinchō,* Aug. 1909, pp. 62–63.

63. Tokuda Shūsei, "Sakka no kosei to chihō iro," *Shinsei,* Jan. 1909, p. 61.

64. Tokuda Shūsei, "Kansō futatsu mitsu," *Bunshō Sekai,* Dec. 1908, p. 94.

65. A lucid and accurate presentation of the debate over narrative perspective and Iwano Hōmei's theoretical position is found in Fowler, *Rhetoric of Confession,* pp. 124–27. For a detailed examination of how Hōmei's views evolved, see Wada Kingo, *Shizenshugi bungaku,* pp. 246–86.

66. Tokuda Shūsei, "Sōsaku zatsuwa," *Shinchō* 13, no. 6 (Dec. 1910): 107.

67. Sōma Tsuneo, *Nihon Shizenshugi saikō,* pp. 175–78.

68. In 1911 Ikuta Chōkō declared that Shūsei was in the first rank as a stylist of the novel together with Mori Ōgai and Natsume Sōseki, and he was simply incredulous that writing as fine as that in *Arajotai* produced sales of fewer than 500 volumes (Ikuta Chōkō, "Tokuda Shūsei-shi o ronzu," in *Tokuda Shūsei shū,* vol. 68 of *Meiji bungaku zenshū* [Chikuma Shobō, 1971], p. 361).

69. Sōma Tsuneo, *Nihon Shizenshugi saikō,* p. 177; Takahama Kyoshi, "Shaseibun to Shizen-ha," *Shumi* 2, no. 9, pp. 69–70.

70. As quoted in Sōma Tsuneo, *Nihon Shizenshugi saikō,* p. 178, from a July 1913 interview with Kyoshi in *Bunshō Sekai.*

71. Noguchi, *Shūsei den,* pp. 335–36.

72. As quoted in Enomoto Takashi, "Shūsei bungaku ron," in a special edition of *Bunshō Kurabu, Tokuda Shūsei Kenkyū Go,* Sept. 1952, p. 15. Shūsei made several similar declarations (Tokuda Shūsei, *Shōsetsu no tsukurikata* [Shinchōsha, 1918], p. 82).

73. Ikuta, "Tokuda Shūsei-shi o ronzu," p. 362.

74. Shūsei showed an early interest in naturalism (Matsumoto Tōru, *Tokuda Shūsei,* pp. 83–84), but it was not until 1908 that Shūsei publicly associated himself with the literary movement. He wrote that he and Oguri Fūyō had made the transition to naturalism (*shizen-ha*) (Tokuda Shūsei, "Kōyō o shite ima no bundan ni arashimeba," *Waseda Bungaku,* Sept. 1908, p. 392). On naturalism as a national literary movement, see Yoshida Seiichi, roundtable discussion, "Tayama Katai to Tokuda Shūsei," pp. 64–65 (410–11).

75. As quoted in Noguchi, *Shūsei den,* p. 156.

Chapter 3. Four Novels about Common Life

1. Kojima Masajirō, "Shōsetsu no kamisama," *Nihon Bungaku Zenshū Geppō* (Shūeisha) 67 (Aug. 1974): 1–2.

2. As quoted in Kōno, *Ronkō Tokuda Shūsei,* pp. 248–49.

3. Funabashi Seiichi, *Tokuda Shūsei* (Kōbundō Shobō, 1941), p. 158.

4. As quoted in Kōno, *Ronkō Tokuda Shūsei,* p. 247.

5. Ibid., pp. 245–58; Uno Kōji and Hirotsu Kazuo, roundtable discussion, "Shūsei o kataru," in *Geirin Kanpo* (special edition *Tokuda Shūsei: hito to bungaku*), Nov. 1947, pp. 48–58; Takami Jun, Takeda Rintarō, Hirotsu Kazuo, and Tokuda Shūsei, roundtable discussion, "Sanbun-seishin o kiku," *Jinmin Bunko* 1, no. 9 (Nov. 1936): 72–90; Chikamatsu Shūkō, "Hito oyobi geijut-suka to shite no Tokuda Shūsei-shi," in *Tokuda Shūsei shū,* vol. 68 of *Meiji bungaku zenshū,* pp. 365–70; Shinoda Hajime, *Nihon no gendai shōsetsu* (Shūeisha, 1980), p. 236. See also Yamamoto Kenkichi, "Tokuda Shūsei no sekai: shōsetsu no saihakken," *Bungakukai* 16, no. 12, pp. 142–45; and the various literary journals commemorating Shūsei's fiftieth birthday: *Bunshō Sekai,* Nov. 1920; *Bunshō Kurabu,* Nov. 1920; *Shinchō* 33, no. 5 (Nov. 1920).

6. Kawabata, "Kaisetsu," in *Tokuda Shūsei,* 1:517.

7. Hirotsu Kazuo, "Shūsei-shi no ayunda michi," *Kaizō,* Jan. 1937, p. 247.

8. Shinoda Hajime, "Tokuda Shūsei," *Subaru,* Sept. 1972, p. 131; Shinoda Hajime, *Nihon no kindai shōsetsu* (Shūeisha, 1973), pp. 222–23. Something like an "explanation" of Shūsei's style is offered in Shinoda Hajime, *Zoku-Nihon no kindai shōsetsu* (Shūeisha, 1975), pp. 72–73, but it is not convincing.

9. Takami Jun, "Shūsei bungaku ni kanren shite," *Geirin Kanpo,* Nov. 1947, p. 30.

10. This formulation owes much to Furui Yoshikichi, "*Arajotai* to wataku-shi," in his *Kotoba no jujutsu* (Sakuhinsha, 1980), pp. 103–6.

11. Ara Masahito, "Shomin-teki seimeikan ni kōshite: Shūsei no sakuhin o tōshite," *Kosei,* Nov. 1949, p. 27 for desire to become *citoyen* and pp. 29–30 for self-revulsion.

The use of *shomin* and *shomin-teki* to describe the class-cultural milieu Shūsei portrayed is so pervasive as to be almost unnoticeable. The following list is from references at hand and is far from complete: Noguchi, *Shūsei nōto,* p. 57; Ino Kenji, "Tokuda Shūsei e no shōmei," in *Tokuda Shūsei shū,* vol. 15 of *Gendai Nihon bungaku taikei* (Chikuma Shobō, 1970), p. 352; Matsubara Shin'ichi, "*Gusha*" *no bungaku* (Tōjusha, 1974), p. 150; Hirotsu Kazuo, "Tokuda Shūsei ron," in *Hirotsu Kazuo zenshū,* 9:401–2; Tokuda Kazuho, "Kaisetsu," in *Tokuda Shūsei shū,* vol. 21 of *Nihon kindai bungaku taikei,* p. 36; Yoshida, *Katai Shūsei,* p. 298; Enomoto Takashi, "*Kabi* no seiritsu to sono imi," *Kokubungaku Kenkyū* 18 (Oct. 1958): 153; Kawabata Yasunari, "Kaisetsu," p. 514; Etō, "Kaisetsu," p. 526; Uno Kōji, "*Arajotai* to *Arakure,*" in *Tokuda Shūsei senshū* (Kengensha, 1952), 2:334; Fukuda Kiyoto and Sasaki Tōru, *Tokuda Shūsei: hito to sakuhin,* Century Books, vol. 41 (Kiyomizu Shoin, 1981).

The *shomin,* or *shomin-teki,* culture these writers and critics refer to is quite different from the pre-Restoration *shomin* culture of old Edo. It is different from the culture described in Takao Kazuhiko, *Kinsei no shomin bunka* (Iwanami Shoten, 1969), and in Yasumaru Toshio, *Nihon no kindaika to minshū shisō* (Aoki Shoten, 1974). This is not because these excellent studies are in any way "mistaken" but rather because in Shūsei's mature works one is beyond concepts or ideologies. Isoda Kōichi, *Shisō to shite no Tokyo: kindai bungakushi nōto* (Kokubunsha, 1978), clarifies what the term *shomin* means in the context of Shūsei's mature fiction. Isoda posits two mass cultures coexisting in the nation's capital. One was relatively indigenous and spoke the local Tokyo dialect, and the other was a newer, immigrant *shomin* culture, which gained dominance at about the turn of the century and began to push the older culture out of Tokyo proper and over the Sumida River. It is this newer mass culture that Shūsei portrayed and that writers and critics refer to as *shomin* or *shomin-teki*. This should become clear in the course of this study.

12. Noguchi, *Shūsei bungaku*, p. 440.

13. I would like to thank Shūsei's son Tokuda Masahiko, who graciously agreed to an interview during my stay in Japan and who later wrote to me providing information about his family and the house in which he was born (letter received from Tokuda Masahiko, 27 Oct. 1987). For other accounts of the cordiality of Shūsei's home under Tokuda Hama's management, see Noguchi, *Shūsei den*, pp. 257–59; Kotera Kikuko, "Tokuda Shūsei Sensei no koto," *Shinsōsaku* 38, special issue in memory of Tokuda Shūsei, pp. 11–15; Mikka Ushio, "Tokuda Shūsei-shi no nichijō," *Bunshō Sekai*, Mar. 1913, pp. 52–55.

14. Takebayashi Musōan, "Omoide futatsu, mitsu," *Geirin Kanpo* 2, no. 8 (Nov. 1947): 1–4.

15. For details on the affair, see Torrance, "Tokuda Shūsei and the Representation of *Shomin* Life," n. 17, pp. 530–31.

16. Takahashi Toshio, "*Arajotai* o yomu: 'risshi' gensō no yukue," in Kōno, *Ronkō Tokuda Shūsei*, pp. 12–15.

17. On the process by which the loan translation for "individualism" was created, see Yanabu Akira, *Honyakugo seiritsu jijō*, Iwanami Shinshō, vol. 189 (Iwanami Shoten, 1982), pp. 21–42.

18. Furui, "*Arajotai* to watakushi," p. 103.

19. Thomas C. Smith, "The Right to Benevolence: Dignity and Japanese Workers, 1890–1920," *Comparative Studies in Society and History* 26, no. 4 (1984): 587–613.

20. Miyachi Masato, *Nichi-Ro sengo seijishi no kenkyū: teikokushugi keiseiki no toshi to nōson* (Tokyo Daigaku Shuppankai, 1973), p. 207. Miyachi argues that much of the poverty came from Western-style innovations, which threw people out of work (pp. 201–9).

21. Takahashi Toshio, "*Arajotai* o yomu," pp. 20–23.

22. Enomoto Takashi, "*Arajotai* ni tsuite," *Meiji Taishō Bungaku Kenkyū* 21 (Mar. 1957): 53–62.

23. Noguchi, *Shūsei den*, pp. 362–66.

24. Tokuda Shūsei, "Nenpu," in *Tokuda Shūsei shū*, vol. 18 of *Gendai Nihon bungaku zenshū* (Kaizōsha, 1928), p. 508.

25. Furui, "*Arajotai* to watakushi," p. 103.

26. Matsubara Iwagorō, *Saiankoku no Tokyo,* ed. Amane Kangōri (1893; reprint, Gendai Shisōsha, 1980).

27. The biographical information about Tokuda Hama and her extended family is taken from Noguchi, *Shūsei bungaku,* pp. 439–60.

28. Ibid., p. 19. As Matsumoto Tōru has argued, it is probably an oversimplification to ascribe the "involution of time" (*sakusō suru jikan*) in *Ashiato* to any one literary technique, be it Noguchi's "reverse narration," Fujii's prolepsis, or "stream of consciousness" narration (Torrance, "Tokuda Shūsei and the Representation of *Shomin* Life," p. 171; Matsumoto Tōru, *Tokuda Shūsei,* pp. 148–51; James A Fujii, "The Subject in Meiji Prose Literature" [Ph.D. diss., University of Chicago, 1986], pp. 104–5). James A. Fujii's *Complicit Fictions* (University of California Press, 1992) appeared shortly after my book had gone to the publisher, and unfortunately I was unable to consult his chapter on Tokuda Shūsei.

29. Matsumoto Tōru, *Tokuda Shūsei,* pp. 152–53.

30. Tokuda Shūsei, "Sōsaku zatsuwa," p. 106.

31. My equation of everyday time with *shomin* life is influenced by Henri Lefebvre, "The Everyday and Everydayness," *Yale French Studies* 73 (1987): 7–11.

32. A special edition of *Gendai Esupuri,* in *Edo/Tokyo Gaku* 5 (Feb. 1987), provides a coherent portrait of how Tokyo grew and how people dealt with the growth. Of particular interest are Fujimori Terunobu, "Meiji no toshi keikaku," pp. 55–69; Hasegawa Tokunosuke, "Taishō ikō no Tokyo no toshi keikaku," pp. 70–95; and Maeda Ai, "Yama-no-te no oku," pp. 143–67.

33. The original—*ta no naka ni mura shibai no tatsu toki ni wa*—probably refers to some form of *dengaku* (a form of ritual theater performed to ensure plentiful harvests).

34. For a photograph of this type of building, see Inagaki Eizō, "Edo Tokyo sumai no utsurikawari," *Kokubungaku Kaishaku to Kanshō* 28, no. 2 (Jan 1963): 93. For an alternative perspective showing how similar buildings were extended back from the street, see *Zusetsu Nihon bunkashi taikei* (Shōgakkan, 1956), vol. 11 (volume for Meiji *jidai*), p. 113.

35. Miyachi, *Nichi-Ro sengo seijishi no kenkyū,* p. 189.

36. This opinion is contradicted by at least one critic, who discovers in Shūsei a reversion to the *chōnin* (Tokugawa merchant) mentality as opposed to the mentality of the free *citoyen*: Kataoka Yoshikazu, *Kataoka Yoshikazu chosaku shū* (Chūō Kōronsha, 1979), 7:278. Kataoka is answered by Noguchi, *Shūsei den,* pp. 501–2.

37. These numbers and estimates are based on *Kindai shomin seikatsu shi* (henceforth abbreviated KSSS), 10 vols. (San'ichi Shobō, 1988), vol. 10 (Kyōraku/sei); and J. E. De Becker, *The Nightless City* (1899; reprint, Charles E. Tuttle, 1971). The figure of over a million guests a year is from De Becker (p. 359). By 1925, for Tokyo as a whole, this number had risen to an annual 3,760,000 men doing a total business of over 15,000,000 yen (KSSS, 10:209–11). On the number of pleasure quarters, houses of assignation, and geisha

houses, see KSSS, 10:263–67. For official police statistics, see KSSS, 10:287. These are only official statistics, and one can assume prostitution was far more widespread. On illegal prostitution, see KSSS, 10:258. On other trades, including nursing, thought to engage in prostitution, see KSSS, 10:274–80.

38. For the view that *Ashiato* represents a move away from the extensive psychological treatment of his protagonists, see Matsumoto Tōru, *Tokuda Shūsei*, pp. 81–105. A comparison of this passage and a similar situation Shūsei created in his *Nijū-shi-go* (Twenty-four or Twenty-five, 1909–10), which he finished some six months before starting *Ashiato,* reveals how condensed and abbreviated his prose had become. Renko, the heroine of *Nijū-shi-go,* agonizes over whether to return to her husband or not (SZ, 16:571–72).

39. Takami, "Shūsei bungaku ni kanren shite," p. 29.

40. Shimazaki Tōson, *Shimazaki Tōson shū,* vol. 7 of *Nihon bungaku zenshū* (Shinchōsha, 1962), 2:237.

41. Tōson's portrayal of Minoru does not contradict the state's official utopian vision of a Japanese people united as a nation to meet the challenge of "internationalization." The official vision is contained in the Boshin Rescript of 1908:

Civilization now advances with each passing day and month, and East and West draw closer, sharing mutual communication; and there is thus born profit and benefit for both. We shall promote diplomatic relations and the spirit of sincere friendship in hopes of participating with other nations far into the future in this fortunate state of affairs. On reflection, however, We discover that We must await the national development necessary to keep abreast with this steady progress in the world and to share in the benefits of civilization. . . . The high and the low must act with one heart, faithfully submitting to your vocations, devoting yourselves with thrift and diligence to production. Through mutual sincerity and probity, cultivate Our traditional custom of warmheartedness, discard the frivolous for the substantial, admonish those who would neglect their work and indulge in indolence, and never cease to exert your most strenuous efforts at self-improvement. ("Boshin Shōsho," as quoted in Sumiya Mikio, *Dai-Nihon Teikoku no shiren,* vol. 22 of *Nihon no rekishi,* in Chūō Bunko series [Chūō Kōronsha, 1974], pp. 345–46)

This language of authority provides a clear model for the average Japanese citizen: warmhearted, sincere, hardworking, persevering, and perhaps a little stupid. Shūsei's subversive and radical vision of common life testifies to an utterly different society.

42. Shinoda, "Tokuda Shūsei," p. 145.

43. Enomoto, "*Kabi* no seiritsu to sono imi," pp. 150–62.

44. Natsume Sōseki, Letter 1361, *Sōseki zenshū* (Iwanami Shoten, 1967), 15:82.

45. Etō, "Kaisetsu," pp. 518–19.

46 Tokuda Shūsei, "Sōsaku zatsuwa," p. 106.

47. Tayama Katai, "Chikagoro yonda shōsetsu ni tsuite no kansō," *Bunshō Sekai* 7, no. 6 (May 1912): 9.

48. Shimazaki Tōson, "*Kabi* no hihyō," *Shinchō* 16, no. 2 (Feb. 1912): 5–6.

49. Masamune Hakuchō, "*Kabi* no hihyō," *Shinchō* 16, no. 2 (Feb. 1912):

7. In the same issue, Shimamura Hōgetsu praises *Kabi* as one of the finest novels created in the previous year (p. 53). Tamura Toshiko devotes her entire review to a condemnation of the "vulgar" Ogin's deportment and manners. "I have learned a great deal from this novel about the slyness of uneducated women," she writes (Tamura Toshiko, "*Kabi* no Ogin," *Shinchō* 16, no. 3 [Mar. 1912]: 66–71; quotation from p. 71).

50. On the real-life continuities between *Ashiato* and *Kabi,* see Torrance, "Tokuda Shūsei and the Representation of *Shomin* Life," pp. 216–17.

51. Natsume Sōseki, *The Miner,* trans. Jay Rubin (Stanford University Press, 1988), p. 16.

52. Terada Tōru, "Tokuda Shūsei," in *Tokuda Shūsei shū,* vol. 68 of *Meiji bungaku zenshū,* p. 372.

53. Matsumoto Tōru, *Tokuda Shūsei,* p. 178.

54. Noguchi, *Shūsei bungaku,* p. 134; Noguchi, *Shūsei den,* p. 560.

55. Yozo Watanabe, "The Family and the Law," in Arthur Taylor von Mehren, ed., *Law in Japan: The Legal Order in a Changing Society* (Harvard University Press, 1963), pp. 364–72. It was not until 1915 that the Great Court of Judicature held that the breach of a promise of marriage constituted a default of obligation.

56. Noguchi, *Shūsei bungaku,* pp. 140–47.

57. Shimamura, "*Kabi* no hihyō," p. 53.

58. Fujii, "The Subject in Meiji Prose Literature," p. 118.

59. Something of a myth had grown up about the circumstances of Ozaki Kōyō's death. The *Japan Times* reported that he had died in a particularly heroic way. See the introduction to Ozaki Kōyō, *The Gold Demon,* trans. A. Lloyd (Seibundō, 1917), p. xi. Shūsei was violating this myth. On the complex relationship between Shūsei and Izumi Kyōka, see Yoshimura Hakunin, "Tokuda Shūsei no mita Izumi Kyōka: *Onna keizu* to 'Wakai' to o megutte," *Meiji Taishō Bungaku Kenkyū* 21 (Mar. 1957): 71–79. Shūsei had a strange capacity for feeling affection for people who disliked him.

60. Shūsei defends himself and his relationship with Kōyō most effectively in Tokuda Shūsei, "Waga bundan seikatsu no sanjūnen," *Shinchō* 26, no. 5 (May 1926): 38–39.

Chapter 4. Rough Living

1. Nakamura Seiko, Nogami Shirakawa, and Sōma Gyofū, "*Arakure* no hihyō," *Shinchō* 23, no. 4 (Oct. 1915): 102–5; Kisha, "*Arakure,*" *Waseda Bungaku,* Oct. 1915, pp. 8–9; Kisha, "*Arakure,*" *Bunshō Sekai* 10, no. 12 (Nov. 1915): 222–31; Okada Hachiyo, "*Arakure* no Oshima," *Shinchō* 23, no. 5 (Nov. 1915): 82; A. B. C., "Shūsei no geijutsu," *Shinchō,* Nov. 1915, pp. 36–39; Chikamatsu Shūkō, "Shūsei-shi no sakufū," *Bunshō Sekai* 11, no. 6 (June 1916): 58–63.

2. On Sōseki's opinions about giving interviews, see Komiya Toyotaka,

"Kaisetsu," in *Sōseki zenshū,* 16:837–39. On the reprinting of the interview, see Matsumoto Tōru, *Tokuda Shūsei,* p. 197.

3. For a description of Sōseki's standing in the literary world at this time, see Inagaki Tasurō and Shimomura Fujio, eds., *Ningen sanka,* vol. 11 of *Nihon bungaku no rekishi* (Kadokawa Shoten, 1968), pp. 92–98.

4. *Honryū* is found in SZ, 4:269–574.

5. Natsume, Letter 2059, *Sōseki zenshū,* 15:490–91.

6. Natsume, "Bundan no kono goro," *Sōseki zenshū,* 16:725.

7. Natsume, *Sōseki zenshū,* 16:723–24.

8. Ibid., p. 724.

9. Ibid.

10. Matsumoto Tōru, *Tokuda Shūsei,* pp. 197 and 201–3.

11. As quoted in ibid., p. 198.

12. This formulation owes much to Maurice Blanchot, "Everyday Speech," *Yale French Studies* 73 (1987): 12–20; and Georg Lukacs, *History and Class Consciousness,* trans. Rodney Livingstone (Cambridge: MIT Press, 1971), p. 52.

13. As quoted in Noguchi, *Shūsei den,* p. 404. For a complete translation of the quotation, see Torrance, "Tokuda Shūsei and the Representation of *Shomin* Life," pp. 252–53.

14. For a complete chronology of the events in *Arakure* based on a close reading of the novel, see Torrance, "Tokuda Shūsei and the Representation of *Shomin* Life," pp. 354–56.

15. Noguchi, *Shūsei den,* p. 405. Shūsei's "Shōhai" (Victory or Defeat, 1921) traces Suzuki Chiyo's life up until her divorce from Shūsei's brother-in-law (SZ, 5:349–98).

16. Matsumoto Tōru, *Tokuda Shūsei,* pp. 207–19.

17. This discussion owes much to Etō Jun, "Tokuda Shūsei to 'jūjitsu shita kanji': 'katachi' to 'suji' to 'jisshitsu,' " *Gunzō,* Mar. 1990, pp. 172–82.

18. Shōwa Joshi Daigaku Hifukugaku Kenkyūshitsu, ed., *Kindai Nihon fukusōshi* (Kindai Bunka Kenkyūjo, 1971), pp. 7, 49, 63, and 281–82; Miyachi, *Nicho-Ro sengo seijishi no kenkyū,* pp. 173–87. On the large profits to be made from Western-style clothing, see Shōwa Joshi Daigaku Hifukugaku Kenkyūshitsu, *Kindai Nihon fukusōshi,* p. 314.

19. Shōwa Joshi Daigaku Hifukugaku Kenkyūshitsu, *Kindai Nihon fukusōshi,* pp. 115–16. Of course, the spread of Western-style clothing was generally limited to men's clothing and to those men who worked in white-collar positions (ibid., pp. 314–15).

20. On the creation of the loan translation *ren'ai* and its opposition to the vulgarity of native terms for physical love, see Yanabu Akira, *Honyakugo seiritsu jijō,* pp. 89–105.

21. Funabashi Seiichi remembers his father's shocked disapproval on discovering that Seiichi had underlined the "sexy" parts of *Arakure* (Funabashi, *Tokuda Shūsei,* pp. 2–3).

22. Lefebvre, "The Everyday and Everydayness," p. 10.

23. Kimura is referring to the Japanese women who go to Hawaii, learn Western magic tricks, and return to Japan to perform on the street ("Sukunaku to mo, Hawai atari kara kaette kita tejina-shi gurai ni wa fumemasu ze").

24. Fukuda and Sasaki, *Tokuda Shūsei,* pp. 156–60.

25. Tokuda Shūsei, *"Tadare* to *Aradure* no moderu," *Shinchō* 23, no. 4 (Oct. 1915): 13.

26. Ao Zukin, "Shūsei-shi no *Tadare,*" *Shinchō* 19, no. 2 (Aug. 1913): 94–97.

27. Shojo Hō, "Shigatsu bundan no saku to hyōron," *Bunshō Sekai* 8, no. 6 (May 1913): 77.

28. Kisha, *"Arakure," Waseda Bungaku,* Oct. 1915, pp. 8–9.

29. See n. 1 above. These reviews can also be found in Inagaki Tatsurō et al., eds., *Kindai bungaku hyōron taikei,* 10 vols. (Kadokawa Shoten, 1971–75).

30. Chikamatsu, "Shūsei-shi no sakufū," *Bunshō Sekai* 11, no. 6 (June 1916): 58–59. See also Chikamatsu Shūkō, "Mikaiketsu no shōsetsu: Shūsei no *Arakure," Yomiuri Shinbun,* 17 Oct. 1915, p. 7.

31. E.g., see Tanaka Jun, "Tokuda Shūsei ron," *Waseda Bungaku,* Feb. 1917, p. 34.

32. Hirotsu, "Tokuda Shūsei ron," in *Hirotsu Kazuo zenshū,* 9:401.

33. Masamune, *Shizenshugi seisuishi,* in *Masamune Hakuchō shū,* p. 263.

34. Mikhail M. Bakhtin, *The Dialogic Imagination: Four Essays,* trans. Caryl Emerson and Michael Holquist (Austin: University of Texas Press, 1981), pp. 84–85.

35. Isoda Kōichi and Takahashi Hideo, "Taidan," *Tokyo Shinbun,* 21 Dec. 1977, p. 3; Nakagami Kenji, *Da'in* (Kawade Shobō Shinsha, 1977), pp. 33–82. For a rather tentative argument that Shūsei is still influential, see Matsumoto Tōru, *Tokuda Shūsei,* p. 2.

Chapter 5. In Disguise, 1915–1938

1. Funabashi, *Tokuda Shūsei,* p. 132.

2. Shibundō Henshūbu, *Bundanshi jiten* (Shibundō, 1972), pp. 75–76.

3. Yoshiya Nobuko, "Tokuda Shūsei," in *Yoshiya Nobuko zenshū* (Asahi Shinbunsha, 1976), 12:117–21; Funabashi, *Tokuda Shūsei,* pp. 138–43.

4. Kanai Keiko, *"Kasō jinbutsu* ron: fūzoko to sakka shutai no kakawari ni tsuite," in Kōno, *Ronkō Tokuda Shūsei,* pp. 109–10.

5. Tanigawa Tetsuzō, *Shizenshugi no sakka,* fourth pamphlet in Iwanami Kōza Nihon Bungaku series (Iwanami Shoten, 1931), p. 22.

6. For an excellent summary of the 1927–32 Marxist debate on the nature of Japanese capitalism, see Germaine Hoston, *Marxism and the Crisis of Development in Prewar Japan* (Princeton University Press, 1986).

7. Nakamura Mitsuo, *Meiji bungakushi,* pp. 211–17; Kataoka Yoshikazu, *Kataoka Yoshikazu chosaku shū,* 7:215–82; Itō Sei, *Shōsetsu no hōhō,* in *Itō Sei zenshū* (Shinchōsha, 1973), vol. 16, esp. pp. 44–50.

8. Kenshiro Homma, *The Literature of Naturalism: An East-West Comparative Study* (Kyoto: Yamaguchi Publishing House, 1983), p. 346.

9. Shinoda, *Nihon no gendai shōsetsu,* p. 240.

10. Kanai, "*Kasō jinbutsu* ron," p. 109.

11. Donald Keene, "Tokuda Shūsei: hito to sakuhin," in vol. 2 of *Shōwa bungaku zenshū* (Shōgakkan, 1988), p. 959.

12. Noguchi, *Shūsei den,* p. 414.

13. Satomi Ton, "Futari no sakka" (Two Novelists, 1950), in *Satomi Ton zenshū* (Chikuma Shobō, 1978), 9:208.

14. "What is a *shinkyō shōsetsu*?" Tokuda Shūsei asks in a roundtable discussion in 1924 ("*Shinchō* gappyō kai," *Shinchō* 40, no. 2 [Feb. 1924]: 41).

15. My discussion of Shūsei's personal fiction as eulogy has been influenced by Matsumoto Tōru, *Tokuda Shūsei,* pp. 223–39; and Tōya Ryūnosuke, " 'Machi no odoriba' ron," in Kōno, *Ronkō Tokuda Shūsei,* pp. 95–97. For a more detailed discussion of this subgenre and a listing of the locations of these works, see Torrance, "Tokuda Shūsei and the Representation of *Shomin* Life," pp. 326–30 and n. 26, p. 545.

16. Kawabata Yasunari, *Kawabata Yasunari zenshū* (Shinchōsha, 1982), 31:82.

17. Tokuda Shūsei, *Furusato no yuki* (Hakusan Shobō, 1947), pp. 265–70. For a fuller discussion of subgenres of Shūsei's personal fiction, see Torrance, "Tokuda Shūsei and the Representation of *Shomin* Life," pp. 330–33 and n. 30, pp. 546–48.

18. Matsumoto Tōru, *Tokuda Shūsei,* pp. 260–62. Summaries of some of these stories and a plausible description of how Shūsei might have used them to rewrite his love affair with Yamada Junko are contained in Wada Kingo, *Shizenshugi bungaku,* pp. 337–50.

19. Uno Kōji, "Bungaku dangi," *Shinchō* 24, no. 2 (Feb. 1927): 6.

20. As quoted in Wada Kingo, *Shizenshugi bungaku,* p. 340.

21. SZ, 17:159; Tokuda Shūsei, roundtable discussion, "Gappyō: Shūsei-shi no renai geijutsu," *Shinchō* 24, no. 10 (Oct. 1927): 126–29; Fudōchō Gappyō Kai, "Tokuda Shūsei ron," *Fudōchō* 3, no. 5 (Nov. 1926): 68–70; Tokuda Shūsei, "Tokuda Shūsei-shi yori," *Sandē Mainichi* 6, no. 39 (18 Sept. 1927): 8.

22. Enomoto, "Nenpu," in Tokuda Shusei, *Tokuda Shūsei shū,* vol. 21 of *Nihon kindai bungaku taikei,* pp. 485–86. The term "miraculous comeback" is frequently used in the secondary literature to describe this phase of Shūsei's career. See, e.g., Matsumoto Tōru, *Tokuda Shūsei,* p. 331.

23. Takami Jun, *Shōwa bungaku seisuishi* (Bungei Shunjūsha, 1958), 1:13–15.

24. Ibid., p. 15. Kobayashi Hideo, "Shishōsetsu ron," *Kobayashi Hideo zenshū* (Shinchōsha, 1956), 3:100–102.

25. Tokuda Shūsei, "Sakka wa kakumei kibun o motsu," *Shinchō* 38, no. 2 (Feb. 1923): 25–27.

26. Tokuda Shūsei, "Gappyō: Shūsei-shi no ren'ai geijutsu," pp. 127–28. See also Tokuda Shūsei, "Gappyō," *Shinchō* 23, no. 7 (July 1926): 23.

27. He was probably not wrong. See George Tyson Shea, *Leftwing Literature in Japan: A Brief History of the Proletarian Literary Movement* (Hosei University Press, 1964), p. 430; Noguchi, *Shūsei den,* pp. 492–94.

28. Rubin, *Injurious to Public Morals,* pp. 246–47; Inagaki and Shimomura, *Ningen sanka,* pp. 364–65 and 417–18; Senuma Shigeki, *Hon no hyakunen shi* (Shuppan Nyūsusha, 1965), pp. 171–77; Yoshida Seiichi and Inagaki Tatsurō, eds., *Gendai no hatate-tachi,* vol. 12 of *Nihon bungaku no rekishi* (Kadokawa Shoten, 1968), pp. 12–13; Kitani Kimie, "Enpon būmu to bungakusha," in vol. 1 of *Kōza Shōwa bungakushi* (Yūseidō, 1988), pp. 28–39.

29. Tokuda Shūsei, SZ, 15:232, as translated and quoted in Rubin, *Injurious to Public Morals,* p. 253. On Shūsei's interest in writing popular fiction, see Tokuda Shūsei, roundtable discussion, "*Shinchō* gappyō," *Shinchō* 42, no. 3 (Mar. 1925): 49–50, 58, 68, and 75–76.

30. Tokuda Shūsei, "Iwayuru tsūzoku shōsetsu to geijutsu shōsetsu no mondai: jibun no keiken o kiso ni shite," *Shinchō* 30, no. 2 (Feb. 1919): 2–4, esp. p. 2. On Shūsei's aversion to writing popular fiction, see Tokuda Kazuho, "Kaisetsu," in *Tokuda Shūsei shū,* vol. 21 of *Nihon kindai bungaku taikei,* pp. 43–44.

31. Etō, "Kaisetsu," pp. 525–27.

32. Kobayashi Hideo, *Kobayashi Hideo zenshū,* 4:204–7. For the first quotation, see p. 205; for the second, see p. 207.

33. Kanai, "*Kasō jinbutsu* ron," pp. 111–13.

34. Tosaka Jun, *Tosaka Jun zenshū* (Keisō Shobō, 1966), 4:265.

35. Ibid., p. 268. For an interesting examination of the similarities between the thought of Tosaka Jun and that of Kobayashi Hideo and the more philosophical project, as opposed to literary, that led Tosaka to attempt to bridge the gap between the social individual and the self through a critique of the Japanese ideology, see Takahashi Bunzō, "Kaisetsu," in *Tosaka Jun zenshū,* 4:470–80.

36. Tosaka Jun, *Tosaka Jun zenshū,* 4:271.

37. Ibid., p. 282.

38. Kanai, "*Kasō jinbutsu* ron," p. 108. Kanai is particularly critical of Nakamura Mitsuo's *Fūzoku shōsetsu ron.* Clearly Nakamura's "theory of the Japanese novel and Japanese personality" is unequal to the task of engaging the major current of Japanese realism represented by Shūsei's mature fiction. He barely mentions Shūsei (Nakamura Mitsuo, *Fūzoku shōsetsu ron,* Shinchō Bunko series [1950; reprint, Shinchōsha, 1958]).

39. Keene, "Tokuda Shūsei," p. 954.

40. Wada Kingo, *Shizenshugi bungaku,* pp. 337–39.

41. Most of this information about the real-life counterparts of the characters in *Kasō jinbutsu* is taken from Noguchi, *Shūsei bungaku,* pp. 252–354.

42. Katsumoto Seiichirō, roundtable discussion, "Tayama Katai to Tokuda Shūsei: Shizenshugi bungaku, 3," *Bungaku* 28, no. 4 (1960): 79–86 (425–32).

43. Yamada Junko's own fictional account of her affair with Shūsei appeared in several forms. It first appeared in a special edition of *Chūō Kōron* and was then included in a collection of her pieces: Yamada Junko, *Onna deshi* (Yuki Shobō, 1954). It appears in yet another form: Yamada Junko, *Onna deshi* (Amatoriasha, 1955). On Shūsei's stinginess, see the 1955 version, pp. 39 and 77; for quotation, see p. 44.

44. Noguchi, *Shūsei den,* pp. 468–85.

45. Kobayashi Hideo has called the Christmas party scene "highly symbolic." Donald Keene has interpreted the title of the work as follows: "Yōzō remembered his experiences ten years before and wondered how he could have acted so crazily. He compared that time to his present and concluded that, in the past, he had been a *Man in Disguise* ("Tokuda Shusei," p. 955). Kawabata Yasunari has written, "One might say that only the novelist . . . appears undisguised on the stage of life. But, in another sense, a novelist is always in disguise. A novelist cannot live a 'real life.' *Kasō jinbutsu* is the pained confession of a novelist who realizes that he can never remove his mask" (Kawabata, *Kawabata Yasunari zenshū,* 29:460). See also Kobayashi Hideo, *Kobayashi Hideo zenshū,* 4:206.

46. Rubin, *Injurious to Public Morals,* pp. 251–52.

47. A reproduction of this painting is conveniently found at the front of *Kadokawa Nihon-shi jiten,* 2d ed. (Kadokawa Shoten, 1974), fifteenth page of reproductions from the front.

48. This symbol of cheap modernism is cited in Etō Jun's discussion of *Kasō jinbutsu* (Etō, "Kaisetsu," p. 526). As in *Arakure,* this cheap modernism has a grotesque, sadomasochistic quality (Etō Jun, *Onna no kigogaku* [Kadokawa Shoten, 1985], pp. 180–96).

49. Rubin, *Injurious to Public Morals,* pp. 251–52; SZ, 15:19–21, 133–40, 151–55, 222–36, 424–25, and 443. Shūsei apparently tried to encourage the leftist writer Nakano Shigeharu, whose writing had been proscribed by the state (Noguchi, *Shūsei nōto,* p. 102).

50. Katsumoto, "Tayama Katai to Tokuda Shūsei," pp. 427–32; Noguchi, *Shūsei den,* p. 485; Noguchi, *Shūsei nōto,* pp. 214–18.

51. Yoshiya, *Yoshiya Nobuko zenshū,* 12:121.

Chapter 6. Social Realism

1. Shinoda, "Tokuda Shūsei," p. 135. For a young critic who was ambivalent about the idealization and mystification of Shūsei by his contemporary writers and critics, see Furuya Tsunatake, "Tokuda Shūsei ron," in Satō Haruo and Uno Kōji, eds., *Meiji bungaku sakka ron* (Shōgakkan, 1943), 2:224–45, esp. p. 224.

2. On Shūsei's extraordinary generosity to younger writers, see Nakamura Seiko, "Katai Shūsei ryō-shi no inshō," *Ningen* 3, no. 1 (Jan. 1921): 4; Mizumori Kamenosuke, "Katai Shūsei nishi to watakushi," *Ningen* 3, no. 1

(Jan. 1921): 14–15; Takebayashi, "Omoide futatsu, mitsu," 3–4; Hayashi Fumiko, "Shūsei Sensei," *Geirin Kanpo,* Nov. 1947, pp. 44–47; Yoshiya, *Yoshiya Nobuko zenshū,* pp. 117–21.

3. Torrance, "Tokuda Shūsei and the Representation of *Shomin* Life," pp. 404–9.

4. SZ, 8:206; Torrance, "Tokuda Shūsei and the Representation of *Shomin* Life," pp. 407–8.

5. As quoted in Noguchi, *Shūsei den,* p. 532.

6. Tokuda Shūsei, "*Sōwa* shuppan ni nozomite no sakusha no kotoba," *Sōwa* (Sakurai Shoten, 1942), p. 2, located at the end of the volume.

7. Noguchi, *Shūsei den,* pp. 487–89 and 498–99.

8. As quoted in Noguchi, *Shūsei den,* pp. 488–89.

9. Yoshitake Teruko, *Nyonin Yoshiya Nobuko* (Bungei Shunjū, 1982), pp. 97–114; Noguchi, *Shūsei nōto,* pp. 127–30; Wada Yoshie and Noguchi Fujio, roundtable discussion, "Taidan: Shūsei o otte," in Noguchi, *Shūsei nōto,* pp. 240–43; Kawabata, *Kawabata Yasunari zenshū,* 29:452–53 and 468–70; Funabashi, *Tokuda Shūsei,* pp. 142–43; Hayashi, "Shūsei Sensei," pp. 44–47; Kawasaki Chōtarō and Minakami Tsutomu, "Zui o egaku: Tokuda Shūsei to Uno Kōji," *Umi* 10, no. 1 (Jan. 1978): 152–69. In a revealing aside, Kawasaki remembers that Shūsei said that he was aware that the public looked on him as a person playing the role of Jinzaemon, a rather gloomy male character from the kabuki, but that Shūsei himself saw his role as that of Jaku'uemon, the extravagant woman's role (*hanagata*) from the kabuki (Kawasaki and Minakami, "Zui o egaku," p. 158).

10. Torrance, "Tokuda Shūsei and the Representation of *Shomin* Life," pp. 418–19.

11. Satomi, *Satomi Ton zenshū,* 9:215.

12. On Kawabata's description, see Noguchi, *Shūsei den,* p. 515; and Hayashi, "Shūsei Sensei," p. 46. On Yoshiya Nobuko's loan to Kobayashi Masako, "*Shukuzu* no moderu Ginko: Tokuda Shūsei Sensei no omoide," *Yomiuri Hyōron,* May 1950, p. 124. For other accounts of young writers who visited Shūsei in the Hakusan geisha house, see Narasaki Tsutomu, *Sakka no butai ura* (Yomiuri Shinbunsha, 1970), pp. 28–30; Wada Yoshie, *Omokage no hitobito* (Kōdansha, 1958), pp. 97–115; and Yoshiya, *Yoshiya Nobuko zenshū,* p. 120.

13. As quoted in Sugino Yōkichi, *Nakano Shigeharu no kenkyū,* Kasama Sōsho, vol. 123 (Kasama Shoin, 1979), p. 492.

14. The first issue of *Jinmin Bunko* appeared in March 1936 and the magazine folded in January 1938. There were rumors that those who published in the magazine were going to be arrested, and Takeda and Takami decided to close the magazine down to protect themselves and their associates. Takeda's intentions for the periodical are found in his postscript to the first issue (Muramatsu et al., *Shōwa hihyō taikei* [Banchō Shobō, 1968], 2:379).

On the debate between writers associated with *Jinmin Bunko* and those associated with "Nihon roman-ha," see Muramatsu et al., *Shōwa hihyō taikei,* 2:414–

23, esp. p. 423. For one of the more important articles in the original debate, see Hirotsu Kazuo, "Sanbun geijutsu no ichi," in Aono Suikichi et al., eds., *Gendai bungakuron taikei* (Kawade Shobō, 1954), 3:262–64. On the establishment and end of *Jinmin Bunko,* see Takami, *Shōwa bungaku seisuishi,* 2:65–77. Shūsei's attendance at the special roundtable discussion of the "spirit of prose literature" with Takeda Rintarō, Takami Jun, and Hirotsu Kazuo left no doubt about which side of the debate he was on (Tokuda Shūsei, roundtable discussion, "Sanbun seishin o kiku," *Jinmin Bunko* 1, no. 11 [Nov. 1936]: 72–90). In this discussion, Shūsei states that in his *Arakure* he was aiming for "carnivalism" (*kanibuarizumu*) (p. 85). For an account of the Tokuda Shūsei study group, its makeup, and suppression, see Muramatsu et al., *Shōwa hihyō taikei,* 2:546; and Torrance, "Tokuda Shūsei and the Representation of *Shomin* Life," pp. 423–24.

15. Noguchi, *Shūsei den,* p. 519.

16. Ibid., p. 499.

17. Shūsei's "Shashō fufu no shi" is in SZ, 6:247–80. For "Kisha no kamataki," see Nakano Shigeharu, *Nakano Shigeharu zenshū* (Chikuma Shobō, 1977), 2:212–82.

18. The exact revisions ordered by the Cabinet Information Bureau are not known, but Hirotsu Kazuo recalls that Shūsei told him, with a lively laugh, "They were so displeased, so displeased, I'm delighted I made it to the eightieth installment. I planned about fifty more installments, and I think I'll add about that many" (Hirotsu Kazuo, "Kaisetsu *Kasō jinbutsu Shukuzu*," in SSZ, 13:596). When Shūsei began writing *Shukuzu,* he declared in print that he was moved that *Miyako Shinbun* was giving him the opportunity to write for purely artistic ends without consideration for how well his writing would sell, and he vowed to do his best to satisfy his readers and to "write as freely as the times permit." This provision probably indicates that he expected problems from the authorities. Taking this statement together with the one Shūsei made to Hirotsu, one can probably conclude that he was being constantly harassed by censors during the time he was writing the novel, harassment he ignored for as long as he could. Finally, he seems to have been faced with the ultimatum to either change the content of the novel or stop writing. He wrote a letter to his editors at *Miyako Shinbun,* stating, "If I compromise, the work will come to lack any substance [*funuke ni naru*]. I really can't suddenly abandon my position now, and so I think it best to make a firm decision and stop writing" (Tokuda Kazuho, "Batsu," and "Tsuiki," in SSZ, 13:517–20). Shortly after Shūsei ceased serialization of *Shukuzu,* a collection of his short stories, *Nishi no tabi,* was banned by the censors (Noguchi, *Shūsei den,* p. 532).

Shūsei invested a great deal of effort in *Shukuzu.* Tokuda Kazuho remembers how fatigued his father was while he wrote the novel during the hot summer of 1941. Shūsei had every intention of finishing it (Tokuda Kazuho, "Batsu," p. 517). Unfortunately, Shūsei's health declined in 1942 and 1943, and the unfinished *Shukuzu* was his last novel. It is important to remember, however, that Shūsei's literary career came to an end not because of poor health or impaired faculties or because his creativity dried up; rather his career ended because he refused to compromise with the censors and his writing was systematically suppressed by the state (Noguchi, *Shūsei den*, p. 528).

19. Torrance, "Tokuda Shūsei and the Representation of *Shomin* Life," pp. 49–142.

20. See, e.g., Iwanaga Yutaka, "Shūsei *Shukuzu* no kenkyū," in Nihon Bungaku Kenkyū Shiryō Kankōkai, *Shizenshugi bungaku*, pp. 285–94, esp. pp. 292–94. Iwanaga's approach is influenced by Kataoka Yoshikazu.

21. In *Saiankoku no Tokyo* (1893), Matsubara Iwagorō describes a shocking scene in which poor people fiercely compete to buy garbage and rice and vegetables not eaten that day at the tables of military colleges (pp. 39–44). Some fifty years later, Shūsei described a similar situation: hungry children who subsist on leftovers bought from the military and sold to the poor at *zanpanya* (leftover-rice shops).

22. Iwanaga, "Shūsei *Shukuzu* no kenkyū," p. 292.

23. Tanigawa Kenichi, ed., *Kindai minshū no kiroku: shōfu* (Shinjinbutsu Ōraisha, 1971), 3:390–96.

24. Tokuda Shūsei, "Kanojo-tachi no mi no ue," in SZ, 8:103–54.

25. Noguchi, *Shūsei nōto*, p. 222.

26. Noguchi Fujio illustrates just how silly the reductionistic arguments of progressive critics become in their search for "feudal elements" in Shūsei's fiction. Kataoka Yoshikazu maintains that the name Kuramochi Shingo reflects the influence of Ihara Saikaku and the feudal ideology of the *gesaku* tradition (*Kataoka Yoshikazu chosaku shū*, 7:278). Perhaps one can go Kataoka one better and discover prefeudal influence in the name Kuramochi. Wasn't one of the suitors for Kaguyahime in *Taketori monogatari* named Kuramochi?

In fact, the names of characters in Shūsei's fiction are typical in the sense that they usually reflect generational trends in fashion. For example, women born before the turn of the century have personal names with the prefix "*O-*": Osaku, Oshō, Ogin, Omasu, or Oyuki. Women born after the turn of the century reflect the new fashion in women's names, the one that reigns today, and have personal names that end with the suffix "*-ko*": Yōko, Rumiko, Sayoko, Ginko, or Tamiko.

As Noguchi Fujio argues, Shūsei probably took the name Kuramochi from a participant in a sensational incident that made an impression on Kobayashi Masako and that appears as an episode in *Shukuzu*: the sensational double suicide of Yoshikawa Kamako and her chauffeur, Kuramochi Mutsusuke. With one exception (Hitoshi in *Hikari o ōte*), Shūsei was generally not concerned with the allegorical significance of his characters' names. He was far more concerned with keeping the names of his characters realistic in terms of each character's social status and age. To this end, he frequently borrowed the names of real-life people and changed them slightly. Kuramochi was convenient because Kuramochi Mutsusuke was about the same age as *Shukuzu*'s Kuramochi Shingo. Shūsei's choice of the name had nothing to do with the feudal ideology of the *gesaku* tradition (Noguchi, *Shūsei den*, pp. 500–502).

27. Iwanaga, "Shūsei *Shukuzu* no kenkyū," p. 293.

28. Imura Shōkai, "*Arakure* kara *Shukuzu* e," *Bungaku,* Apr. 1953, pp. 42–50 (482–90); see pp. 48–49 (488–89) for quotation.

29. Kobayashi Masako, "*Shukuzu* no moderu Ginko," p. 125; Noguchi, *Shūsei nōto,* p. 233.

Epilogue

1. As quoted in Matsumoto Tōru, *Tokuda Shūsei,* p. 406.

2. As quoted in Tokuda Kazuho, "Batsu," in SSZ, 13:518.

3. Ōhori Taiichirō, "Tokuda Shūsei-shi no byōreki," *Geirin Kanpo,* Nov. 1947, pp. 60–62.

4. Noguchi, *Shūsei den,* p. 541.

5. Ibid., pp. 543–45.

Select Bibliography

Unless specifically noted in the bibliographical entry, listed primary sources are not in the various *Shūsei zenshū* (Complete Works of Tokuda Shūsei). Secondary sources have been cited in conformance with the notes in the forms closest at hand. As in the notes, when the place of publication is Tokyo or obvious, it has been omitted. At present, the definitive bibliography for secondary material on Tokuda Shūsei is Enomoto Takashi, "Sankō bunken," in *Tokuda Shūsei shū*, vol. 21 of *Nihon kindai bungaku taikei*, pp. 464–69. The definitive bibliography for primary sources is Matsumoto Tōru, "Chosaku shoshutsu nenpu," in his *Tokuda Shūsei*, pp. 413–59. Most of the Japanese books and periodicals cited can be found at the Nihon Kindai Bungaku Kan in Tokyo.

Primary Sources

Shūsei zenshū (Complete works of Shūsei). 15 vols. Hibonkaku, 1936–37.
Shūsei zenshū. 6 vols. Sekkasha, 1961–62. Abbreviated in notes as SSZ. See also chap 1, n. 8.
Shūsei zenshū. 18 vols. Kyoto: Rinsen Shoten, 1974–75. Reprint, 1989–91. Abbreviated in notes as SZ. See also chap. 1, n. 8.

Books, articles, essays, short stories, novellas, poetry, interviews, and round-table discussions by Tokuda Shūsei containing cited material not available in *Shūsei zenshū* (entries arranged by date)

"Danpen" [Fragments]. *Seinenbun* 2, no. 2 (Sept. 1895): 43–49; no. 3 (Oct. 1895): 56–61; no. 4 (Nov. 1895): 51–57.
"Shajitsu-ha" [The realist school]. *Waseda Bungaku,* Nov. 1895, p. 242.
"Kaede no shitakage" [In the shade of the maple] (1898). In Tokuda Shūsei, *Kaede no shitakage* (1904), pp. 1–18.
"Nohibari" [Meadowlark] (1898). In Tokuda Shūsei, *Kaede no shitakage* (1904), pp. 109–31.
"Kawanami" [Waves on the river]. *Shinshōsetsu,* June 1899, pp. 68–145.
"Kimaguremono" [Capricious persons]. *Bungei Kurabu* 6, no. 5 (Apr. 1900): 76–117.
Kyōmanji [The haughty child]. Shinseisha, 1902.

Kaede no shitakage [In the shade of the maple]. Edited by Dai-Nihon Jogakukai. Tokyo: n.p., 1904.

"Fugū no kishi Mokuan-kyō o itamu" [Mourning the ill-fated hero Mokuan]. *Uzue* 2, no. 4 (1904).

Hanataba [Bouquet]. Hidaka Yūrindō, 1905.

Shōkazoku [The minor aristocrat]. Shun'yōdō, 1905.

"Jijo" [Author's preface]. In Tokuda Shūsei, *Shōdazoku* (1905), first two pages, unpaginated.

"Shōsetsu to shūchiku" [The novel and collecting sources]. In Nihon Bunshō-gaku, ed., *Shōsetsu sahō*. Shinchōsha, 1906.

"Yakōbune" [The night ferry]. *Shinchō*, Sept. 1906, pp. 9–15.

"Shin no shakai shōsetsu" [The true social novel]. *Bunshō Sekai*, Nov. 1906, pp. 15–19.

"Zetsubō" [Despair] (1907). In Tokuda Shūsei, *Tokuda Shūsei shū*. Vol. 68 of *Meiji bungaku zenshū* (1971), pp. 145–49.

"Happun" [Roused to action] (1907). In Tokuda Shūsei, *Shūsei shu* (1908).

"Ware wa ikani shite shōsetsuka to narishi ka" [How I became a novelist]. *Shinko Bunrin* 3, no. 1 (1907): 56–58.

"Kōyō Sensei no juku" [Kōyō's private school]. *Bunshō Sekai* 2, no. 2 (Feb. 1907): 21–26.

"Ichiyō-joshi no sakubutsu" [The works of Higuchi Ichiyō]. *Chūō Kōron*, June 1907, p. 49.

"Ga no moderu to shōsetsu no moderu" [Models for pictures and models for novels]. *Bunshō Sekai*, Sept. 1907, pp. 21–24.

Shūsei shū [Collected stories of Shūsei]. Ekifūsha, 1908.

"Mienu tokoro wakaranu oku" [At a point that cannot be seen, at unknown depths]. *Waseda Bungaku*, Mar. 1908, pp. 85–86.

"Katai-shi" [Tayama Katai]. *Chūō Kōron*, May 1908, pp. 82–83.

"Yo ga jōkyō tōji" [My first trip to Tokyo]. *Waseda Bungaku*, July 1908, pp. 68–72.

"Kōyō o shite ima no bundan ni arashimeba" [The literary world today if Kōyō had lived]. *Waseda Bungaku*, Sept. 1908, p. 392.

"Kansō futatsu mitsu" [Several impressions]. *Bunshō Sekai*, Dec. 1908, pp. 93–94.

"Oi" [The Nephew] (1908). In Tokuda Shūsei, *Shūsei shū* (1908), pp. 59–79.

"Sakka no kosei to chihō iro" [The author's individuality and local color]. *Shinsei*, Jan. 1909, p. 61.

"Motometsutsu aru mono no imada ataerarezu" [Searching for something we have not yet been given]. *Shinchō*, Feb. 1909, pp. 20–21.

"Shōsetsu keishiki ron" [Theory of the form of the novel]. *Shinchō*, Aug. 1909, pp. 60–63.

"Taika no honyaku yori wa wakai hito no honyaku" [Translations by the young are preferable to translations by the eminent]. *Bunshō Sekai*, Aug. 1910, pp. 36–37.

"Sōsaku zatsuwa" [Random conversations about writing]. *Shinchō* 13, no. 6 (Dec. 1910): 106–7.

Waga ko no ie [My son's family]. Shun'yōdō, 1911.

Jinbutsu byōsha hō [Methods of depicting literary characters]. Shinchōsha, 1912.

"Morikawa-chō yori" [From the Morikawa district]. *Shinchō* 16, no. 3 (Mar. 1912): 7.

"Tansu-chō no juku" [Kōyō's school in the Tansu district]. *Bunshō Sekai* 7, no. 14 (Oct. 1912): 62.

"Karada" [The body] (1912). In Noma Hiroshi, ed., *Nihon puroretari bungaku taikei*, vol. 1 (*jo*):160–66. San'ichi Shobō, 1955.

"Jo" [Preface]. In Taoka Reiun, *Sūkiden* [Biography of a checkered career], pp. 9–11. Genōsha, 1912.

Meiji shōsetsu bunshō hensenshi [A history of stylistic change in the Meiji novel]. Waseda Bungakusha Bungaku Fukyūkai Kan, 1914.

"*Tadare* to *Arakure* no moderu" [Literary models for *Tadare* and *Arakure*]. *Shinchō* 23, no. 4 (Oct. 1915): 11–13.

"Kikumi" [Viewing the chrysanthemums] (1917). In Tokuda Shūsei, *Furusato no yuki* (1947), pp. 227–45.

"Watakushi to yū ningen" [This human being called myself]. *Waseda Bungaku*, Mar. 1917, p. 41.

Shōsetsu no tsukurikata [Ways to write novels]. Shinchōsha, 1918.

"Iwayuru tsūzoku shōsetsu to geijutsu shōsetsu no mondai: jibun no keiken o kiso ni shite" [The so-called conflict between popular and artistic fiction: Based on personal experience]. *Shichō* 30, no. 2 (Feb. 1919): 2–4.

"Watakushi no ayunde kita michi" [The road I have followed]. *Bunshō Sekai*, Nov. 1920, pp. 118–21.

"Sōsaku seikatsu no nijūgonen" [Twenty-five years as a novelist]. *Shinchō* 33, no. 5 (Nov. 1920): 5–7. Also in SZ, 15:343–47.

"Gaikoku bungaku no ishokusha" [Transplanter of foreign literature]. *Shinshōsetsu: rinji sōkan* 27, no. 8 (Aug. 1922): 31–32.

"Yo no isshō o shihai suru hodo no ōkinaru eikyō o ataeshi hito, jiken, oyobi shisō" [People, incidents, and ideas that have formed a great enough influence to govern my whole life]. *Chūō Kōron*, Feb. 1923, p. 101.

"Sakka wa kakumei kibun o motsu" [A writer must possess a revolutionary spirit]. *Shinchō* 38, no. 2 (Feb. 1923): 25–27. Also in SZ, 15:357–58.

Roundtable discussion. "*Shinchō* gappyō kai" [*Shinchō*'s monthly roundtable review]. *Shinchō* 40, no. 2 (Feb. 1924): 30ff.

Roundtable discussion. "*Shinchō* gappyō." *Shinchō* 42, no. 3 (Mar. 1925): 49ff.

"Tokuda Shūsei-shi to bungaku to shumi o kataru: sakka to kisha no ichimon ittō roku 13" [Tokuda Shūsei speaks of literature and his personal interests: A one-on-one interview between the reporter and the author, 13]. *Shinchō* 43, no. 6 (Dec. 1925): 26–36.

"Shinkyō kara kyakukan e" [From mental-state to objective fiction] (1926). In Aono Suekichi et al., eds., *Gendai bungakuron taikei,* 3:312–13. Kawade Shobō, 1954.

Sugiyuku hi [Passing days]. Kaizōsha, 1926.

"Waga bundan seikatsu no sanjūnen" [Thirty years of my life in the literary world]. *Shinchō* 23, no. 1 (1926): 11–21; no. 3 (1926): 24–33; no. 4 (1926): 19–29; no. 5 (1926): 33–39; no. 6 (1926): 26–40.

"Sugiyuku hi" [Passing days] (1926). In Tokuda Shūsei, *Tokuda Shūsei shū,* pp. 395–416. Vol. 21 of *Nihon kindai bungaku shū* (1973).

Roundtable discussion. "Gappyō." *Shinchō* 23, no. 7 (July 1926): 23ff.

"Tokuda Shūsei-shi yori" [Letter to the editors from Tokuda Shūsei]. *Sandē Mainichi* 6, no. 39 (18 Sept. 1927): 8.

Roundtable discussion. "Gappyō: Shūsei-shi no renai geijutsu" [Monthly roundtable: Shūsei's literary art of love]. *Shinchō* 24, no. 10 (Oct. 1927): 126ff.

"Nenpu" [Personal chronology]. In Tokuda Shūsei, *Tokuda Shūsei shū,* pp. 507–9. Vol. 18 of *Gendai Nihon bungaku zenshū*. Kaizōsha, 1928.

"Yū'utsu narishi koro" [A time of despair]. *Bunshō Kurabu* 14 (Mar. 1929): 116–17.

Shimazaki Tōson and Tokuda Shūsei. "Jinsei bungei o kataru Shimazaki Tōson to Tokuda Shūsei" [Shimazaki Tōson and Tokuda Shūsei speak of life and art]. *Shinchō* 29, no. 5 (May 1932): 24–40.

"Baruzakku-kata to Hadēi-kata" [Balzac's form and Hardy's form]. *Bungei Shunjū,* Aug. 1932, pp. 34–35.

Kunshō ["Order of the White Paulownia" and other stories]. Chūō Kōronsha, 1936.

Roundtable discussion. "Sanbun seishin o kiku" [Inquiring about the spirit of prose literature]. *Jinmin Bunko* 1, no. 11 (Nov. 1936): 72–90.

Sandai meisaku zenshū: Tokuda Shūsei shū [Collected great works of three generations: Tokuda Shūsei]. Kawade Shobō, 1942.

Sōwa ["An episode" and other stories]. Sakurai Shoten, 1942.

"Atogaki" [Afterword]. In Tokuda Shūsei, *Sandai meisaku zenshū: Tokuda Shūsei shū* (1942), p. 404.

Furusato no yuki [Snows of home]. Hakusan Shobō, 1947.

Kan no bara [Roses in a cold season]. Tokyo Shuppan Kubashiki Kaisha, 1948.

"Shūsei haiku" [Haiku by Shūsei]. In Tokuda Shūsei, *Tokuda Shūsei shū,* p. 387. Vol. 11 of *Shōwa bungaku zenshū* (1953).

Tokuda Shūsei shū [Tokuda Shūsei anthology]. Vol. 11 of *Shōwa bungaku zenshū*. Kadokawa Shoten, 1953.

Tokuda Shūsei shū [Tokuda Shūsei anthology]. Vol. 68 of *Meiji bungaku zenshū*. Chikuma Shobō, 1971.

Tokuda Shūsei shū [Tokuda Shūsei anthology]. Vol. 21 of *Nihon kindai bungaku taikei*. Kadokawa Shoten, 1973.

Secondary Sources

Books on Tokuda Shūsei and other sources
containing significant material on Tokuda Shūsei

A. B. C. "Shūsei no geijutsu" [Shūsei's art]. *Shinchō*, Nov. 1915, pp. 36–39.

Ao Zukin. "Shūsei-shi no *Tadare*" [Shūsei's *Tadare*]. *Shinchō* 19, no. 2 (Aug. 1913): 94–97.

Aono Suekichi et al., eds. *Gendai bungakuron taikei* [Collected modern literary criticism]. 8 vols. Kawade Shobō, 1954.

Ara Masahito. "Shomin-teki seimeikan ni kōshite: Shūsei no sakuhin o tōshite" [Resisting the commoner's view of life: Reading through Shūsei's works]. *Kosei*, Nov. 1949, pp. 24–33.

Chikamatsu Shūkō. "Mikaiketsu no shōsetsu: Shūsei no *Arakure*" [A novel without resolution: Shūsei's *Arakure*]. *Yomiuri Shinbun*, 17 Oct. 1915, p. 7.

———. "Shūsei-shi no sakufū" [Shūsei's style]. *Bunshō Sekai* 11, no. 6 (June 1916): 58–63.

———. "Hito oyobi geijutsuka to shite no Tokuda Shūsei-shi" [Tokuda Shūsei, the man and the artist] (1921). In Tokuda Shūsei, *Tokuda Shūsei shū*, pp. 365–70. Vol. 68 of *Meiji bungaku zenshū* (1971).

Choin-sei. "Boshin bundan gaikan" [An outside view of the 1908 literary scene]. *Chūō Kōron*, Jan. 1909, pp. 14–15.

Enomoto Takashi. "Shūsei bungaku ron" [On Shūsei's literature]. *Bunshō Kurabu: Tokuda Shūsei Kenkyū Go*, Sept. 1952, pp. 14–17.

———. "Jōkyō tōji no Tokuda Shūsei" [Tokuda Shūsei's first trip to Tokyo]. *Kokubungaku Kenkyū* 14 (1956): 114–26.

———. "*Arajotai* ni tsuite" [Concerning *Arajotai*]. *Meiji Taishō Bungaku Kenkyū* 21 (Mar. 1957): 53–62.

———. "*Kabi* no seiritsu to sono imi" [*Kabi*'s creation and its significance]. *Kokubungaku Kenkyū* 18 (Oct. 1958): 150–62.

———. "Shūsei no shoki no hito-kōsatsu: Kōyō to no kankei o chūshin ni" [A consideration of early Shūsei: Concentrating on his relationship with Kōyō]. *Bungaku Gogaku* 12 (1958): 103–13.

———. "Hochū" [Supplementary notes]. In Tokuda Shūsei, *Tokuda Shūsei shū*, pp. 54–461. Vol. 21 of *Nihon kindai bungaku taikei* (1973).

———. "Sankō bunken" [Bibliography]. In Tokuda Shūsei, *Tokuda Shūsei shū*, pp. 464–69. Vol. 21 of *Nihon kindai bungaku taikei* (1973).

———. "Shūsei nōto 2: Seiyō bungaku juyō" [Note on Shūsei, 2: His reception of Western literature]. *Waseda Daigaku Kyōiku Gakubu Gakujutsu Kenkyū Kokugo Kokubungaku Hen* 28 (1979): 41–50.

———. "Shūsei nōto 3: 'Yabukōji' 'Namakemono' " [Note on Shūsei, 3: "The spearflower" and "A man lacking ambition"]. *Waseda Daigaku Kyōiku Gakubu Gakujutsu Kenkyū Kokugo Kokubungaku Hen* 29 (1980): 29–41.

Etō Jun. "Kaisetsu" [Commentary]. In *Tokuda Shūsei,* 2:514–30. Vol. 10 of *Nihon no bungaku.* Chūō Kōronsha, 1973.

———. *Onna no kigogaku* [A semiology of women]. Kadokawa Shoten, 1985.

———. "Tokuda Shūsei to 'jūjitsu shita kanji': 'katachi' to 'suji' to 'jisshitsu' " [Tokuda Shūsei and a "sense of fulfillment": "Form" and "plot" and "substance"]. *Gunzō,* Mar. 1990, 172–82.

Fudōchō Gappyō Kai. "Tokuda Shūsei ron" [On Tokuda Shūsei]. *Fudōchō* 3, no. 5 (Nov. 1926): 68ff.

Fujii, James A. "The Subject in Meiji Prose Literature." Ph.D. diss., University of Chicago, 1986.

Fukuda Kiyoto and Sasaki Tōru. *Tokuda Shūsei: hito to sakuhin* [Tokuda Shūsei: The man and his work]. Century Books, vol. 41. Kiyomizu Shoin, 1981.

Funabashi Seiichi. *Tokuda Shūsei.* Kōbundō Shobō, 1941.

Furui Yoshikichi. *Kotoba no jujutsu* [The magic of words]. Sakuhinsha, 1980.

Furuya Tsunatake. "Tokuda Shūsei ron" [On Tokuda Shūsei]. In Satō Haruo and Uno Kōji, eds., *Meiji bungaku sakka ron,* 2:224–45. Shōgakkan, 1943.

Gyofū-sei. "Shūsei no *Honoo*" [Shūsei's *Flames*]. *Waseda Bungaku,* Mar. 1908, p. 24.

Haten Kōshi. "Ken'yūsha tsui ni horobu" ["Friends of the Inkstone" has fallen at last]. *Shinsei,* Apr. 1907, pp. 19–20 (391–92).

Hayashi Fumiko. "Shūsei Sensei" [Shūsei]. *Geirin Kanpo,* Nov. 1947, pp. 44–47.

Hirotsu Kazuo. "Shūsei-shi no ayunda michi" [The path Shūsei has followed]. *Kaizō,* Jan. 1937, pp. 247–60.

———. "Kaisetsu *Kasō jinbutsu Shukuzu*" [Commentary on *Kasō jinbutsu Shukuzu*]. In SSZ, 13:591–98.

———. *Hirotsu Kazuo zenshū* [Complete works of Hirotsu Kazuo]. 12 vols. Chūō Kōronsha, 1974.

Homma, Kenshiro. *The Literature of Naturalism: An East-West Comparative Study.* Kyoto: Yamaguchi Publishing House, 1983.

Ikari Akira. *Ken'yūsha to Shizenshugi kenkyū* [Study of the Ken'yūsha and Naturalism]. Ōfūsha, 1975.

Ikuta Chōkō. "Tokuda Shūsei-shi o ronzu" [Considering Tokuda Shūsei]. In Tokuda Shūsei, *Tokuda Shūsei shū,* pp. 357–63. Vol. 68 of *Meiji bungaku zenshū.*

Imura Shōkai. "*Arakure* kara *Shukuzu* e" [From *Arakure* to *Shukuzu*]. *Bungaku,* Apr. 1953, pp. 42–50 (482–90).

Inagaki Tatsurō et al., eds. *Kindai bungaku hyōron taikei* [Collected modern literary criticism]. 10 vols. Kadokawa Shoten, 1971–75.

Inagaki Tatsurō and Shimomura Fujio, eds. *Ningen sanka* [In praise of humanity]. Vol. 11 of *Nihon bungaku no rekishi.* Kadokawa Shoten, 1968.

Ino Kenji. "Tokuda Shūsei e no shōmei" [Illuminating Tokuda Shūsei]. In Tokuda Shūsei, *Tokuda Shūsei shū,* pp. 351–56. Vol. 15 of *Gendai Nihon bungaku taikei.* Chikuma Shobō, 1970.

Ishikawa Gendai Bungaku no Kai, ed. *Furusato to bungaku tanbō: Kyōka, Shūsei, Saisei* [Exploring Kanazawa and its literature: Izumi Kyōka, Tokuda Shūsei, and Murō Saisei]. Kanazawa: Noto Insatsu Shuppanbu, 1985.

Isoda Kōichi and Takahashi Hideo. "Taidan" [A dialogue]. *Tokyo Shinbun,* 21 Dec. 1977, p. 3.

Itō Sei. *Itō Sei zenshū* [Complete works of Itō Sei]. 24 vols. Shinchōsha, 1973.

Iwanaga Yutaka. "*Shūsei roku Muchoan nikki* ni tsuite: Tokuda Shūsei kenkyū shiryō" ["Record of autumn tears," "Diary of a featureless place": Research materials on Tokuda Shūsei]. *Kokugo to Kokubungaku* 31, no. 365 (Sept. 1954): 37–42.

———. "Shūsei *Shukuzu* no kenkyū" [Research into Shūsei's *Shukuzu*]. In Nihon Bungaku Kenkyū Shiryō Kankōkai, ed., *Shizenshugi bungaku,* pp. 284–94.

Jamet, Olivier. "Naturalisme et modernité dans 'Le dancing de la ville' de Tokuda Shūsei." *Tenri Daigaku Gakuhō* 40, no. 2 (Mar. 1989): 171–90.

Kamitsukasa Shōken. "Tokuda Shūsei-shi no inshō" [Impressions of Tokuda Shūsei]. *Shinchō* 26, no. 4 (Apr. 1917): 24–25.

Kanai Keiko. "*Kasō jinbutsu* ron: fūzoku to sakka shutai no kakawari no tsuite" [On *Kasō jinbutsu:* Concerning the relation between popular customs and manners and the author's subjectivity]. In Kōno, ed., *Ronkō Tokuda Shūsei,* pp. 104–31.

———. "Meikyū to shite no toshi: Ranpo, Kawabata, Hirotsu, Shūsei" [The city as labyrinth: Ranpo, Kawabata, Hirotsu, and Shūsei]. In *Kōza Shōwa bungaku shi,* 1:107–16. Yūseidō, 1988.

Kataoka Tsutomu. "Tokuda Shūsei Meiji sanjū nendai no shōsetsu" [Tokuda Shūsei's fiction, 1897–1906]. *Komazawa Kokubun* 16, pp. 15–32.

———. "*Shūsei shū Naraku:* Shūsei no shōsetsu, 2" [*Collected stories of Shūsei Inferno:* Shūsei's fiction, 2]. *Komazawa Kokubun* 17, pp. 73–91.

Kataoka Yoshikazu. *Kataoka Yoshikazu chosaku shū* [Works of Kataoka Yoshikazu]. 11 vols. Chūō Kōronsha, 1979–80.

Katsumoto Seiichirō. Roundtable discussion. "Tayama Katai to Tokuda Shūsei: Shizenshugi bungaku, 3" [Tayama Katai and Tokuda Shūsei: The literature of naturalism, 3]. *Bungaku* 28, no. 4 (1960): 54–88 (400–434).

Kawabata Yasunari. *Kawabata Yasunari zenshū* [Complete works of Kawabata Yasunari]. 19 vols. Shinchōsha, 1969.

———. "Kaisetsu" [Commentary]. In *Tokuda Shūsei,* 1:512–26. Vol. 9 of *Nihon no bungaku.* Chūō Kōronsha, 1973.

———. *Kawabata Yasunari zenshū.* 37 vols. Shinchōsha, 1982.

Kawasaki Chōtarō and Minakami Tsutomu. "Zui o egaku: Tokuda Shūsei to Uno Kōji" [Describing the essence: Tokuda Shūsei and Uno Kōji]. *Umi* 10, no. 1 (Jan. 1978): 152–69.

Keene, Donald. *Dawn to the West.* 2 vols. New York: Holt, Rinehart, and Winston, 1984.

————. "Tokuda Shūsei: hito to sakuhin" [Tokuda Shūsei: Man and works]. In *Shōwa bungaku zenshū*, 2:953–59. Shōgakkan, 1988.

Kisha [reporter/staff critic]. "*Shūsei shū*" [Collected stories of Shūsei]. *Chūō Kōron*, Oct. 1908, p. 150.

————. "*Arakure.*" *Waseda Bungaku*, Oct. 1915, pp. 8–9.

————. "*Arakure.*" *Bunshō Sekai* 10, no. 12 (Nov. 1915): 222–31.

Kobayashi Hideo. *Kobayashi Hideo zenshū* [Complete works of Kobayashi Hideo]. 8 vols. Shinchōsha, 1956.

Kobayashi Masako. "*Shukuzu* no moderu Ginko: Tokuda Shūsei Sensei no omoide" [Ginko, the model for *Shukuzu*: Remembrances of Tokuda Shūsei]. *Yomiuri Hyōron*, May 1950, pp. 119–26.

Kojima Masajirō. "Shōsetsu no kamisama" [The master of the novel]. *Nihon Bungaku Zenshū Geppō* (Shūeisha) 67 (Aug. 1974): 1–2.

Kōno Toshirō. "Hibonkaku *Shūsei zenshū* no naiyō kenbon to geppō" [Review of monthly bulletins and endorsements for Hibonkaku's *Shūsei zenshū*]. In Kōno, ed., *Ronkō Tokuda Shūsei*, pp. 245–58.

————, ed. *Ronkō Tokuda Shūsei* [Studies on Tokuda Shūsei]. Ōfūsha, 1983.

Kotera Kikuko. "Tokuda Shūsei Sensei no koto" [Memories of Tokuda Shūsei]. *Shinsōsaku* 38, pp. 11–15.

Maekawa Ryūnosuke. "Kyōka to Kanazawa" [Izumi Kyōka and Kanazawa]. In Ishikawa Gendai Bungaku no Kai, ed., *Furusato to bungaku tanbō*, pp. 20–21.

Masamune Hakuchō. "*Kabi* no hihyō" [Review of *Kabi*]. *Shinchō* 16, no. 2 (Feb. 1912): 7.

————. "Tayama Tokuda ryō-shi ni tsuite" [Concerning Tayama Katai and Tokuda Shūsei]. *Bunshō Sekai* 15, no. 11 (Nov. 1920): 124–26.

————. *Shizenshugi seisuishi* [The rise and fall of Japanese naturalism]. In *Masamune Hakuchō shū* [An anthology of Masamune Hakuchō]. Vol. 16 of *Gendai Nihon bungaku taikei*. Chikuma Shobō, 1969.

Matsubara Shibun. "Tokuda Shūsei ron" [Thoughts on Tokuda Shūsei]. *Shinchō*, Nov. 1908, pp. 28–32.

Matsubara Shin'ichi. "*Gusha*" *no bungaku* [Literature of "fools"]. Tōjusha, 1974.

Matsumoto Sachiko. "Tokuda Shūsei no kakei nenpu" [A genealogical chronology of Tokuda Shūsei]. In Nihon Bungaku Kenkyū Shiryō Kankōkai, ed., *Shizenshugi bungaku*, pp. 217–26.

Matsumoto Tōru. "Tokuda Shūsei no chosaku shoshutsu nenpu kō" [Study of the chronology of first place of publication of Tokuda Shūsei's works]. *Kinki Daigaku Kyōyōbu Kenkyū Kiyō* 13, no. 3 (1982): 1–35.

————. "Meiji sanjūni, sannen no Shūsei: 'Kawanami,' 'Shiokeburi,' *Kumo no yukue*" [Shūsei in Meiji 32, 33 (1899, 1900): "Waves on the river," "Sea spray," *Where the clouds go*]. *Kinki Daigaku Kyōyōbu Kenkyū Kiyō* 14, no. 2 (1982): 11–22.

————. "Tokuda Shūsei no shajitsu: *Arajotai* o chūshin ni" [Tokuda Shūsei's realism: *Arajotai*]. *Kinki Daigaku Kyōyōbu Kenkyū Kiyō* 15, no. 1 (1983): 1–140.

————. "Tokuda Shūsei no ichisokumen: kore mo seiō taiken, 1" [An aspect of Tokuda Shūsei: This too was an experience of the West, 1]. *Gakutō* 4, no. 6 (1985): 44–47.

————. "Tokuda Shūsei no ichisokumen: sakusō suru jikan, 2 [An aspect of Tokuda Shūsei: The involution of time, 2]. *Gakutō* 4, no. 7 (1985): 44–47.

————. *Tokuda Shūsei*. Kasama Shoin, 1988.

Mikka Ushio. "Tokuda Shūsei-shi no nichijō" [Tokuda Shūsei's daily life]. *Bunshō Sekai*, Mar. 1913, pp. 52–55.

Mizumori Kamenosuke. "Katai Shūsei nishi to watakushi" [Katai Shūsei and myself]. *Ningen* 3, no. 1 (Jan. 1921): 14–15.

Morita Sōhei. "*Kabi* no hihyō" [A review of *Kabi*]. In *Kindai bungaku hyōron taikei*, 3:445.

Nakamura Mitsuo. *Meiji bungakushi* [A history of Meiji literature]. Chikuma Sōsho, vol. 9. Chikuma Shobō, 1963.

Nakamura Seiko. "Katai Shūsei ryō-shi ni tsuite" [Concerning Tayama Katai and Tokuda Shūsei]. *Bunshō Sekai* 15, no. 11 (Nov. 1920): 135.

————. "Katai Shūsei ryō-shi no inshō" [Impressions of Katai and Shūsei]. *Ningen* 3, no. 1 (Jan. 1921): 4.

Nakamura Seiko, Nogami Shirakawa, and Sōma Gyofū. "*Arakure* no hihyō" [Reviews of *Arakure*]. *Shinchō* 23, no. 4 (Oct. 1915): 102–5.

Narasaki Tsutomu. *Sakka no butai ura* [In back of the author's stage]. Yomiuri Shinbunsha, 1970.

Natsume Sōseki. *Sōseki zenshū* [Complete works of Natsume Sōseki]. 18 vols. Iwanami Shoten, 1967.

Nihon Bungaku Kenkyū Shiryō Kankōkai, ed. *Shizenshugi bungaku* [The literature of naturalism]. Nihon Bungaku Kenkyū Shiryō Sōsho series. Yūseidō, 1975.

Noguchi. *Shūsei bungaku*. See Noguchi Fujio, *Tokuda Shūsei no bungaku*.

Noguchi. *Shūsei den*. See Noguchi Fujio, *Tokuda Shūsei den*.

Noguchi. *Shūsei nōto*. See Noguchi Fujio, *Tokuda Shūsei nōto*.

Noguchi Fujio. *Tokuda Shūsei den* [Biography of Tokuda Shūsei]. Chikuma Shobō, 1965.

————. *Tokuda Shūsei nōto* [Notes on Tokuda Shūsei]. Chūō Daigaku Shuppanbu, 1972.

————. *Tokuda Shūsei no bungaku* [Tokuda Shūsei's literature]. Chikuma Shobō, 1979.

Odagiri Hideo, ed. *Hakkin sakuhin shū* [Anthology of banned works]. Hokushindō, 1957.

Ogawa Taketoshi, ed. *Tokuda Shūsei to Iwano Hōmei: Shizenshugi no saikentō*. Vol. 16 of *Nihon bungaku kenkyū shiryō shinshū*. Yūseidō, 1992.

Ōhori Taiichirō. "Tokuda Shūsei-shi no byōreki" [Tokuda Shūsei's medical history]. *Geirin Kanpo*, Nov. 1947, pp. 60–62.

Okada Hachiyo. "*Arakure* no Oshima" [*Arakure*'s Oshima]. *Shinchō* 23, no. 5 (Nov. 1915): 82.

Representative Tales of Japan. Tokyo: Sanko Shoten, 1917.

Rolf, Robert. "Shūsei, Hakuchō, and the Age of Literary Naturalism, 1907–1911." Ph.D. diss., University of Hawaii, 1975.

———. "Tokuda Shūsei." *Kodansha Encyclopedia of Japan.* Kodansha, 1983.

Rubin, Jay. *Injurious to Public Morals: Writers and the Meiji State.* Seattle: University of Washington Press, 1984.

Sakamoto Hiroshi. "Tokuda Shūsei ron" [Concerning Tokuda Shūsei]. *Hyōron* 1, no. 9 (1934): 10–17.

Sasaki Tōru. "Tokuda Shūsei ron" [On Tokuda Shūsei]. In Nihon Bungaku Kenkyū Shiryō Kankōkai, ed., *Shizenshugi bungaku,* pp. 227–51.

Shibundō Henshūbu. *Bundanshi jiten* [Dictionary of the history of the literary world]. Shibundō, 1972.

Shimamura Hōgetsu. "*Kabi* no hihyō" [Review of *Kabi*]. *Shinchō* 16, no. 2 (Feb. 1912): 53.

Shimazaki Tōson. "*Kabi* no hihyō" [Review of *Kabi*]. *Shinchō* 16, no. 2 (Feb. 1912): 2–6.

Shinoda Hajime. "Tokuda Shūsei." *Subaru,* Sept. 1972, pp. 130–45.

———. *Nihon no kindai shōsetsu* [Japan's modern novel]. Shūeisha, 1973.

———. *Zoku-Nihon no kindai shōsetsu* [The second Japan's modern novel]. Shūeisha, 1975.

———. *Nihon no gendai shōsetsu* [Japan's contemporary modern novel]. Shūeisha, 1980.

Shojo Hō. "Shigatsu bundan no saku to hyōron" [Works and criticism on the April literary scene]. *Bunshō Sekai* 8, no. 6 (May 1913): 77.

Sōma Gyofū. "Shinsho zakkan" [Miscellaneous impressions of new works. *Waseda Bungaku,* Nov. 1908, pp. 70–71.

———. "Tōson-shi no *Ie* to Shūsei-shi no *Kabi*" [Tōson's *Ie* and Shūsei's *Kabi*]. *Waseda Bungaku,* Mar. 1912, pp. 55–56.

Sōma Tsuneo. *Nihon Shizenshugi ron* [Discourse on Japanese naturalism]. Yagi Shoten, 1970.

———. *Nihon Shizenshugi saikō* [Rethinking Japanese naturalism]. Yagi Shoten, 1981.

Takahashi Toshio. "*Arajotai* o yomu: 'risshi' gensō no yukue" [Reading *Arajotai:* The outcome of the illusion of the "self-made man"]. In Kōno, ed., *Ronkō Tokuda Shūsei,* pp. 7–34.

Takami Jun. "Shūsei bungaku ni kanren shite" [Concerning Shūsei's literature]. *Geirin Kanpo,* Nov. 1947, pp. 27–30.

———. *Shōwa bungaku seisuishi* [The rise and fall of Shōwa literature]. 2 vols. Bungei Shunjūsha, 1958.

Takami Jun, Takeda Rintarō, Hirotsu Kazuo, and Tokuda Shūsei. Roundtable discussion. "Sanbun seishin o kiku" [Inquiring into the spirit of prose literature]. *Jinmin Bunko* 1, no. 9 (Nov. 1936): 72ff.

Takebayashi Musōan. "Omoide futatsu, mitsu" [A few memories]. *Geirin Kanpo* 2, no. 8 (Nov. 1947): 1–4.

Tamura Toshiko. "*Kabi* no Ogin" [*Kabi*'s Ogin]. *Shinchō* 16, no. 3 (Mar. 1912): 66–71.

Tanaka Jun. "Tokuda Shūsei ron" [On Tokuda Shūsei]. *Waseda Bungaku*, Feb. 1917, pp. 30–40.

Tanigawa Tetsuzō. *Shizenshugi no sakka* [Authors of naturalism]. Fourth pamphlet in Iwanami Kōza Nihon Bungaku series. Iwanami Shoten, 1931.

Tayama Katai. "Chikagoro yonda shōsetsu ni tsuite no kansō" [Feelings about novels I have read recently]. *Bunshō Sekai* 7, no. 6 (May 1912): 2–9.

———. *Kindai no shōsetsu* [The modern novel]. In *Kindai bungaku kaisō shū* [Anthology of memoirs about modern literature]. Vol. 60 of *Nihon kindai bungaku taikei*. Kadokawa Shoten, 1973.

Terada Tōru. "Tokuda Shūsei." In Tokuda Shūsei, *Tokuda Shūsei shū*, pp. 371–80. Vol. 68 of *Meiji bungaku zenshū* (1971).

Tōda Yasutaka. "Tokuda Shūsei: hito to bungaku" [Tokuda Shūsei: Man and literature]. In Ishikawa Gendai Bungaku no Kai, ed., *Furusato to bungaku tanbō*, pp. 114–17.

Tokuda Kazuho. "Kaisetsu" [Commentary]. In Tokuda Shūsei, *Tokuda Shūsei shū*, pp. 388–93. Vol. 11 of *Shōwa bungaku zenshū* (1953).

———. "Kaisetsu *Kōjin*" [Commentary *Kōjin* (Dust by the way)]. In SSZ, 13: 599–601.

———. "Batsu" [Epilogue] and "Tsuiki" [Postscript]. In SSZ, 13:517–20.

———. "Kaisetsu" [Commentary]. In Tokuda Shūsei, *Tokuda Shūsei shū*, pp. 8–50. Vol. 21 of *Nihon kindai bungaku taikei* (1973).

———. "Kaisetsu" [Commentary]. In SZ, 18:401–550.

Tomita Hitoshi. "Tokuda Shūsei to Arufuonsu Dōdē: *Kyōmanji* to *Ru Puchi Shōzu*" [Tokuda Shūsei and Alphonse Daudet: "The haughty child" and "Le petit chose"]. *Hikaku Bungaku Nenshi* 9 (1973): 1–24.

Torrance, Richard. "Tokuda Shūsei and the Representation of *Shomin* Life." Ph.D. diss., Yale University, 1989.

Tōya Ryūnosuke. " 'Machi no odoriba' ron" [Thoughts on "Machi no odoriba"]. In Kōno, ed., *Ronkō Tokuda Shūsei*, pp. 88–103.

Uno Kōji. "Bungei jihyō: shōsetsu no shomondai" [On recent literature: Various problems involving the novel]. *Shinchō* 23, no. 5 (May 1926): 22–32.

———. "Shōsetsu dōkanken: *Moto no eda* to Shūsei-shi" [A personal view on recent novels: "Returning to the branch" and Shūsei]. *Shinchō* 23, no. 11 (Nov. 1926): 99–105.

———. "Bungaku dangi" [Lecture on literature]. *Shinchō* 24, no. 2 (Feb. 1927): 2–6.

———. "*Arajotai* to *Arakure*." In *Tokuda Shūsei senshū*, 2:334–37. Kengensha, 1952.

Uno Kōji and Hirotsu Kazuo. Roundtable discussion. "Shūsei o kataru" [Speaking of Shūsei]. *Geirin Kanpo* (special edition *Tokuda Shūsei: hito to bungaku*), Nov. 1947, pp. 48–58.

Wada Kingo. *Shizenshugi bungaku* [The literature of naturalism]. Shibundō, 1966.

———. *Byōsha no jidai: hitotsu no Shizenshugi bungaku ron* [The age of depiction: A discourse on naturalism]. Sapporo: Hokkaidō Daigaku Tosho Kankōkai, 1975.

Wada Yoshie. *Omokage no hitobito* [Images of people]. Kōdansha, 1958.

Waza Sachiko, ed. *Tokuda Shūsei*. Kanazawa: Noto Insatsu Shuppanbu, 1991.

Yamada Junko. *Onna deshi* [The woman apprentice]. Amatoriasha, 1955.

Yamamoto Kenkichi. "Tokuda Shūsei no sekai: shōsetsu no saihakken" [Tokuda Shūsei's world: Rediscovery of the novel]. *Bungakukai* 16, no. 12, pp. 142–45.

Yamamoto Yoshio. "*Seinenbun* ni okeru Shūsei" [Shūsei's relation to the journal *Young People's Literature*]. *Komazawa Kokubun* 1, no. 1, pp. 61–70.

Yobidashiya. "Bundan hyakunin: Tokuda Shūsei-shi" [A hundred authors in the literary world: Tokuda Shūsei]. *Shinsei*, Apr. 1907, p. 85 (461).

Yoshida Seiichi. *Shizenshugi no kenkyū* [Study of naturalism]. 2 vols. Tokyodō Shuppan, 1955–58.

———. Roundtable discussion. "Tayama Katai to Tokuda Shūsei: shizenshugi bungaku III" [Tayama Katai and Tokuda Shūsei: The literature of naturalism]. *Bungaku* 28, no. 4 (1960): 54–88 (400–434).

———. *Katai Shūsei*. Vol. 8 of *Yoshida Seiichi chosaku shū*. Ōfūsha, 1980.

Yoshimura Hakunin. "Tokuda Shūsei no mita Izumi Kyōka: *Onna keizu* to 'Wakai' to o megutte" [Izumi Kyōka through Tokuda Shūsei's eyes: The circumstances surrounding *Lineage of a woman* and "Reconciliation"]. *Meiji Taishō Bungaku Kenkyū* 21 (Mar. 1957): 71–79.

Yoshitake Teruko. *Nyonin Yoshiya Nobuko*. Bungei Shunjū, 1982.

Yoshiya Nobuko. *Yoshiya Nobuko zenshū* [Complete works of Yoshiya Nobuko]. 12 vols. Asahi Shinbunsha, 1976.

Sources not directly related to Tokuda Shūsei

Bakhtin, Mikhail M. *The Dialogic Imagination: Four Essays*. Translated by Caryl Emerson and Michael Holquist. Austin: University of Texas Press, 1981.

———. *Rabelais and His World*. Translated by Helene Iswolsky. Bloomington: Indiana University Press, 1984.

Barthes, Roland. *Writing Degree Zero*. Translated by Annette Havers and Colin Smith. New York: Hill and Wang, 1968.

Benjamin, Walter. *Illuminations*. Translated by Harry Zohn and edited by Hannah Arendt. New York: Schocken, 1969.

Blanchot, Maurice. "Everyday Speech." *Yale French Studies* 73 (1987): 12–20.

Blaylock, David. "Industrialization and Image of the Merchant in Meiji Japan." Ph.D. diss., Ohio State University, 1992.

Brooks, Peter. *The Melodramatic Imagination: Balzac, Henry James, Melodrama, and the Mode of Excess*. 1976. Reprint. Columbia University Press, 1985.

Cheng, Ching-Mao. "Nagai Kafū and Chinese Tradition." Ph.D. diss., Princeton University, 1970.

De Becker, J. E. *The Nightless City*. 1899. Reprint. Charles E. Tuttle, 1971.

Etō Jun. "Riarizumu no genryū: shaseibun to tasha no mondai" [The origins of realism: Sketch-from-life prose and the problem of the other]. *Shinchō*, Oct. 1971, pp. 217–40.

———. *Jiyū to kinki* [Freedom and taboo]. Kawade Shobō Shinsha, 1984.

Fowler, Edward. *The Rhetoric of Confession: "Shishōsetsu" in Early Twentieth-Century Japanese Fiction*. University of California Press, 1988.

Gluck, Carol. *Japan's Modern Myths: Ideology in the Late Meiji Period*. Princeton University Press, 1985.

Hashimoto Tetsuya and Hayashi Yūichi. *Ishikawa-ken no hyaku-nen* [A hundred years of Ishikawa prefecture's history]. Yamakawa Shuppansha, 1987.

Hirotsu Kazuo. "Sanbun geijutsu no ichi" [The place for prose literary art]. In *Gendai bungakuron taikei*, 3:262–64.

Hoston, Germaine. *Marxism and the Crisis of Development in Prewar Japan*. Princeton University Press, 1986.

Ide Magoroku. *Teikō no shinbunjin Kiryū Yūyū* [Journalist in resistance: Kiryū Yūyū]. Iwanami Shoten, 1980.

Isoda Kōichi. *Shisō to shite no Tokyo: kindai bungakushi nōto* [Tokyo as an idea: Notes on modern literature]. Kokubunsha, 1978.

Kanazawa Shishi Hensan Iinkai, ed. *Kōhon Kanazawa shishi: seijihen* [Official history of Kanazawa city: Politics]. 14 vols. Meicho Shuppan, 1973.

Kanazawa Shishi Hensan Shingi Iinkai, ed. *Kanazawa shishi: gendai-hen* [History of Kanazawa city: Modern period]. 2 vols. Kanazawa: Kanazawa-shi, 1969.

Karatani Kōjin. *Nihon kindai bungaku no kigen* [The origin of modern Japanese literature]. Kōdansha, 1980.

Katagami Tengen. "Sakka no saikin no inshō" [Recent impressions of authors]. *Shumi* 3, no. 10 (Oct. 1908): 62.

Kindai shomin seikatsu shi [History of modern commoner life]. 10 vols. San'ichi Shobō, 1988.

Kiryū Yūyū. *Omoideru mama* [As I remember]. In Ōta Masao, ed., *Kiryū Yūyū jiden*. Gendai Jyānarizumu Shuppankai, 1973.

Kitagawa Tōru. "Shaseibun no ironī: Masaoka Shiki o chūshin ni" [Irony in sketch-from-life prose: Concentrating on Masaoka Shiki]. *Bungaku* 54 (1986): 213–22.

Lefebvre, Henri. "The Everyday and Everydayness." *Yale French Studies* 73 (1987): 7–11.

Lloyd, A. "Introduction." In Ozaki Kōyō, *The Gold Demon*. Translated by A. Lloyd. Seibundō, 1917.

Lukacs, Georg. *History and Class Consciousness*. Translated by Rodney Livingstone. MIT Press, 1971.

McClain, James L. *Kanazawa: A Seventeenth-Century Japanese Castle Town*. Yale University Press, 1982.

————. "Failed Expectations: Kaga Domain on the Eve of the Meiji Restoration." *Journal of Japanese Studies* 14, no. 2 (Summer 1988): 403–47.

Maeda Yūji. *Pen wa shinazu* [The pen shall not die]. Jiji Tsūshinsha, 1964.

Matsubara Iwagorō. *Saiankoku no Tokyo* [Tokyo at its darkest]. Edited by Amane Kangōri. 1893. Reprint. Gendai Shisōsha, 1980.

Matsuura Sōzō, ed. *Genkōryō no kenkyū: sakka jyānarisuto no keizaigaku* [A study of fees per manuscript page: The economics of authors and journalists]. Nihon Jyānarisuto Senmon Gakuin Shuppanbu, 1978.

Mitarai Tatsuo. *Yamagata Aritomo*. 1958. Reprint. Jiji Tsūshinsha, 1985.

Miyachi Masato. *Nichi-Ro sengo seijishi no kenkyū: teikokushugi keiseiki no toshi to nōson* [Research into post-Russo-Japanese War political history: The city and country under imperialism in its formative phase]. Tokyo Daigaku Shuppankai, 1973.

Miyoshi, Masao. "Against the Native Grain: The Japanese Novel and the 'Postmodern' West." *South Atlantic Quarterly* 87, no. 3 (Summer 1988): 525–50.

Muramatsu Takeshi et al., eds. *Shōwa hihyō taikei* [Collected Shōwa literary criticism]. 5 vols. Banchō Shobō, 1968.

Najita, Tetsuo. *Japan*. Modern Nations in Historical Perspective. Englewood Cliffs, N.J.: Prentice-Hall, 1974.

Nakagami Kenji. *Da'in* [Debauchery of Snakes]. Kawade Shobō Shinsha, 1977.

Nakamura Akira. *Hiyu hyōgen jiten* [Dictionary of figurative language]. Kadokawa Shoten, 1977.

Nakamura Mitsuo. *Fūzoku shōsetsu ron* [The novel of customs and manners]. Shinchō Bunko series. 1950. Reprint. Shinchōsha, 1958.

Nakano Shigeharu. *Nakano Shigeharu zenshū* [Complete works of Nakano Shigeharu]. 28 vols. Chikuma Shobō, 1976–80.

Natsume Sōseki. *The Miner*. Translated by Jay Rubin. Stanford University Press, 1988.

Nihon Shiseki Kyōkai, ed. *In'yō-reki taishōhyō* [Comparative tables of lunar and solar calendars]. 1940. Reprint. Tokyo Daigaku Shuppankai, 1978.

Ōta Masao. *Hyōden Kiryū Yūyū: senjika teikō no jyānarisuto* [Biography of Kiryū Yūyū: Wartime journalist in resistance]. Fuji Shuppan, 1987.

Roden, Donald. *Schooldays in Imperial Japan: A Study in the Culture of a Student Elite*. University of California Press, 1980.

Senuma Shigeki. *Hon no hyakunen shi* [A hundred-year history of books]. Shuppan Nyūsusha, 1965.

Shea, George Tyson. *Leftwing Literature in Japan: A Brief History of the Proletarian Literary Movement*. Hosei University Press, 1964.

Shimazaki Tōson. *Shimazaki Tōson shū* [Shimazaki Tōson anthology]. Vol. 7 of *Nihon bungaku zenshū*. Shinchōsha, 1962.

Shōwa Joshi Daigaku Hifukugaku Kenkyūshitsu, ed. *Kindai Nihon fukusōshi* [A history of modern Japanese clothing]. Kindai Bunka Kenkyūjo, 1971.

Smith, Thomas C. "The Right to Benevolence: Dignity and Japanese Workers,

1890–1920." *Comparative Studies in Society and History* 26, no. 4 (1984): 587–613.

Sugino Yōkichi. *Nakano Shigeharu no kenkyū* [A study of Nakano Shigeharu]. Kasama Sōsho, vol. 123. Kasama Shoin, 1979.

Sumiya Mikio. *Dai-Nihon Teikoku no shiren* [The trials of the Japanese empire]. Vol. 22 of *Nihon no rekishi*. Chūō Bunko series. Chūō Kōronsha, 1974.

Suzuki Toshio. *Shuppan: kōfukyōka kōbō no isseiki* [Publishing: A century of the rise and decline in times of prosperity and depression]. Shuppan Nyūsusha, 1970.

Takahama Kyoshi. "Shaseibun to Shizen-ha" [Sketch-from-life and naturalism]. *Shumi* 2, no. 9, pp. 66–70.

Takahashi Bunzō. "Kaisetsu" [Commentary]. In *Tosaka Jun zenshū*, 4:470–80.

Takao Kazuhiko. *Kinsei no shomin bunka* [Early modern commoner culture]. Iwanami Shoten, 1969.

Takazawa Yūichi, ed. *Kyōdoshi jiten Ishikawa-ken* [Dictionary of the local history of Ishikawa prefecture]. Shōheisha, 1980.

Tanigawa Kenichi, ed. *Kindai minshū no kiroku: shōfu* [Records of the modern masses: Prostitutes]. Shinjinbutsu Ōraisha, 1971.

Taoka Reiun. "Karyū no saimin to bunshi" [The impoverished lower classes and men of letters]. In *Gendai bungakuron taikei*, 1:274–75.

Tosaka Jun. *Tosaka Jun zenshū* [Complete works of Tosaka Jun]. 5 vols. Keisō Shobō, 1966.

Uchida Masao. *Nihon rekijitsu genten* [Origins of the Japanese calendar]. Yūsankaku Shuppan, 1975.

Wakabayashi Kisaburō, ed. *Ishikawa-ken no rekishi* [History of Ishikawa prefecture]. Kanazawa: Hokkoku Shuppansha, 1970.

Watanabe, Yozo. "The Family and the Law." In Arthur Taylor von Mehren, ed., *Law in Japan: The Legal Order in a Changing Society,* pp. 364–72. Harvard University Press, 1963.

Williams, Raymond. *Keywords.* Rev. ed. New York: Oxford University Press, 1983.

Yanabu Akira. *Honyakugo seiritsu jijō* [Circumstances surrounding the formation of loan translations]. Iwanami Shinsho, vol. 189. Iwanami Shoten, 1982.

Yasumaru Toshio. *Nihon no kindaika to minshū shisō* [Japan's modernization and the ideology of the masses]. Aoki Shoten, 1974.

Yoshida Seiichi and Inagaki Tatsurō, eds. *Gendai no hatate-tachi* [Banner bearers of modernity]. Vol. 12 of *Nihon bungaku no rekishi*. Kadokawa Shoten, 1968.

Index

Abe Tomoji, 184
Akutagawa Ryūnosuke, 132, 146
Apprenticeship: as sake merchant, 49, 56, 57; traditional system of, 74; unsponsored, 116; as geisha, 193, 199, 206; shoemaking, 198, 199
Ara Masabito, 53, 136
Arakure (literary journal), 135, 184
Arakure-kai (Arakure Society), 184
Arishima Takeo, 146, 186
Asahi Shinbun (daily newspaper), 87, 104, 145, 155
Asakusa (Tokyo ward), 70–71, 74–75, 76–78, 79, 86, 98, 198, 200

Bakhtin, Mikhail, 51
Boshin Rescript of 1908, 235*n41*
Brooks, Peter, 37
Buddhism, 167, 180
Bundan (literary world): importance of, 4, 26, 132, 134, 144, 181–82; development of, 31; collapse of during Taishō period, 146, 150; Yamada Junko and, 154. *See also* Tokuda Shūsei: generosity to younger writers
Bushi (samurai class): in Kanazawa, 6, 7; marginalization of, 8, 12, 14–15, 221–22*n11;* contrasted with commoners, 52–53. *See also* Tokuda Shūsei: family's status; Kanazawa

Chikamatsu Shūkō, 51, 131, 184, 216
Chinese, classical: political philosophy, 24, 195; poetry, 25, 195; novels, 26; Tokuda Shūsei's education in, 27
Chinese students in Japan, 172
Christianity, 23–24, 27, 38, 39, 44, 199
Chuang Tzu, 24
Clothing: tailoring and manufacture of men's Western style, 117–19, 123–26; shoemaking, 199–200
—women's fashions: Japanese-style, 124, 160, 162, 163, 190; Western-style, 128–29, 161, 163, 164–65, 166, 189; Chinese-style, 160–61

Colette, S. G., 158, 172
Common life, commoners. *See Shomin*

Demimonde: in Kanazawa, 12; selling of *bushi* daughters into, 13–14; Ise women and, 61; statistics of, Tokyo, 75–76, 234–35*n37;* in Asakusa, 76–77; prostitution, 77, 89, 98–99, 100–101, 193, 194, 208; in Yoshiwara, 96, 100–101, 193; Tsuge Soyo and, 156; Yamada Junko and, 158; in 1920s, 159–60, 161, 162, 163, 167; Hakusan pleasure district, 184–85, 192; politically powerful and Hakusan, Shinbashi, Yanagibashi, 190, 192, 193, 207; standard three trades of, 192; and foreign brothels, 193, 194, 208; Salvation Army and, 204; in Ikebukuro, 212
—geisha: *kōkō* geisha (prostitution for good of family), 70, 100, 194, 199–201, 203; around Ginza, 189–90; poverty as basis of existence of, 191–92; definition of, 192–93; illegal prostitution and, 193, 209; exploitation of and transferal of contracts of, 194, 201, 204, 206–10; sale of young women as, 199–200, 201–3; in Ishinomaki (Miyagi prefecture), 201–5; economics of management of geisha house, 205–6, 207–11; in Yoshi-chō (Nihonbashi ward), 206–10. *See also* Tokuda Shūsei: as manager of Hakusan geisha house

Economic depression, 80, 120, 123, 153, 159, 195
Enomoto Takashi, 86
Enpon (one-yen-book series), 148, 149, 157, 184
Etō Jun, 87, 149–50

Fascism, 161, 178, 185
Fujin Kōron, 148, 205
Funabashi Seiichi, 51, 134, 184
Funayama Kaoru, 215
Furui Yoshikichi, 57, 63, 232*n10*

263